MOSES

A Man of Selfless Dedication

Books in the Great Lives from God's Word series

David
A Man of Passion and Destiny

Esther
A Woman of Strength and Dignity

Joseph
A Man of Integrity and Forgiveness

Moses
A Man of Selfless Dedication

Elijah
A Man of Heroism and Humility

Paul
A Man of Grace and Grit

Job
A Man of Heroic Endurance

Fascinating Stories of Forgotten Lives
Rediscovering Some Old Testament Characters

Jesus
The Greatest Life of All

Great Days with the Great Lives
Daily Insight from Great Lives of the Bible

GREAT LIVES FROM GOD'S WORD

A Man of Selfless Dedication

MOSES

Profiles in Character from

CHARLES R. SWINDOLL

THOMAS NELSON
Since 1798

NASHVILLE DALLAS MEXICO CITY RIO DE JANEIRO

Published in Nashville, Tennessee. Thomas Nelson is a registered trademark of Thomas Nelson, Inc.

Thomas Nelson, Inc. titles may be purchased in bulk for educational, business, fund-raising, or sales promotional use. For information, please e-mail SpecialMarkets @ThomasNelson.com.

All Scripture quotations in this book, except those noted otherwise, are from the New American Standard Bible © 1960, 1962, 1963, 1971, 1973, 1975, and 1977 by the Lockman Foundation, and are used by permission.

Other Scripture quotations are from the following sources:

The New International Version of the Bible (NIV), © 1983 by the International Bible Society. Used by permission of Zondervan Bible Publishers.

The Living Bible (LB), © 1971 by Tyndale House Publishers, Wheaton, Ill. Used by permission.

The King James Version of the Bible (KJV).

Library of Congress Cataloging-in-Publication Data

Swindoll, Charles R.
    Moses: a man of selfless dedication: profiles in character / from Charles R. Swindoll.
        p. cm.—(Great lives from God's word ; v. 4)
    ISBN: 978-1-4002-0249-2 (TP)
    ISBN: 978-0-8499-1385-3 (HC)
    1. Moses (Biblical leader).   i. Title.   ii. Series: Swindoll, Charles R.
Great lives from God's word.
bs580.m6s9   1999
222'.1092–dc21   97-17106
    [b]   cip

Printed and bound in the United States of America

HB 11.08.2023

DEDICATION

This volume is dedicated, with great respect,
to a man I have admired for four decades

Dr. John F. Walvoord

the distinguished Chancellor of Dallas Theological Seminary,
who served with vision, diligence, and wisdom
as its president and spiritual leader
for thirty-four years.

I know of no one who better represents the
qualities of greatness that characterized Moses
than this man who has remained my mentor and friend
since we first met back in 1959.

I thank my God upon every remembrance of him.

CONTENTS

INTRODUCTION

Moses: A Man of Selfless Dedication

The mere mention of the name Moses arouses different images in the minds of various folks. For example, my thoughts go back to the award-winning film, The Ten Commandments, directed by the late Cecil B. DeMille, in which the famous actor, Charlton Heston, played the leading role. In that role, he was handsome, strong-hearted, and confident; therefore, my earliest ideas about Moses were formed by that classic Hollywood image. Moses, being God's man of the hour, must have been all the above and so much more.

Today's generation would place that production among the archives of the film industry. The Ten Commandments has now been eclipsed by The Prince of Egypt, an entertaining, animated film that presents another image of Moses. He is sleek and trim, quick-witted, fun-loving, and virtually ageless. Whether in a chariot race with Ramses, blowing up swirling clouds of dust all around Pharaoh's Egyptian palace, or leading the people through the walled-up Red Sea, the tanned superstar is everybody's hero. Kids and adults alike find delight in the fantasy portrayal of a man who looks the same in his teenage years as he does in his eighties. I mean, who wouldn't want to drink from the same Fountain of Youth as the debonair Prince of Egypt?

But wait. There is something conspicuous by its absence in both those characters. They got the name right, and the original country is correct, but something of much greater importance is missing. It's called reality.

When you turn to the most reliable source document on Moses' life (the Bible) from which you're able to form an accurate opinion of the man God used in such remarkable ways, you come away with an understanding that is both realistic and believable. And when you mix those two ingredients together, an accurate image of the man emerges, which is what this book is all about.

Throughout my ministry of thirty-five-plus years and for as long as I have been writing, more than twenty of those years, I have pursued the twin goals of biblical accuracy and practical realism with a passion. For this reason, I've never been all that interested in fantasy portrayals or imaginative characterizations of real people who lived in a real world. I realize by my making that admission, some of my readers immediately feel pity for me and would consider my approach much too rigid and confining. There is so much creativity I am missing, they would claim. So be it. In my world of inescapable, face-to-face, gut-level reality, there's not a lot of room left for daydreaming, certainly not if you hope to help real people get on with real life. And that is exactly what I desire to do. To make matters worse, I'm not all that crazy about novels, either. So, while you're feeling sorry for me, that ought to give you sufficient grounds to question my whole philosophy of communication.

On the other hand, if you're the type who is looking for straight-from-the-shoulder, hard-hitting facts, based squarely on the truth revealed in God's Word, without much time or space reserved for unrealistic concepts floating in and out of a field of dreams, then this down-to-earth study is for you. Like my other three biographical works, *David, Esther,* and *Joseph,* this volume on Moses will bring you back again and again to reality. Furthermore, it will help you relate to a man who lived in your kind of world, faced your kinds of struggles and didn't always handle them correctly, but who, in spite of his sins and shortcomings, became useful in God's hands for God's sovereign purposes, in keeping with God's perfect timing and plan.

Over and over you will find yourself nodding with understanding and compassion, thinking, *Been there, done that.* Time and again you will smile as you find yourself portrayed in the life of a very ordinary human being who, by God's matchless grace, was able to accomplish some pretty remarkable things. So then, if it's a boost of hope you need these days when your energy is drying up and your money is running short, this is a book for you. Moses: A Man of Selfless Dedication, rather than overwhelming you with off-the-chart accomplishments and guilt-giving expectations, will provide you with fresh wings to soar into the new century, confident in God's strength, not your own.

Who knows? That Red Sea test out in front of you that seems so stormy and deep and frightening at the moment, may open up while you're turning these pages. And when it does, you will find yourself as grateful and humbled as Moses once was. Reality says, maybe it won't. Either way, you will be better prepared to handle it as you get reacquainted with a real man who was neither a handsome superstar nor some fantasy character who looked like he was thirty-eight when he was actually eighty.

If it's reality you're searching for, welcome to my kind of world and God's way of working.

CHUCK SWINDOLL
Dallas, Texas

A Man of Selfless Dedication

MOSES

CHAPTER ONE

Misery, Midwives, and Murder

Imagine some scholarly historian in the distant future, probing ancient archives and peering into dim and dusty records for clues about a life in the past.

Your life.

As he lays all the puzzle pieces on the table—the faded photographs, the curled pages of a journal, the accounts of your driving record, and credit reports—he begins to draw conclusions about who you were and what you were all about. What factors might that researcher consider as he pulls together his report?

If he is wise, he will remember that you are a product of your time. All of us are. That's an important point to keep in mind when you're considering *anyone's* life. We cannot and must not separate a person from his or her times. Our moment in history and our unique, individual circumstances become the anvil upon which our character is beaten out and formed. We will either rise to the challenge of our times, or we will remain stuck on the sidelines.

Moses became God's man for a transitional epoch in history. When the divine call came to assume a crucial role in the destiny of men and nations, Moses stepped into the gap. He may have been reluctant. He may have been frightened. He may have been filled with regret and self-doubt. But in the end, he yielded...and became God's instrument in his own generation.

It is the same in *this* generation, at this epochal moment at the turn of a millennium. God is still looking for the man or woman who will believe Him, despite weaknesses and doubts, and become a mighty tool in His hand...an instrument of His purpose.

AT THE HINGE OF HISTORY

Baby Moses opened his eyes on a world very different from our own. Although neither his mother nor father knew it, the birth of this man-child launched a series of events that would change the course of nations and shape the destiny of millions. History would turn like a hinge on that birth. The world would never be the same again.

The very title of the book where Moses' story begins tips us off that great and climactic events are in the works.

Exodus

The word means "departure, going out," and that certainly describes the major theme of this second book of the Old Testament. It records the departure of the Israelites from Egypt, where they had lived for more than four hundred years. They had entered the land as a little family; they departed as a huge nation. When Pharaoh finally let God's people go, they took their leave of Egypt and began (what turned out to be) a long, long journey to their own land, the land of Canaan.

Exodus records great events and high drama. It actually continues the Book of Genesis, with a lapse of several centuries in between. Exodus picks up where Genesis leaves off, some three hundred fifty years later. And the connection *between* those two books is one of the most fascinating accounts in all of history.

THE TRANSITIONAL MAN

The main character toward the end of Genesis is a man named Joseph.

(For a fuller telling of his story, you might enjoy another volume in this series, *Joseph: A Man of Integrity and Forgiveness.*) Hated and mistreated by jealous brothers, Joseph was kidnapped as a naïve teenager and sold as a slave to a passing caravan bound for Egypt. Through time and a chain of incredible events, God greatly honored this young man and promoted him out of slavery, out of the bowels of an Egyptian dungeon, to the right hand of Pharaoh himself. Against all odds, he became prime minister of the most powerful nation in the ancient world.

And here's the big surprise: Joseph, the remarkable ex-slave who rose to such stellar heights of power and prestige, was a Jew, a Hebrew like his father and brothers.

And what a name this young man made for himself! Time and again Joseph showed his brilliance. God gave him insight to handle vast and perplexing problems. Pharaoh quickly recognized this and exalted him, putting him in charge of the agriculture and economy of the nation.

And it was a good thing, too, because just at that time a terrible famine swept the land. Warned by God, Joseph saw it coming and prepared for it. Not so with Jacob and his sons back in Canaan. They would have died of starvation had they stayed put. Instead, several of them traveled to Egypt seeking grain and eventually came before the ruler of that land—their own long-lost younger brother. After a warm and moving family reunion, Joseph invited his brothers and father to move to Egypt so they might enjoy plenty of grain and a fine spread of land where they could raise crops and graze their flocks.

If you hope to appreciate the exodus, you must understand how the Hebrews got to this foreign land in the first place. The children of Jacob were not made for Egypt! They were made for Canaan, that rich and renewed land of promise that awaited their return.

Pharaoh responded to the arrival of Jacob's family with open and generous hands:

> Then Pharaoh said to Joseph, "Your father and your brothers have
> come to you. The land of Egypt is at your disposal; settle your father
> and your brothers in the best of the land, let them live in the land of

Goshen; and if you know any capable men among them, then put
them in charge of my livestock."

Genesis 47:5–6

What an astounding offer! It reveals how highly Pharaoh regarded his
right-hand man. The king said to Joseph, "Your family has come. That's
wonderful. Give them the best of the land! Let them settle in Goshen. Let
them graze their animals and help me tend my own my livestock while
they're at it. I accept them wholeheartedly, Joseph."

Because of Pharaoh's kindness, Joseph could welcome his family to this
alien land and provide them with a beautiful layout beyond anything they
might have imagined. He told them, "So therefore, do not be afraid; I will
provide for you and your little ones." So he comforted them and spoke
kindly to them" (Genesis 50:21).

But as great as it was, the king's magnanimous offer of refuge and provision wasn't the most amazing part of this story. Even more remarkable
was the lack of bitterness in Joseph's heart toward the brothers who had
hated and mistreated him. He said to them, "Don't worry. Be at peace.
All is well. Come on in and I'll take care of you and your families." And
so through such strange and marvelous circumstances, the sons of Israel
came to live in Egypt.

At that time, of course, they were only an extended family, a small band
of bewildered refugees. You could have loaded the whole tribe on a couple
of Greyhound buses. But since such transport wasn't available, these brothers and their elderly father gathered their belongings and began the long
walk to the south. Yet even when they arrived at the border as foreigners,
the Egyptians didn't stick them in some fenced-off refugee camp to ferret
out a meager life as best they could. They were given choice real estate, a
prime slice of Egyptian heartland, where they might live and raise their
families in peace.

CHANGE ON THE HORIZON

For about seventy-one years after that radical relocation, life rolled along
like the lazy Nile River. Scripture tells us, "Now Joseph stayed in Egypt,

he and his father's household, and Joseph lived one hundred and ten years" (47:22). Joseph was probably thirty-nine years old when his family set up shop in Egypt. He lived for seventy-one years after that, then breathed his last. The very last verse of the Book of Genesis says it succinctly: "So Joseph died at the age of a hundred and ten years; and he was embalmed and placed in a coffin in Egypt" (50:26).

That worthy man's quiet passing marked the beginning of the end of the *good life* for the Hebrews in Egypt. With Joseph lying in his coffin, life began to change for these transplanted Jews—subtle changes at first (they usually are), but soon the Israelites' fortunes plunged like the stock market of October 1929—all the way to the bottom.

By this time, the population of Jews in Egypt had exploded. The offspring of Jacob's sons grew in number until they became a mighty people in Egypt... to the growing dismay of Egyptian officials.

With Joseph no longer on the scene to represent and put in a good word for his kinfolk, the Egyptian attitude toward these "foreign Hebrews" soured. The native population began to look upon Israel with narrowed eyes and growing suspicion. And as we know all too well from our world's bloody history, mounting suspicion toward a people group is only a step away from prejudice... yet another step away from persecution... and but a stone's throw from genocide.

Where did that prejudice come from? I think we can identify at least two sources for it.

LOATHSOME SHEPHERDS

Many years before, Joseph had warned his brothers about something very specific in the Egyptian culture. It's a *little* thing, easy for us to miss—and I strongly suspect that Joseph's brothers missed it, too.

Now, when you're given a *heads up* about living in a foreign culture, you'd better pay close attention. When I was a young Marine, about to enter Japan for the first time, I'll never forget how our colonel stood before us, describing the new way of life into which we were stepping. This was not going to be like driving the highways of North Carolina, strolling the streets of some dusty town in Texas, or kicking back on the beaches in

Southern California. We were guests in another land. We would be regarded with suspicion by some, hostility by others. Many of us had never before been *foreigners*.

That's the way it was when Joseph gave his brothers the inside scoop about Egypt. Listen to his counsel:

> Joseph said to his brothers and to his father's household... "When Pharaoh calls you and says, 'What is your occupation?' you shall say, 'Your servants have been keepers of livestock from our youth even until now, both we and our fathers,' that you may live in the land of Goshen; for every shepherd is loathsome to the Egyptians." (46:31, 33–34)

Joseph told them, "Whatever you do, guys, don't tell Pharaoh you're shepherds! Keep that part under your hats, all right? Just tell him you're keepers of livestock."

Now, why would he say that? Because Joseph knew that shepherds were "loathsome to the Egyptians."

Let me add a little background here. At that time, the Egyptian culture had risen to a high water mark. Its residents were expected to display a certain level of sophistication. You might say it was the Nob Hill of that era. Educationally, it topped the pile. The Egyptians' advanced hieroglyphics, their fine universities, and their enviable economic situation all made them look askance at any group of refugees or expatriates who might corrupt their good fortune. And they certainly didn't want to *import* a group of lowly shepherds who could tarnish their nation's high-gloss image. (There goes the neighborhood!)

Old Testament scholars Keil and Delitzsch add this interesting insight:

> The dislike of the Egyptians to shepherds arose from the fact that the more completely the foundations of Egypt rested upon agricul-ture, the more did the Egyptians associate the idea of rudeness and barbarism with the very name of a shepherd. This is... attested in various ways by the monuments on which shepherds are constantly

depicted as lanky and withered, distorted, emaciated, and sometimes almost ghostly figures.[1]

In other words, shepherds were the low-lifes. Strictly bush-leaguers. And to use the shepherd-word at this tender point in the relationship with Pharaoh would definitely mean starting off on the wrong sandal.

Think back to the days when portions of the American West were being settled, and you'll get a similar picture. Beef barons and sheep ranchers competed for land and profits, and these guys never joined the same bowling teams, I promise you. If you visited a cow town, you didn't walk into a crowd of cowboys and announce you were a shepherd with a big flock of woolies grazing on the outskirts of town. One of the cowboys would probably sniff the air and say, "Ah smell *sheep*." At that point, you would need to either fight, duck, shoot, or flee. Fast!

Pharaoh, apparently, ran cattle, while Jacob's boys were sheep-herders. So Joseph told them, "Look, when the king asks you what you do for a living, just tell him you handle livestock. Keep it generic, and that'll work great. Don't announce that you're shepherds."

Sadly, they either forgot their brother's advice or disregarded it. When Pharaoh asked them to name their occupations, they piped up, "Your servants are shepherds, just as our fathers were." As time passed, the growing number of Jewish shepherds became an Issue (with a capital "I") among the people of Egypt.

That's one source of the prejudice the Israelites eventually ran up against. But I believe something even deeper than that caused the real problems.

THE FORGOTTEN MAN

The first chapter of Exodus reveals a strong second reason why times became so hard for the Hebrews. Not only were they tenders of sheep in a land that hated shepherds, but Scripture also tells us, "Now a new king arose over Egypt, who did not know Joseph" (Exodus 1:8).

The day came, after the deaths of Joseph and the Pharaoh who had promoted him, that a new Pharaoh stepped onto the throne. He too ruled, then passed the crown to the next Pharaoh. Finally, after several centuries, the name Joseph became virtually unknown. No one remembered the famine. No one recalled the golden oceans of stored grain. No one recollected how a wise, young Jewish prime minister had stepped out of obscurity to save the day. That was ancient history. Irrelevant. And the bilateral policy established between Joseph and some long-gone Pharaoh? Completely forgotten.

This new Pharaoh despised the growing Hebrew population. How had they even come to be there? No one knew for sure; the reports had been filed away in some forgotten basement archive.

But one thing about these multiplying Hebrews could not be ignored: They seemed to pose a threat. And a threatened Pharaoh was not a pleasant Pharaoh to have around. He said to his people,

> "Behold, the people of the sons of Israel are more and mightier than
> we. Come, let us deal wisely with them, or else they will multiply
> and in the event of war, they will also join themselves to those who
> hate us, and fight against us and depart from the land." (vv. 9–10)

And so a whole new way of life came to pass for the Hebrews. Notice the change. It's a sad scene. "So they appointed taskmasters over them to afflict them with hard labor. And they built for Pharaoh storage cities, Pithom and Raamses" (v. 11).

As I read those ominous words, I can't help but recall the dark days prior to World War II when the fortunes of Jewish people in another land—Germany—changed so drastically under a hateful new ruler named Adolph Hitler. Not only were Jews murdered and huddled into death camps, they were also forced into cruel corporate slavery by some of the Reich's largest companies. Housed in inhuman conditions, many of these modern-era slaves were simply worked to death.

What happened in Egypt seems a strange foreshadowing of that tragic era. A whole new scene took place in the land of the Nile, the likes of which none of us could imagine. All too suddenly for the bewildered Israelites, a devastating new policy came into effect . . . and life would never be the same.

Exit: ease, abundance, and prosperity.

Enter: taskmasters and the whip.

Archaeologists have greatly helped us to understand this portion of Scripture. They have unearthed obelisks and monuments and columns, etched with all manner of figures and hieroglyphics. One interesting discovery featured a mural, depicting a large group of laborers working under two superior officers armed with heavy lashes. Their task? Making bricks. The two holding the whips were portrayed as crying out, *"Work without fainting!"*

Think of that! As long as Joseph lived, the Israelites knew peace and joy and relaxation in the sunny fields of Goshen. But then the wind shifted. Clouds began to darken the horizon, and a chill crept into the air. Their Egyptian neighbors began to look at them differently—at first with suspicion and distaste, then with outright hatred.

Before anyone could figure out what had gone wrong and what they might do, the taskmasters appeared on the scene, like an angry troop of jack-booted SS officers. Gone were the idyllic days of shepherding. Henceforth they were to make bricks under the snarl of slave drivers and the crack of the lash.

AN ENDURING PROMISE

And so it might have remained until the Hebrews were ground into the Egyptian dust. Scripture says, "The Israelites groaned in their slavery and cried out, and their cry for help...went up to God" (Exodus 3:23, NIV).

God heard that cry. He had not been sleeping. His attention had not drifted. He well remembered His promise to the sons and daughters of Jacob. Way back, centuries before Exodus chapter 1, God spoke to Abram, the father of the Hebrews, and unveiled a prophecy regarding that man's descendants:

> God said to Abram, "Know for certain that your descendants will be strangers in a land that is not theirs, where they will be enslaved and oppressed four hundred years. But I will also judge the nation whom they will serve, and afterward they will come out [Exodus!] with many possessions."

> Genesis 15:13–14

9

"My son," God told Abram, "your progeny will grow in number, and they will enter a land where they were not born. They will be strangers in that foreign land and they will be abused and enslaved. But they won't stay there forever! After several hundred years under the yoke of that brutal people, they will be delivered. They will leave that land."

A deliverer would come, a man hand-picked by God Himself—a leader uniquely prepared to deal with both Israelites and the Pharaoh himself.

His name would be *Moses*.

DESPERATE MEASURES

Return with me to the first chapter of Exodus for a moment. Let's look at life under the pharaohs and the taskmasters. With whips at their backs, the Israelites built two new cities for the Egyptians. You would think all of that hard labor and bitter persecution might have put a crimp in the Israelite baby boom. Not so! These folks were prolific: "But the more they were oppressed, the more they multiplied and spread; so the Egyptians came to dread the Israelites and worked them ruthlessly" (1:12–13, NIV).

The Egyptians looked upon the growing number of Israelites (a "mighty people," Pharaoh called them) with dread. The Hebrew word translated "dread" is *kootz*. It means "to have an abhorrence for and horror, a sickening feeling." When the officers of Egypt noted the swelling population of Hebrews from month to month and year to year, they felt sick in the pit of their stomachs. Had there been coffee shops in those days, John and Jane Egyptian might have sat at those little round tables and said over their lattes, "Man, this thing is getting out of hand. Our plan isn't working. We've got to stop that growth! If we don't put the hammer on these foreigners now, they'll be running the country in a few years."

And so the brutality increased.

So many times when you read about brutality in Scripture, you find strong emotion behind it. Roll back the rock of brutality, and fear crawls out from underneath. The Egyptians' insecurity and abhorrence for their Jewish neighbors eventually led to savagery.

I find that interesting. It strikes me that if you are prone to violent anger and brutality, it might be wise for you to back off and ask yourself what you're afraid of. Throughout my years of ministry, I have sadly noted how brutal people are often driven by fear. Fear of loss. Fear of humiliation. Fear of exposure. Fear of weakness. Fear of losing control.

The Egyptians wallowed in that kind of fear. Fear of losing their land drove them to ever more vicious acts of injustice. Once you've decided to starve or beat or mistreat one person, it becomes easy to persecute a whole population. Note what happened next: "The Egyptians compelled the sons of Israel to labor rigorously; and they made their lives bitter with hard labor in mortar and bricks and at all kinds of labor in the field, all their labors which they rigorously imposed on them" (vv. 12–13).

When this work-'em-to-death tactic didn't accomplish Pharaoh's objectives, however, he unleashed yet another, even darker plan. Again, I am reminded of the Nazi tactics in our own Twentieth Century. First came the denunciations of Jews in the popular press. Second, the denial of privileges. Next, the wanton destruction of Jewish shops and property. Then the indignity and humiliation of making Jews wear special badges, marking them as enemies. And last, the crowded boxcars, the concentration camps…and the ovens.

When Pharaoh saw that the harsh conditions of slavery didn't achieve his ends, he turned up the persecution dial yet one more terrible notch.

Infanticide.

Murder.

> Then the king of Egypt spoke to the Hebrew midwives, one of whom
> was named Shiphrah and the other was named Puah…. (1:15)

These two women apparently oversaw all the Jewish midwives. And here's what Pharaoh said: "When you are helping the Hebrew women to give birth and see them upon the birthstool, if it is a son, then you shall put him to death; but if it is a daughter, then she shall live" (v. 16).

Before we look at their response, let's consider these instructions. Pharaoh, acting under the compulsion of fear, holds a private conference with these representative midwives. I can hear the king's assistants telling him, "Just haul these women into the royal chambers before your royal presence, and they'll be blown away. They'll be intimidated into doing whatever you say!"

Not *those* women!

Before modern obstetrics clinics opened their doors, expectant moms received care in the home. Birth took place through the help of midwives (a practice that has returned to favor in our own era).

That little word "birthstool" in the passage above jumps out at me. I'm not even sure I want to know what that looked like! If the truth were known, I get a little queasy when considering certain intimate subjects. When my own children were born, I had zero desire to be on the scene. I've heard all about this new breed of dad that enters the delivery room with a party hat, a camcorder, and a Domino's pizza... but that wasn't my style at all.

I left it totally up to Cynthia whether she wanted an anesthetic. (I would have preferred anesthetic, myself, but they didn't offer it to the guys.) When it comes to those career placement tests, I'm afraid I wouldn't have scored very well in the midwife category.

According to Pharaoh's instructions, the Hebrew midwife was to watch closely as the baby emerged. She was immediately to discover the sex of the child as it came forth from the womb and to snuff out its life if she noticed it was a male—possibly suffocating the little boy before he ever uttered his first cry.

Then the midwife could say, "Oh, I'm so sorry. This one was stillborn."

What a heinous, murderous plan! Frankly, it comes very close—within a few seconds, as a matter of fact—to the present heinous practice known as "partial birth abortion." These midwives however, remained staunchly pro-life! Notice their action and their subsequent conference with a frustrated Pharaoh:

> But the midwives feared God, and did not do as the king of Egypt had commanded them, but let the boys live. So the king of Egypt called for the midwives and said to them, "Why have you done this thing, and let the boys live?" The midwives said to Pharaoh, "Because the Hebrew women are not as the Egyptian women; for they are vigorous

and give birth before the midwife can get to them."

So God was good to the midwives, and the people multiplied, and became very mighty. And it came about because the midwives feared God, that He established households for them. (vv. 17–21)

What heroines! These ladies feared God more than they feared the laws of the king. Actually, their alibi contained some humor. (Though I'm not sure I could have done any better, given the circumstances.) The word "vigorous" literally means "lively." They told a frowning, unhappy Pharaoh, "Man oh man, King, these women are fast. When we hear they're about to give birth, we rush over to the house and *zip, pop,* it's *over!* The baby's already there, and then what can we do?"

Pharaoh, who may not have appreciated the graphic details of childbirth any more than I do, bought the whole thing. Who was he to argue with a couple of midwives? Thankfully, these courageous women, as Scripture would later say of Moses' own parents, "were not afraid of the king's edict" (Hebrews 11:23).

Praise God for such courageous people of faith. To this day, from Africa to China to the Middle East, that same courage shines out like a beacon. All over the world as you read these words, God's people are being hounded and persecuted for their allegiance to Jesus Christ. And they are standing fast in the face of edicts from kings, presidents, generals, and party commissars. They are saying, "No, we won't do the things you are asking us to do. We refuse to deny our Lord." And they are paying the price.

NO "BLANKET SUBMISSION"

Scripture is careful to instruct God's people to be subject to authority, to pay taxes, and to live quiet, responsible lives. A sweet, submissive spirit characterizes Christ's man and Christ's woman.

- "Wives, submit to your husbands as to the Lord." (Ephesians 5:22, NIV)

- "Children, obey your parents in the Lord, for this is right." (Ephesians 6:1)

13

- "Everyone must submit himself to the governing authorities." (Romans 13:1, NIV)

- "Urge bondslaves to be subject to their own masters in everything." (Titus 2:9)

- "Submit to one another out of reverence for Christ." (Ephesians 5:21, NIV)

But then we come to passages like the first chapter of Exodus, and we are reminded that God's law always comes before man's law. Scripture does not teach *blanket submission*. The fact is, there is a time to submit and a time to resist.

Before we run with that principle too far, however, a word of caution may be in order. The Exodus passage does not teach children to disobey their parents, wives to usurp their husband's leadership in the home, or anyone to reject ethical authority. But the passage does make one thing clear: Submission to civil authority has limits. As Peter once told the Jewish ruling council, "We must obey God rather than men" (Acts 5:29).

In other words, when the king's edict directly violates God's clearly stated will, we ought to fear God, even as a couple of brave ladies named Shiphrah and Puah feared God. And they, being dead, still speak. Scripture tells us that God honored the faith of these midwives. It says, "... the people multiplied, and became mighty. And it came about because the midwives feared God, that He established households for them" (1:20–21).

I'm not sure what that last phrase implies. Perhaps it means they found husbands, married, and had homes and families of their own. Whatever happened, these women were protected and rewarded by God Himself.

The midwives valued God's favor more than that of Pharaoh. Motivated by a deep and abiding reverence for the living God, they refused to obey the king's wicked edict. When that king told them to violate God's basic principle, the preservation of life, they refused to do so.

Stop and think for a moment. The foundations of evangelical

Christianity—and even of our very nation—rest upon resistance and rebellion. We rebelled against a mother church that said, "Believe this and worship in the way we tell you." Our fathers back in the Reformation said, "We will not. We will obey the Word of God." Many of them were exiled, imprisoned, and even martyred for taking that stand.

At the birth of our nation, our fathers rebelled against a king who said, "You do this and you do it my way." Our ancestors said, "We will not do that. We will do it God's way." Because of these courageous men and women who resisted ungodly authority, you and I can look back on the twin births of religious freedom and national freedom.

Even so, I must agree with Augustine, who wrote of these Hebrew women, "God rewarded them for their piety, not their deceit." I do not believe their deceitful response pleased God; but I do believe that, despite that, He rewarded them for doing what was right in His eyes. (And there's always the possibility those Hebrew moms really *were* fast!)

Unfortunately, Israel's problems did not end with the midwives's courageous refusal. The king's murderous fury knew no restraint. Frustrated and angry, Pharaoh issued yet another command: "Pharaoh commanded the people, saying, 'Every son who is born you are to cast into the Nile, and every daughter you are to keep alive'" (v. 22).

Pharaoh's directive, barbarous as it was, has its contemporary equivalent . . . in reverse. In Communist China today, couples are allowed only one child. When many women learn the sexes of their babies, they either carry them to term or immediately abort. If it's a boy, he lives. If it's a baby girl, she is frequently terminated.

The date on the calendar may have changed since the days of the Exodus, but human nature has not. Apart from the redeeming work of Christ, our hearts are desperately wicked. Cruelty existed in Moses' day, and cruelty exists now. Tyrants ruled in the ancient world, and tyrants rule today. Injustice hurt the innocent in Pharaoh's time, in Herod's time, and still in our *sophisticated* world today.

But in the days of Exodus there also lived men and women ready to stand alone for righteousness, even in the face of death, just as there are today. God always has His witnesses!

LESSONS TO PONDER

As I ponder this panoramic portion of Scripture, I am struck by three strong and life-sustaining truths—truths that surface again and again as we consider the life of Moses.

Hard times don't erase God's promises.

These people found themselves in terrible straits, but God had promised, "I'll send a deliverer." When times grow hard it is easy to leap to the conclusion that God has forgotten His promises. The Book of Exodus shows us that when God says, "I promise you something," He *never* forgets it. You may forget. I may forget. The whole nation may forget. But God cannot forget.

In this era of decadence and moral decay, at a time when our nation's capital reels with scandal and is ripped with partisan politics, don't think for a moment that God has taken a vacation or misplaced His promises. He hasn't fallen asleep at the switch. He doesn't need CNN to keep up with the latest developments. At the proper moment, at the time determined before the foundation of the world, He will send forth His Son . . . again. The mighty King of kings will return to deliver His blood-bought people. He will return with justice. The earth may melt, and the stars may fall from the heavens, but the living God will not forget what He has promised. And that's just the first lesson.

Harsh treatment doesn't escape God's notice.

In Exodus chapter three, God later said to Moses,

> "I have indeed seen the misery of my people in Egypt. I have heard them crying out because of their slave drivers, and I am concerned about their suffering. So I have come down to rescue them from the hand of the Egyptians. . . ." (vv. 7–8, NIV)

Do you ever imagine that your hard, harsh moments and tests escape God's notice? You may become so discouraged, so filled with acute pain, that you begin to think God couldn't be aware of your circumstances, or, if He is aware, then He doesn't care. That's a lie from the evil one himself.

God is *always* aware. And He cares very deeply. As we will see, He will do whatever it takes to rescue His people. It may be by calling you home to Himself, or it may be by splitting an ocean right down the middle so you can walk through on dry ground. His deliverance may not arrive on your timetable or in the manner you expect it, but it will arrive at the best time, the right time. He will not abandon His own.

Heavy tests don't eclipse God's concern.

Regardless of the severity of the test you may be facing, it can never overshadow His concern. Remember how God rewarded those midwives? He misses nothing. Nothing!

Perhaps this has been a difficult year for you. The future stretching out before you may seem gloomy or threatening. You want very much to be God's man or God's woman, but you find yourself under the gun. In your rare moments of quiet, you may wonder, *Where is God?*

He's right there at your side, my friend. He has never left. He has never removed His eye from you, nor has His attention wandered to other matters. Not even for a heartbeat. He has never ceased caring for you, thinking about you, considering your situation, and loving you with a passion and intensity beyond comprehension.

Hudson Taylor wrote on one occasion, "It doesn't matter how great the pressure is; what really matters is where the pressure lies. Whether it comes between you and God or presses you nearer His heart."[2]

It was no accident that you were born into this particular era, at this very juncture of history in our nation and our world. God is looking for a man or woman, who will yield to His purposes and seize the day for His glory.

Yes, you may feel unqualified, uneducated, untrained, under-gifted, or even unworthy. Yet, as we will see in the coming chapters, those are excellent qualifications for God to do a mighty work.

CHAPTER TWO

Born After Midnight

The God we worship and serve is perfect in every aspect of His being. He is also realistic. He tells Isaiah, "For My thoughts are not your thoughts, nor are your ways My ways...for as the heavens are higher than the earth, so are My ways higher than your ways and My thoughts than your thoughts" (Isaiah 55:8–9).

David reminds us, "For He Himself knows our frame; He is mindful that we are but dust" (Psalm 103:14). God knows very well that His thoughts and ways infinitely surpass our own. He is mindful that He created us as finite beings out of a few pounds of garden soil. He understands that. He knows how to work with those limited in comprehension and frail of frame.

My question is, why don't *we* understand it? Why do we expect perfection of ourselves and of our associates?

Through all my years of studying biblical characters, I have not encountered a single episode of instant effectiveness for God. Among all the biblical heroes, only Daniel (and possibly Joseph and Joshua) makes it to the pages of holy writ without recorded lapses and failures. And in my own experience, spanning more than thirty-five years of ministry, I cannot recall one believer who simply lifted off the runway and soared into the spiritual stratosphere, staying there until death.

You and I, however, become terribly impatient with our own shortcomings and limitations and with each other. We despair because we think we ought to be in spiritual orbit by this time, when we're barely skimming the treetops, or still trying to lift off the runway. We think we ought instantly, constantly, and effectively to conquer vast territories for the kingdom, like some spiritual Alexander the Great. And when it doesn't happen—when victory seems elusive—we grow discouraged.

Whenever I start feeling like that, I need to revisit the life of Moses. He helps me to take heart. Here was a man who didn't become effective for God until he was *eighty*. Long after most of us would be riding a rocking chair or pushing up daisies, Moses began his spiritual career. And guess what? God used him mightily.

The life of Moses, according to the Book of Acts, chapter 7, may be divided into three 40-year segments. He spent his first forty years in Egypt, nursed by his mother and taught by the Egyptian schools. He spent his second forty years in the desert, nursed by solitude and taught by God. He spent his final forty years with the Hebrew people in the wilderness, nursed by trials, discouragements, and tests, and taught by the Law, which he received from God's own hand.

Dwight L. Moody gave his own spin on this remarkable biography. "Moses," Moody observed, "spent his first forty years thinking he was somebody. He spent his second forty years learning he was a nobody. He spent his third forty years discovering what God can do with a nobody."[1]

You and I, though we may never achieve the age of one hundred and twenty, live in one of those three stages at this very moment. We either think we're somebody, or we have advanced enough to realize we are nobody, or we have finally discovered what God can do with a nobody! It's kind of encouraging, isn't it? God never gives up on us!

The best of the three, of course, is the final phase. Moses had already blown out eighty candles on his birthday cake before that last fact began to take root in his soul (and then only after a stubborn argument with the Almighty). After he learned it, however—after the truth of heaven's desire and ability to use him finally gripped his heart—the very earth would shake, and the seas would boil with the power of God radiating through his life.

If we observe nothing else in this sojourn with Moses, we're going to learn about the first few steps of a man who discovered late in life (but not too late!) what it meant to count for God, regardless of his age.

I've titled this chapter "Born After Midnight," which suggests an untimely birth. And so it was.

AN UNENVIABLE BIRTH

For most of my adult life, I have been a fan of Sir Winston Churchill. His life, his recorded speeches, and his ringing prose never fail to inspire me. Recently I recalled his address to the House of Commons on the seventeenth of April, 1945, five days after the passing of his friend, President Franklin D. Roosevelt.

Churchill said this to Parliament: "In Franklin Roosevelt there died the greatest American friend the islands have ever known. He died in the harness, and we may well say in *battle* harness. What an enviable death was his."[2]

In Churchill's mind, that famous president died at an enviable time. Hitler was dead, his evil empire in smoking ruins. The war in the Pacific was rolling on toward victory. The forces of tyranny would not swallow up the free world. Roosevelt slipped into eternity while seeing his goals fulfilled.

As enviable a death as FDR may have had, Moses, at the other end of the spectrum, endured a most *unenviable* birth. Born as a Jew into a land ruled by an anti-Semitic despot, Moses entered the world in desperate conditions. His people, the Hebrews, suffered horribly under the whip. They were oppressed, hated, misused, maligned. Many were murdered by Pharaoh, the Hitler of Moses' day.

DESPERATE TIMES

Baby Moses entered a world of cruelty and pain, slavery and despair. He began life in a dark era, long after midnight... the darkest day of Hebrew history to that point. Nevertheless, life went on for the Jewish people. Men and women married, cradled young ones, and tried to carve out a family

life in the crucible of oppression and brutality. Oh, they enjoyed brief moments of relief—perhaps the occasional feast of the inevitable "leeks and
garlics"—but fear and dread shadowed even the best of times.

In the early verses of Exodus chapter 2, we read of a marriage celebrated
under these stressful conditions. "Now a man from the house of Levi went
and married a daughter of Levi. The woman conceived and bore a son; and
when she saw that he was beautiful, she hid him for three months" (vv. 1–2).

Moses became a great man of faith because his father and mother were
people of faith. They were Levites, evidently committed to the things of
God. We know that because of what we read in Hebrews chapter 11. "By
faith Moses, when he was born, was hidden for three months by his parents,
because they saw he was a beautiful child; and they were not afraid of the
king's edict" (v. 23).

That king was Pharaoh, the iron-fisted ruler of Egypt. We're told here
that this baby was protected for three months by *faith*. His mother and
father feared the God of heaven more than they feared a king of earth.
And it must have been no easy task to hide that healthy boy. But out of
a deep reverence for God, an abiding confidence in the living Lord, they
did just that.

Though Exodus 2 doesn't mention it, Moses was not the firstborn. He
had an older sister named Miriam, who was not yet a teenager, and an older
brother named Aaron, who was three years older than Moses.

As we read in the second verse, Moses' parents hid their third child
for three months because they saw he was a good (or well-formed) baby.
The Hebrew word can mean several things. Many of our best translations
render the word "beautiful." Some people take it to mean that Amram,
the father, and Jochebed, the mother, looked at the boy and saw a unique
beauty in him. Frankly, that doesn't surprise me. Most parents, when they
look at their little baby, see a unique beauty.

At times I have looked down into the pinched, red face of some little
newborn and have been hard-pressed to say, "My, isn't he beautiful." Sometimes it's difficult for a pastor to know *what* to say. ("Yes, that's a baby, all
right.") But all new parents the world over see nothing but beauty in their
own babies.

Yet I don't think that sort of prejudiced response is what Scripture means here. I believe the Bible is telling us that little Moses really *was* beautiful, way down deep in his tiny soul. Possibly, his godly parents saw in him something more than physical beauty. Perhaps God revealed to them in the secrecy of their hearts that this boy had a very special destiny.

Whatever they may have thought about his birth, they knew immediately that grave danger faced their baby. To keep the child alive, his father and mother would have to risk everything. Had they not carefully hidden him, Pharaoh's troops would have seized the boy and fed him to the crocodiles, at the king's command.

How would you like to try hiding a baby for three months in a miserable little hut? I remember well that our own firstborn never slept through the night for eighteen weary months. At times I longed for a basket and a Nile River nearby! (Just kidding, Curt.) How could we have concealed that boy of ours for three months? With the set of lungs he had, you couldn't have concealed him for three minutes.

In Moses' case, the day soon arrived when he could no longer be concealed. His hiding place would have to change. Can you imagine the tension and fear in that little household? "Keep that baby quiet! Miriam, you *have* to keep him still or we'll lose him. Aaron, you just keep away from the baby. You mustn't tease him or he'll cry. Shh! Quiet! I think someone might be coming down the path!"

Perhaps the Egyptians had instituted house-to-house searches on the rumor of hidden babies. Undoubtedly at least a few Hebrews cooperated with the authorities, in fear of their own lives. Whatever the reason, Moses' parents arrived at a terrible conclusion: They could not keep the secret any longer. Something had to be done. In that moment of agony, somewhere between grief and despair, Jochebed devised a creative plan.

DESPERATE MEASURES

But when she could hide him no longer, she got him a wicker basket and covered it over with tar and pitch. Then she put the child into it and set it among the reeds by the bank of the Nile. (v. 3)

With great care and tenderness, Jochebed mixed a tar-like substance from the banks of the Nile and covered the sides of a little wicker basket, rendering it watertight. We can assume she placed some soft pieces of cloth into that floating bassinet, and perhaps a bit of hay. And then, with what must have been a breaking heart, she set that little basket among the reeds along the bank of the river.

All my life, until I began digging more deeply into this passage, I visualized Jochebed thrusting that basket out into the current of the Nile, until it happened to come to rest where the princess came out to bathe. But that's not what the text says. It says, "She put the child into it, and *set it among the reeds by the bank*" (italics mine).

I have never seen the Nile River, but I have seen plenty of river reeds. Perhaps you have, too. For all their flexibility, those reeds are rather sturdy plants. Moses' mother apparently waded out a ways into the water and secured this little floating basket in a very special place. She didn't merely push it out into the current, singing, "*Que sera, sera*, whatever will be, will be. . . . " She positioned that little basket precisely where she wanted it. As I said, Jochebed had a plan.

Here we meet a woman with great faith in God. But it was not foolish faith! On the contrary, she took steps to devise the very best plan she could under those terrible circumstances, leaving the ultimate results to a sovereign God.

As I ponder this passage, I am confident that this wise mother had identified certain habits of Pharaoh's daughter. She knew that in a certain place, at a certain time, the princess came to the river to bathe. She also reasoned that, if she placed that basket in just the right spot, at just the right time, the princess and her attendants would see it, or at least hear the baby crying, which is precisely what transpired.

> His sister stood at a distance to find out what would happen to him.
> The daughter of Pharaoh came down to bathe at the Nile, with her
> maidens walking alongside the Nile. . . . (vv. 4–5)

You'll never convince me that Jochebed didn't rehearse the whole plan with Miriam time and again—where Miriam would stand, how she would act, what she would say. I can just hear Jochebed's voice: "Make it look like a surprise, Miriam. Make it seem spontaneous. You can do it, honey; I know you can. And I'll be waiting. I'll be right there, ready to come."

At that juncture in the history of Egypt, two daughters of the Pharaoh reigned for a time as co-regents over a section of the Nile. It may be that Jochebed knew that and deliberately placed her precious bundle near one of those co-regents. Jochebed hoped that the princess, who carried a lot of clout, might see the helpless baby and take pity on him. Egyptians, after all, considered the Nile one of their gods. Would the princess believe that the river god had delivered the child to her? Jochebed thought she might, but how could she know for sure? She could only place her baby and herself at God's mercy. Nothing else could be done.

And then the moment came. As if on cue, the princess strode down to the Nile to bathe. "And she saw the basket among the reeds and sent her maid, and she brought it to her" (v. 5).

No mother reading these words has any trouble imagining the feelings of Jochebed at that moment. Can't you see her, behind a tree or perhaps behind some reeds at a distance...standing on tip-toe...clutching her hands together...holding her breath? Can't you imagine her dry throat? Her heart pounding in her chest? How could she know what the Egyptian woman would do? She might have her hunches, but how could she *know?* The princess might just as easily obey her father's stern decree, plunge the baby into the water, and drown him right there. There were no guarantees. All Jochebed could do was trust God to give that Egyptian woman a mother-heart.

Through archaeological digs in recent years, researchers have uncovered an ancient religious ritual associated with the god of the Nile. It included a statement of trust that many Egyptians may have repeated. The statement read, "I have afflicted no man. I have not made any man weep. I have not withheld milk from the mouths of sucklings."

Could the princess have taken such an oath? It's certainly possible. Perhaps she took that baby among the reeds as from the womb of the river itself. Scripture simply says this: "When she opened it she saw the child, and behold, the boy was crying. And she had pity on him and said, "This is one of the Hebrews' children" (v. 6).

When the princess saw the baby, she recognized him as a Hebrew, perhaps belonging to some mother who didn't have the heart to drown her own child. But now, what was a daughter of Pharaoh to do? She had a baby on her hands. And he was hungry.

Josephus adds an interesting thought here. I have no idea whether it's true, but it is interesting. The ancient historian said the princess took the baby to several of her maidens to see if one of them could nurse the child, without success. Only at that point did Miriam come forward to deliver the little speech she had so carefully memorized.

Now that makes a neat little story, but it's not found in Scripture. Here is what the Bible says: "Then [Moses'] sister said to Pharaoh's daughter, "Shall I go and call a nurse for you from the Hebrew women that she may nurse the child for you" (v. 7)?

Miriam never mentioned that the Hebrew nurse happened to be the baby's own mother. Certainly not! The girl had practiced making it all seem casual and impromptu, as though she were saying, "Oh goodness me, look at that. Perhaps I could find someone to help, your highness." "Pharaoh's daughter said to her, 'Go ahead.' So the girl went and called the child's mother" (v. 8).

Now can you picture Jochebed? In her eagerness, she must have longed to *sprint* to that river bank. But she had to play the part of a respectful but disinterested female slave. She had to remain cool. She couldn't show any signs of recognition. She mustn't allow her eyes to shine with love and tenderness for that crying infant. No trembling hands. No quick breathing. No catch in her voice or tears in her eyes. The life of her little son was at stake!

And here's what happened next: "Then Pharaoh's daughter said to her, 'Take this child away and nurse him for me and I will give you your wages.' So the woman took the child and nursed him" (v. 9).

Wow! That's terrific, isn't it? You not only get your child back from the edge of the grave, you not only get the official sanction and protection of Pharaoh's daughter, but you get *paid* to raise him! That, my friend, is no coincidence. That is the hand of God. Scripture tells us, "When a man's ways are pleasing to the LORD, he makes even his enemies live at peace with him" (Proverbs 16:7, NIV). Never doubt that. When your ways really please the Lord, He'll take care of those enemies one by one, day by day.

FAITH AND PLANNING

Jochebed had faith. She also thought through a very creative plan.

I'd like to pause to reflect on this tension between careful planning and full-hearted faith. Are they mutually exclusive? Not on your life! Yet to talk to some believers, you might be led to think otherwise.

I've counseled with unemployed men and women who tell me, "I'm just waiting on the Lord to provide a job."

"Fine," I reply. "And where have you placed your resumé?"

"Well, I'm not going that route. I'm just waiting on God."

"Oh really?" I say. "Then I hope you don't mind going hungry for awhile."

The old motto of soldiers during the Revolutionary War applies to many areas of life: "Trust in God, but keep your powder dry!" In other words, place your life in the Savior's hands, but stay at the ready. Do all that you can to prepare yourself for battle, understanding that the ultimate outcome rests with the Lord God.

To walk by faith does not mean you stop *thinking*. To trust God does not imply becoming slovenly or lazy or apathetic. What a distortion of biblical faith! You and I need to trust God for our finances, but that is no license to spend foolishly. You and I ought to trust God for safety in the car, but we're not wise to pass on a blind curve. We trust God for our health, but that doesn't mean we can chain smoke, stay up half the night, and subsist on potato chips and Twinkies without consequences.

Acting foolishly or thoughtlessly, expecting God to bail you out if things go amiss, isn't faith at all. It is *presumption*. Wisdom says, do all you can within your strength, then trust Him to do what you cannot do, to accomplish what you cannot accomplish. Faith and careful planning go hand-in-hand. They always have.

Susanna Wesley, that great Christian lady of yesteryear, gave birth to nineteen children. Now you might well be a woman of great faith, but if you have children, you'd better have more than faith going in your home. Can you imagine feeding such a brood? (Actually, a number of the Wesley children died as infants.) But the fifteenth child born into that home was a fellow named John... John Wesley. The youngest boy, Charles, ultimately penned over eight thousand hymns. At the height of his career, Charles declared that he owed much to the faith and example of his mother.

If you study the life of Mrs. Wesley, however, you'll discover she was more than a woman of faith. Here was a thoughtful, clear-eyed mom with carefully developed strategies for rearing her children. In fact, she employed twenty-one principles in bringing up her boys and girls. Here is one of them: "When my child turns one year old, and some of them before then, he is taught to fear the rod and cry softly, by which he escapes an abundance of correction which he might otherwise have had."

That's a plan, isn't it? She not only trusted in the Lord, she employed the rod when necessary. You don't raise nineteen kids without a rod, by the way. You can have all the faith in the world, but if you have no consistent plan for discipline, you run a *circus,* not a family. Susanna Wesley had both a deep, abiding faith in God and a plan.

That's what impresses me about Jochebed. She trusted the Lord so fully that the Holy Spirit includes her in the Hebrews 11 "Hall of Faith." What Moses drank into his life, he most likely imbibed from his mother.

But on that dark morning when Jochebed placed her little one in a tiny basket coated with pitch and tar, she also had a plan. It may have been desperate, but these were desperate times. And she put her plan into action, fully realizing the results lay completely in God's good hands.

The result? God rewarded her faith beyond her fondest hopes. Pharaoh's daughter paid Jochebed to rear her own son. *Paid!* How many others among the multitudes of Hebrew slaves were paid for their labors? The greatest part of all, however, was to get her baby boy back in her arms again. She took that little one and "nursed him," as it says in verse 9.

We're not told how long she kept the child. But the next verse begins with an intriguing hint. "The child grew, and she brought him to Pharaoh's daughter and he became her son" (v. 10).

This record suggests that she had the boy longer than the age of weaning, at three or four. She had the child while he was *growing*. In God's grace and in His plan, Moses may have been allowed to remain with his family long enough to firmly establish his Hebrew roots and learn of the God of Abraham, Isaac, and Jacob.

We know that Jochebed did not have him until he was full grown, because of what we read in verse 11: "Now it came about in those days, when Moses had grown up, that he went out to his brethren and looked on their hard labors...."

So Moses wasn't grown up by the time he left home; but he was growing. Jochebed undoubtedly had him during what we would call the preschool years. You can bet that mother treasured every one of those days with her youngest boy. Would that mothers of our own era treasured those years with their little ones to the same degree.

OUT ON A LIMB

I may be going out on a limb here, but so be it. (I've been there before, and I will likely be there again.) Considering the example of Jochebed before us, I feel constrained to say that, if you are a mother of preschoolers, you ought to think and pray long and hard before you turn your children over to someone else to rear.

I have no desire to stir up controversy or raise guilt. I simply want to declare what I see to be biblical principles—principles that ought to be soberly, carefully considered. I'm not writing here to single moms...nor am I addressing every working mother. I'm not really addressing working mothers with older children in school. I am writing especially to mothers with *preschool* children. I am calling on you to think very carefully about those crucial, irretrievable years of your child's life and development. If you must work, if no other option exists, then I strongly urge you to work the bare minimum and make sure your child enjoys the best possible care. Having said that, I still maintain it is better to sacrifice almost any material goal—short of food on the table and a roof overhead—than to sacrifice those precious years of opportunity with your little ones.

I cannot help but be impressed with how God exalts the role of the mother. Not once is Moses' father mentioned in these first few verses of Exodus chapter 2. Hebrews 11:23 certainly indicates that he participated in the decision to hide baby Moses and that he was willing to trust God in the face of great risk to his own life. But it is Jochebed who plays the major role in saving and nurturing the child. And that underlines my point: Nobody can take the place of the mother with a preschool child. Nobody.

A STRANGE NEW HOME

> So the woman took the child and nursed him. The child grew, and she brought him to Pharaoh's daughter and he became her son. And she named him Moses, and said, "Because I drew him out of the water." (v. 9-10)

A deep sea of emotions surges beneath these two verses. The boy Moses suddenly had a new home. And what a change of scene! From the security of his own loving family to a lonely and unfamiliar place of strangers. From slave quarters to a palace. From the simple and the familiar to the strange and overwhelming. This wasn't like moving down the block, into another neighborhood, or across the state to a new city; this was like relocating to a different planet.

Perhaps somewhere along the way you have endured such a radical, upsetting change. You may have suffered the crushing fracture of your home by the divorce of your parents. You shifted from one home to another and the memory of those days will stay with you for the rest of your life. Perhaps you spent time in a foster home and found yourself living with total strangers. I have known some who were shuttled in and out of more than a *dozen* homes in their growing up years. Coming from a stable home as I did, I struggle even to imagine such an experience.

Those must have been difficult, lonely years for young Moses. I imagine he must have wept night after night in the privacy of his palace room, his tears soaking into those royal linen sheets. No soothing touch from his mother. No comforting word from his father. No smile of sister Miriam or antics of brother Aaron. Though Scripture draws a curtain over those years, it is easy to imagine the lad pouring out his heart to the God he had learned to seek.

But Moses wasn't the only one to suffer. A mother wept, too. Picture, if you can, Jochebed taking her little son by the hand and walking away from that little hut in the slave quarters of the Hebrew slum. Within the shelter of their humble home, she had nursed him and reared him and taught him what she knew of the one true God, the God of heaven and earth. She had taught him his Hebrew roots, and perhaps planted in his imagination a picture of a beautiful land to the north...a land promised to their fathers...a land called Canaan.

For all Jochebed knew, she would never see her little boy again. After all, what reason could she claim for visiting him? She was only his *nurse*. A female slave. A member of a despised, rejected race. Nevertheless, when the royal summons came, she cleaned him up, washed one last time behind his ears, tenderly slicked down his hair, and dressed him in his best tunic (probably a homespun hand-me-down from Aaron). Like boys the world over, little Moses would have wanted to take some of his own treasures along...the ancient equivalent, I suppose, to a bag of marbles and a few comic books.

And down the path they went toward the palace.

With tenderness, F. B. Meyer writes, "The mother's heart must have suffered bitterly as she let her boy go into the unknown world within the great palace gate; and very lonely must the little household have felt when the last kisses had been exchanged, the last instruction given, and the last prayer offered. What a crowd of tender thoughts, curious speculations, and eager yearnings must have followed the little nursling of the Hebrew home, as his mother took him and brought him to Pharaoh's daughter, and he became her son!"[3]

Just picture that sad scene. Moses became the son of another woman with a completely different set of values. A stranger. An idolater. A foreigner.

As we will discover a bit later in the story, Moses became an eager student in a whole new school of learning, designed to prepare him for the throne. I am convinced that the daughter of Pharaoh had in her heart the desire, someday, to make Moses the Pharaoh of Egypt. And it almost happened.

The adopted son of the princess stepped into a whole new world. On top of everything else, he was given a new name, which seems to be a mixture of two words: an Egyptian word that means "son," and a Hebrew word that means "to draw out." The daughter of Pharaoh "drew out her son" and named him Moses. He didn't bear that name until she gave it to him.

The amazing irony of God's divine plan was that this one whom the princess renamed, nurtured, reared, and educated in all the ways of the Egyptians, became the instrument of judgment in the very court where he grew up.

NO ACCIDENTS WITH GOD

Perhaps these images have stirred some memories of your own that haven't been nudged for awhile. You may feel some pain in recalling certain aspects of your childhood. Maybe you, too, feel as though you were "born after midnight." Perhaps you never knew what it was to nestle securely in a parent's love. Your home life may have been strained or even fractured from your earliest memory. From a human point of view, your birth might have come at a difficult or awkward time in the lives of your parents. It may be that you've never known the reassurance of a faithful mother and father who built their faith into your heart. When you think back on your growing-up years, you realize you don't have much to shout about.

I'd like to deliver a beautiful message to you, my friend. God's hand on your life may be just beginning to make its mark. That steep hill you've been climbing for such a long time may be the ramp to a destiny beyond your dreams. I do not believe there is any such thing as an accidental or ill-timed birth. You may have arrived in a home that was financially strapped. You may have known brokenness, hurt, and insecurity since your earliest days—but please hear me on this: *You were not an accident.*

At some point in my youth (and no doubt with the best of intentions), my parents informed me that I was an *accident,* an unintended child. So I figured if I was *born* an accident, I might as well *live* like an accident. And that's precisely what I did. That knowledge greatly shaped my early life.

And then one day I learned that God can use so-called *accidents.* God uses those who seem ill-fitted for a significant life. All of a sudden the pieces began to fall together. I began to realize He had a specific reason and purpose for me to be alive. To my parents, I may have been an accident, but in His eyes, I wasn't an accident at all. I began to understand some of the same things that struck the heart of David, insights which led him to pen these words of awe and worship:

> You made all the delicate, inner parts of my body and knit them together in my mother's womb.
>
> Thank you for making me so wonderfully complex! It is amazing to think about. Your workmanship is marvelous—and how well I know it.
>
> You were there while I was being formed in utter seclusion!
>
> You saw me before I was born and scheduled each day of my life before I began to breathe. Every day was recorded in your book!
>
> How precious it is, Lord, to realize that you are thinking about me constantly! I can't even count how many times a day your thoughts turn toward me. And when I waken in the morning, you are still thinking of me! (Psalm 139:13–17, TLB)

Even though my life hadn't been everything I wanted it to be, or everything it should or could or might have been, God wasn't finished with me yet!

And the good news is this: He isn't finished with you, either. Not by a long shot.

Moses could very well have turned into a bitter, angry young man. He could have held a grudge against his birth mother, despised his new situation, fought the system, and never become the man destined for greatness. But he didn't. Instead, he stayed, he learned, he grew, he trusted, and he never forgot his roots in an eternal, sovereign God.

As you read these words, you may look back on a record as black as midnight. But I've got great hope for you. "Weeping may endure for a night, but joy comes in the morning" (Psalm 30:5). We will see that demonstrated in astonishing ways in the life of Moses. And you too will experience that morning in your life, as you refuse to live in the bitterness of the past, trust a sovereign God, drink deeply of His grace, and wait for Him to use you in His great plan.

He makes no mistakes, my friend. And He is able to take your life, with all of the heartache, all of the pain, all of the regret, all of the missed opportunities, and use you for His glory.

Never forget His promise: Joy comes in the morning. Look! The sun is already starting to rise.

CHAPTER THREE

God's Will, My Way

I t is one thing to do the will of God. It is another thing entirely to do it God's way in God's time. Let's imagine God calls you into vocational Christian service. You know in your heart it is His plan for you one day to embrace some aspect of full-time ministry. But if you aren't careful, you could easily begin to pull strings behind the scenes. You could find yourself competing for some plum assignment or prestigious pulpit. You could even begin to push and shove and manipulate, until over time you actually prostituted the calling you received from God.

You wanted to do the will of God, but bent on carrying out that plan in your own way, you took matters into your own hands and wound up losing His blessing.

Let's make it a little more personal. God has made it clear to you that He neither desires nor requires you to remain single. He knows you are lonely, knows you do not possess the gift of celibacy, and knows that time is passing and prospects are narrowing.

At some point, if you do not guard your heart, you may say to the Lord, in effect, "Okay, God, I know Your plan. You want me married. Now, please just step aside for a few months. When I get to the altar, I'll whistle. At that time, I'd like You to come back and bless the union, and we'll slip back into Your plans and pursue Your will."

You see how that works? You say you want the will of God, but through manipulation, compromise, matchmaking, and game-playing, you get the one of *your* choice. Only then do you suddenly *rediscover* God and pray, "O Lord, please bless this union. Make it strong and great because, as You have led me, I am getting married today."

AN OLD PATTERN

Now it may bring you a bit of comfort to know that this is nothing new. It goes as far back as a man who worked to become highly qualified in his field of endeavor but proved himself completely useless, despite his credentials as a polished, capable, well-educated leader of men. As you've probably guessed, I'm referring to Moses.

Let's pick up the biblical account back in Exodus chapter 2.

> Now it came about in those days, when Moses had grown up, that he went out to his brethren and looked on their hard labors; and he saw an Egyptian beating a Hebrew, one of his brethren. So he looked this way and that, and when he saw there was no one around he struck down the Egyptian and hid him in the sand. He went out the next day, and behold, two Hebrews were fighting with each other; and he said to the offender, "Why are you striking your companion?"
>
> But he said, "Who made you a prince or a judge over us? Are you intending to kill me as you killed the Egyptian?" Then Moses was afraid and said, "Surely the matter has become known."
>
> When Pharaoh heard of this matter, he tried to kill Moses. But Moses fled from the presence of Pharaoh and settled in the land of Midian, and he sat down by a well. (Exodus 2:11–15)

Before we move on, we need to take a look at the same event from a different angle, through the lens of another camera. In the New Testament book of Acts, Stephen the deacon also gives an inspired account of the same story. Take time to read his words carefully:

It was at this time that Moses was born; and he was lovely in the sight of God, and he was nurtured three months in his father's home. And after he had been set outside, Pharaoh's daughter took him away and nurtured him as her own son. Moses was educated in all the learning of the Egyptians, and he was a man of power in words and deeds.

But when he was approaching the age of forty, it entered his mind to visit his brethren, the sons of Israel. And when he saw one of them being treated unjustly, he defended him and took vengeance for the oppressed by striking down the Egyptian. And he supposed that his brethren understood that God was granting them deliverance through him, but they did not understand. On the following day he appeared to them as they were fighting together, and he tried to reconcile them in peace, saying, "Men, you are brethren, why do you injure one another?"

But the one who was injuring his neighbor pushed him away, saying, "Who made you a ruler and judge over us? You do not mean to kill me as you killed the Egyptian yesterday, do you?" At this remark, Moses fled and became an alien in the land of Midian. (Acts 7:20–29)

After Pharaoh's daughter adopted Moses, she immediately began to prepare him for a proper life in Pharaoh's court. The historian Josephus tells us that because the Pharaoh had no son and heir, Moses was being nurtured for the throne. That seems like a sound assumption; no doubt, historians bear this out. Whatever the case, Moses experienced a radical change of lifestyle. Consider these two verses, one immediately following the other:

He was born; . . . he was nurtured three months in his father's home. After he was exposed, [Pharaoh's] daughter took him away and nurtured him as her own son. (Acts 7:20–21)

The word nurture means *to rear, to educate, to train*. Pharaoh's daughter put him through the training of an Egyptian home, a wholly different proposition from a Hebrew home. Moses moved from a humble little shack in what we might call the ghetto of Goshen, where his mom and dad lived, to the stately and elegant court of the king.

It taxes the imagination to identify a similar, contemporary situation. We might think, for instance, of an abandoned child from the gutters of Calcutta suddenly whisked by military aircraft to the White House to be adopted by the President and First Lady. But even that doesn't do justice to the contrast. What happened, according to the account in the Book of Exodus simply astonishes and can only be attributed to the hand of a sovereign God.

Little Moses probably got not only his own room, but a suite of rooms. No longer home-schooled under the care of Jochebed, he fell into the hands of polished Egyptian tutors. They immediately began to instruct the bewildered young lad in the protocol, lifestyle, and culture of Egyptian life. He endured a whole process of reorientation in his preparation for the throne.

The next verse tells us that "Moses was educated in all the learning of the Egyptians" (Acts 7:22). The original text says, "in all the wisdom of the Egyptians." In a colloquialism of that day, people referred to a brilliant person as having "the wisdom of the Egyptians."

A boy reared in Egypt with a silver spoon in his mouth attended the Temple of the Sun. Archaeologists and historians have done us a great service in unearthing and bringing to our attention some facts concerning this premier educational center.

The Temple of the Sun has been called by some "the Oxford of the ancient world." The course of study at Sun Temple U began with what we would call Hieroglyphics 101. Some have said that this language is the most difficult ever put into writing. It does not use characters; it uses pictographs—highly stylized symbols that represent complex ideas.

While working my way through this portion of Scripture, I pulled a book off my study shelf to look for a sample of this unique writing. It's incredible! I have seen many computer fonts while playing with my word processing program, but I have never seen a font like that. Just for fun, I picked out one line to see if I might make anything of it. The line began with three pelican-type creatures, followed by a crow's foot, three dashes, and a disembodied head.

My translation would have read, "Take a hike, Chuck. You'll never get it!" One scholar of antiquities says it takes some people a lifetime to master hieroglyphics. I am now convinced of that.

Moses began to learn the language of the Egyptians at the temple. He also would have plunged into the sciences, medicine, astronomy, chemistry, theology, philosophy, and law. He most certainly took the Egyptian equivalent of ROTC, studying the battles, combat tactics, and foes of that nation's proud military history. On top of that, he would have dabbled in the arts—sculpture, music, and painting. The whole world of Egyptian literature was opened to him. The adopted son of the princess found himself immersed in Egyptian learning. It became his life.

Although it isn't verified in Scripture, some historians claim Moses was a quick study. It didn't take long for the former Hebrew slave to grasp the content of these heavy courses. For one thing, he found few distractions at the Temple of the Sun. This was no party school. With such a heavy course load, who could find time for sports contests, fraternity functions, or chariot races? And *no one* majored in basket-weaving, line dancing, or other such light fare. You really had to *study* back then. So Moses became a keen-thinking man, learned in "all the wisdom of the Egyptians."

The Bible also tells us that Moses' diligent study and preparation made him into a man "mighty in words and deeds." He made a name for himself and earned the Egyptians' respect. Early on, it became obvious that this son of the princess wielded both power and influence. By the time he reached thirty, extrabiblical historians tell us, he had already led the Egyptian army to a smashing victory over the Ethiopians. A bold military strategist. Highly valued. Bronzed by the sun. Scarred by battle. Wise in worldly matters. Competent as a leader. And inspiring to boot.

Yes, this certainly was one highly qualified young man.

When the text calls him "a man of power in words and deeds," it implies an ability to sway the masses. It means he not only possessed intellect, he oozed charisma. He spoke with ease, and his walk backed up his talk. Everyone knew about his courage and heroism. Moses—primed for the throne. The pride of Egypt!

But he was also *vulnerable*.

He had no idea *how* vulnerable. But that would soon become obvious to the whole nation.

Some teachers suggest Moses did not know the will of God for his life until his encounter at the burning bush, at age eighty. That's what I heard all through my growing-up years, and I believed it. Everyone assumed that Moses first realized he was to deliver Israel at that amazing moment in the desert of Midian when the voice of God called to him from the flames.

I no longer believe that to be true. Though I don't have a specific verse to back up my position, I believe Scripture strongly implies Moses had begun to understand his destiny while still a young man being educated in the Egyptian court. Before he reached the age of forty, I am convinced God had already put it into Moses' mind that he would one day, through some as-yet-unrevealed manner, lead his people out of bondage.

He *knew* God's will. But the problem was, he did not bother to seek God's way and God's timing. Instead, Moses began to carry out that plan according to *Moses'* way and *Moses'* schedule. As he did, sadly, many things came unraveled for him. Allow me to explain the steps that led me to this conclusion.

STEP ONE: AN IDEA INITIATED BY MOSES, NOT GOD

> But when he was approaching the age of forty, it entered his mind to
> visit his brethren, the sons of Israel. (Acts 7:23)

This couldn't have been the first time such a thought occurred to Moses. He had certainly seen Hebrews before. How could you miss them? They were all over the place—building, carrying, chopping, sweeping, shoveling, hauling, dragging stones, and working the landscape. In short, they were doing all the Egyptians' dirty work. And why not? They were slaves of Egypt.

Somewhere along the line, Scripture doesn't say when, a plan began to form in this powerful young man's mind. The trouble is, when you know the ultimate will of God for your life and things aren't happening fast enough to suit you, you become anxious. You begin looking for ways to jumpstart the process. You will not read in Acts or Exodus or in any other portion of Scripture that God led Moses to kill an Egyptian. Moses was strictly a freelance murderer. Verse 23 tells us, "It entered *his* mind to visit his brethren, the sons of Israel" (italics mine).

Without realizing it, Moses entered a vulnerable, dangerous time of life. While I'm convinced he knew he was to redeem Israel, I also believe he grew antsy about it. Anxious. Impatient. And in that state of mind, he launched a premature strike that resulted in disaster…and a forty-year setback. Desiring to carry out the will of God, eager to do great things for God, he forced a situation, which led to personal disaster. Notice again what it says in verse 11: "He saw an Egyptian beating a Hebrew, one of his brethren."

Because the mistreated slave also descended from Jacob, Moses' heart went out to him. Suddenly it happened. Moses gripped the wheel of his life and flipped it over at high speed, like a car hitting a patch of black ice and careening over a bank. There was no going back.

It would be easy to explain it all by saying something suddenly *snapped*. But that's not how Scripture explains it. Moses acted deliberately according to plan. *His* plan. Verse 12 tells us that "he looked this way and that." Picture that in your mind. In that moment, Moses became *man-conscious*. He saw abuse going on and he thought, *Now's my chance to make my move.* So he rolled up his sleeves and took on the inequity. Enough of all this unfair treatment!

> So he looked this way and that, and when he saw there was no one around, he struck down the Egyptian and hid him in the sand. (v.12)

STEP TWO: A PROCEDURE ENERGIZED BY THE FLESH

Did Moses pinion the man with the practiced toss of a spear? Did he run him through from behind with a sword? Did he strike him with a killing blow from a powerful fist? The Bible doesn't say. Yet it is clear the idea came from and was implemented by Moses, energized by the flesh. Nowhere do you read where *God* said to Moses, "Move into this situation and make it right." Moses made that decision on his own. He looked this way, and he looked that way...then reacted swiftly, viciously.

Having established that fact, we need to be a little careful here. We ought not to go overboard criticizing the motives of this young man's heart. I'm convinced Moses was doing more than grandstanding. I believe he was absolutely sincere. He didn't see himself murdering a cruel slave-driver as much as courageously striking a blow for God's people. The desire to do something right overcame him. His problem? *He dedicated himself to the will of God, but not to the God whose will it was.*

Let that thought sink in. You and I can become so dedicated to the will of God, we can be so driven by a false sense of purpose, that we might inadvertently take matters into our own hands and leave God completely out of the loop. Been there, done that?

Did that cruel taskmaster need to be punished? Yes. Was it wrong to beat that Hebrew as he did? Certainly. But when Moses stepped in and began his own Operation Deliverance, he was energized by the flesh, not the Spirit.

How easily this can happen to good people, to men and women with the highest motives and the best of intentions. Picture this: You're a gifted and highly qualified teacher. In your heart, you *ache* to be in front of a classroom again. With all your soul, you want to feel that lectern beneath your hands and the minds of those eager students absorbing your knowledge. And suddenly, seemingly out of the blue, an opportunity presents itself. If you don't watch it, my friend, you'll find yourself elbowing your way through that "open door."

But all the while, God waits for you to seek His counsel. If you act without discerning His timing, you may lose the smile of divine favor. He will not bless what He has not ordained. You may truly sense that God has something for you to accomplish in a certain area. But if you aren't vigilant, if you aren't daily humbling yourself before Him, seeking His face, discerning His timing, operating under the Spirit's control, you may push and shove and force your way prematurely into that place where God wanted you, but you will not have arrived in His own time.

How critical is this issue of God's timing! A later biblical hero, who well understood his crucial role, once asked a frightened child of God, "Who knows but that you have come to royal position *for such a time as this*" (Esther 4:14)? And the apostle Paul deepened our appreciation for this mystery when he wrote of Christ's birth, "But *when the time had fully come*, God sent his Son, born of a woman, born under law, to redeem those under law, that we might receive the full rights of sons" (Galatians 4:4–5). At the right time, untold blessing! But at the wrong time....

Moses looked this way, and he looked that way. Isn't it interesting? He didn't look *up*, did he? He looked in both directions horizontally, but left the vertical completely out of it. And what did he do with the results of his murderous anger? Scripture says "he hid the Egyptian in the sand."

Invariably, when you act in the flesh, you have something to cover up. You have to bury your motive. You have to hide a contact you made to manipulate the plan. You have to conceal a lie or half-truth. You have to backtrack on a boast. You have to cover up the corpse your fleshly procedure has created. It's just a matter of time before truth catches up with you. The sand always yields its secrets.

This is a good time to emphasize that the capable and gifted are also cursed with vulnerability. The highly qualified live on the cutting edge of the enemy's subtle attack—the very adversary who prods you to act in the flesh, to do the *right* thing at the *wrong* time. And how does he operate? Most of us know the drill.

You find yourself moved by a sense of *need*. You utter a foolish vow, like Jepthah, and live to keenly regret it for the rest of your days. You hurry the process along, as Abram and Sarai did, and later find yourself with an Ishmael on your hands, mocking the child of promise.

Neglecting to ask God's counsel, neglecting to seek God's timing, you step in to *handle* things. And by and by, you've got a mess on your hands. You're stuck with a corpse, with a shovel in your hands and a shallow grave at your feet.

You know the odd thing about it all? Most of us aren't very clever at cover-ups anyway. It amazes me that Moses couldn't even bury an Egyptian right. Makes me wonder if he left the guy's toes sticking out of the sand. He failed simply to cover up the corpse.

But what about years and years later, when God took charge and Moses acted according to His timing? Was *God* able to cover up the Egyptians? God buried their entire army under the Red Sea, horses, weapons, chariots, and all! When God's in it, the job gets done. With the Lord in charge, failure flees.

When the flesh rules, however, you can't even *bury* the consequences. They haunt you! They dog your steps! That is why Moses "looked this way and that." Operating in the flesh, he had to make sure the coast was clear before he acted. But it caught up with him.

STEP THREE: AN ACT LEADING TO
CONFUSION AND FAILURE

Don't miss this point. This is where the misery really kicks in. Up to this point, Moses may have felt as if he'd pulled off something pretty slick. He'd made a bold gesture and felt pretty good about it. He had no idea that confusion, failure, and grief lurked like a leopard just around the corner.

Let me remind you again that Moses thought he was doing God's will.

> And when he saw one of them being treated unjustly, he defended
> him and took vengeance for the oppressed by striking down the
> Egyptian. And he supposed that his brethren understood that God
> was granting them deliverance through him, but they did not un-
> derstand. (Acts 7:24–25)

Moses believed he was to be the deliverer, many years before he received his recommission at the burning bush. He assumed everyone else would realize it, too. He thought all he had to do was start the ball rolling and the Hebrews would rally around him, hailing him as their champion. "All right, Prince Moses, let's march on the palace! Grab those hammers and pitchforks, everybody. Let's go! Lead us, O mighty Prince!" But what does Scripture say? It reports, "They did not understand."

They didn't put it together. Then their confusion spread to Moses. He knew God desired to use him mightily; so why wasn't this working? He'd struck the match, but the wood refused to burn. What could possibly have gone wrong? How could he have miscalculated? Confusion replaced confidence. What was happening?

The passage goes on to tell us, "On the following day he appeared to them as they were fighting... (Acts 7:26).

Now why did he go back to the scene of the crime? I think he returned to carry out his plan. He'd proved his loyalty to the Hebrews by striking down an Egyptian official. That was Plan A. Now for Plan B. He would return to the scene of his action and rally the troops.

As it happened, however, he arrived in the middle of a fight. Can't you see him frowning as he stepped down out of his official chariot? *Fighting*? That wasn't in the script. The grateful population should have been gathering themselves together, readying themselves for the Great Rebellion.

"Here now," he said as he bulled into their midst. "This shouldn't be happening. We've got to work together, men." But they didn't listen to his counsel. In fact, they didn't respect him at all. "But the one who was injuring his neighbor pushed him away, saying, 'Who made you a ruler and judge over us'" (Acts 7:27)?

What a crushing put-down! "Hey, Fancy Boy, back off. Who died and left you in charge? Where do you get off? You're not our leader. Who do you think you are, anyway?"

How those words must have stung a man who had just risked *everything*.

In her book *D. E. Hoste*, Phyllis Thompson does a masterful job describing the characteristics of spiritual leadership. She wrote, "I suppose if you really want to know who is a spiritual leader, you ought to look around and see how many who are spiritual are following him."[1]

It's a pretty simple plan, isn't it? A meat-and-potatoes sort of proposition. If you're a spiritual leader, spiritual people will follow you. That's true of any leader. If you've got the goods, people follow. But they didn't follow Moses. At that point, the prince of Egypt led a lonely one-man parade. The bills of the flesh are now coming due.

Let's level with each other. Have you ever experienced something like that? Most of us have been there. You get all ready to pull off something big for God. You set goals. You spend time and money. You tell a bunch of people. But as painful as it may be for us to admit it, goals not bathed in prayer or brought in humility before the Lord turn out to be downright useless. They don't go anywhere. They don't accomplish anything. They generate heat but no light. And you're left with confusion and defeat.

Maybe you make plans for a big Bible class in your home. You send out the invitations—7:30 P.M. sharp—you talk it up. The night comes and you have the living room all arranged—flowers on the table, fire on the grate, refreshments in the kitchen.

Then 7:30 comes . . . and goes. The clock in the hall tolls eight bells, and still nobody shows. The hands grind around to 8:30 and silence reigns. The fire dies down. The fizz goes out of the punch. The coffee gets cold. The refreshments dry up on the table. And your heart sinks.

A fellow told me some time ago about planning a big rally with a group of collegians. "Man," he said, "we made all sorts of arrangements. Neat stuff. Arranged for a room that seated two hundred fifty people. Publicized it like crazy. We had huge plans and record-breaking ideas. And eight people showed up."

Talk about confusion! That sort of thing will set you back on your heels. And frankly, it ought to! That's the time when you need to face the music, get quiet, fall back to your knees, and ask, "Lord, are You in this? Or is this just someone's great idea?"

Let me pass along an old motto of mine. It's guided me for well over thirty years and remains as appropriate now as the day it first slapped me alongside the head.

I try, I fail.
I trust, He succeeds!

Isn't that true? What simple counsel. Only eight words, yet how profound. Bottom line: If you are moving in the energy of the flesh, you're doomed to fail. The old hymn says it well: "The arm of flesh will fail you, you cannot trust your own." It's just a matter of time before they'll dig up the corpse, with your fingerprints all over the knife. But when you trust the Lord God to give you the next step, when you wait in humility upon Him, *He* will open the doors or close them, and you'll get to rest and relax until He says, "Go."

STEP FOUR: AN UNBEARABLE RESULT

Then Moses was afraid and said, "Surely the matter has become known" (Exodus 2:14).

First surprise. Next confusion, followed by fear, like icy fingers around the heart. When Moses' well-kept secret hit the primetime networks, he got the shakes. And acting on fear, the biblical account states that "he fled from the presence of Pharaoh."

Why did he run? Verse 15 tells us, "Pharaoh tried to kill Moses." Now that Moses had tipped his hand and shown his true loyalties, Pharaoh couldn't stomach having such a man around. In the king's eyes, a disloyal and out-of-control prince was better off dead. What awful repercussions grew out of Moses' ill-considered action.

It is very possible that you, too, have been forced to deal with such consequences. Your track record may reflect a pattern of great ambition but little knowledge. Great desire but little discernment. Great aspirations but little humility. Great zeal and energy but little wisdom. And so you have to run the rabbit trails right to the bitter dead-ends, one after another. You've run faster each time, but never succeeded. None has taken you where you wanted to go. And if the truth were known, your impulsive actions have resulted in an unbearable situation.

In my book, there's only one thing worse than being at the end of a self-directed life, and that's being in the middle of one.

You say, "Well, I'm in my thirties, I ought to know better than *that*."

Moses was forty.

You say, "Hey, I'm no novice! I've got education and training like you wouldn't believe!"

Better than Moses? Remember, by this time in his career, he was "educated in all the learning of the Egyptians."

You see, our impressive resumé is part of the problem. Sometimes we're educated beyond our own intelligence. We know more than we're safe to handle! The truth is, when you rely on the flesh to get a job done, you don't need more schooling. You don't need another degree. You don't need

47

more training seminars. Plain and simple, you need *wisdom*. So do I. So do all of God's people.

But discerning wisdom takes time. It takes some major bumps in the road. It takes enduring some failures and swallowing big and bitter doses of humility.

FROM THE PALACE TO THE WILDERNESS

Finding himself highly qualified to be completely useless, Moses tucked up his royal robes and ran like a scared coyote. Did he take off on foot, throw himself on the back of a horse, or borrow a royal chariot and ride it until the wheels fell off? Scripture doesn't say. We're told only that he "settled in the land of Midian; and sat down by a well" (Exodus 2:15).

Years ago, my sister Luci gave me a book titled *God's Wilderness*. It's a huge, coffee-table volume filled with pictures of the Sinai desert, from Midian all the way up to the slopes of Mt. Sinai. As I pondered this portion of Scripture, I dragged it off my shelf and thumbed through it, wondering just where Moses landed when he finally stopped running. What was that Midian desert like?

You wouldn't believe the photographs. They remind me of those Viking shots from the surface of Mars. What a bleak, desolate place! Maybe our government didn't need to spend all that money to put a little robot on the red planet. They could have saved a bundle by dropping that same robot out of a Piper Cub somewhere north of the Arabian peninsula. Midian! It makes the desert around Palm Springs look like British Columbia.

Incredibly barren. Hot, arid sand and gravel, punctuated by craggy chunks of rock, with an occasional scraggly bush somehow clinging to life.

Can you visualize Moses stumbling through that wasteland, catching his tailored clothing on thorns, tripping and lurching over half submerged rocks, picking his way through that tortured wilderness?

Moses wasn't strutting down the road singing, "I Did It My Way." He was a frightened and disillusioned fugitive running, escaping for his very life. His vaunted education now meant nothing to him. His knowledge of hieroglyphics and Egyptian poetry gave him no comfort. His military victories seemed hollow. Thanks to his rash act of violence, that same military wanted to kill him. And with every step, he probably groaned within himself over his untimely deed, saying things like, "Life is over. God can never, *never* use me. I'm *absolutely* finished."

He was wrong, of course. But it would be many weary years before he fully realized that fact.

Maybe that's where you are today as you read these words. This man Moses lived thousands of years ago, but the situation I've just described may seem as contemporary to you as today's stale bread in your kitchen. You say, "I've worked so hard. Tried so many things. Pushed myself so relentlessly. But it's gotten me nowhere. Nothing has worked for me. It's curtains."

Believe it or not, you may be closer than ever in your life to a spiritual breakthrough. Before we wrap up this chapter, I'd like to share two final thoughts.

First: *When the self-life has run its course, we settle in a desert.* You won't quit running in the flesh until you get to the endless, waterless sand dunes. When you finally get there, when you finally stumble to a stop in the pitiful shade of some sun-scorched rock, you will be saying to yourself, "Will God ever, ever use me?" And there you'll sit.

But did you notice *where* Moses sat down? The Bible tells us it was "by a well." Doesn't that seem significant?

Second: *When the self-life finally sits down, the well of a new life lies near.* When will we ever learn that? Highly qualified, capable people prefer to be on the move; sitting down goes against the grain. Yet when that broken forty-year-old named Moses finally slumped to the ground at the end of a self-driven life, fresh, cool drinking water was available right next to him.

Years ago, in a situation very much like what I've just described, I came across these poignant observations.

> Moses was out of touch with God. So he fled, and crossed the desert that lay between him and the eastern frontier; threaded the mountain passes of the Sinaitic peninsula, through which in after years he was to lead his people; and at last sat wearily down by a well in the land of Midian.[2]

....

Such experiences come to us all. We rush forward, thinking to carry all before us; we strike a few blows in vain; we are staggered with disappointment, and reel back; we are afraid at the first breath of human disapprobation; we flee from the scene...to hide ourselves in chagrin. Then we are hidden in the secret of God's presence from the pride of man. And there our vision clears; the silt drops from the current of our life...our self-life dies down; our spirit drinks of the river of God, which is full of water; our faith begins to grasp His arm, to be the channel for the manifestation of His power; and thus at last we emerge to be His hand to lead an Exodus.[3]

I close this third chapter with a strange but strong request.

Sit down. That's right, my friend, *sit down!*

You have run far enough. You have stood long enough. You have fought, pushed, and manipulated your way for too many years. God has finally grabbed your attention. He is saying, "Quit! Stop! Let Me handle it! Sit there on the hot sands of the desert where you have brought yourself. Look at what lies next to you. It is a well, full of fresh water." Soon it will be God's delight to bring that bucket up and refresh your soul. Sit still. Stay there. Be quiet.

Perhaps for the first time in your adult life, obey His words: "Cease striving and know that I am God" (Psalm 46:10).

Cease all the striving. Relax. Be contented by that well, and drink deeply. You are thirstier than you realize.

CHAPTER FOUR

Lessons Learned From Failure

"Happily ever after" belongs at the end of a fairy tale, not in a description of the Christian life. Life in Christ is *real*. It isn't plastic, it isn't stained-glass, it isn't saccharine, it isn't fantasy-land. In all my years of walking with the Lord, I have yet to meet one Christian who has "lived happily ever after." On the other hand, I have met a great many significant saints who have endured affliction, loss, disappointment, setbacks, failures, and incredible pain through the years. And I have seen many of those same men, women, and even a few adolescents cling to their joy, radiate hope, and sustain a winsome spirit... even through heartache... even through tears... even at death's door.

Living as we do in a product-oriented culture, we like to package our faith, too. We prefer to sell a slick, shrink-wrapped version of salvation that includes happiness and peace, and happiness here and now, and heaven by and by. While there is nothing wrong with good marketing techniques or teaching principles of authentic success, there is something wrong if we neglect to mention the *process*, which must inevitably include times of defeat and failure.

I wouldn't have to go back very far on my calendar to describe a week where I missed the mark—missed the whole target—more than I hit close to the bull's eye. And I don't have to be a prophet to proclaim that you have experienced the same. Of course you have. You may be having such a week even as you read these words.

What I'd like to know is who erected such a happily-ever-after standard of perfection in the first place? God knows very well we aren't able to produce perfection; that's why Jesus, the perfect Son of God, placed us into His family. That's why He gave us a position of perfect righteousness in Him, reminding us by contrast that our own daily experience will constantly fall short.

If you're waiting for a seamless, blemish-free week, friend, you're going to wait in vain. There is no such thing. And until we learn how to derive lessons from seasons of failure and loss, we will keep repeating those failures—digging ourselves into an ever deeper hole—rather than moving on as we grow up.

What you and I need is a *process* that leads to times of victory and success. Then, with memories of those golden moments shining in our minds, we'll learn how to avoid some of those valleys, or how to climb out of them more quickly. That process, I believe, is every bit as important as the product.

THE PSALMIST TAKES HIS LUMPS

Please glance with me at two of my favorite verses in Psalm 119:

> Before I was afflicted I went astray, but now I keep Your word.
> (v. 67)

> It is good for me that I was afflicted, that I may learn Your statutes.
> The law of your mouth is better to me than thousands of gold and
> silver pieces. (vv. 71–72)

What a mature perspective! In his Living Bible paraphrase, Ken Taylor captures the sense of these verses in a startling way: "I used to wander off until you punished me; now I closely follow all you say. . . . The punishment you gave me was the best thing that could have happened to me, for it taught me to pay attention to your laws. They are more valuable to me than millions in silver and gold!"

Don't miss the thought here. The psalmist has been hurting for some period of time. He doesn't tell us what causes his pain, nor does he tell us how long he has endured it. He simply tells us that it happened. He describes to us the dark and dismal backwash of failure, and the serious affliction he experienced at the hands of the Lord.

Looking back with twenty-twenty vision after the affliction has run its course, the psalmist reflects, "There are two things I can say about failure...."

EXPERIENCING FAILURE PROMOTES
AN OBEDIENT LIFE

First, when I go through times of failure, I am more than ever prompted to live in obedience. When I emerge from dark passages of walking and acting in the flesh and (finally) come to the end of that ugly scene, my heart cries out for purity. For light. I hunger for it! I am disgusted with my selfishness, more determined than ever to stay on the right path, walking closer than ever to Christ. Times of failure bring me to a place of wanting to live in uncompromising obedience.

There's a second principle of equal importance.

EXPERIENCING FAILURE PROMPTS
A TEACHABLE SPIRIT

It was good for me to be afflicted *so that I might learn*....(v. 71, NIV)

Can you name people today who seem to listen carefully to God—people whose hearts are especially sensitive to the Holy Spirit? I can almost guarantee that those are men and women who know what it is to be broken and bruised. They have the scars to prove it.

Perhaps as you read these words you bear the marks of a carnal week, day after day in which you've gone your own way and grieved the Spirit of

God. And now you come to these pages with desperation to change in your heart—to learn from God and renew your fellowship with Him. Do you realize what's happened? Your failure has given you a sensitive, teachable spirit. It has broken the pride barrier in your life. It is what Paul called a "godly sorrow" (2 Corinthians 7:10).

Yet for all of that, one of the hardest things for you and me to do is own up to our own failures. Whether we're talking to our spouses, our kids, our employers, or with our Lord Himself, it goes against the grain to come clean and admit our offenses. The knee-jerk response every time is to employ defense mechanisms: to deny, to excuse, to rationalize, to *reinterpret* our shortfalls.

The best and healthiest course is to 'fess up. To call failure, "failure." To name sin for what it is. To admit we were wrong, and having declared it, to learn what God may have to teach us from the experience.

It was Sir Winston Churchill, in the midst of Nazi bombings, who said to the people of London, "This is not the end. It is not even the beginning of the end. But it is, perhaps, the end of the beginning."[1] He was the one who offered the best definition of success I've ever read: "Success is moving from one failure to another with no loss of enthusiasm."

Churchill's words speak very well to our failures in the Christian life. This isn't the end! It's not even the beginning of the end. But it is, perhaps, the end of the beginning. In other words, as you begin to interpret failure correctly, you will take your first giant step toward maturity.

Fiorello La Guardia, Mayor of New York City during the 1930s, used to say, "I don't fail often. But when I do, it's a beaut!" Maybe that's the way you feel. "Chuck, I don't stumble all that often, but boy, when I do, it's a royal belly-flop."

All right, so it's a royal flop, but royal flops can lead to royal lessons learned. If you fail only slightly, you'll only get a slight lesson. But if the bottom drops out and you fall forty stories, that's when you begin to learn. Actually, it isn't the fall that hurts...it's that sudden stop at the bottom!

Moses took a forty-story fall just like that. And as we pick up the biblical account, he's a heavy-hearted, bruised-and-battered soul who has come to a sudden stop at the bottom. In a matter of mere days, he has stepped off the top of the pyramid as Pharaoh-designate and down to a bedraggled, penniless fugitive on the backside of Zipville.

I've just come through an extremely difficult week myself. You don't need to know the details; suffice it to say, I've been blindsided by a couple of things while I was looking in another direction. I didn't even hear the footsteps! I feel like a quarterback who drops back to watch his receiver run a pattern way down field and gets steam-rolled by a two-hundred-eighty-pound linebacker somebody forgot to block. After getting crunched, you find yourself looking out the ear hole in your helmet wondering, *What happened?*

Last night, as I was screwing my head back on straight and licking my wounds a little, I was thinking through this chapter. And I found myself thinking, *Thanks, Lord... I guess I needed that. Now it will be easier for me to write what I need to write.* (Seems a shame a guy has to pay such a price in order to gain a little insight. I'm glad I wasn't writing about the crucifixion!)

Exodus 2:15 tells us that Moses "sat down by a well." At that moment, he felt as if he was at the *bottom* of the well, looking up. A well in Midian, of all places. That was as far as he was going to run. It certainly must have been the lowest ebb of his life. Perhaps you've arrived at a similar place during this past year, or even this past season of the year. You think to yourself, *God's had enough with this cowboy. He's through with me. I'll never be useful to Him!*

Dazed and exhausted, Moses may very well have stared into the depths of that well on that hot desert afternoon, musing on lessons from his recent past. Let me suggest four such thoughts he might have considered in those reflective moments. The first lesson emerges from the previous chapter.

SPIRITUAL ENDS ARE NEVER
ACHIEVED BY CARNAL MEANS

Back in Egypt, as you may recall, Moses had "looked this way and that," then murdered an Egyptian and buried him with sand. As we have already noted, Moses may have thought he was following God's plan in that moment, but he never bothered to check signals. He certainly never prayed before he struck the blow. We have no record that he sought God's face before taking that significant step. As a result, the bottom fell out of Moses' dreams like a soggy cardboard box. It was the biggest setback of his life.

The fact is, you cannot sow a fleshly seed and reap a spiritual plant. You cannot plant a carnal act and grow spiritual fruit. If you manipulate and connive and scheme and lie to get yourself to the top, don't thank God for the promotion! God knows, as you know, that you maneuvered and pulled strings and buried those carnal carcasses in the soil to get yourself promoted. So when you get that bigger office and the key to the executive washroom, don't give Him the credit. He doesn't want it. Your fingerprints are all over that scheme, not His.

At times we say to the Lord, "Thanks for that, Father." And the Lord must answer back, "Who? Me? I didn't pull that off. That was *your* doing." You cheat on an exam, make a good grade, and thank God for the "A." You fudge on your income tax, get a nice refund and thank Him for the extra cash you can give to the building fund.

It doesn't work that way, friend. He says to you, "This isn't My doing. This is your plan."

As Moses was sitting by that well, I can imagine a still, small voice cutting through his musings. "Don't thank Me, Moses, that an Egyptian lies buried in the sand. *You* did that. And fleshly acts like that can never advance My plans. It was carnal, Moses, from start to finish. And you know it."

He did know it. He realized it most keenly when he had come back to the Hebrews the next day and tried to take leadership . . . only to be mocked and rejected. And then the whole scheme came unglued, and he had to take to his heels. Thankfully, Moses learned that first lesson well. And I think he learned another one, too.

TIMING IS AS IMPORTANT AS ACTION

Sometimes I think it's *more* important. How many times have I done the right thing at the wrong time . . . and had it blow up in my face? I'm embarrassed to think back and remember how often that's happened. The fact is, God not only plans what we are to do, He has arranged the right time for us to do it.

As Moses looked back over that incident with the Egyptian (he must have rehearsed it in his mind a thousand times through the intervening years), he could have written one word over the entire carnal experience: *premature*. He jumped into that scene. He vaulted into rebellion. He pushed his way in. He forced the door. And everything backfired.

Years ago, I latched onto a simple principle that has given me untold help through countless situations. I'd like to give it to you, if only to keep you from stubbing your toe as often as I've stubbed mine. Here it is:

When God's in it ... it flows.
When the flesh is in it ... it's forced.

Do you find yourself trying to hammer a square peg into a round hole? Are you pushing and straining and dumping loads of emotional freight to get something going? You'd better call time out and check with the Coach! When God's in something, it flows.

Let's say you had it in your heart to get into some kind of ministry at your place of employment. You'd like the opportunity to sit down with some co-workers and maybe spend fifteen minutes together around the Scriptures at lunch. Great idea! But don't force it. Lay it before God and let Him open the doors. If He is in it, it's remarkable how approval will be granted, how a growing interest will percolate, and how the timing will fall right into place. It will come together almost in spite of you.

Timing is as important as action. I think this is where wisdom comes in. Knowledge tells me what to do; wisdom tells me when to do it and how to carry it out. The longer I live, the more I believe the words of the sage who wrote, "One blow struck when the time is right is worth a thousand struck in premature eagerness." God has no limitations in His ability to pull something off, but He's going to do it in His time and not before.

What if Joshua had said something like this? "Let's walk *five* times around Jericho, then blow our trumpets. Seven laps seems excessive to me." Do you think the walls would still have fallen?

What if David had seen King Saul vulnerable in the cave, and had said, "Now's my chance to cut years off this exhausting hide-n-seek chase through the wilderness. I'll just dispatch the old boy right now and claim the crown. After all, God said it would be mine." Do you suppose God would have blessed such a short cut?

We've all fumed with frustration, feeling as though heaven was chugging along in first gear when we needed to be in overdrive. In our darker moments, we may have felt like saying to the Lord, "Hey, this is *serious*. Can't You move it up a notch or two on Your priority list? Can't You get something moving down here? Hurry up, Lord! I've been talking to You for weeks."

The problem, of course, is not that God is too slow. It's that we are too fast. Too fast for our own good.

Ever seen an untrained dog on a leash? It's kind of funny, unless you're the one who's attached to the other end of that leash. There's young Fido, straining mightily at his tether, eyes bulging, tongue hanging out, jerking here, tugging there, panting and wheezing along with a half-collapsed windpipe. What's the problem with that picture? Does the fault lie with that poor guy who's getting his arm dislocated out of the socket? Is he being cruel and unreasonable for walking instead of galloping hither and yon at the dog's pace? Or could it be that the dog needs to learn some new words like, "heel" and "sit?"

We had a dog like that in our previous neighborhood. I'd usually see him in the morning when I'd step out on the porch in the California sunshine to collect my *L.A. Times*. You could always tell that particular critter was coming because you could hear him way up the block—wheezing and gagging and choking, his feet slipping and scraping along the sidewalk. The owner was invariably being wrenched this way and that, while the dog craned his neck and pulled as if he were on the trail of a wounded jackrabbit. It was like that every morning, and neither dog nor owner seemed to be enjoying themselves.

One day, after observing that spectacle once again, I remember thinking, *That scene reminds me of me!* I want to get way out ahead of God, pulling and straining, choking on my own eagerness, not having much fun at all.

And God is saying, "Slow down. Take it easy. Heel! You're only hurting yourself. Let's enjoy the morning. Let's enjoy this walk together."

Moses was too strong. Too educated. Too cultured. Too gifted. Too advantaged. He was straining at the leash and had to learn that waiting—pacing himself—was not a sign of weakness but of strength. Maybe, as you read these words, you have to admit that you haven't learned that, either. You're straining and gagging and kicking up lots of anxiety dust because life isn't moving rapidly enough; circumstances aren't changing at a fast enough clip.

I'm afraid I have some sad news for you. If that is your mindset, you will *always* be frustrated. Why? Because life will move along at its own pace. No matter how much you may will it to be so, circumstances will simply not conform themselves to your expectations or time schedule. If you try to force *events*, you will only give yourself blisters, ulcers, or an early heart attack. If you try to force *people*, they will never measure up; they will end up resenting you, avoiding you, or worse still, simply ignoring you. No one likes to be pushed.

Here's another thought that may have occurred to our weary friend by the well.

HIDING WRONG DOESN'T ERASE WRONG; IT ONLY POSTPONES ITS DISCOVERY

According to Exodus 2:12, Moses hid the body of the slain Egyptian. But by the next day, it was all over the papers. They found the Egyptian. Five inches of loose sand hid nothing.

Hiding wrong, Moses now had to admit, does nothing to *erase* wrong. And I am convinced that from that moment on Moses determined never to hide anything again. He would be transparent. He would speak his heart, regardless of the risks of vulnerability. He would no longer hide.

The most Adamic muscle in all of us is the "hiding muscle." It goes all the way back to the Garden of Eden. It was (and is) the classic reflex response of sinners the world over. Isn't that interesting? The first thing Adam and Eve did was hide behind some bushes when they heard God walking in the garden. The next thing they did was to sew together a couple of ridiculous fig-leaf bikinis to hide their nakedness.

Remember the scene? God came to walk with His man and woman in the cool of the day, just as He had always done. But where was the pinnacle of Creation? Where was the man he had formed from the dust of the ground? He was hiding. Crouching behind a blooming rhododendron bush, peering through the leaves. And we've been hiding ever since. We hide the consequences of acting in the flesh. We hide from ourselves the truth about ourselves. As Mark Twain put it, "We're all like the moon. We have a dark side we don't want anybody to see."

Why not? Because you and I consider it vastly, supremely important to emphasize image and appearance. How we appear to others completely overshadows who we really are. What I want to know is *why*.

Sometime in my ministry, I am going to gather up enough courage to have a testimony time where the only thing we'll share is our failures. Wouldn't that be different? Ever been to a testimony meeting where everybody else seemed to be on Cloud 39 and you were in Tunnel Number 7? One after another is talking about soaring in the heavenlies, while you're counting gum wrappers in the gutter. Why don't we visit the other side? Why not hand the microphone around and say, "When was the last time you took a nosedive? Can you share with others what it was like to experience a major disappointment?"

Far from being a downer, I've got a hunch that might prove to be a major encouragement to a group of people who feel all alone in their struggles. So many of us feel as though we have to hide our failures, believing no one else could have possibly failed as we have. Some are even afraid to tell God about it, fearing He might be as put off as we imagine others will be.

But He isn't like that at all, is He? When we take a tumble, and cry out to Him in our shame and our distress, the psalmist says He "inclines His ear" to us. He bends over to listen. We say, "Oh, Father, I've failed! I've failed terribly. Look at what I've done!" And then He puts His arms around us, just as a loving earthly father would do. He then says, "I accept you just as you are. I acknowledge that what you have done was wrong, as you've confessed it to Me. Now, My son, My daughter, let's move on."

Some of the most tender experiences of my life as a father have come when my children have honestly said to me, "Daddy, I want to tell you that what I did was wrong." And some of the hardest times of a father's life come when the child won't admit to wrong and tries to cover it up.

Moses, I'm convinced, never covered up again. He learned that lesson from failure. He learned a fourth lesson, too.

SPIRITUAL LEADERSHIP IS GOD-APPOINTED, NOT SELF-ASSUMED

This is such a foreign concept in the secular world. How do you get promoted in the world system? Well, you have to assume an air of total confidence. You work up a killer resumé, dancing near the edge of exaggeration. Then you present yourself in full burnished armor, banners flying, as capable of handling whatever the job may be, from chief executive right on down to assistant manager (preferably the former).

That's not the way it is in the family of God, but Moses hadn't understood that... not yet at least. He was a *summa cum laude* graduate of Sun Temple U. He'd earned his stars in a distinguished military career. It was only a matter of time before he would be proclaimed Pharaoh Moses the First (think of that!). He'd pulled himself up through the ranks (or so he imagined) by his own sandal straps. With such confidence in his own capability, jumpstarting a rebellion seemed like something well within his range of competence. He just went out and did it. And why not? It came natural.

In the spiritual life, however, it has to come *super*natural.

The same principle holds true in the selection of church leaders. Here's what I mean: We often feel that because a person has been very successful in business, he's a slam dunk to be successful as an officer in the church. But that simply isn't true. Some men and women who have conquered and accomplished much in the corporate area are *pitiful* when it comes to leadership roles in a local assembly. We aren't looking for "natural leaders" in the Body of Christ, we are looking for spiritual, God-appointed leaders. And these folks may look very, very different from their secular counterparts.

If you are a pastor-in-the-making, don't kid yourself into thinking you'll get to the top of the pile and have any church you want just because you're loaded with charisma, and you've pulled the right strings or dropped the right names. It's never like that. More often than not, God will call you to the very church you *didn't* want.

It's amazing how many times Cynthia and I have had to eat our words through our years of ministry together. Early on, we thought we had it all nailed down. We told the Lord, "We're ready to serve you, Lord, wherever You want us to go, with the exceptions of the Dallas area, New England, and California." We thought that was reasonable enough; those were three places where we simply didn't want to live. Obviously, God wouldn't put us where we would choose not to be.

Guess what? Yeah, you're right on the money, and you're smiling. We've had pastorates in all of those areas, one after another, and God placed us in all three. Now we're back in Dallas, the first place we said we "didn't want to go." I can remember Cynthia looking at me one time and saying, "Chuck, you won't hear me praying not to go to Alaska! Because as soon as I say, 'Not Alaska, Lord,' then you'd better pack your long-johns and woolen mittens.'" We both laughed out loud. And, by the way, we've never said, "Not Alaska!"

It's remarkable how God appoints and directs as He wills, and we have very little to say about it. Moses learned that lesson from failure.

A. W. Tozer says, "A true and safe leader is likely one who has no desire to lead, but is forced into a position of leadership by the inward pressure of the Holy Spirit and by the press of the external situation."[2] Such was the case with David and the Old Testament prophets. Even Saul, Israel's first king, hid among the baggage so that he wouldn't be drafted. A shorter man might have pulled it off, but Saul was a big guy and they nailed him.

And in the church, I can't think of a great leader from Paul to the present day who wasn't drafted by the Holy Spirit for the task. Most of the great church leaders didn't look up into the stars and say, "Ahh, there lies my destiny. I'm going to climb to the top and breathe that rarified air." More often than not, God's leadership candidates are aghast at their selection. They look with chagrin at the assignment before them. They can hardly believe their ears when God says, "You are the man," or "You are the woman."

Author Os Guinness reminds us of Martin Luther's unusual experience, which vividly illustrates the man's surprise at being used by God to lead so many others into a reformation that swept across Europe. He writes,

> Painfully climbing up the steps of a medieval cathedral in the dark, he reached for the stair rope to steady himself and was amazed to hear the bell ring out above him—he had inadvertently pulled the bell rope and woken up the whole countryside.
>
> Far from a man with a comprehensive vision of reform and a well-calculated plan for carrying it out, Luther struggled painfully for salvation before God and was surprised to set off the cataclysmic sixteenth-century movement we now simply call the Reformation.[3]

Do you know how I know Moses learned this lesson in humility? Because forty years later, at the burning bush, when God said, "You're the man to deliver the people from Egypt," Moses responded, in effect, "You've got to be kidding, Lord. Not me. Wrong guy, wrong address. You probably meant to appear in a different bush to someone else, right? Remember me? I'm the failure. I'm the washout. Forty years ago I couldn't pull it off, and I surely can't do it now. Not me, Lord."

"Yes, Moses. You."

"No! No! I can't even talk. I stutter all over the place."

"I'll use your mouth."

"But I can't lead. I have trouble enough with a few lousy sheep."

"I'll show you how to lead."

"You don't understand, I can't speak in public."

"I'll use your brother. He'll speak for you."

"Uh . . . well, if You insist. . . . "

The eighty-year-old Moses ran himself right out of excuses. And then he reluctantly said (with great reservations), "Oh, all right, Lord. *But it won't work.*"

Yet it did work. God worked. And Moses became the most magnificent leader Israel ever had—God appointed, not self-assumed. (We'll look at that in greater depth in chapters 6 and 7.) That was the secret, plain and simple.

Did he change? Were there any strategic changes in Moses' life? Yes, I think there were a few. As I ponder the man's transformation, I discover at least three.

HE DEVELOPED A SERVANT'S ATTITUDE

Now the priest of Midian had seven daughters; and they came to draw water and filled the troughs to water their father's flock. Then the shepherds came and drove them away, but Moses stood up and helped them and watered their flock. (Exodus 2:16–17)

Moses, the Prince of Egypt, alias Prince Charming, watering animals? Why?

Because Moses had just choked down the biggest wedge of humble pie you can imagine. By now, the man was ready to do anything. Isn't it interesting, though, that in this incident Moses was allowed to be a deliverer on an immensely smaller scale? Earlier, he had thought he was going to deliver a nation. He had grand dreams and mighty schemes. But this time God said, "You want a job as deliverer? Then stand up and do it, son. *Start here*. There are seven women here in Midian who need a champion at this moment."

Moses could have shrugged it off. He could have said, "Aw forget it. I'm out of the delivery business. Let someone else do the job." But he didn't. It was here Moses took his first steps in becoming a man of selfless dedication.

The young women would later tell their father, "An Egyptian delivered us from the hand of the shepherds, and what is more, he even drew the water for us and watered the flock" (v. 19).

It wasn't Cecil B. DeMille with a cast of thousands surrounding the hero, it was just one small act of courage. Of this incident, Matthew Henry writes, "He loved to be doing justice, and appearing in the defense of such as he saw injured, which every man ought to do as far as it is in the power of his hand to do it. He loved to be doing good. Wherever the Providence of God casts us, we should desire and endeavor to be useful; and, when we cannot do the good we would, we must be ready to do the good we can. And he that is faithful in a little shall be entrusted with more."[4]

That thought moves me. If you can't do the good you *would,* do the good you *can.* You may have had big-time plans in your life—major league dreams that haven't panned out. You were going to write a best-selling book, but the opportunities just haven't come along. Are you willing to write for your church newsletter? Believe it or not, some of my most satisfying moments as a writer came many years ago as I labored over a weekly column in a church newsletter. It wasn't the *Los Angeles Times* or *Christianity Today,* but God gave me a great deal of joy and heart satisfaction in that task. And later, to my absolute surprise, He was pleased to bless those efforts in a wider way.

Maybe you wanted to teach in seminary or Bible school, but the pressures of life forced you in a different direction. Are you willing to teach a Sunday School class? Are you up for leading a small group Bible study? Is it really the teaching that draws your heart, or is it the prestige that goes along with the position?

Maybe you'd hoped to be a missionary and bring the word of Christ to distant portions of the globe, but for one reason or another, that door has never opened. Are you willing to start an evangelistic Bible study in your neighborhood? Are you open to working with Hispanic or Vietnamese people in your own city? Are you willing to befriend a few lonely international students?

Failure, you see, teaches us a servant's attitude. And what does a servant do? He does "the next task." She does what is available and ready for her to do. Those without such an attitude resist getting their hands dirty. They never want to get involved in the messy part of working with people. They always want the polished part, the fun part. But the tough stuff behind the scenes? Well, give that to someone else.

God, however, will use our failures and setbacks to cultivate within us a servant's heart. That's all part of the process.

I noticed something else that changed in Moses, too.

HE WAS WILLING TO BE OBSCURE

Now the priest of Midian had seven daughters; and they came to draw water and filled the troughs to water their father's flock. Then the shepherds came and drove them away, but Moses stood up and helped them and watered their flock. When they came to Reuel their father, he said, "Why have you come back so soon today?" So they said, "An Egyptian delivered us from the hand of the shepherds, and what is more, he even drew the water for us and watered the flock." He said to his daughters, "Where is he then? Why is it that you have left the man behind? Invite him to have something to eat." Moses was willing to dwell with the man.... (vv. 16–21)

Pay close attention to that last sentence. "Moses was willing to dwell with the man." How good that is. Here is a man he had never met; an obscure desert priest and shepherd, who had spent a lifetime raising sheep (and daughters!) in the desolate patch of land known as Midian. "And he gave his daughter Zipporah to Moses. Then she gave birth to a son, and he named him Gershom, for he said, "I have been a sojourner in a foreign land" (vv. 21–22).

Moses, who would have been in line to marry an exotic Cleopatra-type beauty back in Egypt, settled down with a shepherdess. And when she gave birth to their firstborn, Moses gave him an unusual name: Gershom. It means "a sojourner." That's what Moses had become—a sojourner in a distant land, forgotten and obscure. He came into Midian not knowing anyone, not knowing the ropes, not even knowing where he was going to live. But when Jethro said, "Young man, would you like to live with us?" Moses replied, "Yes, I would. I'll live anywhere."

Let me ask you directly: Are you willing to be obscure? A servant's mindset will teach you what that attitude is all about. To put it in simple terms, in the Body of Christ some people are called to be the toes. Not everyone can be a right hand, an eye, or an ear. Some people have to be the toe, or the heel, or the kidney, or the liver. These members are (hopefully) seldom seen. But just let one of them stop functioning for awhile and watch out! The whole body is in trouble.

Moses was willing to be obscure, to dwell apart from the limelight, to accept his new status. I ask again: Are you? God will use failure in your life to break down that strong desire in your heart to see your name in lights. And when he finally breaks you of that lust for recognition, He may place you before the lights like you've never imagined. But then it won't matter. You won't care if you're prime time or small time, center stage or backstage, leading the charge or packing the baggage. You're just part of the King's army. People of selfless dedication are mainly... available. That's plenty!

There is yet another lesson Moses learned from his failure.

HE LEARNED TO REST AND RELY ON GOD

The last three verses of Exodus 2 are both heavy with sadness and alive with hope.

> Now it came about in the course of those many days that the king of Egypt died. And the sons of Israel sighed because of the bondage, and they cried out; and their cry for help because of {their} bondage rose up to God. So God heard their groaning; and God remembered His covenant with Abraham, Isaac, and Jacob. God saw the sons of Israel, and God took notice of them. (vv. 23–25)

You'd better believe that Moses, though tucked away in a corner of that wasteland, heard that news from the travelers in caravans making their way up from Egypt through the Midian desert. When Moses learned the Hebrews were crying out, his heart must have turned over within him. But unlike before, he rested and relied upon God. He didn't try to organize a rescue party. He didn't slip back into Egypt as an assassin or saboteur. Not him! He'd learned that lesson. Now he simply said in his heart, *God knows all about it. When He's ready, He will work. I must leave it at that.* Rather than rushing back into battle, he relied on and rested in God.

Some years ago, I was reading a Navigator publication and came across the writing of Ruth Myers. She and her first husband, Dean Denler, had traveled across Southeast Asia and Far Eastern islands, bringing music and the Word of God wherever they went. Dean, however, lost a vicious battle with cancer, leaving Ruth as a widow with two little children. Subsequently remarried to Warren Myers, she paused one day and looked back on that dark chapter in her life. As a result of that reflection, she penned these words:

I remember one spring when I was a widow. Both of my children were facing excruciating problems. I would lie in bed at night harassed by anxiety. Even though I prayed about their needs, my worries kept returning. Why was I so anxious? At the time, I was afraid of failure as a mother—my number one responsibility. I didn't even have their father to share the blame with. I was seeking identity in successful performance.

When I realized that, I prayed with new insight. I said, "Lord, I confess my persistent anxiety and reliance on successful performance and the approval of others. Thank You for Your forgiveness. The children are dedicated to You. If their difficult experiences will glorify You, even if I seem to be a failure as their mother, You have my permission. Even if it means my appearing to the world around me as a failure, You have my permission." My gnawing anxiety evaporated.

Do you know who it is who keeps erecting all those unrealistic standards in your life? Do you know who keeps raising the bar beyond all hope of clearing it?

It's you. You do. And so do I. Our Heavenly Father doesn't. The psalmist tells us, He knows our frame. He remembers that we are dust. We think we're finished because of our failures, but God says, "No, you're just getting started. Press on!"

Our problem isn't that we've failed. Our problem is that we haven't failed enough. We haven't been brought low enough to learn what God wants us to learn. We're still trying to redeem Egypt single-handedly.

Remember one of the songs from the Seventies we used to sing again and again? It mentioned how we learned to trust in Jesus and to trust in God by going "through it all." Not around it. *Through* it.

Through it *all*. That's the ticket! Through the victories and the failures. Through the Egypts and the Midians. Through the brilliant days of accomplishment and the broken days beside the well. Through the heady days of laughter and success and those nameless intervals of setback and blank despair. Through it all, He is with us, leading us, teaching us, humbling us, preparing us.

As I wrap up this chapter, I'm grateful that in one area of life—no matter who we are and no matter what our backgrounds—we are all on the same level. We all qualify as failures. *All of us!*

So what are you trying to prove? Who are you trying to impress? Why don't you step off that treadmill and just be yourself? Plead with the Spirit of God to prepare you, then use you, however He pleases, dark side and all. You'll be amazed how that takes the pressure off.

This very moment, you and I are the recipients of a gift from One who loves us just the way we are, warts, cracks, failures, and all. Since it is a gift, you might as well open your hands and receive it. Look, there—that's your name on the tag, just underneath the ribbon.

The gift is called grace.

CHAPTER FIVE

The Desert: School of Self-Discovery

O ne by one, clad in cap and gown, each of the Swindoll children has marched across the platform, taken high school diploma in hand, and walked down the stairs into the next chapter of life.

Before that moment, however, before the majestic strains of "Pomp and Circumstance" filled the auditorium, before Dad and Mom had a chance to get swept along on a strong current of nostalgia, each of our tribe had already been wrestling with the question of college.

To go or not to go. To work awhile, play awhile, or plunge right in, hammer 'n tongs. To live at home for a time, or to venture forth where no Swindoll has gone before. Private college or Christian college, or state college or community college, large college or small college, or no college at all. Which would it be?

If you've ever been through it, you know it's a sometimes exciting, sometimes agonizing process. Our family has seen it all: the brochures, the catalogs, the campus visits, the phone calls from the recruitment office, the trauma of decision pressures, the sudden deviations and gut-wrenching mid-course corrections.

By and by, the candidate list narrows, the far-out options evaporate in the relentless heat of realism ("No son, I'm not sure at all about the University of Fiji"), and the best choice becomes increasingly obvious and logical.

Then comes that moment in the driveway when the car is packed to the gills, and that young man, that young lady, walks out of the house. We all hesitate at the car door, knowing life must change when that car drives away. There are hugs, kisses, last-minute items to remember, stern admonitions, more hugs...and tears. And then the car drives away, and Mom and Dad stand arm-in-arm in the empty driveway, wondering where all the years went.

That's the usual college routine.

God has a school, too. Did you know that? And there isn't anything *usual* about it. It doesn't have dormitories, a science lab, or a football field. It isn't listed in any catalog, magazine, or website. The high school counselor may know nothing about it. Yet it is one of the most profound institutions of learning you could ever attend.

I know. I'm an alum. I've been there...more than once. Maybe you've taken some courses there as well. As a father who loves his kids, I can't say I'm excited about any of my children spending time in *that* school. On the other hand, life being what it is, I know they most likely will. Since I have experienced the voice and presence of the Lord God in that place, I can't help longing for each of my sons and daughters to know Him as I have known Him, to hear His voice as I have heard His voice. Yet, in my father's heart, I would spare them from the tuition. It can be extremely high.

I am referring to God's school in the desert, and I don't mean Arizona State or UNLV. I speak of that arid, often barren campus in which God places His children to prepare them for a particular task in life. There's nothing glamorous, colorful, or attractive about this particular desert. It was never designed to be. It's not Palm Desert or Sedona, believe me. In fact, it's probably more like the Sahara or the Serengeti.

It's a place of desolation: craggy rocks, trackless sand, life-sapping heat. Some people spend a few weeks in that wilderness. Others, many months. Moses walked those barren lands for forty years. That's f-o-r-t-y years; you read it correctly.

THE DESERT'S MANY FACES

It may help you to know that the Hebrew word for "desert" is *midbaar*. It's from the word *dahbaar*, meaning "to speak." Let me draw from that root term and suggest that the desert is the place where God speaks, where He communicates some of His most important messages to us.

Apart from that desert experience, you and I might live out our lives without ever hearing or knowing what the God of the universe desires to tell us. The wilderness-like desert changes that. In that lonely place, you find yourself stripped of all the things you hang on to for comfort—all the stuff you felt you needed through life but really didn't need at all.

It gets very quiet in those wide, sandy wastes—so quiet you can hear your pulse pound in your ears, so quiet you can hear the voice of God.

I remember finding myself in a desert—a literal one—some years ago. I'd been asked to join a group of elders from another church for a planning meeting. To get to that rendezvous, I had to drive quite a number of miles through a stretch of southern California desert. On the way home, just on a whim, I pulled off the highway onto a little side road that wound its way out into that wild and solitary terrain. Climbing out into the late afternoon heat, I took a little hike through the sand and scrub brush, finally reaching a point where I could see neither road nor car.

I can't tell you what it was that drew me. Maybe I felt the need to soak up some of that rare solitude for a few minutes. And that's what I did. I just stood there for awhile, all alone.

A desert wind came up, howling across those miles of empty land. There was no other sound at all. Nothing. I felt the sun bear down on me, and the bite of wind-whipped sand. Squinting against the glare, I scanned far horizons, shimmering with heat. It was a scorched and desolate place. No fruit. No shrubbery. No lush, verdant lawns. No orchards, heavy with fruit. No stream singing in its banks. Even though I knew the car and the highway were right around the corner from me, I felt strangely removed into another world. Loneliness began to press in all around me the longer I stayed in that deserted place. Silence wrapped me like a second skin.

Your desert interlude may not occur in a literal desert at all. It might be in a logging camp in Alaska, a trailer court in Georgia, a farmhouse in Kansas, or a posh, hilltop apartment in Seattle. Your wilderness experience might involve caring for an ailing family member or an elderly parent over an extended time, with no help at hand and no relief in sight. Your sojourn in the dry lands might be a stubborn physical condition that keeps you confined. It could be that deep soul-ache that comes with an unfaithful spouse, or a rebellious teenager. It may be moving from an area where you had numerous friends and deep family ties to a place that seems strange and alien, where you don't know anyone at all. You feel displaced...shelved. It may be a failure at school, an estrangement from an old friend, a boring, thankless job, or a deadline that grinds down on you like a coarse millstone.

The desert wears many faces.

It may be crowded with people, yet it is lonely.

It may rain day and night without reprieve, yet it is barren.

Flowers may bloom and trees may blossom all around you, yet it is desolate.

Does God know? Does He understand? He understands very well, my friend. After all, He's the One who *put* you there. His schooling includes time in the wilderness. That's where He gets our attention.

WILDERNESS 101

In Deuteronomy 32, the Holy Spirit pens these words about the nation Israel. With your permission, I'd like to apply them in a very personal way. "He found him in a desert land, and in the howling waste of a wilderness; He encircled him, He cared for him, He guarded him as the pupil of His eye" (v. 10).

The "He" of this verse is God, and the "him" is a reference to the Jews. But let's personalize our Lord's words here. Let's place your name in the verse in place of "him." God found __(you)__ in a desert land...God found __(you)__ in the howling waste of a wilderness. God encircled you. Cared for you. And guarded you as the pupil of His eye.

The Lord, who set you down in that desert land, knows precisely what manner of wasteland experience you need. He knows the very place where the distractions of life will be silenced, and you will be able to hear His voice. Your "howling wilderness" may look very different from mine. God knows each of us in our inmost hearts; He understands what it will take to strip us of the crutches that keep us from running in His will and the noises that keep us from hearing His words of counsel and tender love. He knows how to oversee our curriculum in this school of the desert, building character qualities into our lives that we would not otherwise gain.

Isolation is always part of the wilderness experience. Never forget that. Once God finds the desert that you need, He ushers you off the bus and drives away. At least it seems that way. And the instant feeling you get is, *God's gone! Where is He? He's left me in this place!* In the midst of this painful experience, you find you are no longer able to do things you once were able to do. Fear sets in. You say to yourself, *I'm going to lose my gifts. I'm going to lose my usefulness. I'm forgotten! God's left me behind. Time is running out. Opportunities are passing me by. I'll never get out of this place.*

The nation of Israel, as it wandered in the Sinai Desert, must have felt that way. And Moses in mid-life, so far away from the only land he'd ever known, with no chance (or so he thought) of going back, certainly experienced some of those thoughts and emotions.

Before we give way to feelings of abandonment, however, we need to take a closer, more personal look at this verse in Deuteronomy. In the "howling waste of a wilderness," God does four things. If you happen to have your Bible open, I'd recommend taking a pen and highlighting each one.

First, He *encircles* us. Second, He *cares for us.* Third, He *guards us as the pupil of His eye.* Isn't that beautiful? When you think about it, you realize the pupil of your eye is the most protected part of your body. You won't let anything touch it. You shield it with great care. You safeguard it from the sun. You care for it constantly. If the tiniest speck touches its membrane, you take instant measures to get rid of it.

In the desert, *you* are the pupil of God's eye. And to your own amazement, you will ultimately discover that God has neither abandoned nor forsaken you. In fact, He has been caring for you more than at any other time of your life. Let that thought encourage you, friend, if you find yourself in a desert today.

75

Note the two verses that follow verse 10: "Like an eagle that stirs up its nest, that hovers over its young, He spread His wings and caught them, He carried them on His pinions. The LORD alone guided him..." (vv. 11–12).

The fourth thing He does is to *guide us.* Whether you have known it or not, felt it or not, even believed it or not, God has not taken His hand off your life. You have felt naked and exposed in that empty land, yet all along He has spread His wings over you. You have been sheltered by the pinions of the Most High God.

I'm attracted to that little word "alone" in verse 12. He alone is guiding you. There's no one else to lead you through the desert. There are no sign-posts, no information kiosks, no maps with arrows that say "You Are Here." As a matter of fact, you don't know *where* you are. You don't *when* (or if) you'll ever leave that oppressive wilderness. Yet the Bible tells us He alone will guide you. You are reserved for God alone.

DOORWAYS INTO THE DESERT

Perhaps I'm writing to someone who enjoyed an enviable education and had several handsome prospects coming out of college. But now, for whatever reason, you find yourself dead-ended.

Maybe you're a student athlete, and you've worked for years sharpening your skills only to be benched in your senior year because some hot-shot underclassman has grabbed your spot in the starting lineup.

It could be that you've enjoyed good health and strength through most of your life, and suddenly the doctor tells you, "You know, I've noticed a spot on your lung. Frankly, I don't like the looks of it." Or, "We've checked the biopsy, and it doesn't look good. In fact, there's a malignancy."

Information like that sends you reeling, and in your heart you cry out, *Where is God? How can I cope? How can I handle this?*

It could be you're a single person, waiting (and waiting) for that right person to step into your life. As the months and years slip by, that hope you've cherished like a secret candle flame begins to flicker. Years ago, I clipped a piece of writing out of a Christian magazine. The writer, Natalie Ray, captures the feelings of rejection in a poem called, "No Lover."

No lover makes my kiss his daily quest.
No hand across the table reaches mine.
No precious baby nestles at my breast.
No one needs my love.
Where is the sign
That God, my Father, loves Me? Surely He
Creates this wealth of love to overflow.
How could it be that none who wanted me
Has become mine? Why did I tell them, "No"?

But do they really matter, all the Why's?
Could all the answers take away the pain,
Or all the reasons really dry my eyes,
Though from heaven's court? No, I would weep again.
My God, You saved me from Hell's black abyss;
Oh, save me from the tyranny of bitterness![1]

There is a woman seeking to hear God's voice in her desert.

For others, it is the unrelenting anguish of a loved one who has walked out the door, with no hope that he or she will ever return. It may have begun the day you came home from work to discover your wife had left you a note. Her closet and drawers were empty. She was gone. And the howling winds began to blow. Or you discovered through a chain of events that your husband had been unfaithful to you. Another doorway into the desert!

It's dry. It's lonely. You feel dismal and sad. But whatever your emotions may be telling you, the Bible says you are *not* alone. God is there. He encircles you. Cares for you. Guards you like the pupil of His eye. And He promises to guide you through that strange habitation with neither landmark nor path. You have not left Him, nor has He left you. In fact, He may be closer to you at this moment than He has ever been before.

A DESERT, TAILOR-MADE

As I was putting the finishing touches on this chapter, I thought to myself, how interesting that God put Moses through forty years in a desert, then had him turn around and lead the children of Israel for forty more years, right back in the desert. (And the time he spent in Egypt in between was no holiday interlude!) Have you ever thought about that? Moses had a four-decade course of study in the wilderness so that He might know how to lead a whole nation through a similar wilderness.

Listen to what Moses told the Israelites as they were about to enter the Promised Land: "You shall remember all the way which the LORD your God has led you in the wilderness these forty years, that He might humble you, testing you, to know what was in your heart, whether you would keep His commandments or not" (Deuteronomy 8:2).

Why does God lead us through desert places? Let's get the answer from Moses, who had advanced degrees from God's School of the Wilderness. It is so that He might humble us, that He might test us, and that the true condition of our heart might be revealed. Not that *God* might come to know you (He already does), but that *you* might come to know you. There's nothing like the desert to help you discover the real you. When you strip away all of the trappings, peel off all the masks, and shed all the phony costumes, you begin to see a true identity—a face that hasn't emerged for years. Maybe never.

That's what the desert did for Moses. That is what it has done for me, in the wilderness sojourns of my own life. It will humble you. It will show you your strengths and weaknesses. It will help you discover yourself as never before.

The classic hymn, "How Firm a Foundation" (1787), expresses this thought well. My favorite stanza reads:

> When through fiery trials thy pathway shall lie,
> My grace all sufficient, shall be thy supply;
> The flames shall not hurt thee, I only design,
> Thy dross to consume, thy gold to refine.[2]

God never puts us through the blast furnace in the desert to ruin us. He does it to refine us. And in the midst of that howling wilderness, through the process of time, the stinging sand bites through the rust and corrosion, and we become a usable tool in His hands.

There have been numerous times in my past when I have had the joyful experience of rubbing shoulders with men and women who have been tempered in such a desert. You can always tell—sometimes within moments—when you have met individuals so refined by God. They are some of the most secure, genuinely humble, gracious, honest individuals one can imagine. It took the desert to do it. As the hymn states so eloquently, their dross has been consumed, and their gold has been refined.

That's the kind of life the psalmist longed for, when he penned the words below. He had experienced affliction. The Lord had sent him through a prolonged course of study in an unnamed wilderness. But he had this hope: At the end of it all, he wanted to be the kind of man who could bring courage and hope to God's people.

> May those who fear you rejoice when they see me, for I have put my hope in your word. . . .

> May those who fear you turn to me, those who understand your statutes (Psalm 119:74,79, NIV).

Before we go any further in this chapter on God's school of self-discovery, let's return to the narrative with Moses once again.

IN THE SHADOW OF SINAI

> Now Moses was pasturing the flock of Jethro his father-in-law, the priest of Midian; and he led the flock to the west side of the wilderness and came to Horeb, the mountain of God. (Exodus 3:1)

Moses was in the shadow of Sinai, the very mountain where God would come down with cloud and fire and earthquake to meet with the children of Israel. At the time, however, Moses probably wasn't thinking about anything so profound or cataclysmic. With a shepherd's keen eye, he was most likely scouring that desolate place for a little grass to sustain that flock of woolies.

In the photographic book I mentioned to you earlier, there is a picture of the place where Moses most likely wandered that day. And if you can see any grass in that sun-seared acreage, you have better eyes than I! Beno Rothenberg, author of *God's Wilderness*, calls it a place where "time stood still." It is an area of no shrubbery, as forlorn and forbidding as a moonscape. Here and there large chunks of rock rest helter-skelter like pieces from some bomb-blasted temple. You could hardly step where you wouldn't stumble over rocks.

I remember an old credit card commercial where some strange, grizzled-looking shopkeeper behind a counter in a ramshackle building greets a customer with the words, "Welcome . . . to the last place on earth." The idea of the commercial was that even *there*, they will take Visa.

Those are the words that run through my mind as I study this photograph of Midian: *the last place on earth*—a place where even a Visa card wouldn't buy you a cold drink. If ever a place could be called "the backside of the desert," this was it.

The Hebrews had an interesting way of referring to location. They faced east, and everything behind them, the west area, was called "the backside." North, south, east, and west were determined on the basis of the direction they were facing. They faced east, toward the rising sun, to determine what was north, south, or west. Moses at that moment was in the west or backside of the desert.

He didn't come there on an air-conditioned tour bus. He didn't show up to have a fun week of riding camels, collecting rocks, and capturing the quaint landscape with his video camera before climbing back into the soft-cushioned motor coach. No, Moses had come to that place to *live*. The desert was his address.

Have you ever been driving through some forsaken stretch of land and turned to your spouse or friend and said, "Boy, aren't you glad we don't live *here?*" And without thinking, you press the accelerator a little harder and zoom on through that section of no-man's-land to get back to the comforts of home.

For Moses, there was no escaping the desolation; this *was* home. The son of Amram and Jochebed came to Midian and unloaded his sea bag.

That's where he would sink his mailbox in the ground, even though he'd left no forwarding address.

His location wasn't very attractive. Neither was his vocation. He was a shepherd for his father-in-law. He didn't even have his own flock. He married the man's daughter, borrowed a second-hand shepherd's staff, and said, "Okay, so where are the sheep?" Along the way, he fathered a couple of kids—two sons, we're told in Acts 7:29. So Moses went about living out his three roles: husband, father, and shepherd. And that was that. He and monotony became soulmates.

NO SHORTCUTS

Can you believe it? A man with advanced knowledge in hieroglyphics, science, literature, and military tactics was now eking out his existence on the backside of the desert, living with his father-in-law, raising a couple of boys, and watching over little flocks of sheep.

That, my friend, is a desert.

One author has wisely stated: "Time is no object with God, who demands quality at all costs. There is therefore no point in chafing under the discipline of the training years, or in endeavoring to take a shortcut. It will inevitably prove to be a cul-de-sac."[3]

How true. If you try to shortcut your journey through the desert, you will lead yourself into a dead-end. Do you remember those old Westerns, where the bad guys would be riding way out in front of the posse? One of the deputies would inevitably shout, "They're gettin' away, Marshal!" And the lawman would smile and say, "Them sorry dudes are ridin' right into a box canyon. We got 'em!"

There's no way out of a box canyon or a cul-de-sac, except by the way you came in. You cannot get through. In the same way, there are no shortcuts out of the desert where God has placed you; all those anticipated escape routes end in cul-de-sacs. Many people spend their time running from one cul-de-sac to another, getting dizzy in the process. God says, "You're going to stay right where I put you until I move you."

Moses, the former high and mighty Prince of Egypt, learned what it was like to share life with a wife and two little boys. Can't you imagine what wild-eyed little squirts those boys must have been, growing up in a place like that? The truth is, there's nothing like little children to humble the most advanced in education. A Ph.D. is no help at all when you're trying to corral a couple of high-spirited lads bent on mischief.

But there was Moses, with degrees as long as your arm, changing diapers, playin' peek-a-boo, and trying to get food into those babies' mouths. You know, experts can tell you the whole scientific background of the stuff that goes into baby food, how it came to be processed, and how it gets digested. But they still don't tell you how to get food in the mouth of an infant. You're on your own when you try to spoon that stuff in there.

That's all part of the desert. In the desert you learn to do things you never dreamed you would have to do. You learn to tolerate inconveniences and bear with the situation; you learn to accept a set of circumstances you never imagined being a part of your life. That's all part of the training. That's just a phase in the curriculum at God's wilderness university.

Did I tell you about the course offerings in that school? You won't find a selection like it anywhere else! There are four majors in this place of higher learning.

A MAJOR IN OBSCURITY

As I mentioned in the previous chapter, the desert is a place of obscurity. Moses had to cope with being a nobody. All his adolescent and adult life, he had been a big-time somebody. The spotlight followed his every move, much as the contemporary spotlight follows Britain's Prince William and Prince Harry. Every time Moses stood, people looked up expectantly. Every time he addressed them, people stopped talking and listened. Every time he strolled through the streets, heads turned.

Sheep don't do that.

You can say whatever you want, you can turn backflips while reciting poetry, and the flock won't be impressed at all. They'll go right on feeding their faces. As much as you and I may appreciate wool sweaters and wool socks, sheep are basically unintelligent and unresponsive animals. And

Moses had the pleasure of their company for four long decades of his life.

"He pastured the flock of Jethro his father-in-law." Isn't that humiliating? Imagine an old friend of Moses' younger days coming up to Midian to visit with the ex-prince—maybe one of his fraternity buddies from Sun Temple U. And as the friend steps out of his flashy chariot, he looks Moses up and down, noticing the shaggy hair, the beard, and the simple, homespun garments.

"So, Prince Moses, what do you do for a living now?"

"I, um, well, I'm a shepherd."

"Really? Who would have thought it! You have your own flock, then? A big operation?"

"No. These aren't my sheep. I work for my wife's father."

"You work for *your father-in-law?*"

"Uh-huh."

"And, let me get this straight, you walk alongside sheep. That's what you do."

"That's right."

"Well, I really don't know what to say, Moses. Good night, man, what about all of your training? You were the best!"

"I have nothing to say about it. All I know is, this is where God wants me. This is where I stay."

Perhaps you identify with this situation. As you read, you're nodding your head. You are taking some course work in obscurity, yourself; you find yourself struggling every day with the limitations you've had to endure. You have been forced by the very nature of the desert to give up many of the privileges, perks, and activities you held most dear. Now you're "just getting by," subsisting on the basics of life.

That is God's plan, my friend. And if you would graduate from His school of the desert, you must take classes in obscurity; it is the first required course of the school.

Amy Carmichael, one of my favorite poets, wrote these words:

> Before the winds that blow do cease,
> Teach me to dwell within Thy calm:

Before the pain has passed in peace,
Give me, my God, to sing a psalm.
Let me not lose the chance to prove
The fullness of enabling love.
Oh, love of God, do this for me:
Maintain a constant victory.[4]

Here is the unvarnished truth: If you don't learn to live peacefully with obscurity, you will repeat that course until you do. You cannot skip this one and still graduate.

In the movie *The Hiding Place* one scene portrays Corrie Ten Boom telling the Lord she wants Him to use her in whatever way He pleases, even if it means in obscurity. Soon after that, she is taken prisoner by the Nazis, along with her father, from whom she is separated. Her father dies in the death camp, and then she is forcibly removed from her beloved sister. The Nazis shove Corrie into a cold, damp cell in Germany.

As the scene closes, she is lying in a corner, shivering. And with tear-filled eyes she whispers to the Lord, "But God, I didn't know I would have to be *alone*."

That's obscurity.

We can handle almost anything as long as there are people around to encourage and help us shoulder the load. But in God's desert school, the campus is empty. There's no one in the student union but you, a textbook titled *Obscurity*, and lots of time to read it.

A MAJOR IN TIME

Moses fled and became an alien in the land of Midian, where he became the father of two sons.

After forty years had passed... (Acts 7:29–30).

In my Bible, I have underlined the words "forty years" just because I don't want the impact of that phrase to escape my notice. He came to the desert as an alien, and *forty years later*, school was out. I remember, at age forty, preaching a series on Moses in my previous pastorate. At that time, it hit me that Moses spent the entire length of my life in the Midian wilderness. He entered the desert at forty and didn't leave until he was eighty. So during those years—considered by many the most productive years of a person's life—Moses herded sheep on what might as well have been the front yard of Hades.

Are you between age forty and eighty and find yourself in a desert? Welcome aboard. It's part of His plan. God not only plans the breadth of a test, He plans the length as well. His timing is every bit as significant as His testing. He knows when you need the desert, and He knows when you are ready to move on.

We live today in a microwave culture. If it takes longer than five minutes to fix lunch, that's long! In earlier days, you even had to wait for a TV set to warm up. Can you imagine? And you couldn't push a single button on your phone to call home on a pre-set number, you had to *dial* it...with your finger, for pity's sake. Talk about the stone age! I remember driving by a vacant lot some time ago, then going by the same corner several weeks later. Where there had been nothing but grass and weeds, empty beer cans, and trash just days before, there was now a huge warehouse, assembled from pre-fab sections, ready to receive goods.

That's the way life is today. Fast. Compressed. Condensed. Slam-bang-it's-done. Not so in God's wilderness schooling. When it comes to walking with God, there is no such thing as instant maturity. God doesn't mass produce His saints. He hand tools each one, and it always takes longer than we expected.

An impatient activist like Moses needed those years in the desert to unwind—to climb off the *fast* track and find *God's* track. God's work was painstakingly slow, yes; but in order to shape Moses, and then use him as no man had been used before.

A MAJOR IN SOLITUDE

You and I are strangers to silence. That's why we almost panic when we find ourselves alone. That's why some people can hardly bear to ride in a car or sit in a room without electronic noise in the background. It used to amaze me to see people jogging on the track or walking through the neighborhood with headphones over their ears. Now I hardly notice it; it's too common.

When I got out of my car in the desert that time, and walked away from the highway (just far enough for me to know I didn't want to be there very long), the first thing that struck me was the utter silence. Until that wind came moaning across the sand, there wasn't a sound—not so much as the chirp of a cricket or the buzz of a fly. I just stood there and absorbed it for awhile.

Solitude has an interesting sound. I'd almost forgotten what it was like. If you, too, have forgotten, you need to take a trip. Go as far as you need to go to get away from the buzz and hum and chatter of civilization. Not to the beach, for that is a place of constant, crashing sound. No, you need to go high up into the mountains, or to the desert, or out on the wide prairie somewhere. And please, leave your Walkman and CD player behind. Take time to be still and listen to the profound sound of silence.

It's remarkable. Stay there long enough, and you may begin to gain a sensitivity for things you had forgotten. Your thoughts will begin to probe beneath that shallow, surface level where most of us spend our waking hours. Given enough time in that environment, you find yourself growing deeper.

Through the years, it has been my observation that most of the world's great people have been lonely people. Many of the artists and artisans of the world, those who have left us a legacy of their art and music, have been people of solitude and loneliness. Some of the world's greatest leaders have been people who lived lonely lives.

In Moses' long career as a leader, he would be questioned, attacked, accused, hated, and betrayed. Through it all, he would stand alone. How could he do it? How could he endure it? He had been trained to handle it. He had graduated from God's school of the desert with a major in solitude. He had learned those lessons well. He no longer needed anyone to pat him on the back. He could go right on doing what God had called him to do, even in the face of bitter opposition.

A MAJOR IN DISCOMFORT

Mark it down, there was nothing comfortable about Midian.

It was a hard place, oppressively hot and notably deficient in creature comforts. Moses, who had been drawn out of the Nile River as an infant and lived near that great river for most of his forty years, had to adjust to a place where water was a precious commodity. He learned to live with a dry throat, cracked lips, and a perpetual squint to his eyes, shielding himself from the glare of the naked sun.

That was the curriculum of God's college in the wilderness: four major courses of study in order to graduate. Notice carefully how the process took place through those years of desert learning, because it is the same with you and me. God must break through several hard, exterior barriers in our lives before He can renovate our souls. His persistent goal is to break through to the inner person. As David acknowledged, "Behold, You desire truth in the innermost being, and in the hidden part You will make me know wisdom" (Psalm 51:6).

What are those resistant layers in our hearts, and how does He break through to that *hidden part?* First, He finds pride. And He uses the sandpaper of obscurity to remove it ever so gradually.

Then He finds us gripped by fear—dread of our past, anxiety over our present, and terror over what may lie ahead—and He uses the passing of time to remove that fear. We learn that things aren't out of hand at all; they're in *His* hand.

He next encounters the barrier of resentment—the tyranny of bitterness. He breaks down that layer with solitude. In the silence of His presence, we gain a fresh perspective, gradually release our cherished *rights,* and let go of the expectations that held us hostage.

Finally, He gets down to the basic habits of living, so close to our inner person, and there He brings discomfort and hardship to buff away that last layer of resistance. Why? So that He might renovate us at the very core of our being. "Our dross to consume . . . our gold to refine."

V. Raymond Edman was the president of Wheaton College for a number of years, before his sudden death. In a small book called *In Quietness and Confidence,* Dr. Edman describes a desert experience of his own.

Something painful happened to me. This is how I met it: I was quiet for a while with the Lord, and then I wrote these words for myself:

First, He brought me here. It is by His will I am in this strait place: in that fact I will rest.

Next, He will keep me here in His love, and give me grace as His child.

Then, He will make the trial a blessing, teaching me the lessons He intends me to learn, and working in me the grace He needs to bestow.

Last, in His good time He can bring me out again—how and when only He knows.

Let me say I am here, first, by God's appointment; second, in His keeping; third, under His training; fourth, for His time."[5]

Now there is a *magna cum laude* graduate of God's Desert University! You can spot one every time. Not all of us, however, have reached that level of maturity in our walk with Jesus Christ. In fact, I have discovered that there are three different responses we can offer when finding ourselves in the wilderness. I admit, with a measure of embarrassment, that I have given all three rejoinders to God at various times in my life.

First, *"I don't need it."* That's the response of pride. "My neighbor needs an experience like this. My friend needs it. My wife needs it. My husband needs it. My kids need it. My roommate needs it. My boss certainly needs it! But me? I don't need it."

Second, *"I'm tired of it."* That's the response of shortsightedness. You may have uttered those words this very day. You might say to me, "Chuck, if you only knew! I've been in the desert so long I can't remember what the other side even looks like."

The third response is the one God is waiting to hear: *"I accept it."* That is the response of maturity.

> Pain knocked upon my door and said
> That she had come to stay;
> And though I would not welcome her
> But bade her go away,

She entered in. And like my own shade
She followed after me,
And from her stabbing, stinging sword,
No moment was I free.

And then one day another knocked
Most gently at my door.
I said, "No, Pain is here.
There's not room for more."
And then I heard His tender voice,
"It is I, be not afraid."
And from the day He entered in—
Ah, the difference He made![6]

There have been times when I have stood before a congregation on Sunday morning and felt as though we were singing empty, hollow words. Beautiful music, majestic words, but drained of authentic life content. We sing "All hail the power of Jesus' name;...crown Him Lord of all!"

Do we really? Or do we crown Him Lord of everything but the desert?

Do you ever find yourself saying something like this? "Lord, I give You my life, but I'm weary to death of this irritation, this person, this circumstance, this uncomfortable situation. I feel trapped, Lord. I want relief—I *must* have relief! And if You don't bring it soon...well, I've had it. I feel like walking away from it all."

You may walk, my friend, but there are no shortcuts. Here's a better plan: Reach for the hand of your Guide! He is Lord of the desert. Even your desert. The most precious object of God's love is His child in the desert. If it were possible, you mean more to Him during this time than at any other time. You are as the pupil of His eye. You are His beloved student taking his toughest courses. He loves you with an infinite amount of love.

Jesus went through the worst desert of all for you. He was alone as no man has ever been alone. He was rejected. He lived in obscurity. He suffered the worst earth and hell could hurl at Him. On the cross He said, "I thirst." And when that desert night was the darkest, He screamed, "My

God, My God, Why have You forsaken Me?"

Jesus walked through the desert first. He felt its heat. He tasted its loneliness. He accepted its obscurity. He faced down Satan himself while the desert winds howled around Him. And He will never, ever forget or forsake the one who follows Him across the sand.

CHAPTER SIX

Burning Bushes and Second Chances

J ust because a saying is old doesn't make it reliable. There are venerable and ancient lies floating around out there that are every bit as dangerous and deceptive now as the day when they were first passed off as truth.

I'm thinking of a Nineteenth Century proverb which has come down the pike and fallen into our ears on a number of occasions. Through the years, it has been frequently quoted and generally believed. You have undoubtedly heard it: *The bird with the broken piñion never soars as high again.*[1]

In other words, once you have failed, you will never, ever attain the heights you did before. It's a sad, bittersweet bit of poetic prose, dripping with disappointment. People who hear it may gravely nod their heads, press their lips together, and say, "Hmmm."

The only problem with the saying is that it isn't true. It's never been true.

I did a little study on that proverb at one time, and found out it was penned over a hundred years ago by a man named Hezekiah Butterworth. No kidding. That's really all I know about him, and all I *want* to know about him. He originated one of those phrases that *sounds* like wisdom, until you turn the powerful searchlight of Scripture on it, and it evaporates in a little puff of purple mist.

THE HALL OF BROKEN PIÑIONS

Think about it. Father Abraham was a liar. He uttered blatant lies on more than one occasion to save his skin. But even after he lied, he came to be known as the "friend of God," an intimate of the Almighty. With a "broken piñion," Abraham soared higher than he (or perhaps anyone else) had ever been before.

Jacob was a chiseler and a cheat who talked his own twin brother out of his birthright. What a sneaky, despicable thing to do! Yet even though he was a deceiver, God lifted Jacob to such heights that his old name couldn't even contain the glory; he was given the new name of "Israel." So much for Jacob's broken piñion.

And Rahab? What of her notable failures? She had been a well known resident of Jericho's red-light district. That's correct; Rahab was a prostitute. Yet God selected her as His choice instrument to preserve the lives of His two courageous servants. Following that, she was accorded the unspeakable dual honors of having her name listed in the Hebrews 11 "Hall of Faith," and being included in the very ancestry and lineage of Jesus Christ. When have broken piñions ever soared so high?

How about those notable missionary dropouts, Jonah and John Mark? Jonah never really *dropped in,* you know; he was a refugee from the will of God from Day One. After he made that curious amphibious landing there on the shores, he hurried to Nineveh and preached in the greatest revival of all time. An entire city—the capital of a mighty empire—repented. Every human being in that vast municipality fasted and prayed. Even the animals were required to fast. Think of it! Every man, woman, and child in that great metropolis donned sackcloth, including the animals.

After he had fled from God, rebelling against God's clearly-stated will, that old prophet had all kinds of broken piñions (and wet ones, too). Yet God said, "Jonah, I still want to use you. Let's get back on track." And Jonah went on to lead a spiritual awakening that shook the ancient world.

John Mark had a similar, if less dramatic, turnaround. He bailed on the apostle Paul and went home in the middle of a crucial missionary enterprise. Paul was ready to write the young man off as a bad investment. But not God. Mark came back into the service of Christ with a roar. He authored the second gospel, the one that bears his name, and was considered profitable for Paul's ministry. Said who? Paul himself. "Only Luke is with me. Get Mark and bring him with you, because he is helpful to me in my ministry" (2 Timothy 4:11, NIV).

I'll tell you something else. If birds with broken piñions could never fly as high again, you wouldn't be reading this book. I don't know what you would be doing, but you wouldn't be doing this, I can promise you. And while I'm at it, I need to add that this author wouldn't even be an author. You see, old Hezekiah Butterworth's proverb may be good for birds of the sky, but it's not good for men and women of God, because God doesn't deal with His servants in that way. As a matter of fact, even though it may sound like a maverick idea, God seems to *prefer* using people with broken piñions.

Isn't that great? Takes all the strain out of it, doesn't it? I *qualify* for His service, just as I am, failures and all. And so do you. No matter what your past may have been, the future is brighter than you can imagine. Why? Because our God specializes in using broken vessels. That's His preferred plan.

Remember what Paul (another bird with broken piñions) wrote to the Corinthians? "But we have this treasure in earthen vessels, so that the surpassing greatness of the power will be of God and not from ourselves" (2 Corinthians 4:7). Do you know what an earthen vessel is? It's nothing more than a clay pot. A "common, earthenware jar," as J. B. Phillips renders it. That's a reference to our bodies and our abilities in the strength of our flesh. That is all you and I have to offer God . . . a pot. A perishable container.

You may be like brittle, delicate china. You break and chip easily, and you could show the glue marks because of those broken times. Then again, you may be a rugged, scarred hunk of heavy pottery—not very attractive, but boy, are you useful. Or you may be composed of clay that hasn't yet been fired in the kiln; you are still being molded and shaped for use. As my mentor, Ray Stedman, used to say, "We're all clay pots, and all of us are being molded. Only some are moldier than others!"

To tell you the truth, it isn't the condition of the pot that's most important. What's important is the treasure inside—the light and glory of Christ's salvation. What's a few dings, or even a crack or two? If others can see the glory inside through the cracks, so much the better.

All this brings us back to our story. Moses, after his major, life-shattering failure and all those years of obscurity that followed, certainly must have felt like an unusable vessel. He couldn't imagine God's picking up a rejected utensil such as himself, and finding any use in it. To him, the idea was ludicrous. And then one normal, ordinary, desert day, he stopped to look at a particular bush, and nothing was ever normal and ordinary for him again.

Exodus 3, verses 1 through 10, is a passage that revolves around a day, a bush, a need, and a call. Let's consider each in turn.

THE DAY

> Now Moses was pasturing the flock of Jethro his father-in-law, the
> priest of Midian; and he led the flock to the west side of the wilderness
> and came to Horeb, the mountain of God. (Exodus 3:1)

This was a day when God was going to break a forty-year silence.

Pause and let that sink in! Through four decades in Midian, we have no record of God's speaking to Moses. Not even once. The day that was going to shatter that silence, however, dawned like every other day in the wilderness. The night before, as he was sleeping out under those bright desert stars with his flock, perhaps under the looming shoulder of Sinai, he saw no meteor flash across the sky. He heard no voice. No angel tapped him on the shoulder at breakfast that morning and said, "Pay attention, Moses. God speaks today."

There were no hints, no premonitions, no special signs to alert him to the fact that God Himself would break the silence that day and that life would change forever. It was just your common, ordinary, garden-variety day-shift with the sheep. Nothing more. Nothing less. Nothing else. Just another day at the wilderness office, under the shadow of Mount Horeb.

The sun came up, the sheep grazed, and Moses chalked off his 14,600[th] day as Jethro's assistant shepherd.

That is the way God works. Without even a hint of warning, He speaks to ordinary people, on ordinary days.

You may be catching a bus tomorrow morning. Or climbing into a big rig for a 900-mile stretch of monotonous highway. Or facing a classroom full of students. Or slipping behind the wheel of your patrol car. Or lifting the baby out of the crib, while another little one clings to your leg.

That's your day. That's your routine. That's your Mount Horeb. And it may be that on such a normal, standard-issue day, God will choose to speak to you as He has never spoken before. It may be the day when He communicates to you something great on His heart, something that pertains to your destiny.

You would have never guessed it when you rolled out of bed. You couldn't have predicted it when you shaved your face for the umpteenth time or put on your makeup. It didn't feel any different at all.

Do you remember what Scripture says about our Lord's second coming? The Bible says it will be just like "the days of Noah. For as in those days before the flood they were eating and drinking, marrying and giving in marriage, until the day that Noah entered the ark, and they did not understand until the flood came and took them all away" (Matthew 24:37–39).

In other words, it will happen on an ordinary day. People will be getting married and buried. There will be problems, and there will be needs. Some people will be driving buses, others will be riding in them. Some will be on the way home from work, tuned in to talk radio. Others will be in the checkout line at the grocery store, impatiently wondering why the person ahead of them is taking so long to write that check. Some will be boarding an airplane, others stepping out of a subway.

And suddenly, the Son will come! There will be a flash in the sky, a shout, the staccato blast of a trumpet, and in the twinkling of an eye it will be over. There will be no previous warning.

That's God's method, you see. He doesn't need a P. R. department or a slick advance team. His plan doesn't require a drum roll or crashing cymbals. He doesn't use neon signs blinking, "Get ready! Get ready! Today's the day I do something big in your life."

That's not His style. Don't look for some brilliant aura to come over you early in the morning, and a booming angelic voice announcing, "This is the day!" If that happened, you might pull the covers over your head and never get out of bed.

God works by simply stepping into an ordinary day of life and saying what He wants to say. It's a meat-and-potatoes kind of proposition. Here's what needs doing, and you're the person who's going to do it, *so let's get after it!*

THE BUSH

> The angel of the LORD appeared to him in a blazing fire from the midst of a bush; and he looked, and behold, the bush was burning with fire, yet the bush was not consumed.
>
> So Moses said, "I must turn aside now and see this marvelous sight, why the bush is not burned up." (vv. 2–3)

A remarkable thing happened to Moses on that otherwise unremarkable morning. The eighty-year-old shepherd was kicking his sandals in the sand, roustin' those old woolies out of the briers, pushing them toward a little bit of grass, and suddenly a bush ignited.

I have seen artists' conceptions of this occurrence, and I don't much care for them. The bush looks more like it belongs in an art museum than in a motley patch of desert. And the flames in some of these pictures look like the exploding end of a rocket thruster.

I don't think it was that way at all. I think this was your basic desert scrub bush, like countless others dotting that landscape. The Hebrew word names it as "a thorny shrub." That's all it was. One of millions in Midian.

The *bush* wasn't different or remarkable, but what was *happening* to it certainly was different and remarkable. That's an important point to note. The text says the angel of the Lord appeared to him in the midst of the bush. The bush wasn't God; the bush happened to be chosen by God and was set on fire. And the fire was inextinguishable.

96

Moses, of course, was curious. There usually wasn't much to write home about on the backside of that desert. But this was something else! Verse 2 tells us that he did two things: First, he looked; and second, he said something to himself. I have every reason to believe you and I would have done the same thing had we been in his shoes that day. It's not every day that you see bushes suddenly kindle themselves, especially when the fire doesn't go out.

Through the years, Moses may have seen a bush or two catch fire, perhaps after a lightning strike. And in that arid place, it would take only a few seconds for the bush to resemble burnt toast. The fire would flare up, then rapidly burn itself out, leaving a little pile of smoldering sticks and ash. But this one didn't.

Moses stood there for a minute watching, and it kept burning and burning and burning. He thought to himself, *How strange that is!* The bush wasn't strange, but the fire was. It kept blazing and didn't die down. Now if it had been me, I would have felt a little spooky about it in that moment. Maybe I would have heard the theme from *The Twilight Zone* playing in my brain. This was really strange and, wouldn't you know it, there wasn't a soul within miles he could tell about it. At that moment, I don't believe he had the foggiest idea that God was in the bush. He was simply curious, as any of us would have been.

This is also God's method. In the common, ordinary, everyday circumstances of our lives, He occasionally does something altogether extraordinary. He burns a bush, as it were. We call some of these unusual occurrences "coincidences."

I think that's an unfortunate expression. Let me hasten to add, I'm not saying that every *coincidence* is God's burning bush in your life. But I am saying this: God may use an extraordinary event or circumstance to tap you on the shoulder, in order to grab your undivided attention. He may use something like that to intrude into your daily life and say, "Wait a minute. Stop. Be still. I have something to say to you."

When you and I come across extremely unusual events, it's a good idea to ask, "Could God be saying something to me now?"

Years ago, I remember sitting in my study with a young couple, discussing their plans for marriage. Suddenly there was a strong knock on my door. No one was expecting it, and we all jumped a little.

"Come in," I said.

A man came through the door—a total stranger—and walked right up to me, maybe two feet away from where I sat. "Is your name Swindoll?" he asked.

"Yes," I said, "it is."

"I just came to know Jesus because of you," he said. "It all happened because of this." And he pulled a cassette tape out of his jacket pocket.

It turns out the man was a race car driver, known up and down the West Coast. Waving the cassette at me, he said, "I have a friend who kept giving me these things." (I'm sure he must have thought at first that they were music tapes. What a surprise!)

In the course of his racing, this man had just recently experienced a couple of near brushes with death, and it had started him thinking about some issues he'd never concerned himself with before.

"Suddenly," he said, "I just popped this thing in the player as I was driving and started listening to you. Do you remember a message called, 'God's Will, My Way'?"

"Yes," I replied, "I do."

"Well, I listened to it. And that message—well, I don't know who *you* thought you were talking to. But I know you were talking to me. I thought to myself, *Lord, I need You. This is more than coincidence. This is for me.*"

That man came to know Jesus Christ that very day. He pushed a tape at random into the cassette deck, and the words spoke exactly to where he was in life. He'd stared death eyeball to eyeball, and now here was this message that offered him eternal life. That was a burning bush in that man's life. His life changed *forever* because of that encounter.

I think of Jack, a long-time friend of mine who was a bombardier in the belly of a B-17 plane during World War II. After one bombing run over Germany, the big bird didn't quite make it back to base. It crashed clumsily into a residential apartment building in Britain, killing many, many people. The whole crew also perished in the crash. All except Jack.

My friend walked away from that unbelievable scene of flaming mayhem with hardly a scratch, even though he was belted into the mid-section of that doomed aircraft. The incident haunted him. Why should he live when so many died? Why should he be spared? Jack went to his chaplain and spread it out on the table.

"Why Chaplain?" he asked. "Why me? Why did I live when my entire crew died?"

The chaplain's answer was a shallow one and didn't satisfy: "Well, Jack, let's just say you were lucky."

It was more than luck. It had to be! Restlessly curious, Jack persisted in asking his questions. Finally, someone had the right answer. Jack was spared so that he could surrender his life to the Lord of the universe, Jesus Christ. And he did. He could not—he would not—walk away from that *burning bush* the same man.

Mark it down, things do not "just happen." Ours is not a random, whistle-in-the-dark universe. There is a God-arranged plan for this world of ours, which includes a specific plan for you. And through every ordinary day and every extraordinary moment, there is a God who constantly seeks you.

You're walking through the desert with the sheep one Tuesday morning, and you suddenly encounter one event among the countless myriad of events that happen every day and every night. All of a sudden, life changes. Something's different. And never doubt it! The God who loves us and redeemed us uses those moments to advance His purposes. He is there, and He is not silent.

He doesn't speak vocally from heaven, shouting down His Word at you. He uses His Book, He uses His people, and He uses events in your life. And through the blending of those unusual events, He says, "*Listen* to Me. Heed this burning bush. Pay attention, and I will speak to you. Answer My call, and I will use you."

Frankly, in this rushed, frantic world of ours, that doesn't happen very often. All that is needed is a hushed spirit and a listening heart. Moses possessed these; therefore he heard the voice of God.

THE NEED

> When the LORD saw that he turned aside to look, God called to him
> from the midst of the bush and said, "Moses, Moses!" And he said,
> "Here I am." (v. 4)

I think one of the most important words in this verse is the very first one. *When*. The Hebrew word means "at the same time." That goes back to verse 3, where Moses said, "I must turn aside."

When did God speak to Moses? At the same moment when he turned aside. Now that's simple, isn't it? Moses stopped his forward motion, stepped aside from his responsibilities for only a few brief seconds and headed in another direction. He moved toward the event that had captured his attention.

It isn't easy to get people to do that. Bushes burn, planes crash, cars are totaled, lives are taken and spared, questions cry out for answers, and strange events pass across the landscape of our lives like the shadows of wind-driven clouds. And what do most folks do? They shrug it all off, chalking it up as *coincidence*. They traffic right through the midst of these events as though surrounded by a thick hide of leather. If there is a bush burning, they don't trouble themselves with it; somebody else will put it out. If there is a voice speaking, they're too busy to pay any attention. Why bother? It means nothing. They've got more important things on their minds.

And God says, "What's it going to take? What will finally persuade you to stop in your tracks for a minute, turn aside, and consider this event in your life?" What's it going to take before you say, "I'm going to check this out. I'm going to find out what all of this might be saying to me."

Moses did just that, and when he did, he came face to face with his destiny. It was not until Moses turned aside that God spoke. Yet even at that moment, I do not believe it had dawned on the man that God was speaking. As far as Moses was concerned, a *bush* was speaking. God hadn't introduced himself yet. Moses had simply heard his name coming out of a flaming shrub and answered back.

"Moses! Moses!" the voice said.

And do you know what Moses answered? The original Hebrew reveals that he spoke only one word: *hinaynee*, which could be rendered, "I'm here," or, in our terms, "It's me."

That's all he said! I find that refreshingly disarming. Forty years before, he would have hauled out his resumé. "Need someone special? Glad you located me, God. I was thinking You might. You want to check out my work experience? Honors and awards? References? I've got about three pages here." Back then, he would have *expected* a divine summons.

Not now. He's had forty years of obscurity and silence in God's school of the desert. He's become a nobody. So when the call comes, his only response is a quiet and reluctant, "I'm here."

Believe it or not, that's all God wanted to hear. It's still true today. That's all He wants to hear from you when He speaks. Don't kid yourself; He's not impressed with *you*; He's checking out your humility, your sensitivity, your availability. He's looking for someone who will slow down long enough to check out a burning bush. And when He calls, all He asks is a simple acknowledgement. *I'm here, Lord. All present and accounted for.* "Then He said, 'Do not come near here; remove your sandals from your feet, for the place on which you are standing is holy ground'" (v. 5).

I like to think about a couple of the words in verses 4 and 5. Verse 4 says, "*When* the LORD saw that he turned aside to look...." And verse 5 says, "*Then* He said...." I believe the *when* and the *then* are connected. After Moses stopped in his tracks and said, "Here I am, Lord," the voice came across with specific instructions.

"The place where you are standing is holy ground...."

The Hebrew word translated "holy" means, literally, "separated." God was saying to him, "Moses, I want you to separate yourself from your past. Futhermore, I want you to remove from your mind your immediate responsibilities. Give me your undivided attention. I want you to listen only to what I am saying right now. Separate yourself from every human thing. Draw an imaginary perimeter around yourself and stand still, Moses."

I had read this passage all my life, yet until I made a real study of it, I always thought the *bush* was holy. After all, God was in that bush. But that's not what it says. The text tells us that the place where Moses stood was holy. That's why the Lord told him, "Get those sandals off, Moses."

Now why did He say that? If Moses' sandals were dirty, it's a cinch his feet were dirty, too. If you walk around on the dirty rocks and in the desert sand with sweaty feet, you're going to wear some of that sand and dirt. So why the command to shed the shoes?

In many parts of Asia, it's a custom to remove your shoes before entering someone's home. During my months overseas in Okinawa and Japan, I learned that unique cultural practice. You don't stomp into someone's home with your shoes or boots on; it would be an affront to your host.

But this was more than a custom, because Moses wasn't in a home, he was out in the middle of the sand and gravel in the Midian desert under a great vault of blue sky. Apparently, God saw this moment as so holy and precious that He wanted nothing between Moses and Himself. "Take those sandals off, Moses, and stand on the hot ground." There was no argument or question. Without hesitation Moses did precisely as he was told. "He said also, 'I am the God of your father, the God of Abraham, the God of Isaac, and the God of Jacob.' Then Moses hid his face, for he was afraid to look at God" (v. 6).

Look at that list: Abraham, Isaac, Jacob. Whenever we read those names, we think we're dealing with the starting lineup of Bible superstars—the heavy hitters. It's as if these were men who floated through life in a bubble and never soiled their feet by walking on the dirty ground. Not so! If you ever do a study on their lives, you'll find that these men were people just like us. Yes, their names are in the Bible, but each one of these men had broken piñions, too. Had it not been for God's grace, not one of them would have accomplished anything worth remembering.

So God is saying, in effect, "Moses, I'm the God of men who have failed. I'm the God of ordinary men who have accomplished some extraordinary things in their lives."

The sacred record says Moses hid his face, and that he was afraid to look at God. What do you think flashed through his mind in those moments?

Back in the earliest days of television, there was a popular program called *This Is Your Life*. Some man or woman would be standing on stage with the host, and you would hear an amplified voice from backstage saying, "Remember me? I taught you your fractions when you were a fifth grader."

Or, "Remember me? We were in the same military outfit together overseas. Remember how you always used to borrow my shaving cream?" Then there would be a series of on-camera reunions as the life of the individual in the spotlight was recreated before his or her eyes.

At the bush, Moses was hearing a voice saying, "Remember Me? I'm the One who told you that you would redeem My people Israel someday. I'm the God of your fathers."

Moses had thought all that was behind him. He'd thought all the bridges had been burned. He thought he was going to live out his days pushing scrawny sheep around the rocks in Midian. Moses had tried mightily to forget the past. And forty years in Wilderness University had helped a lot. The desert winds had sandblasted the pain away from some of those memories and regrets. But now...? The past must have washed over the once-handsome prince of Egypt like a tidal wave. He hid his wrinkled, rugged face, probably groaning within himself. *Oh no! It can't be! I can't believe this!*

He felt so humiliated, so unworthy, so "bushy," if you know what I mean. But that is precisely the way God wanted him to be, because that is precisely the kind of person God can use. And so the Lord of heaven did not hesitate in revealing His plans to the man before Him—the man whose face was hidden in his hands.

As you read these words, you may find yourself in a situation that seems terribly unfair. Your immediate circumstances are harsh and hard to handle. Your heart aches as events beyond your control roll across your landscape like heavy boulders. If that is your situation, I want you to take note of the next verses: "The LORD said, 'I have surely seen the affliction of My people who are in Egypt, and have given heed to their cry because of their taskmasters, for I am aware of their sufferings. So I have come down to deliver them from the power of the Egyptians....'" (vv. 7–8).

Linger over the phrases of this passage. If you've ever doubted the heart of God for His own, read these words until the Holy Spirit convinces you otherwise.

"I have surely seen..."
"I have given heed to their cry..."

"I am aware of the sufferings..."
"I have come down to deliver..."

The Lord was reassuring Moses, "I've been watching this situation. I'm aware of what's happening. I've seen My people weeping at night. I've heard the crack of the whip and the cries of the little ones. I've seen the bodies alongside the road, or flung into the Nile like so many beasts of burden. None of it has escaped my notice. Now, behold, the cry of the sons of Israel has come to Me; furthermore, I have seen the oppression with which the Egyptians are oppressing them" (v. 9).

God knows, right down to the final nub, exactly where you are in life. He sees. He cares. He is aware. And best of all, He is touched by it.

The enemy of our souls wants you to think differently. *God doesn't care. He's left you in this mess for so many months. How unfair! Those around you, those at work, your neighbors, live like the devil, and they're making it fine. And here you don't even have a job. You don't even have enough to cover the credit card bills. What kind of God is that?*

Or maybe some young mother-to-be, stretched to the limit already with other young children and crushing responsibilities, cries out in her heart, "My situation is more than I can bear!" And God replies, "My daughter, I know what I am doing. I know the pain of your heart right now. I know you feel overwhelmed, overloaded, pressed down. But believe Me, I am touched with your situation. And I have a plan! I am working out the details of your deliverance even now. Trust Me!"

As the Lord told Jeremiah, "For I know the plans I have for you... plans to prosper you and not to harm you, plans to give you hope and a future" (Jeremiah 29:11, NIV). The God of Jeremiah still lives, and cares, and delivers.

Now keep in mind, Moses is simply in neutral at this point. A voice is coming out of the bush, out of the undying flames, and he's standing there barefoot, mouth wide open, all ears. The Lord hasn't said anything about *his* part in the operation yet. You see, the problem with us is that we've read the story. (We may have even seen the movie!) But Moses at this point is living the story; he's never read Exodus. He's never watched

The Ten Commandments or *The Prince of Egypt*. He doesn't have a clue what's coming next.

The voice had said, "I know what's going on in Egypt." And Moses was thinking, *Yes, I've heard, too. It's terrible. Maybe the Lord will do something.*

Suddenly Moses hears words that stun him like a jolt from a high-voltage wire. "Therefore, come now, and I will send you to Pharaoh, so that you may bring My people, the sons of Israel, out of Egypt" (v. 10).

Say what? Send me to *Pharaoh?* To do *what?*

Before we consider Moses' response at that bush in greater depth (that's the next chapter) I'd like to linger a little longer here and look at this call of the Lord from a different camera angle.

ANY OLD BUSH WILL DO

What was God's larger message to Moses in that moment? Release your imagination for a few moments. It might have included some thoughts such as these:

"Moses, forty years ago you were a fine looking bush, impressed with all your own foliage. You had impressive, strong branches and lush, green leaves. But when your bush started burning, it was gone in less than forty-eight hours. Your grand scheme went up in flames, charring your dreams and consuming your ambitions along with it. There was nothing left, was there? That was your life, Moses. And then you ran like a scared rabbit across the border to get away from the Egyptian lynch mob.

"You thought you were a choice, top-quality bush before that happened, and now you don't think you're worth much at all. Listen, man, *any bush will do as long as I, the great God of all grace, am in the bush!* I want to use *you,* Moses. Stand still, and let Me set you on fire!"

What does it take to qualify as a bush that God will use? You have to be dried up and thorny. *Okay, I qualify.* You have to be dusty and dirty. *All right, I'm there.* You've got to be ordinary. *Right. That's me all over. What else, Lord?*

You have to be burnable. God is looking for flammable bushes. There are some good looking bushes and shrubs out there in Christendom that won't burn at all. They're made out of asbestos. You couldn't set 'em on fire with a welding torch. Napalm wouldn't even do the job. These are beautiful replicas of beautiful plants, but they won't burn. Which means they are of no use to God.

The truth is, any old bush will do as long as God is in the bush. That's what He was saying to Moses. "I want you to burn for Me as no man has burned before. You've been dried out and well-seasoned in this howling wasteland through these years. I wanted you dried out! And I have pruned away from you all those things you used to hang on to, and that meant so much to you. I have reduced you to a simple love for Me. That's all you have to offer now, Moses, and that is all I want."

We will explore Moses' responses in chapter seven, but before we leave the subject of responding to the call of God, I'd like to have you ponder some lingering lessons. Let me suggest three of the most common mistakes among us bushes who are candidates for God's match.

WE RUN BEFORE WE ARE SENT

That's the first major mistake we make. A younger, more confident, more headstrong Moses had done that forty years before the encounter at the bush. God hadn't sent him—not yet—but he ran ahead anyway. This problem is caused by *intensity*; we run ahead in our own strength before we've been given the divinely appointed go-ahead. Sometimes we're just champing at the bit, straining at the reins, ready to gallop out and do God's will. We can't wait for God to set things up. We can't wait for events to fall into place. We can't wait for the Spirit's nod. So we don't wait, we run! And God says, "Whoa! I haven't sent you yet. Hold on until I give the word."

WE RETREAT AFTER WE HAVE FAILED

Having run before we were sent, we end up in the ditch. Then what do we do? We try to find the very smallest mousehole we can crawl into and hide ourselves away, preferably, forever. This problem is prompted by *insecurity*.

We simply cannot stand the thought of failure. Yet who ever said you and I had to succeed at everything we attempt? That's an artificial standard set up by men, not by God. As we've already seen, failure, though a painful pedagogue, can be an outstanding instructor.

WE RESIST WHEN WE ARE CALLED

Intensity causes us to run before we are sent. Insecurity causes us to retreat when we haven't met our standard. And that brings us to a third mistake: We resist when God actually does call us. That's brought about by the feeling of *inferiority*, which is definitely not the same thing as humility.

Moses wasn't simply humble as he began to argue with God's call; he felt inferior. And that borders on a neurosis. You may be one who has clearly received the call of God, but you are closing your ears to that summons because you feel of such little value. Your broken piñon declares, "I'm not worthy!" Yet all God asks of any of us is that we be available and burnable. He doesn't ask us to be spectacular, just ready to yield.

Because of the misunderstandings I've described above, I believe there are many who have not yet responded to God's call on their lives—many who may miss opportunities to flame brightly for Him, like a radiant city shining on a hilltop. I speak to so many who are waiting for some kind of curious sign in the heavens, some engraved invitation hand delivered by an angel, some wondrous, mystical moment. And all God is waiting for is to hear you say, "I'm here, Lord. I'm Yours, thorns and all. Just set me afire."

In one of her more inspiring moments, Amy Carmichael wrote this:

> Give me the love that leads the way,
> The faith that nothing can dismay,
> The hope no disappointments tire,
> The passion that will burn like fire,
> Let me not sink to be a clod:
> Make me Thy fuel, flame of God.[2]

107

VENITA'S STORY

The name Venita Schlopfeldt will not mean anything to most who read these pages. But to our God, this name represents a bright light in His kingdom, who at one time in her life felt like an ordinary, forgotten bush.

Venita is confined to a wheelchair, paralyzed from the shoulders down. She is also the wife of a godly man named Larry. They once served the Lord as missionaries in Caracas, Venezuela.

Larry and Venita began their marriage together with strong determination, desirous of doing God's will, but in their own way and in their own time. Early in their marriage they were traveling in a car with some relatives, but never arrived at their destination. Their car ran head-on into another. Venita was thrown from the back seat, her spinal cord severed at the neck.

From that moment on, Venita suffered from inescapable paralysis. Talk about broken piñions! Through a series of operations and analyses, several competent doctors told Larry the hard truth. "You will have to live with the fact that your wife will be in a wheelchair for the rest of her life. She will never be able to bear children. And frankly, you will have to care for her as you would for a child." Larry remembered their wedding vows and determined to keep them, regardless. He stayed by her side.

When they want to travel together, Larry lifts her into the car, folding up her wheelchair in the trunk. At night, Larry dresses her for bed and tucks her in. In the morning, he lifts her from bed, places her in the chair, and feeds her breakfast.

Together, for several years, they were engaged in a bookstore ministry in Caracas, faithfully sharing the gospel of Jesus Christ at every opportunity. Larry and Venita, who worked through the shock and grief and bitterness of her condition, came out trusting God on the other side. They remain, to this day, highly effective tools for Jesus Christ. In my mind, this man and woman are among the most attractive, winsome examples of burning bushes that I've ever met. And contrary to what the doctors told Larry at the beginning, Venita has borne three healthy children.

Larry came to the Lord one day, as did Venita, and said, "We may not be much, but we are available, thorns and all. We're just a couple of ordinary bushes, Lord. Set us on fire for your glory!"

And He has.

Back when I first met them in Venezuela, Larry told me, "Chuck, you can't imagine the ministry that woman has as she wheels around that bookstore and in different places in downtown Caracas. She speaks fluent Spanish and is always leading people to Christ." And Larry himself, as far as I am able to tell, lives free of all bitterness, all rancor, all resentment. I have never once heard this man say, "Why me?"

If this choice missionary couple can burn so brightly for Jesus Christ, so can you. God wants to use you in His service, thorns and all. Your past doesn't matter. Your resumé isn't the issue. Your training and education, in the long run, won't tell the story. God is looking for someone with ears to hear His voice, hands ready to do His work, and a heart that is willing to respond.

Any old bush will do, but He must fuel the fire. Moses, after forty long years—no, make that eighty!—was finally ready and willing.

How long will it take for you?

CHAPTER SEVEN

Who? Me, Lord?

You've heard of God's children referred to as sheep. It isn't a bad picture, all things considered. The image conjures up visions of green pastures, still waters, and a gentle Shepherd, keeping watch over the flock.

But He also refers to us as mules. Sometimes, I think that's the better analogy.

Remember what the Lord said in the Psalms? "Do not be as the horse or as the mule which have no understanding, whose trappings include bit and bridle to hold them in check, otherwise they will not come near to you" (Psalm 32:9).

Don't be like a balky mule! Don't be stubborn when God speaks. Don't continually fight and resist Him. Don't keep running away from Him so that He can't speak to you. Don't force Him to lasso you before you'll let Him draw near.

Why do we resist such a magnificent God who loves us? It makes no sense! As we noted in the last chapter, we often turn away from His call because we feel so inferior. We've failed again and again, and we can't imagine His wanting to use us. We nurse our broken piñions and refuse to risk soaring across the skies once again. When the Lord says, "My son, My daughter, you are My choice for this task," we turn away. We tell ourselves that since we made such a mess of it before, we simply can't go through the disappointment and shame all over again. That's when our mule-like tendencies kick in. We stubbornly resist even the thought of getting back into the action.

I am reminded of those times many years ago when our youngest son Chuck would bring me one of his shoes with a knot in the lace. He must have been four, maybe five at the time, and nobody but nobody could get a knot in a shoestring like our little guy. He had this strange approach to dealing with the knot: He pulled on the strings with all his might. He tugged and strained and cinched that knot until it was a hard little ball. You couldn't tell where one string ended and the other began.

Rather than bringing the problem to me earlier, he would bring it to me later...after he'd tried to fix it, after the knot was so tiny and tight it would take an act of God to untie it. I had told him time and again, "Son, when you pull the strings and it won't open like it's supposed to, *don't jerk harder*. Come get me, and I'll help you." And he would usually reply, "Well, I keep thinking I *can* get it out. That's why I pull harder."

What an appropriate picture of our life with God. We get ourselves into a tangled mess and refuse to admit it's a self-made knot. So we pull harder and harder, until it takes (literally) an act of God to get us out of it.

Some time ago, I came across this apt bit of verse:

> With thoughtlessness and impatient hands,
> We tangle up the plans the Lord hath wrought.
> And when we cry in pain, He says,
> "Be quiet, My child, while I untie the knot."[1]

That's what God wanted to do with Moses. His life had been one great knot of self-effort—hard, sincere labor in the energy of the flesh. And when it became so tangled and complicated, he finally retreated into the desert, where he stayed for forty years. Then came the great day when

God spoke to Moses and said, in effect, "Moses, I want to use you again. I have a job for you."

That was when Moses the mule dug in his hooves.

"LORD, DID I HEAR YOU RIGHT?"

Moses had been resistant for forty years, telling himself all that time that his was a lost cause. Now, when God came with a direct, simple call, the old shepherd couldn't handle it. In fact, he wouldn't let himself believe he might still be useful to God. "Therefore, come now, and I will send you to Pharaoh, so that you may bring My people, the sons of Israel, out of Egypt" (Exodus 3:10).

Now that wasn't complicated, was it? The Lord spoke in a tongue Moses could understand. He gave him a simple, two-fold command. First, He said to Moses, "I will send you." And second, "You will bring My people out." That was the plan.

Notice, please, that this was not a multiple choice arrangement. It wasn't even an invitation. *It was a call.* God does not speak and ask our advice regarding His plan. God makes declarations; He doesn't open up the scene for a rap session or a dialogue. He doesn't call in a blue-ribbon panel of consultants to suggest viable options.

He speaks, and that is that.

At very unique junctures of our lives, God says to us, "Now, My child, I have *this* in mind for you. I know that you have knotted things up in the past. And I know that you may knot things up in the future. But as far as today, right now, this is My plan for you. Now go. I'm sending you, and I will be with you."

That's what He told Moses, but Moses didn't want any part of it. Why did he resist? I am convinced in my heart that Moses wasn't hearing God correctly. Moses, I believe, thought God intended *him* to be the deliverer of Israel, and that blew all his circuit breakers.

But God didn't tell him that! God told him that he would be an instrument in the deliverance, but *God Himself* would be the deliverer. Huge difference. In God's calling, He has a plan; but He never expects *you* to carry out that plan. He's going to pull it off. He simply wants you to be the instrument of action. After all, it is His reputation that's at stake, not yours. All He asks is that you give yourself to Him as a tool He can pick up and use. That's all.

Moses didn't get it: "But Moses said to God, 'Who am I, that I should go to Pharaoh, and that I should bring the sons of Israel out of Egypt'" (v. 11)?

I can just hear God replying, "Wait a minute, Moses. Time out. You didn't get the plan. That's not what I said! All you have to do is be in the right place at the right time and watch Me work. It will be great! You just keep your heart prepared, make sure you're walking in obedience, and then watch Me as I deliver those Israelites out of Egypt."

When Moses said, "Lord, who am I to do this?" it sounds like a humble, polite reply, doesn't it? As a matter of fact, it was a most inappropriate question to ask the Lord. He should have responded, "Whatever You say, Lord. I'm available. I am flammable, like this bush. Just strike the match. I'm ready to go." "And He said, 'Certainly I will be with you, and this shall be the sign to you that it is I who have sent you: when you have brought the people out of Egypt, you shall worship God at this mountain'" (v. 12).

What mountain? Mount Sinai, mentioned in verse 1. If you were to travel to that massive mountain of gray stone today, you would see that it towers some 8,000 feet above the earth. At that moment, it's easy to visualize Moses stepping back and looking up to the crown of that rugged peak. I have a hunch that a strange feeling swept over him as he heard those words. God had said, "Moses, the sign you can count on will be this: when you lead those people out of Egypt and come right back to this mountain, you're going to come to worship Me with them by your side."

In that moment, I believe Moses knew in his heart he was a goner. There was no way he was going to talk God out of that plan.

Have you ever tried to talk God out of a plan? It's the most frustrating experience I can imagine. You think you're being "persistent," but all you're doing is yanking those knots tighter. You and I need to work *with* God, even as we're working *for* God. When He lays His plan on us, there is really no other alternative.

The problem with that arrangement is that His choices often seem so illogical from our point of view. We tell ourselves it can't be what He *really* means. Honestly, now, would you have chosen Jonah to be the evangelist at Nineveh, especially when you knew he hated those Ninevites with all his heart? Of course not. You would have ruled him out immediately. Surely most any first-year seminary student would be a better choice than someone with a bitter, racist attitude toward the citizens.

God thought otherwise; Jonah was his man, all the way.

Would you have picked Gideon to lead a revolution against a powerful occupying army? Scripture says of that mighty force, "The vast armies of Midian, Amalek, and the other nations of the Mideast were crowded across the valley like locusts—yes, like the sand upon the seashore" (Judges 6:12, TLB). And *Gideon* would lead the charge? What a joke! The angel of the Lord had to track down this *mighty warrior* who, in great fear of the enemy, threshed grain as he crouched in a winepress.

And how about Moses? Would you have singled out a sun-withered, eighty-year-old shepherd to face down one of the mightiest kings in the world? Moses had been out to pasture for forty years. He had completely lost touch with his people. He'd been raising a little family, living with and working for his father-in-law. In four decades the man couldn't scrape together enough shekels to build a little place of his own. Admit it, doesn't he seem like a highly unlikely prospect for the job of delivering an entire people group from the clutches of a mighty nation?

It certainly seemed so to Moses. It made about as much logical sense as a desert bush that burns and burns but never burns up. That's the way he felt on that banner day when the Lord met him in the desert. And that's the way you and I often feel, too. We don't see things the way heaven sees them. God says to us, "You don't look at people the way I look at people. You look at a person's outward appearance and draw your conclusions from that. Not Me. I look beneath the surface—deep into the heart. I look to find some very specific qualities within an individual, and then I make My choice."

Look at the words of Hanani, the seer: "For the eyes of the LORD move to and fro throughout the earth that He may strongly support those whose heart is completely His" (2 Chronicles 16:9).

Mark that verse well. At some point in your life, you may be able to use those words in the life of someone who comes to you for counsel and encouragement. God's eyes roam across the planet to find specific individuals whose hearts are just right for a particular task He has in mind. And when He finds them, watch out! He plunges them into the stream of action, upholding them with His mighty hand.

Moses did not view himself as God viewed him. He became mulish in his resistance. He set his jaw, bowed his neck, and refused to believe what the Lord was telling him. In the process, he served up several weak excuses. Let's consider each of these four inadequate responses. I should warn you, they will sound very familiar as you read them.

EXCUSE #1: "I DON'T HAVE ALL THE ANSWERS."

> Then Moses said to God, "Behold, I am going to the sons of Israel, and I will say to them, 'The God of your fathers has sent me to you.' Now they may say to me, 'What is His name?' What shall I say to them?" (v. 13)

"But Lord," Moses was saying, "I can't be Your spokesman in this situation. Why, I wouldn't have any answers when those guys started firing questions at me."

Before we consider the Lord's response, stop and think about that lame excuse for a moment. It has a familiar ring to it, doesn't it? It's a pretext mouthed by many believers today. "Lord, I can't do that, because I'll get in a verbal corner and won't know how to handle it. Somebody will ask me, 'What about the heathen in Africa?' or 'How did they fit dinosaurs into Noah's ark?' I'll get tongue-tied. I won't know what to say, and I'll appear ridiculous and foolish in the eyes of other people. No, I can't do that, Lord. You can see that, can't You? I just don't have all the answers."

Maybe you remember what it was like in high school or college to have a teacher or professor who stranded himself out on a logical limb. He found himself in the wrong, everyone knew it, and yet he stubbornly refused to admit it. What did you do? Chances are, you began to bear down on him, sawing off that flimsy limb with a set of sharp-toothed facts. Why did you do that? Because there is something inside of us that wants the other person simply to admit, "Yeah, I was wrong."

I have never lost respect for any individual who replied to a question with the answer, "I just don't know." On the other hand, I have lost a great deal of respect for those who knew they were wrong, and knew that I knew they were wrong, but could not bring themselves to admit it.

Direct question: Why do we feel we have to have all the answers at our fingertips? Straight answer: Pride. Pride says, "If I don't have a ready come-back, if I say 'I don't know,' they'll laugh at me." But that's not true at all. Intelligent, thoughtful people won't laugh; they will realize that *no one* has all the answers.

When Moses gave God that first miserable excuse and said, "I won't have all the answers," God had an immediate reply: *"Perhaps not, but you will have all of Me."*

> God said to Moses, "I AM WHO I AM"; and He said, "Thus you shall say to the sons of Israel, 'I AM has sent me to you.'" (v. 14)

What does that mean? English readers of an English Bible run their eyes across those words and wonder why in the world that answer was significant and why it seemed to satisfy Moses.

Probing a little deeper into the original language, we discover that these words, "I AM WHO I AM," are the very characters in Hebrew that spell out the name *Yahweh.* Here is what God was saying, "The only self-existent, infinite Being in all of the universe has dispatched you, Moses. You represent Him. I AM has sent you. You tell them *that.*"

The word *"Yahweh"* is the most intimate term for the living Lord in the Hebrew vocabulary. God was saying, "Moses, when you stand before those elders of Israel, you let them know that the intimate God of Israel has sent you to be His representative."

God went on to give Moses two promises, to aid him in his introduction to the elders, and then to Pharaoh himself. In verse 18, God tells Moses that the leaders of the Israelites "will pay heed to what you say." Moses had

God's promise on that. And when it came time to deal with Pharaoh, the Lord made a second promise: "So I will stretch out My hand and strike Egypt with all My miracles which I shall do in the midst of it; and after that he will let you go" (v. 20).

What assurance! It was already a done deal. The Lord told Moses, not only will the elders of Israel hear you and believe you, but Pharaoh himself will fall in line and unlock the gate to freedom. It's going to happen; He'll let Israel go. So you've got My promises to stand on, Moses. I won't let you down. You feel as if you don't have all the answers, but you'll have all of Me. You represent I AM, and you represent My unfailing promises."

You would think that would have sealed the deal, right? I mean, what else did Moses need to hear? Instead, it led to yet another weak excuse.

EXCUSE #2: "I MAY NOT HAVE THEIR RESPECT."

> Then Moses said, "What if they will not believe me or listen to what
> I say? For they may say, 'The LORD has not appeared to you.'" (4:1)

With this reaction, Moses shows how deeply he fears ridicule. More than anything else, perhaps, he is deathly afraid of appearing as a silly old man. He says, in effect, "Lord, I've been to Egypt. I know what it's like there. And You say I'm going to come waltzing back into the capital city—an old, run-down-at-the-heels shepherd out of the backside of the desert? What kind of reception do you think I'll get? Look at these clothes! Look at this wrinkled mug of mine. And You say I'm going to walk right into the core of sophistication and culture—stroll up to the golden throne of Pharaoh holding this knobby old staff of mine? And I'm going to talk that stubborn monarch into letting me lead all of his slaves out the back door like a flock of sheep? Who would believe it, Lord? I'd feel like a redneck who just fell off of the turnip truck saying something like that."

It isn't any fun to feel foolish in front of people, is it? For most of us, that would be like the old nightmare where you're giving a report to your class and suddenly notice you're standing there in your underwear. Moses feared that level of embarrassment. In the solitude of his desert retreat, at least, he still had his dignity. He might be obscure, he might be a nobody, he might be over the hill, but he was safe. At least no one was *laughing* at him.

It's obvious from Moses' answer that he had ignored what God had just said. Somehow, the words out of that fiery bush had sailed right over his shaggy head. The Lord had already told him, *"They will pay heed to what you say."* And now here he is, only moments later, saying, "What if they do not pay heed to what I say?"

There's a disconnect there somewhere! Moses' second excuse was actually an open denial of God's clear promise.

"Moses, when you go, they're going to listen."

"Right Lord, but what if they don't listen?"

I can't help but wonder if somewhere inside of that bush, God was shaking His head. *Didn't the man hear what I just said?* The problem? Moses was in his mule mode. And you can't reason with a mule.

"Moses, you will have all My power. That's my answer."

"Yeah, but I may not have all their respect."

"Of course you will! I just told you you'd have all My power!"

Here's another thought: Moses' second excuse was totally hypothetical. It began with the words, "What if...?" Those are, and always will be, the words of worriers. Every worry-wart in the family of God lives on those two words. *What if* such and such occurs? *What if* so and so does this or that? *What if* thus and so takes place?

Many people feed their minds on the uncertainty of tomorrow, allowing the "What If" monster to keep a grip around their throats. That's what Moses was doing. He was so worried about what *might* happen, he didn't hear God tell him what *would* happen. His mind was filled with imaginary scenarios. He pictured himself back in the lush, Nile-watered lands of Egypt. He visualized the opulence and splendor of the Egyptian court and all those well-dressed, sophisticated, worldly men and women. *They won't respect* me. *How could they? They'll stare at* me *like some curious old relic, and laugh* me *off.* Obviously, Moses was preoccupied with himself.

Knowing Moses' thoughts and fears, the Lord graciously and patiently told him, "Let Me show you what I am able to do."

> The LORD said to him, "What is that in your hand?" And he said,
> "A staff."
>
> Then He said, "Throw it on the ground." So he threw it on the
> ground, and it became a serpent; and Moses fled from it.
>
> But the LORD said to Moses, "Stretch out your hand and grasp it
> by its tail"—so he stretched out his hand and caught it, and it became
> a staff in his hand.... (vv. 2–4)

Wow! Don't you think he was relieved at that moment? He had a slithering, venomous serpent by the tail, and God turned it back into a hunk of wood. The lesson? "Look, Moses, I'm able to turn a wooden staff into a live snake, then back into a wooden staff again. That's something right there in your hand you can make use of. I'm not sending you before the king like a silly clown with little rings or boxes or a bag of cheap tricks. I'm the Lord of heaven and earth. I'm sending you with mighty signs to perform."

The Lord certainly had Moses' attention at that moment. So He went on:

> The LORD furthermore said to him, "Now put your hand into your
> bosom." So he put his hand into his bosom, and when he took it out,
> behold, his hand was leprous like snow.
>
> Then He said, "Put your hand into your bosom again." So he put
> his hand into his bosom again, and when he took it out of his bosom,
> behold, it was restored like the rest of his flesh. (vv. 6–7)

Think of that! Moses looked down at his own hand and it was leprous—the most dreaded of all diseases. What a shock! But on God's command, when he stuck it back into the folds of his desert tunic and pulled it out again, it was restored like the rest of his flesh.

Remarkable! Yet that was nothing for the Lord of the universe. He could (and would) do many more miraculous signs and wonders in Egypt. He would turn the mighty Nile itself into blood. He would cover the land with lice, and grasshoppers, and frogs, and gnats, and nasty, painful boils. He would eclipse the sun and plunge the nation into thick darkness. Finally, He would snuff out the life of every firstborn male in all of Egypt. He is

Lord, meaning He could do whatever He pleased. All He asked of Moses was to stand before the king, deliver the message, then just get out of the way as God shook the whole country with His awesome power.

That makes me excited just to think about being Moses! When had God ever placed such power into the hands of one man? Surely, he was now convinced.

No, he was not. Amazingly, instead of falling on his knees in awe and obedience, he hid behind another lame excuse.

EXCUSE #3: "I'M SLOW IN MY EXPRESSIONS."

> Then Moses said to the LORD, "Please, Lord, I have never been elo-quent, neither recently nor in time past, nor since You have spoken to Your servant; for I am slow of speech and slow of tongue." (v. 10)

The Living Bible paraphrases this third excuse: "O Lord, I'm just not a good speaker. I never have been, and I'm not now, even after you have spoken to me, for I have a speech impediment."

Moses was saying, "Lord, I just don't get my thoughts together very easily. And even if I do get 'em together, I can't get 'em *out*. My tongue is slow on the draw."

Perhaps you identify with Moses in this. You say, "Oh man, I . . . I get in front of a group and . . . ummm . . . I can't get my stuff said. I get scared. My knees knock. I want to throw up. To make matters worse, I never know what to say. I may get a couple good thoughts now and then, but I don't know how to string them together."

That was Moses' complaint. He was telling the Lord, "I've been keeping company with sheep for all these years. All I'm good at now is 'baaa, baaa, baaa.' That's about it! But you're pushing me to stand up in front of all those educated, official people in Pharaoh's court and be eloquent. I . . . I just can't manage that . . . can't do it. Sorry. You understand, don't You, Lord?"

My friend and mentor, Dr. Howard Hendricks, taught a Dale Carnegie course years ago. He told me about two of the men in his class who were petrified at the thought of saying something in front of anybody. One man was so frightened he literally hid under his desk when it was his turn to go up front and say his little piece. The other fella dismissed himself to go to the bathroom when his turn came up and didn't return to class. Neither of these guys could handle the idea of standing in front of even a few sympathetic listeners.

That's the way Moses felt. He'd lost the knack. Have you ever felt like that? You find yourself with an opportunity to say a few words for your Lord in a public setting, you feel the nudge of the Holy Spirit whispering *Go ahead*, but your flesh just shrinks at the thought. The excuse is, "Lord, I don't have the ability. I can't pull it off. I can't cope with that kind of assignment. I'm not a preacher."

Let me share with you something about the apostle Paul that may surprise you. Just the mention of the great apostle's name calls into the mind of most believers the image of a great public speaker—kind of a Winston Churchill, Ronald Reagan, and Billy Graham all rolled into one package. Most of us imagine his sweeping into a city, banners flying, like a combination of Napoleon and Alexander the Great, preaching with great eloquence and founding churches at the snap of his fingers.

While it could certainly be argued that he was a great apostle, he was by no means a great orator. Read his own words on the subject, to the church in Corinth: "When I came to you, brothers, I did not come with eloquence or superior wisdom as I proclaimed to you the testimony about God" (1 Corinthians 2:1, NIV).

In context, Paul was talking about worldly wisdom. He was saying, "As you know, brothers and sisters, I didn't walk in the door with a swagger. I didn't come on with the suave, scintillating style you Greeks love to celebrate. You've heard plenty of eloquent speakers and orators, but I wasn't like that among you. You know that. Here is the way it was.... I came to you in weakness and fear, and with much trembling" (v. 3, NIV).

Can you believe that? Paul was so nervous that one knee said to the other knee, "Let's shake!" He could hear 'em knocking together beneath his robe. *The apostle Paul? Could it be?* You'd expect him to walk into a room and just take charge, like a pro. But that's not the way it was. He was with them in weakness. In fear. In much trembling. As a matter of fact, he goes on to admit, "My message and my preaching were not with wise and persuasive words, but with a demonstration of the Spirit's power, so that your faith might not rest on men's wisdom, but on God's power" (vv. 4–5, NIV).

Back in the first century, why didn't God choose a more powerful, eloquent spokesman? He had a good reason for that. He didn't want people hung up on the man's speaking style and craft. The Lord knew what He was doing. He didn't want men and women walking away from Paul's meetings saying, "Am I impressed! What a communicator. What an awesome speaker!"

When the apostle Paul finished, people had met God. When he stepped away from the podium, men and women had heard from the living Savior. When Paul penned a letter to a church, it was as if God's own hand had written it. Their faith became anchored to the solid rock of God's power, not the shifting sand of human personality. Paul, himself, was never the attraction. In public speaking skills he couldn't hold a candle to a man like Apollos.

That's not the common mental image we cherish of the great apostle, is it? Why, we have the idea that he was as Demosthenes. He was not. As in the case of Moses, we have developed the mental image of a leader as a persuasive, dynamic man or woman with a well-modulated voice who never stutters, stammers, or slides past a single word. Accustomed as we've become to television media types, we think true leaders ought to be in a handsome suit or tailored dress, without a blemish, beautiful, straight teeth, every hair in place, and staring into the audience with sharp eyes, speaking with confidence. (Never mind that he or she is reading from a teleprompter!)

God, with continuing patience, says to Moses, "I hear what you're saying, and here is what I will do." The LORD said to him, "Who has made man's mouth? Or who makes him mute or deaf, or seeing or blind? Is it not I, the LORD? Now then go, and I, even I, will be with your mouth, and teach you what you are to say" (vv. 11–12).

Now that's divine speech therapy! *I will be in between your lips. I will be right on your tongue. And I will give you the necessary words as you need them.*

Do you know what I've discovered about the Lord? He doesn't give wisdom on credit. He doesn't advance you a bundle of insight, or slip you several Spirit-filled phrases to tuck away and use in an emergency. Do you know when He gives us words and wisdom and insight? *Right when we need them.* At the very instant they are required.

If you're a parent, you may have experienced this phenomenon. You find yourself in a situation you never anticipated, and couldn't prepare for. Suddenly, you're at one of the critical junctures of life where you're the mom or dad, and your child is looking into your eyes, depending on you for a right answer. Not always, but often, you are given the words you need. Later you realize that they were words beyond your own wisdom. At that quiet moment, you breathe a little prayer of thanks. "Praise You, Lord. That's exactly what needed to be said." You couldn't have planned for it, you couldn't have prepared for it; but when the moment came, the Lord gave you the wisdom and the words you required.

That's what God, in His gentleness, was trying to get across to a man with a severe case of mule-itis. "This is how it will be, Moses. I will be with your mouth, and I will guide your tongue, and I will give you the very words you need precisely when they are needed." Isn't that a great plan? But don't forget, it demands faith. God was saying, "I want you to be willing to *trust* Me, Moses. I want you to be willing to step into that situation and rely on Me for the words."

In verse 14, it almost sounds as if Moses is saying, "All right, I'm ready to go." Unfortunately, that's not what he meant. Instead, it is yet another excuse. The mule is still stuck.

EXCUSE #4: "I'M NOT AS QUALIFIED AS OTHERS."

> But he said, "Please, Lord, now send the message by whomever You will." (Exodus 4:13)

In other words, *anybody but me, Lord!*

The New International Version renders this verse, "O Lord, please send someone else to do it." *The Modern Language Bible* makes me smile: "O Lord, please send *anyone* else."

"Oh Lord, I'm just not qualified. That land of Egypt is shot through with capable people who know the culture and the lingo like the back of their hands. I used to, but no longer. I'm out of touch. You just haven't looked very far, Lord. There are all kinds of people who could move in and handle this job with ease and efficiency. Have You considered taking out an ad? There's probably some young buck in Egypt who's wonderfully qualified. Use him! Why come out here to this forsaken patch of wilderness and speak to a sun-baked, leather-skinned old desert-dweller? I haven't set foot in Egypt for forty long years. I don't even know my way around Goshen anymore. Everything's probably changed. Don't you get it, Lord? There are so many others more qualified than I."

Do you ever feel like that? The Lord puts His finger on you, and you immediately glance around and say, "Who? Me, Lord? Look at that guy in the next row. Look at the classy lady over there. He's got his degree in that area. She's been a *consultant*, for goodness' sake. He speaks to groups all the time. She has led a women's Bible study for eighteen years. His family has all grown up and gone. She's been in this church twenty-three years. Look at her ability! Me? I've got kids at home...I've got debt...I've got high blood pressure...I've got crooked teeth...I'm overweight...never been to seminary...I don't have anything decent to wear...I don't do well in front of people."

And the Lord comes back and says to us, "I know every one of those things. But you are still My choice. My call is clear and final." That's His answer. You see, if you think *you* are persistent, you haven't done business with God lately. He doesn't give up on us. (Thank goodness!)

But He does become angry at times. Maybe you had parents like mine, who were patient up to a point, and from that point on weren't patient at all.

SECOND BEST

Then the anger of the LORD burned against Moses, and He said, "Is there not your brother Aaron the Levite? I know that he speaks fluently. And moreover, behold, he is coming out to meet you; when he sees you, he will be glad in his heart. You are to speak to him and put the words in his mouth; and I, even I, will be with your mouth and his mouth, and I will teach you what you are to do. Moreover, he shall speak for you to the people; and he will be as a mouth for you and you will be as God to him. You shall take in your hand this staff, with which you shall perform the signs. (vv. 14–17)

Do you know what God did? He accommodated Moses' desire. But the compromise was less than the best; brother Aaron proved to be an albatross around his neck. It was Aaron who got impatient while Moses was on the mountain and created a golden calf for the people to worship. It was he who told the people, "This is your god, O Israel, who brought you up from the land of Egypt" (Exodus 32:4).

As you read these words, you may sense God's nudge to step out on faith in a plan that seems risky at best. You don't have all the answers. You don't know the hows and whys and wherefores of what God has in mind. From a human point of view, the prospects look rather bleak. Do you know what our tendency is? It's to take someone with us. Somehow, that keeps us from having to put our full trust in the Lord's plan; we can lean on that gifted friend or companion we've brought along with us.

How many men have gone into a business partnership and lived to regret the day they chose that partner? How many women have engaged in pursuits with a companion they wish they had never asked to join them? God's call is a serious, individual matter. While I believe with all my heart in accountability, God's call does not lend itself to the buddy system, or to group excursions. And before you bring any other individual along with you to fulfill that call, or before you join a team, you must make absolutely certain in your heart that each one has the same vision beating in his or her heart that you do.

If not, then take this advice, my friend: Go it alone. Follow God's voice without distraction.

God was finally willing to say to Moses, "All right, all right, have it your way. I'll send Aaron, too, but it isn't My best, Moses. The day will come when you will wish you'd followed My call on your own. You don't really need Aaron; all you need is Me."

"I NEED A LEAVE OF ABSENCE, JETHRO."

Verse 18 features a glimpse into Moses' humanity and God's patience.

> Then Moses departed and returned to Jethro his father-in-law and said to him, "Please, let me go, that I may return to my brethren who are in Egypt, and see if they are still alive." And Jethro said to Moses, "Go in peace."

Moses left *just a few things* out of that account, don't you think? Moses says, "Dad, I want to go see if any of my buddies down in Egypt are still alive. I've been at this forty years now. Do you mind if I take a little time off? You know, check out the pyramids, take a ride on the Nile, that kind of stuff."

And Jethro says, "Fine. Have a good time. Take off, son."

Somehow, Moses couldn't bring himself to say, "Uh, Jethro, there was this bush out in the desert, and there was this voice in the bush, and well, the upshot is I'm going to lead the whole nation of Israel in an Exodus out of slavery and deliver them to Canaan." He just couldn't say that. But God, in His grace, doesn't slap Moses' hand. He doesn't say, "Knock it off, Moses! Tell him the whole story." He lets Moses cover his departure with kind of a broad-brush, nebulous explanation.

Somehow, that touches my heart. God is full of grace. Moses was packing his bags for Egypt, and God let it go at that. All He asks of us is a willing heart. He doesn't expect perfection. He doesn't expect you to have all the answers, all the ability, or all the courage. He doesn't even require you to spell out each detail of His call. He just asks you to be available, and take that first step of faith in the direction He's pointing.

THREE FINAL CAUTIONS

Once you've quit resisting, once you've shed the mule mentality and decided in your heart to respond to the Lord, you need to exercise three cautions.

First, *be certain it is God's voice.* Many people in pursuit of God's glory seem to think God's opinion has nothing to do with it. They're on a roll, they're on a lark, they're feeling a throb of adventure in their quest, and they don't want to slow down for anybody, even God Himself.

God's voice isn't all that difficult to hear. In fact, you almost have to be closing your eyes and stopping your ears to miss it. He sometimes shouts through our pain, whispers to us while we're relaxing on vacation, occasionally He sings to us in a song, and warns us through the sixty-six books of His written Word. It's right there, ink on paper. Count on it—that book will never lead you astray.

In addition to His unfailing source of wisdom, He has given you wise counselors, friends, acquaintances, parents, teachers, and mentors who have earned your love and respect through long years. Screen what you believe to be the will of God through their thoughts, their perspectives. Does your conviction about the direction you're headed grow, or are you seeing lots of red flags and caution signs? Before you undertake a major life-direction change, be very careful that it is God's voice, that it is God's call you are hearing.

Second, *be confident in His power*. Don't turn aside from the task, saying to yourself, "I'm not strong enough for this. I don't have the power." Listen, you don't *have* to be powerful. You're a clay pot, remember? You're a common, earthenware jar made to contain His power. He doesn't ask you to be cute, clever, lucid, or persuasive. He doesn't expect you to be mighty in word and deed. He just asks that you place your confidence in Him.

As good King Jehoshaphat prayed, "O our God . . . we have no power to face this vast army that is attacking us. We do not know what to do, but our eyes are upon you" (2 Chronicles 20:6, NIV).

Third, *Be comfortable with His plan*. Take it the way He gives it to you. Accept His arrangement. Don't tinker with this and mess with that or think that by throwing an Aaron into the mix you'll improve things and make the plan more effective. Take the hard road rather than the easier, compromise road. In the end, you'll bless the Lord again and again that you did.

As I wrestled with the content of this chapter, I kept asking myself, "What does it mean to be willing? What does it mean to give up that old, mule-headed stubbornness and start yielding to the Lord's voice? As I pondered those questions, I came across a prayer that says it all and says it well.

"Lord, I am willing.
I am willing to receive what You give.
I am willing to lack what You withhold.
I am willing to relinquish what You take.
I am willing to suffer what You require."[2]

That's how to curb our tendency to resist. That's how to shed that uncomfortable mule suit and run like a deer.

Don't keep yanking on those loose strings of your life, thinking your own plan is best. Bring the whole tangled knot to Him. Bring Him your failures, your false starts, and your well-intentioned crusades that landed you on the backside of a lonely desert. Let Him sort through the details of your life, and give you fresh direction.

No one unties knots like the Lord.

CHAPTER EIGHT

God's Will, God's Way

Tucked away in the third chapter of Proverbs are a couple of verses you may know from memory. "Trust in the LORD with all your heart and do not lean on your own understanding. In all your ways acknowledge Him, and He will make your paths straight" (Proverbs 3:5–6).

This is what I call a "before-and-after" proverb. Certain things need to take place beforehand, so that something might occur afterward.

The *before* part, in verse 5, urges us to "trust in the Lord." That suggests relying on Him, letting Him take the lead, and yielding the steering wheel of our lives. The verse also notes that we are to do this with all of our hearts. This is not something done half-heartedly, reluctantly, or with reservations. It's an all-out, go-for-broke proposition.

At that point, however, Solomon adds a warning: "Be careful not to lean on your own understanding." In other words, don't rely on crutches of your own making. Don't attempt to limp along on your own strength. Instead, lean hard. And while leaning, fully "acknowledge Him." That word "acknowledge" includes the meaning "to recognize." *In all your ways recognize Him.*

That's the *before* part. Our part. Trust Him whole-heartedly, in every corner of your life, recognizing that He is the One in charge.

Now comes the *after* part. *His* part. "He will make your paths straight." The word means "smooth," "straight," or "even." In other words, He will smooth out your path. He'll take care of each of those obstacles on the trail ahead of you.

Another proverb, later on in that book, reads like a kissing cousin to Proverbs 3:5–6. Solomon writes, "When a man's ways are pleasing to the LORD, He makes even his enemies to be at peace with him" (Proverbs 16:7).

Another great promise! When your path is smooth as a result of your walking in obedience, He will make even your enemies to be at peace with you.

"IT'S YOUR PROBLEM, LORD"

I'm reminded of a man in our former church, who was trying to buy a home in that community. He had told the Lord from the beginning, "Lord, this is Your project. This is going to be Your home. And so I'm not going to worry and fret and connive and manipulate to get that home in my name. I want it very much, as You know, Lord, but I refuse to let it be the god of my life. I leave it with You to take care of every barrier."

He meant it. And if you've bought or sold a home recently, you know all about the barriers and obstacles that can block your path. As this man leaned hard and trusted fully in the Lord, however, he and his family saw each of those obstacles removed, one by one. Then, on the very last day when he and his wife were getting dressed to go down and sign papers on that home, the loan company called.

"I'm sorry," the loan officer said, "but we've determined that your salary is insufficient. We won't be able to loan you the money."

At that point, many of us would have exploded with anger or crawled into a cavern of depression and rolled a rock in front of the opening. But this man, even in the midst of this crushing disappointment, remembered his agreement with the Lord. After he hung up the phone, he went to his knees and said, "Lord, I've said all along this is going to be *Your* home. And if You don't want me to have it, so be it. But it's *Your* problem. I refuse to be upset about it." He then rested his spirit. He recognized that God was God, period.

Within a few hours, his phone rang again. Same loan company. Same loan officer. "Something has happened for the first time in my experience here," the man on the phone said. "We've made a mistake! In fact, we made some miscalculations in our figuring. Your salary is certainly sufficient. Do you still want the home?"

You'd better believe he did! And as soon as he hung up the phone with the loan company, he dialed my number. "Pastor Chuck," he said, "I've gotta rejoice with somebody, so you're the one who came to my mind!" And he went on to describe to me what God had just done.

"You know," I told him with a smile, "that reminds me of a proverb. 'When a man's ways please the Lord, He makes even the loan company to be at peace with him.'"

"Where is that proverb?" he yelled into the phone. "Where is it?"

As with all the proverbs, this is an observation of something generally true in life. Please keep in mind, it is not an iron-clad promise. It won't always work out in your favor. God isn't a tooth fairy, always leaving gifts under our pillow anytime we "wish upon a star." You won't always get the loan, or the job, or the passing grade, or the cash settlement, or the blessing of your in-laws. Don't misread this proverb; it isn't some bargaining tool you can use to leverage God your way.

But what a beautiful way to live. It's beautiful when you can say, "Lord, I'm not going to sweat this whole process. I'm not going to wake up every morning with a knot in my gut. It's *Your* baby. I'm going to do it *Your* way to the best of my ability and walk in *Your* revealed will. I'm trusting You to take care of the obstacles."

When we do our part, it's remarkable how the barriers come down, and in the most surprising ways. In Exodus chapter 4, we approach that major life intersection with Moses. Standing barefoot beside the burning bush, he had said to the Lord in so many words, "Okay, God, You win. If You want to use me as Your instrument of deliverance, then here I am at Your disposal.

In the days that followed, Moses began to experience what it was to trust in the Lord with all his heart, refusing to lean any longer on his own manmade crutches. And as he did, he began to see God smooth the way before him.

BRINGING THE FAMILY ALONG

Moses, you'll remember, approached his father-in-law Jethro and asked permission to return to Egypt. He certainly didn't tell Jethro everything at that point, but he let the man know there was something stirring in his heart. After years and years of virtual silence about his life and background back in Egypt, Moses said to Jethro, "It's time for me to go back. There's some unfinished business that needs attention."

When you have heard the voice of God calling you in a new direction—confirming that direction through His Word, through events, and through the wisdom of godly counselors—the result of that thought process needs to be communicated with your family. This is especially true if you are young. Why? *Because your family has not had the benefit of the burning bush.* You've heard God's voice; that's not true for them. They may not know or understand what God has said to you. They still feel like you should be going in a previously agreed-upon direction, and now you seem to be talking about a whole new set of plans. Those kinds of major course changes can seem upsetting, or even frightening, to those who care about you, especially parents. You need to be gracious enough to give them some helpful information on how God has changed your direction.

That holds true for your employer as well. Jethro depended on Moses; they had worked shoulder to shoulder through all those years. Moses took time to inform the older gentleman. It was a wise and gracious thing for him to do. Your employer has made an investment in you; he or she has provided you with employment, allowing you to make a living while you considered God's will and plan for your life. It would be unwise and rash for you, no matter how zealous you may be, suddenly to vacate your position with a hasty explanation that "God has called me to be somewhere else."

It doesn't really matter if your family or your employer are believers or not. You still owe it to them to be prudent, wise, and gracious during the time of life transition.

Because he handled it well, when Moses asked permission to leave for Egypt, his father-in-law replied, "Go in peace" (Exodus 4:18). Jethro used the lovely Hebrew expression *shalom*. "*Shalom*, Moses. Peace be with you." The Living Bible paraphrases it, "Go with my blessing." I like that. Jethro was saying, "Son, it's not only fine for you to leave, please know that you go with my smile and my best wishes."

COVERING HOME BASE

This exchange between these two men leads me to two principles worth considering. First of all, when God crystallizes a plan for your life, perhaps nudging you in a new direction, be very, very sensitive how you communicate that to others. Don't assume they know all you know about the process. Don't expect them to greet the idea with immediate acceptance and open arms. Give them the courtesy of time and space to think things through. Communicate your thoughts with tenderness, care, and concern. This is especially true for those led into missionary endeavors. Pushing and rushing into a plan without concern for parental understanding and blessing can create relational roadblocks that may shadow and hamper the effectiveness of future ministry.

The second thing to notice is that this plan flowed. When you are in the center of God's will, my friend, it *flows*. It doesn't have to be forced. Moses said, "Jethro, may I go?" And Jethro replied, "Go in peace." Moses could move into what would prove to be a difficult ministry knowing things back home were just fine.

May I paraphrase a proverb I quoted earlier? "When a man's ways please the Lord, he makes even his *in-laws* to be at peace with him." Are you having major problems and strife with your in-laws? It may be time to step back and ask why. Begin on your knees, asking , "Father, are my ways pleasing to You? Is there something I'm missing or overlooking here?" And then be open and sensitive in your heart. Those self-examination sessions before the Lord, painful as they might be, may yield benefit and fruit for years to come.

It is a very humbling experience to be moving in the direct current of God's will. But it can also bring fresh assurance. I think the late Theodore Epp put it best when he wrote, "Once a person is satisfied that he is in the center of God's plan and God is working out His will through him, that person is invincible."

Perhaps that's where you are at this moment. You *know* you are in the center of His will, and you feel invincible! It is a humbling place to live but the best place in the whole world.

Earlier in my ministry, I remember speaking for a week of meetings at a small Christian college. In the very first meeting, during my first contact with that student body, they did something for me that hasn't happened to me before or since. Remember the old chorus, "Spirit of the living God, fall afresh on me"?[1] They personalized that song with my name, and sang it quietly as a prayer.

As I stood before those five hundred-plus students, preparing to speak to them, they sang, "Spirit of the living God, fall afresh on Chuck. Melt him, mold him, fill him, use him." In a very real sense, when they finished that prayerful song, I felt invincible! Not proud. No, there wasn't an ounce of pride in that feeling of exhilaration and joy. I felt as Moses might have felt beside that bush: *"He's going to use me this week."* And He was pleased to do just that.

To communicate that invincibility, however, is a very delicate matter. You can't hurry through it. You must not allow impatience or a haughty spirit to dampen your joy or offend those who care about you. Moses didn't, and the journey to Egypt got off on the right footing. Before Moses led a whole nation into exodus from Egypt, he handled his own exodus from home in a considerate, respectful way.

YOU ARE HIS CONCERN

Now the LORD said to Moses in Midian, "Go back to Egypt, for all the men who were seeking your life are dead." So Moses took his wife and his sons and mounted them on a donkey, and returned to the land of Egypt. Moses also took the staff of God in his hand. (Exodus 4: 19–20)

Isn't God gracious? We have a Lord who knows our hearts, knows our thoughts, and knows our fears. When Moses had left Egypt forty years before there were those who sought his life. The king of Egypt put a price on Moses' princely head; he was probably featured at the top of the Egyptian version of The Ten Most Wanted list.

Naturally, Moses had not forgotten. He was a family man now, headin' west with the wife and kids, and that potential danger must have been weighing on his mind. It was part of the reason he had been reluctant to go in the first place. But when he finally made the decision to embrace God's will, he determined to make the journey in spite of those concerns. He told the Lord, in effect, "Lord, I'm going to trust You with all my heart. I'm not going to lean on my own understanding. In all my ways I'm going to recognize You and let You take care of the obstacles."

So he set his face toward Egypt and began putting one foot in front of another, in obedience to God. Before he stepped outside the borders of Midian, however, the Lord did something for His servant. He said to him, "Oh, by the way, Moses, you remember all those who sought your life in Egypt? Don't be anxious about them. They're all dead. They can't hurt you now."

Wow! What a relief that must have been! And how wonderful that God personally cares about those things that worry us and prey upon our thoughts. He cares about them more than we care about them. Not a single nagging, aching, worrisome, stomach-tensing, blood-pressure-raising thought escapes His notice. As the apostle Peter wrote, "Cast all your anxiety on him because he cares for you" (1 Peter 5:7, NIV). The Phillips translation renders the verse, "You can throw the whole weight of your anxieties upon him, for you are his personal concern."

Isn't that good? He genuinely cares. He is able to bear all the weight of your worry. Because you are His personal concern, you never disappear from His radar screen.

He removed an anchor from Moses' heart when He said, "Don't give those men another thought. They're all in the grave." Moses probably felt like singing in that moment. He probably slapped the donkey on the rump and said, "Let's get after it, Cleopatra! We've got work to do."

What a sight that little family must have been as they headed down the desert road. His wife, Zipporah, was on the donkey, the two kids were cavorting on ahead, and a few of the family's belongings were probably tied on the donkey's back. They were on their way, leaving a steady job, family, security, and the familiarity of their surroundings. Midian wasn't much, but it had been their home for many years. And now they were on their way to Egypt—on their way to the Exodus. What faith!

Have you stepped out on faith like that lately? Have you made a move, followed the nudging of God, into realms you wouldn't have even dreamed of five years ago? He will honor your faith if you trust Him in that kind of walk. Those who remain in the false security of Midian never get to experience what Moses experienced on that winding highway to Egypt— the sense of moving in the very current of God's will and plan.

THE STAFF OF GOD

Notice again how verse 20 closes: "Moses also took the staff of God in his hand." Wait a minute! That's the same piece of wood described in verse 2 as simply "a staff." It was Moses' staff—part of his shepherd's equipment. But now in verse 20, it is "the staff of God." What happened between verse 2 and verse 20?

A miracle. That's the very staff that God turned into a writhing snake. Then, after commanding Moses to catch the serpent by the tail, He turned it back into a staff again. But it was no longer the staff of Moses. Now it was the staff of God, because God had touched it.

Let me tell you this, my friend. When your life is marked by God, whatever you use for Him becomes His property. If you're working in the office of a Christian organization, or wherever it may be, your hands that touch the keyboard in service to Him become the hands of God. If you become a faithful witness on your campus, on your job, or in your neighborhood, your voice becomes the voice of God. If you open up your home in a special way, dedicating your hospitality for His glory, your address becomes God's address; your house becomes the house of God. It's marked from then on, just like the staff. Moses took the staff God had touched and made his way to Egypt. F. B. Meyer describes that scene with these words:

Imagine the setting forth that day. Zipporah sitting on the donkey, perhaps nursing a little babe, new-born, while that husband and father walked beside. And in his hand was the sacred rod—only a shepherd's crook, but now the rod of God—destined to be employed for deeds of transcendent power, always reminding Moses what weak things could do when wielded by strong hands behind them.[2]

I imagine Moses held fast to that sturdy rod of wood because it was a tangible reminder of God's presence. He needed that at this moment. He's eighty, remember.

> The LORD said to Moses, "When you go back to Egypt see that you perform before Pharaoh all the wonders which I have put in your power; but I will harden his heart so that he will not let the people go." (Exodus 4:21)

The Lord gave Moses both a command and a reminder in that verse. He was to perform all of the miracles God led him to perform, but he was also to remember that Pharaoh wasn't going to be impressed. The king would harden his heart and resist God's voice, and God was informing Moses of that fact in advance.

I can't imagine any person who doesn't scratch his or her head over verse 21, and say, "What in the world is God doing? He selects an eighty-year-old shepherd to lead His people out of Egypt, and on top of that, He hardens Pharaoh's heart to say, 'Not a chance. I won't let 'em go.' What gives here?"

In my Bible, I have penned "Romans 11:33–34" in the margin by Exodus 4:21. Here is what that reference says:

> Oh, the depth of the riches of the wisdom and knowledge of God! How unsearchable his judgments, and his paths beyond tracing out! Who has known the mind of the Lord? Or who has been his counselor? (NIV)

The New American Standard declares, "How unfathomable His ways!"

Maybe you've come to discover this in your own experience. You've tried to "trace out His path" and you can't pull it off. You've tried to fathom His "unfathomable" ways and you can't. It just doesn't compute. It blows your microprocessor. You have begun to walk with God like never before in your life, but in that path of obedience, you have come across situations that simply defy explanation—you have encountered situations that seem to be contradictory. That's how God works; accept it! It may not make sense to you for years, *if ever*. But that's okay. I've come to realize I wouldn't understand His thought processes and planned procedures, even if He took time to explain them to me.

It was a wonderful day for me when I finally realized I don't have to *explain* the will of God. That's not my task. My job is simply to obey it. When I was a student at Dallas Seminary, President John Walvoord used to say, "We spend too much of our time trying to unscrew the inscrutable." What a waste. You and I can't do that. It isn't even worth the effort.

God was saying to his servant (who may have been understandably bewildered), "Moses, you simply go before Pharaoh and deliver the goods. He won't like it. He won't want it. Just bear in mind that even his stubborn, hardened heart is not outside My will." In the following verse, the Lord gave Moses specific instructions what to say when he rammed into that brick wall. "Then you shall say to Pharaoh, 'Thus says the LORD, "Israel is My son, My firstborn. So I said to you, 'Let My son go that he may serve Me'; but you have refused to let him go. Behold, I will kill your son, your firstborn"'" (Exodus 4:22–23).

To put it into the vernacular, that was a gutsy message, wasn't it? You walk out of the desert into a new land, get an audience with the king, look him eyeball to eyeball and say, "Pharaoh, God says to let His people go. But because you will refuse to do that, your own son will die."

Wow! What a tough thing to say. Yet, it was the Lord's own words. It was a good thing Moses had already settled the issue of obedience to the Lord back in Midian. Moses didn't argue; Scripture doesn't report so much as a flinch. Forty years in the wilderness had changed the man. He was ready to be God's mouthpiece, whatever the consequences. In fact, from that moment on, he seemed to have a quiet confidence in his dealings with the feisty Pharaoh. Knowing he was in the nucleus of God's will, he felt that *invincibility* I mentioned earlier.

A verse in the Book of Isaiah helps to explain Moses' calm spirit at that moment. "And the work of righteousness will be peace, and the service of righteousness, quietness and confidence forever" (Isaiah 32:17).

Perhaps you've never noticed that reference before. It deserves your close examination. We could call any work done in the will of God "the work of righteousness." And in doing that work, you will be surrounded by peace. Deep within you, in the very outworking of that service and that obedient walk, you will enjoy quietness and confidence. The original Hebrew term rendered "confidence" here might be better termed "security." The old King James translates it "assurance."

In other words, there will be a quiet, secure confidence when you are walking in His will. There will be an invincible sense of inner assurance, quietly and humbly accepted. Every believer in Jesus Christ longs to experience such assurance, and it comes from being in the flowing current of His will. All this envelopes us when we do God's will, God's way.

THE DANGER OF NEGLECT

When you have truly made the decision to trust Him with all your heart, to live your life in availability to His will, not leaning on your own crutches, not turning to panic when you don't get your way, then God will begin to dig deeply and deal with areas of your life that have been neglected. The following verses illustrate that phenomenon. "Now it came about at the lodging place on the way that the Lord met [Moses] and sought to put him to death" (Exodus 4:24).

Moses was struck with a severe illness—sick to the point of death. What a frightening experience that must have been for the family. "Then Zipporah [Moses' wife] took a flint and cut off her son's foreskin and threw it at Moses' feet, and she said, 'You are indeed a bridegroom of blood to me'" (v. 25).

The Hebrew says, "A bloody groom you are to me." "So [God] let him alone. At that time she said, 'You are a bridegroom of blood'—because of the circumcision" (v. 26).

At that juncture, no doubt, Zipporah left and went back home to Midian and to Jethro. We may surmise this because of what is recorded in Exodus 18:2, where we read that she and the two boys travel to Egypt along with Jethro. Most likely, the circumcision of the boy left him in such pain he could no longer travel. Zipporah had to take him home and spend time with Grampa Jethro as the young lad healed.

What did all this mean? It meant Moses had overlooked a part of the covenant that demonstrated obedience to God. Every godly Jew was to circumcise the male child; he was to see to it that this was done properly and without exception. Moses would have known that well. Gentiles were known as the uncircumcised ones. But Jews? This was a physical mark of their obedience before God, who planned and designed the procedure. In this unique demonstration, a man said to God, "My family, my heart, and my home are dedicated to You and set apart for You, O God of Israel."

Moses had neglected to do that. We are never told why. It had simply been an oversight but one God refused to overlook. As Moses was on his way to do the will of God, the Lord stopped him in his tracks. He was saying, "Hold it right where you are, Moses. You will become My instrument before Gentiles and before their king and rulers. But before you do, there's a very private area of neglect you need to remedy. It's something I don't take lightly, and I don't want you to take it lightly, either."

As a matter of fact, it was Zipporah who sensed the area of wrong and took care of it herself. Moses may have been too sick at heart to carry out this very delicate act.

What was happening here? Think of it like this: You come to the place in your life where you say, "Lord, I want to be in the center of Your will. I want to do *my* part without reservation. I want every area of my life to be committed to You, with no reservations. I'm sick of wading in the shallows, getting my toes wet. I want to swim in Your plan! I want to jump into the deep end. I'm weary of this half-hearted, hypocritical life. I want to be clean and open before You. I want You to take my tongue and help me know how to use it as a devoted instrument. Take my eyes and keep them focused straight ahead. Take my motives and shape them as You please."

Churchy, superficial people never pray like that. Churchy people put on their pious faces on Sunday, then live the rest of the week just as they please. But the godly man or woman says, "Lord, I'm concerned about areas of my life that used to be out on periphery but now keep coming to my attention. Locked closets. Under-the-rug trash. Hidden secrets. Let's clean out those areas, too, Lord."

Moses wanted to be a man of God. And on his way—in the midst of his obedience—the Lord met him. That encounter was deadly serious. The Lord said to him, "Moses, here is one area nobody else may know about, but I know about it, and you haven't taken care of it."

I don't want to skim over Zipporah's involvement in this incident. It wasn't pleasant or easy for her. It probably shook her to the core. But she got involved, stepped into the situation, and as far as we can tell from Scripture, saved her husband's life.

It may well be that God will use the reproof of a spouse to bring areas of serious spiritual neglect to our attention. I remember talking to a young woman about this subject a number of years ago. She was a married student at a Christian college. As we sat together in the dining hall, talking about different discipleship issues, I mentioned the role of the mate in our growth in Christ. I told her that some of the best counsel I have ever received is from my wife; and Cynthia tells me that some of the best counsel she receives has been from me. We've worked heart-to-heart for many years now.

This young woman shook her head sadly. "It's amazing," she said. "I can take counsel from just about anybody, but I can't take it from my husband." She admitted to a feeling of defensiveness. "I just can't handle his criticism," she told me. I tried to clarify my remarks at that point, explaining that it wasn't just criticism; it was "iron sharpening iron." It's a simple fact that no one knows our blind spots like our mates. But even after the clarification she said, "I'm really not open to my husband."

"Then there is an area," I told her, "that needs some attention."

I have to say something in favor of Moses, here. He willingly took the reproof from his wife. He wasn't defensive. In the Living Bible, Zipporah says to him, "What a blood-smeared husband you've turned out to be!" That wouldn't be easy to take from any spouse, but Moses took it from Zipporah. He left that lodging place shaken but a better man for it.

If you are married, some of the best counsel available to you today could very easily come from the one who knows you better than anyone else. Do you have the courage to say something like this to your spouse? "Honey, I'm wanting very much to place my life in the Lord's hands without reservation. I would like for you to help me see some of the blind spots in my life. I'd like you to help me see areas of neglect that may hinder my walk with God, things I may not even be aware of. I give you the green light to do this, to share whatever you wish. And I promise to be open."

I think that kind of vulnerability would do wonders for domestic relationships. But let me be very frank. I have seen it happen only on the rarest of occasions. It's remarkable how few Christians are open to the counsel of their mates. Tragically, our pride and personal insecurities rob us of a perspective that could benefit our lives.

SOUL BROTHERS

Suddenly, Moses is all alone. Zipporah and the boys have taken the donkey and headed back to Midian. The exciting family adventure has turned into a lonely solo journey into the unknown, but I want you to see how the Lord continues to smooth the path ahead of His servant.

> Now the LORD said to Aaron, "Go to meet Moses in the wilderness."
> So he went and met him at the mountain of God and kissed him.
> Moses told Aaron all the words of the LORD with which He had sent
> him, and all the signs that He had commanded him to do. (Exodus
> 4:27–28)

Do you know what I love about the Lord? He's working on ten trillion fronts at any given moment of the day or night. He's the sovereign God, the Lord of time and eternity, and as I trust Him, He moves people and circumstances like pieces on a chess board to meet needs and to advance His plan.

God knew Moses felt lonely in that moment. God knew His man needed some human companionship. Perhaps before Moses felt his first pang of loneliness, God was already moving to meet his need. Aaron was Moses' big brother, his senior by three years. And the Lord sought this brother out and said to him, "Aaron, go to Moses' side now. He's on a long, wilderness road, heading for Egypt. Your brother has been through some tough things. He needs a soul brother, right now."

So they met and embraced and kissed. They stood there under that desert sun and just held each other for awhile.

It's wonderful to have a sibling relationship like that. My own brother, Orville, is also three years older than I am, and through our adult lives, I've been away from him much more than I've been with him. But every once in awhile, all too seldom, our paths cross and we find ourselves in a good, long, brotherly embrace. (Can't remember its including a kiss, however.) It's just a great thing to sit together and talk until the wee hours about what the Lord has been doing in both our lives. The years seem to melt away, and our hearts beat together again like when we were kids.

That's what Aaron and Moses did that night, under the stars, perhaps by a crackling campfire, in the shadow of Sinai. They shared their lives. This is the first time I read that Moses was able to tell anyone else about the burning bush. And he told every detail, while Aaron listened and took it all in. "Moses told Aaron all the words of the LORD with which He had sent him, and all the signs that He had commanded him to do" (v. 28).

He said, "Aaron, listen to this. You'll never believe it. There I was, out with the sheep one day, just like a thousand other days before. And all of sudden—whoosh!—this bush caught fire, and it wouldn't stop burning. So I stopped and stared. And as I got closer—Aaron, listen to this, man—*God* was speaking from that bush! And here's what He told me...."

If Aaron doubted a single word of the account, Scripture never mentions it. In fact, he was already prepared to believe every word Moses told him. Hadn't God called him out of Egypt to meet his younger brother in the desert? So Aaron listened, nodded his head, and said, "Wow! That's great, Moses. I'm with you, bro."

Do you have a soul brother or a kindred spirit in your sister? Do you have a friend with whom you can pour out your life? Women lead men in this intimate friendship department by a country mile. For years and years, generations of men were brought up to believe that the only masculine course was the rocky path of rugged individualism. How sad. And worse, how untrue. (One of the best outcomes of the Promise Keeper movement over the last number of years has been the shattering of that unbiblical myth.) Men need close friends, just as women do.

You may have lots of friendships in your life, but you'll probably never have more than a couple of friends on that deeper, spiritual, soul-to-soul level. You can tell such a friend anything that God is doing in your life, and you'll find a warm reception and deep appreciation. If you don't have such a friendship, tell God about your longing. He's the same God who moved Aaron's heart down in Egypt while Moses was walking alone on the desert road. And remember, the best way to find such a friend is to *be* such a friend.

HIGH-LEVEL MEETINGS

Once in Egypt, Moses and Aaron didn't let any grass grow under their feet. Israel had been in bondage for four hundred years; it was time to begin an exodus. "Then Moses and Aaron went and assembled all the elders of the sons of Israel; and Aaron spoke all the words which the LORD had spoken to Moses. He then performed the signs in the sight of the people" (Exodus 4:29–30).

Remember now, God had agreed at Moses' insistence to let Aaron be spokesman. Scripture never tells us, but I can't help wondering if Moses found himself wishing he had never made that arrangement with Aaron. Now that he was walking in the Lord's will, I have a hunch the words were slowly beginning to burn within him. But he had to stand back and let his brother take the lead, vocally.

What a scene that must have been! The elders gathered all around and listened to this stranger, Moses, and his brother Aaron, whom they knew. Who performed the signs? I understand the "he" in verse 30 to refer to Moses. I can't imagine him handing off the staff of God to anyone else, can you? And I can't imagine Aaron being really excited about catching a big snake by the tail. These men of Israel witnessed the miracles—the snake, the leprous hand, and the water turned into blood. And weary though they were from their forced labor, these men were on their tiptoes, standing on the brink of faith.

And what did they do? How did they respond? Verse 31 says it all: "So the people believed; and when they heard that the LORD was concerned about the sons of Israel and that He had seen their affliction, then they bowed low and worshiped."

They believed! How that must have lifted Moses' heart. The elders of Israel responded just as the Lord had told him they would back at the burning bush. To paraphrase the proverb (again), "When a man's ways please the Lord, He makes even the host of Hebrews to be at peace with him." Moses had done *his* part; now God was doing His. What a thrill!

THE HOUR OF DECISION

It may be, at this very moment, that you are close to one of the most important decisions you will ever make as a child of God. Through the days of your religious past, you've sung the hymn by Adelaide Pollard, *Have Thine Own Way*:

> Have Thine own way, Lord! Have Thine own way.
> Thou art the potter, I am the clay.
> Mold me and make me After Thy will,
> While I am waiting, Yielded and still.[3]

How many times have you mouthed those words? For many of us, it's been year after year. But maybe here of late you've begun to take those statements more seriously. You've begun to say to the Lord, "God, I mean business. I'm tired of leaning on the weak crutch of my own understanding. I want to trust You with *all* my heart. I don't want to just say something different, I want to *be* something different. I'm tired of the old status quo."

I remember the morning when a man knocked on the door of my study—it was hardly more than a tap—and before I could even say, "Come in," he was through that door and slumping down in a chair. Immediately, he began to shake and sob.

"What can I do?" I asked him.

Through his sobs, he said, "I've come to a turning point in my entire life. When I was eighteen, I left home. My dad gave me five dollars and said, "Okay, Son, make it on your own." And I walked away from that farm and financed my whole education—college, post-graduate work, all of it. Today, this morning, I've come to the place of success and prosperity in the eyes of the world. I've reached the top.

"But Pastor, just this week I've been falsely accused. I've been misjudged, misquoted, misunderstood. I've had to stand before the court, and those accusations against me are false. And suddenly—suddenly I find myself completely dependent. From age eighteen I've been able to do it all myself. But now, for the first time in my adult life, all the crutches are gone." Those were his exact words.

Tears kept pouring down his face as he talked, his big shoulders shaking. "I'm confident I'm in the right, Pastor, but if I'm indicted today, my career will be changed. My family will be hurt. My whole life will be altered."

He looked up at me through eyes red with weeping. "But I'll tell you something. Right now—right now I am willing to trust God *totally*. I've never said that before, but I'm saying it now."

We prayed before he left. He walked out of my study and down the stairs into the chapel to pray some more. I had to gather my things and leave for an appointment. I have no idea how long he stayed in the chapel pouring out his heart to God.

The following Sunday I saw him. "How did it go?" I asked him. "How did it come out?"

"Well," he said with a smile, "they did not indict me. But you know something? *That was the best thing in the world that could have happened to me.* Now, for the first time in my life, I can honestly say I want to get my priorities straight. I want my Lord to be first. Not business. Not success. Not money. Not even my family. I want *Him* to be first."

What that man was saying to me was, "I want to do God's will, God's way. Not my way. No matter how much it costs, no matter what I have to give up or change, I want to be God's man."

Is that your heartbeat? Perhaps the Holy Spirit has His finger on an area of neglect in your life—an area that is as intimate and personal to you as circumcision was to Moses and Zipporah. And He is telling you, "You cannot advance further in My will until you deal with this. I cannot tolerate it any longer. It's time for you to lay that before Me, deal with it, claim My forgiveness, and I will use you. *But not until then.*"

Are you weary of a wavering, half-hearted walk with Christ? Are you willing to open your life to His powerful searchlight? Are you willing to trust Him without reservation, no matter what? Are you *finally* determined to do God's will, God's way?

If that's your decision, I must warn you: The path before you will be costly—more than you can even imagine right now. But shunning that path will be more costly still.

CHAPTER NINE

Going from Bad to Worse

Ever had one of those days that started out bad and only got worse as the day wore on? I hear you! I heard a story recently that reminds me (as if I needed reminding!) of how a day like that can play out. It goes something like this: After just a few years of marriage filled with disagreements and arguments, a young man and his wife decided the only way to save their marriage was to try counseling. Things had slipped from bad to worse as the months passed, turning their marriage into a marathon of misery. They had been at each other's throats for so long that counseling seemed like their only hope.

He was incredibly insensitive and dull, while she was hyperactive and dominant. That's never a good mix.

When they arrived at the designated office, the counselor jumped right in and opened the floor for discussion. "Well," he began, "what seems to be the problem?"

Immediately, the husband slumped in his chair, assuming a defeated posture. He stared down at the carpet, finally managing a shrug of the shoulders. He had nothing to say. In contrast, his wife launched immediately into her script, talking ninety miles an hour, describing all the wrongs within their marriage. And every problem could be traced back to *him*—his failures, his insensitivities, his failure to communicate. And so it went.

After fifteen minutes of listening to the non-stop wife, the counselor stood up without saying a word, walked over to her, and while she was still in mid-sentence, picked her up by her shoulders, gave her a big hug, kissed her passionately, then sat her back down. She sat in stunned silence.

The counselor looked over at her husband, who sat there staring in disbelief. He then said to the husband, "Listen to me, now. Your wife needs *that* at least twice a week—every week!"

The husband blinked, and scratched his head. "Well," he replied, "I guess I could bring her here on Tuesdays and Thursdays."

Believe it or not, I've met guys who are that out of touch. In this case, it contributed to what was already a bad day for a harried marriage counselor.

You may feel like Evander Holyfield after his bout with Mike Tyson. It's bad enough when you have to stand in a ring with a guy who's trying to beat you into insensibility for fifteen rounds. It's worse when your opponent holds you in a clinch and bites off pieces of both your ears. That night as he was applying ointment and fresh bandages to his ears, Holyfield was probably wondering, "Why in the world did I get out of bed this morning?"

Maybe you've had a day like that recently. If you have, it may help a bit to realize you're not alone. As a matter of fact, a man as mighty and impressive as Moses experienced such a day. In our minds, we have a Michelangelo-inspired image of the man. We tend to think of him as some sort of chiseled stone saint or oversized marble statue.

Not so. He was a human being, just like you and me, subject to the same drives and impulses, highs and lows, ups and downs as the common run of humanity. He crawled out of bed in the morning and put on his sandals one at a time, just as we do.

I remember receiving a letter some time ago from a lady who had been listening to tapes of the sermon series I preached on Moses. She wrote, "I'm beginning to know Moses so well he no longer looks like Charlton Heston."

I like that. Cecil B. DeMille, fabled and famous as that film director may have been, did not call the shots in Moses' life. I have a feeling that the real Moses was so far removed from the movie version that they might as well be different people.

The real Moses was a man's man, but he had his weaknesses. And in this chapter, we're going to be looking at one of those days he probably wished he could erase from memory. It started out bad and rapidly deteriorated to worse.

A BAD DAY IN EGYPT

Woven into the fabric of Exodus chapters 5 and 6 are three major personalities: Pharaoh, Moses, and Yahweh—the Lord Himself. The predominant personality, of course, is the Lord. The predominant human personality is Moses. But the catalyst between these two is Pharaoh. He's the reason things got bent out of shape for the man from Midian.

It all began when the king granted Moses and Aaron an audience. Moses and Aaron came and said to Pharaoh, "Thus says the LORD, the God of Israel, 'Let My people go that they may celebrate a feast to Me in the wilderness'" (v. 1).

At this point, the two brothers were coming off a spiritual high. They'd just emerged from a tremendous "Bible conference" with the people of Israel, who had affirmed their plans. The elders had declared, "We believe in you, Moses. We'll stand behind you. Praise God He hasn't forgotten us. We'll trust Him to work through your leadership to get us out of slavery."

Perhaps those Hebrew elders thought it was going to be a quick-and-easy slam-dunk. They imagined Moses walking into Pharaoh's court, blowing him and his counselors away with a few miraculous signs, and then the gates would swing open, and the Israelites would be on their merry way.

It wasn't going to work that way. And Moses, if he had stopped to think about it, already knew it wasn't going to be easy. God had clearly told him there would be major difficulties with Pharaoh.

But you know how it is with people like us. We don't want to think about *that* part of the plan. We just want to think about the glorious deliverance God has promised at the end of it all. We prefer the sweet then-and-there to the miserable here-and-now.

Fresh off that marvelous experience with the Israelite leaders, riding that crest of emotion and euphoria, Moses and Aaron appear before the god of the land, Pharaoh himself. Their mandate was clear and direct. It was not a request; it was a simple declaration—a command, in fact: "Pharaoh, let the Hebrews go."

Now you've got to appreciate, even though neither you nor I can fully enter into it, the powerful presence and impact of a personality like Pharaoh. Remember he was considered a *god* in this land. He was worshipped. Colossal structures and sculptures bearing his name towered into the blue Egyptian skies. What this man said was law, and there was no appeal. He held life and death in the casual snap of his fingers. Most likely, demonic powers resided in him and his courtiers. He was no man to mess with.

Moses and Aaron, however, had just come from bowing before the all-powerful King. And they had His words to deliver. When they gave that first command directly from the mouth of the living Lord, I'm sure Moses thought that was pretty much the whole ballgame—a lightning score in sudden-death overtime. He thought to himself, *Now it's going to happen*.

But it didn't. Nothing happened. At least, nothing positive. Note Pharaoh's arrogant response: "But Pharaoh said, 'Who is the Lord that I should obey His voice to let Israel go? I do not know the Lord, and besides, I will not let Israel go'" (Exodus 5:2).

That was the start of a bad day. And it was all downhill from there. It reminds me of a friend who got off the city bus in Portland, Oregon, unaware that a glaze of ice gripped those city streets. He started down the sidewalk toward his place of employment, took one step, and his legs went out from under him. He threw his briefcase straight in the air, and slid half a block, downhill, on his pin-striped posterior. He arrived at the bottom of the hill just about the time his briefcase caught up with him.

Moses, blissfully unaware, was about to take that first step onto the ice. He had been expecting a positive affirmation, but the king replied, "In your dreams, shepherd."

Have you ever been planning to approach someone with an idea or a proposal, and you were so excited about it, you had your hopes built up so high, you just knew your words would carry the day? You plotted out the perfect timing, and uttered those statements you'd been practicing all day, believing with all your heart the response would be nothing but positive. And then...the response jumps straight out of the freezer. An icy shutdown. "Nope. Not interested. Catch ya later."

How discouraging! It's like taking your emotions skydiving without a parachute.

Moses took Pharaoh's hard rebuff on the chin, shook off the blow, and stepped back into the ring for round two. "Then they said, 'The God of the Hebrews has met with us. Please, let us go a three days' journey into the wilderness that we may sacrifice to the LORD our God, otherwise He will fall upon us with pestilence or with the sword'" (v. 3).

He came back with a modified proposal. He was saying, in effect, "Hey, Pharaoh, if you won't let us all go, at least give us a three-day's journey so we can get away for awhile and worship our God. We're just talking about a little spiritual retreat here. If you won't release us, at least grant us a leave of absence for a few days."

That is exactly what God had told Moses to say. Here is what the Lord had instructed him earlier: "You with the elders of Israel will come to the king of Egypt and you will say to him, 'The LORD, the God of the Hebrews, has met with us. So now, please, let us go a three days' journey into the wilderness, that we may sacrifice to the LORD our God'" (3:18).

Moses was God's man with God's message in God's time, pleading before Pharaoh. But Pharaoh continued to say no.

> The king of Egypt said to them, "Moses and Aaron, why do you draw the people away from their work? Get back to your labors!" Again Pharaoh said, "Look, the people of the land are now many, and you would have them cease from their labors!" So the same day Pharaoh commanded the taskmasters over the people and their foremen.... (5:4–6)

The Egyptian taskmasters superintended the work. The foremen were turn-coat Hebrews, pulled out of the ranks of slaves to serve as leaders over the people. Pharaoh called both groups before him, and the news wasn't good.

> "You are no longer to give the people straw to make brick as previously; let them go and gather straw for themselves. But the quota of bricks which they were making previously, you shall impose on them; you are not to reduce any of it. Because they are lazy, therefore they cry out, 'Let us go and sacrifice to our God.'" (vv. 7–8)

"Look," Pharaoh convinced the slave-drivers and foremen, "all this talk of sacrifice is just a smokescreen. I'm the only god these people need to deal with, and I've got a special word for these slackers. From now on, there will be no more deliveries of straw. Find your own, however you will. But we're not reducing the quota by a single brick. Now move it! Make tracks!"

Please take note of a little phrase in verse 7: "So the same day...." All of these developments were taking place within the very same twenty-four hours. And Moses' high hopes for a quick exodus began to crumble like a sandcastle in the incoming tide.

Pharaoh wasn't done yet either. "Make the work harder for the men so that they keep working and pay no attention to lies" (v. 9, NIV).

Harder? Scripture says the Hebrews were already sighing, groaning, and crying out in their cruel labors. Desperate as their situation had been, though, it was about to become much worse. "So the taskmasters of the people and their foremen went out and spoke to the people... " (v. 10).

I wouldn't want to be one of those foremen. How would you like to deliver *that* message? You walk up to some guys ankle deep in mud and mortar, pressing it out, preparing the bricks. They look up at you expectantly, waiting for good news. And this is what you have to say:

> "Thus says Pharaoh, 'I am not going to give you any straw. You go and get straw for yourselves wherever you can find it but none of your labor will be reduced.'" So the people scattered through all the land of Egypt to gather stubble for straw. The taskmasters pressed them, saying, "Complete your work quota, your daily amount, just as when you had straw." (vv. 10-13)

It wasn't simply a more difficult task they now faced; it was an *impossible* task. They couldn't do it. Nobody could do it. As a result, the foremen were beaten without mercy.

> Moreover, the foremen of the sons of Israel, whom Pharaoh's task-masters had set over them, were beaten and were asked, "Why have you not completed your required amount either yesterday or today in making brick as previously?" Then the foremen of the sons of Israel came and cried out to Pharaoh.... (vv. 14–15)

The foremen wanted to do a little labor negotiation with management. Trouble was, management didn't care a fig for what the rank-and-file had to say. If a few thousand Hebrews died under these harsh new conditions, so be it. From the Egyptians point of view, there were too many Hebrews anyway.

Not even the foremen could believe this horrid turn of events. They pleaded their case with Pharaoh: "Why do you deal this way with your servants? There is no straw given to your servants, yet they keep saying to us, 'Make bricks!' And behold, your servants are being beaten; but it is the fault of your own people" (vv. 15–16).

Utterly bewildered, these men had no idea why they'd been deprived of straw. They hadn't put it together yet, until Pharaoh flung his answer right into their stunned faces. "You are lazy, very lazy; therefore you say, 'Let us go and sacrifice to the Lord.' So go now and work; for you will be given no straw, yet you must deliver the quota of bricks" (vv. 17–18).

The king was in no mood to compromise. He shot his answer back at them with a curled lip, his voice dripping with defiance. At that dark moment, I believe, realization dawned in the minds of these foremen. *It's Moses! It's Aaron! It's because of something that happened when they went to Pharaoh. Now* we're *the ones taking the heat!*

These men were both sick with fear and, on top of that, boiling with anger.

> The foremen of the sons of Israel saw that they were in trouble because they were told, "You must not reduce your daily amount of bricks."

When they left Pharaoh's presence, they met Moses and Aaron as they were waiting for them. They said to them, "May the LORD look upon you and judge you, for you have made us odious in Pharaoh's sight and in the sight of his servants, to put a sword in their hand to kill us." (vv. 19–21)

A bad day just got worse! Moses couldn't believe it. Disappointment turned to disillusionment. Where had he gone wrong? He had taken God at His word, stood before Pharaoh, and repeated—almost word perfectly—what God had told him to say. He said the right words, at the right time, spoken in the right way. And now the wheels seemed to be falling off the wagon. The very people he had longed to help (for over forty years) were now cursing him for increasing their hardships and anguish. "Why did you come, Moses? It was bad enough before you showed up. Now, our lives are in danger."

MISUNDERSTOOD

Being misunderstood hurts all the way to the bone. Maybe you've felt those pangs recently. You did the right things in the right way, but someone misjudged you, reading motives into your acts or words that you never intended. And you must live under that cloud, unable to change the minds of those who have turned against you.

There isn't a leader in the world who holds that post very long without being compelled to stand alone. One writer calls these the "lonely hours of anguish." You've been misunderstood by a boss, by an old friend, by a close relative, by a neighbor, maybe even by your own mate (or a former mate).

In his book, *Spiritual Leadership*, J. Oswald Sanders writes, "The leader must be one who, while welcoming the friendship and support of all who can offer it, has sufficient resources to stand alone, even in the face of fierce opposition, in the discharge of his responsibilities. He or she must be prepared to have 'no one but God.'"[1]

In that dark moment, on that gut-wrenching day in Egypt, that's all Moses had. Scripture says, "Then Moses returned to the LORD" (v. 22). Suddenly finding himself under bitter attack, the aging shepherd-turned-leader had no where else to go. He had no personal friends in Egypt to meet his needs. His wife was in Midian with the kids. Jethro was tending sheep back on the old range. Brother Aaron was apparently clueless. So Moses went back to the One who had commissioned him in the first place. He turned to the Lord and passionately poured out his heart.

"O Lord, why have You brought harm to this people? Why did You ever send me" (v. 22)?

Sounds familiar, doesn't it? Moses' constant doubts about his fitness for the task were like a knee-jerk reflex. Scripture doesn't say, but I can well imagine some tears being shed at this stressful moment. "I told You back at the bush that I'm not the guy for this job, and You kept saying, 'Moses, you're the man.' I told You and told You, 'No I'm not! I'm not cut out for this kind of thing. I'll fail.' But You kept saying, 'Yes, you are. You're My choice.' So I reluctantly gave in. I walked all the way from Midian—left my home and my job. And here I am, Lord, in trouble with Pharaoh and hated by the very people I wanted to help. *See?* I told You I wasn't the one for the job! I did exactly what You said—used Your very words—and Pharaoh kicked sand in my face! And these poor people are worse off and about to die because I've made all the officials so angry."

TWO COMMON QUESTIONS

Moses came before the Lord asking those two questions so many of us ask when we find ourselves under intolerable pressure. *Why?* and *How?*

We begin by saying, "Why? Why me? Why now? Why this?" And then we ask, "How? How in the world am I going to get through this or out of this?"

As you read these words, you probably find yourself nodding your head. You're thinking, "Chuck, I guess you've been lookin' in my window. Those are about the same words I've been using. I've been saying to the Lord *Why?* and *How?* for days now."

As one who has also spoken those words numerous times in my life's journey, I find myself very encouraged by how the Lord responded to Moses. He didn't say, "Back off, Moses. You should be ashamed of yourself." I love that about the Lord. He never slaps you or shames you when you come to Him. He never pushes you away when you bring an aching, honest question that cries out for an answer.

Then the LORD said to Moses, "Now you will see what I will do to Pharaoh...." (6:1, NIV).

Isn't that good? Instead of criticizing Moses for asking "Why?" the Lord says, "Just you wait, son. Pharaoh's been reading too many of his own press clippings. He thinks he's a god, but there is only one God, and he'll find that out soon enough. Maybe for a brief period it will seem to you that he's in charge. But don't kid yourself, Moses. I am the Lord."

"Because of my mighty hand he will let them go; because of my mighty hand he will drive them out of his country." God also said to Moses, "I am the LORD..." (vv. 1–2, NIV).

The Lord was telling Moses, "I've hardly started, My son. I'm not even warmed up. You haven't seen the first movement of My mighty hand. There will come a day when Pharaoh will *push* Israel out the door. Believe it Moses: I'm the Lord. I'm the One who called you from that burning bush. Hang in there with Me."

Moses took that word of encouragement to the Israelites, but this time it was no sale. Scriptures says, "So Moses spoke thus to the sons of Israel, but they did not listen to Moses on account of their despondency and cruel bondage" (v. 9).

HANG THE PREACHER

In spite of the Lord's assurances, things kept going from bad to worse for Moses. He'd already gotten the worst of it in a meeting with Pharaoh, and now, in a subsequent parley with the Israelites, he found himself fresh out of credibility. They would no longer listen to him.

Why wouldn't they? Verse 9 offers two reasons. First, they refused to hear the Lord's words "on account of their despondency." The word "despondency" means "shortness of spirit." They were irritated, impatient, filled with resentment. And when you're mad at the preacher, you don't accept the message. They didn't want to listen to the man who had caused them to forfeit their supply of straw. Moses stood up to repeat the Lord's strong words of assurance, and they waved him off. "Take a hike, preacher. We're not listening. We don't care about what you have to say."

The verse also states they didn't listen because of the "cruel bondage." They held Moses responsible for that. It had been barely tolerable before this so-called "deliverer" walked out of the desert. Now, since Moses and Aaron had twitted Pharaoh's nose, circumstances had become impossible.

So, what do you do when a bad day takes a turn for the worse? You can't beat Moses' plan. He came back to the Lord. Moses may have been discouraged, he may have been sick at heart, he may have felt frustrated and lonely, but he kept coming back. And the Lord met him every time. "But Moses spoke before the LORD, saying, 'Behold, the sons of Israel have not listened to me; how then will Pharaoh listen to me, for I am unskilled in speech'" (v. 12)?

The New International Version says, "I speak with faltering lips." Moses was still obsessed by that issue. He said, "I get tongue-tied, Lord. It seems like I'm doing fine one minute, and the next thing I know I'm stammering like a school kid standing in front of the class. I just don't have it." Moses' discouragement was intensifying by the minute.

During my pastorate in California, I remember receiving a letter from a young man who had grown up in the church but was now away at college. He, too, was discouraged and told me, "Pastor, I just can't get it together. I feel like a yo-yo, up and down, up and down." He wanted me to know about it, but he didn't want a sermon. "I kind of know what you're going to write back to me," he said, "so I want you to know that just a verse or two isn't what I need."

It's interesting how most folks think the only thing pastors know how to do is speak in Bible verses. But this young collegian was in for a surprise. I had a neat little message for him that had nothing to do with a verse of Scripture or a sermon with three points and a poem. No clichés. No religious assignments. My first words to him were, "Welcome to the club! A lot of us know about life on the yo-yo, including yours truly. You'd be surprised how many of us have days when we can't get it together." I went on to suggest a few things that had helped me in handling a similar situation laced with what I hoped were words of encouragement.

"WATCH ME WORK"

Moses felt as low as a slug's belly. Way down there. He still hadn't rid himself of the idea that *he* was supposed to be the deliverer, and that *he* was somehow failing. How many times had God explained it to him? Yet, like many of us, he had trouble keeping a grip on the Lord's assurances.

What was Moses to do now? The message was a rerun of the last one: "Go, tell Pharaoh king of Egypt to let the sons of Israel go out of his land" (v. 11).

"Go to *Pharaoh*, Lord? My own people just bought me a one-way ticket caravan back to Midian, and You want me to go back to Pharaoh? R-r-r-e—m-m-m-em—ber m-m-me? I'm the guy who can't t-t-t-talk. Shoot, I'd mess up a rock fight, Lord. I can't get it together. I'm at the end of my rope. How in the world are You going to pull this off?"

Moses didn't know it at the moment, but he'd put before the Lord the best proposition yet. *I'm at the end of my rope. How are you going to do it?*

Before we go any further, I'd like to underline a major truth in this world of ours that I don't pretend to understand. Here it is: The best framework for the Lord God to do His most ideal work is when things are absolutely impossible and we feel totally unqualified to handle it. That's His favorite circumstance. Those are His ideal working conditions.

As I said, I couldn't begin to explain this phenomenon. I simply affirm—from Scripture, and from the experience of countless thousands of His saints—that this is true. God does His most magnificent work when the situation seems totally impossible from a human point of view, and we feel absolutely unprepared and unable to do anything about it, *yet our eyes are on Him.* I can't number the times I've been right there. That's when God rolls up His big sleeves and says, "Swindoll, step back out of the way a moment, and watch Me work."

Time after time, He brings us to our absolute end and then proves Himself faithful. That, my friend, is not only the story of my life, it's the story of the Bible in a nutshell.

Moses would learn that lesson, too... eventually. Not too many days in advance of that discouraging day in Egypt, he would stand cornered at the edge of the Red Sea, Egyptian chariots thundering toward him in the distance, and say, "Do not be afraid. Stand still, and see the salvation of the LORD, which He will accomplish for you today" (Exodus 14:13, NKJV).

SHORTCUTS TO FUTILITY

So many times, however, you and I miss the opportunity to watch the Lord work in mighty and miraculous ways. Why? Because instead of "standing still" and watching Him pull off our deliverance, we seek out the carnal alternative. We look for the back door, the fleshly shortcut.

The enemy of our souls comes to us at the moment of our greatest pain and says, *"Your wife did that to you? There's no reason to take this hassle anymore. Leave her."*

"Your husband broke his promise again? You don't have to take that! Pack your bags. This marriage isn't worth it."

"Your boss gave you *what* to finish by *when?* Man, you need a little shot of liquid courage this evening. Where's that bottle, anyway? Or how about checking out those hot pictures on that website the guys told you about? C'mon, kick back a little. You deserve a break."

"The kids in school keep treating you like garbage? Then why not *act* like garbage? Maybe doing some drugs wouldn't be such a bad thing, you know?"

In that weak moment, we hear the tempter's voice and take matters into our own hands instead of staying with the Lord's plan and waiting for Him to work. But after we take that shortcut, that temporary escape route so close at hand, there's hell to pay (for real!). And life really does descend from bad to worse.

"WHY AM I THE TARGET, LORD?"

Moses didn't have a corner on that "Why?" question in Scripture. Look with me for a moment at a passage from Job chapter 16. Read these hand-scratched notes from the journal of a broken man:

"I was at ease, but He [God] shattered me, and He has grasped me
by the neck and shaken me to pieces; He has also set me up as His
target. His arrows surround me. Without mercy He splits my kidneys
open; He pours out my gall on the ground." (vv. 12–13)

That's pretty vivid, isn't it? But Job isn't finished....

"He breaks through me with breach after breach [it's relentless!]; He
runs at me like a warrior. I have sewed sackcloth over my skin and
thrust my horn in the dust." (vv. 14–15)

The word "sackcloth" suggests the idea of being totally bankrupt. Job
was saying, "Man, I'm not only wearing this stuff; it's become a part of
me like a layer of skin. That's the condition I'm in." The NIV renders the
next phrase "I have ... buried my brow in the dust." Face down in the dirt!
You can't get much lower than that without a shovel. "My face is flushed
from weeping, and deep darkness is on my eyelids" (v. 16).

Now, note this comment: "Although there is no violence in my hands,
and my prayer is pure" (v.17).

Wow! Do you hear what the man is saying? "I'm innocent. Didn't do
anything to deserve this, but I'm the target." That's a great description of
how Moses felt on that dark day we've been describing in this chapter. It
started out bad and went down from there. First Pharaoh rejected him,
then his own people did, and then God told him to *go back!*

Notice how God handled His man, Moses. (He had a pretty effective
way of dealing with Job, too, but that's a different story.) Without rebuke,
the Lord gave Moses two pieces of counsel. One related to His person;
the other related to His work. He told Moses who He was, and then He
told him what He was going to do. And the *order* in that expression is as
important as the facts themselves.

Right off the top, He repeated the message from the burning bush,
saying, "I am" five different times in Exodus chapter 6.

• "I am the LORD ..." (v. 2)

- "I am the LORD..." (v. 6)

- "I am the LORD..." (v. 7)

- "I am the LORD..." (v. 8)

- "I am the LORD..." (v. 29)

Time after time He punctuated His message to Moses by saying, "Look, Moses, your eyes are in the wrong place (again). Get your eyes back on Me (again). Remember who I am (again)."

Who is the Lord? Ask the prophet Isaiah. Troubled and sick at heart over the moral condition of his nation, Isaiah glanced toward the sky one day and "saw the Lord sitting on a throne, high and lifted up" (Isaiah 6:1, NKJV). That's all he needed to see. He fixed his eyes on the Lord, and, just that suddenly, his whole perspective changed.

If you have been a believer for any length of time, you will have heard these words over and over. But that's all right; here they are again. (I'll throw 'em in for free, and won't add it to the cost of this book.) *Until your eyes are fixed on the Lord, you will not be able to endure those days that go from bad to worse.*

> Therefore, holy brothers, who share in the heavenly calling, fix your thoughts on Jesus.... (Hebrews 3:1, NIV)

> Let us fix our eyes on Jesus, the author and perfecter of our faith. (Hebrews 12:2, NIV)

There is no better therapy. There is no substitute that replaces this. There is no neat, clever little saying or motto that states it any better. Fix your eyes on the Lord! Do it once. Do it daily. Do it ten thousand times ten thousand times. Do it constantly. When your schedule presses, when your prospects thin, when your hope burns low, when people disappoint you, when events turn against you, when dreams die, when the walls close in, when the prognosis seems grim, when your heart breaks, *look at the Lord, and keep on looking at Him.*

Who is He? He is Yahweh, the eternal I AM, the sovereign Lord of the universe. He cannot do what is unjust; it is against His nature. He has never lost control. He is always faithful. Changeless. All powerful. All knowing. Good. Compassionate. Gracious. Wise. Loving. Sovereign. Reliable.

As Peter put it, "Lord, to whom shall we go? You have words of eternal life" (John 6:68). He's right. There really is nowhere else to turn and no one else to turn to.

I remember sitting with Cynthia at our kitchen table, spending time with a couple who were absolutely broken. Both were in tears, and they just unloaded their hearts before us that night. These two had reached the end of their strength, the end of their answers.

The woman looked across the table and said, "What do you say to people who come to you and just don't know where to turn?"

"It's not an easy answer," I said slowly. "But I'll tell you one thing I try to do. I try to remind them of who's in charge of their lives. I try to remind them that God is the one who calls the shots. He's in control. No matter how it appears, the situation is never out of control. He is the Lord."

That helped her, just to know she wasn't the one who had to piece together a massive puzzle with no matching parts. She needed to quit looking down at that impossible tangle for awhile and spend some time looking at the Lord. He knows how it all fits, even in those moments when we can't imagine how it could *ever* come together.

After the Lord told Moses "I am" five times, He told him "I will" eight times!

- "See what I will do..." (v. 1)

- "I will bring..." (v. 6)

- "I will deliver..." (v. 6)

- "I will redeem..." (v. 6)

- "I will take..." (v. 7)

- "I will be..." (v. 7)

- "I will bring..." (v. 8)

• "I will give..." (v. 8)

You know what this repetition says to me? I hear the Lord saying, "Because I am who I am, I will do what is best for you." That's the theme, I believe, of God's great message to Moses and to you and me as well.

The day I really begin to believe that fact is the day when my experience goes from bad, to worse, to *better*. My yo-yo snaps out of the "sleep" position and comes back up again. I say to myself, "*Chuck!* (Sometimes I have to speak loudly to get my own attention.) Chuck, get the wax out of your ears and listen to this. God knows what He is doing. It isn't a mistake. Right now, He chooses to allow this, whatever it is. And because He is who He is, He does what is best for you."

Maybe you need to have a similar conversation with yourself. I advise you to live with that basic theme, and it will help you get better when everything else gets worse.

Right after God told Moses what He would do, He said to him, "You must believe it. I command you to do this thing." "Now the LORD spoke to Moses and Aaron about the Israelites and Pharaoh king of Egypt, and he commanded them to bring the Israelites out of Egypt" (v. 13, NIV).

God was saying, "This *is* going to happen. The Israelites *will* come out of Egypt. This isn't wishful thinking or a nice sentiment. I intend to bring it to pass. Get ready to execute the plan."

So often the arrow that penetrates the believer at the weakest point is our unbelief. We know in our heads what God has said, but it takes faith to put it into gear, to get out there and start practicing what He has told us to do. Then and there, at that split-second of hesitation, the battle is won or lost.

This is how we need to pray, even when we feel as if we never want to pray again: "Lord, I don't feel like praying right now, but hear my prayer, anyway, Lord. I will believe You, even though the tide is rising, and I'm already on tip-toe. I will believe You, even though it seems like it's taking You forever to keep Your promise. I will believe You, even though I've come to the ragged end of my strength, the dregs of my hope, the broken shards of my plans. I will not look for a shortcut. I will not take a carnal option. I will not retreat from the battle. I will believe You!"

THREE CONCLUDING PRINCIPLES

Three timely and timeless principles come to mind as we wrap up this chapter. They're arranged like three standing dominoes, each one falling into the next.

Circumstances that turn against us force dependence. When you find yourself in a situation that suddenly reverses field and begins going in a direction you did not want it to go, you are humbled, and that forces you into a position of dependence upon the Lord. That's precisely where God wants you. His wise approach is to keep us within the circle of His protection and provision.

Circumstances that force dependence teach us patience. Ah, that dreaded "P" word. But how we need it! When the first principle does its work, we become dependent. Then, in that dependent position, we must wait and learn patience.

Circumstances that teach us patience make us wise. Wisdom becomes the gold crown of our adverse circumstances. The wisdom we glean from our experiences and from our testing of the Lord's promises will stay with us and bless us the rest of our lives.

The remarkable pilgrimage of English poet William Cowper comes to mind whenever I think of a man coming to the end of his rope. Cowper found himself so deep in discouragement and despair he tried to put an end to it all by drinking poison. But God graciously led someone to find him. His stomach was pumped, and he was delivered.

As soon as he recovered, the despairing writer hired a coach to take him down to the Thames River where he intended to plunge himself into the dark, swirling waters. The driver of the coach, however, would have none of it. He restrained Cowper, got him back into the coach, and drove him home.

Frustrated with that attempt, he found a knife in the privacy of his home and attempted to fall upon it. If you can believe it, the blade broke.

Still not deterred, he rigged up a rope in the basement, put his neck in the noose, and dropped into thin air. But someone found him before he strangled and took him down. He couldn't even kill himself! Finally, in the depth of sorrow, he drove himself to the Book of Romans. In the pages of that book, he found a passage which brought him to his knees, and to faith in Jesus Christ.

Years later, as a mature man of God, Cowper penned this now-familiar hymn:

> God moves in a mysterious way,
> His wonders to perform;
> He plants his footsteps in the sea,
> And rides upon the storm.
> Deep in unfathomable mines
> Of never-failing skill,
> He treasures up his bright designs,
> And works his sov'reign will.[2]

James adds his "amen" to these thoughts with words I have returned to more times than I can number.

> When all kinds of trials crowd into your lives, my brothers, don't resist them as intruders, but welcome them as friends. Realize that they come to test your faith and to produce in you the quality of endurance. But let the process go on until that endurance is fully developed, and you will find you have become men and women of mature character, with the right sort of independence. And if, in the process, any of you does not know how to meet any particular problem he has only to ask God—who gives generously to all men without making them feel foolish or guilty—and he may be quite sure that the necessary wisdom will be given him. (James 1:2–5, PHILLIPS)

God's promise to Moses is the same to us: "Because I am who I am, I will do what is best for you." There isn't a day on this side of eternity, no matter how grim, that can't be improved by clinging to that reassuring thought.

CHAPTER TEN

Plagues that Preach

There are four great eras of miracles in the Bible. Three have already transpired. One is yet to come. During those periods, the eternal God stepped into the stream of time and space with mighty manifestations of His power. The first era of miracles came in the days of Moses. The second, in the days of Elijah. The third, when Jesus walked on our planet as the God-man. One more era remains, yet in the future. During that time, God will visit this old earth with a series of devastating judgments, meting out righteous wrath on a world that has rejected His Son, His Word, and His ways.

It is interesting to me that the first and fourth eras of multiple miracles, the one that was and the one that is yet to be, are heavy in judgments upon the earth. And following each of those wrath-storms, a fresh era dawns—a beautiful new lifestyle, previously unknown by those people who lived through that time.

In the days of Moses, as we shall see, the Israelites who witnessed God's devastating power in the plagues would enter into a new land, under a new leader, to begin a new way of life as a nation. And in the future, those who turn to Christ and endure the period of Tribulation will enter into the millennial kingdom, an era of incredible peace and prosperity, fulfilling God's promises to the nation of Israel. The period of future judgment will lead into a new era of kingdom life during which Jesus Christ Himself will serve as King of kings and Lord of lords. God will forget neither His people nor His promises.

As we survey the plagues in this chapter and their effect on Moses as a leader, I want to draw your attention to three central facts.

GOD'S VOICE PREDICTED THE PLAGUES

The plagues were not afterthoughts, reflexive reactions, or last-minute exceptions in God's plan. In fact, they served as part of His deliberate strategy. Back at the burning bush in Midian, the Lord explained how it would take place:

> "But I know that the king of Egypt will not permit you to go, except under compulsion. So I will stretch out My hand and strike Egypt with all My miracles which I shall do in the midst of it; and after that he will let you go." (Exodus 3:19–20)

Again in Exodus 4, while Moses was packing his bags for the long walk west, the Lord repeated to His servant what the outcome would be. "When you go back to Egypt see that you perform before Pharaoh all the wonders which I have put in your power; but I will harden his heart so that he will not let the people go" (Exodus 4:21).

God knew what Pharaoh's response would be. He knew the plagues would follow. They were as much a part of His plan as the calling of Moses, or the Exodus itself.

PHARAOH'S NATURE REQUIRED THE PLAGUES

This was one stubborn king. His heart was carved out of knotted oak. The only way God could have ever gained his attention was through the presence of these devastating plagues. Nothing less would have penetrated the man's consciousness. Look, for example, at his first response to the words of the Lord as delivered by Moses and Aaron: "But Pharaoh said, 'Who is the LORD that I should obey His voice to let Israel go? I do not know the LORD, and besides, I will not let Israel go'" (Exodus 5:2).

Who is the Lord...? As I read those words I want to shout, "Watch out, Pharaoh! You're in over your head, buddy. You don't even know what you're saying. You're talking about the God of heaven. He has the final say. Better go with the flow, man."

But Pharaoh had a stubborn heart. It's an old saying that you must fight poison with poison. In other words, in order to deal with those who are stubborn and bullheaded, you have to be equally determined.

Counselors understand that dynamic very well. When you speak with stubborn individuals, they usually don't hear you when you use tender, sensitive, quiet phrases. Sometimes, you have to find ways of getting their attention. Not with a two-by-four (attractive as that prospect might be sometimes), but often with confrontive words that would break the heart and spirit of a more sensitive individual. If you really want to get through, you occasionally have to raise your voice, or slap the table once or twice, or make a few blunt statements, detailing consequences.

That's what God did with Pharaoh. The Searcher of hearts knows a hard heart when He encounters one. At one point He told Moses, "Pharaoh's heart is stubborn; he refuses to let the people go" (Exodus 7:14). Pharaoh's nature being what it was, the plagues were essential.

MOSES' QUESTION PROMPTED THE PLAGUES

Moses asked the Lord a question, and God's answer came in the form of ten plagues. (Be careful what you ask!) Here is how Scripture records it:

> Now the LORD spoke to Moses, saying, "Go, tell Pharaoh king of Egypt to let the sons of Israel go out of his land." But Moses spoke before the LORD, saying, "Behold, the sons of Israel have not listened to me; how then will Pharaoh listen to me, for I am unskilled in speech?" (Exodus 6:10–12)

"But Lord," Moses protested, "if the Israelites don't respect my message, how in the world will I get a hard-headed king like Pharaoh to listen?"

"Ah," the Lord replied. "Glad you asked, Moses. I just happen to have a few tools at My disposal. Don't worry, we'll get Pharaoh's attention." And the Lord of heaven rolled up His sleeves and moved in on the stubborn king of Egypt.

EACH PLAGUE REACHED *ALL* THE EGYPTIANS

The whole nation suffered as a result of Pharaoh's callus, obdurate response to the Lord. As your eye skims across the text covering the plagues that shook the land, you will see the word "all" again and again. "*All* the land, *all* the livestock, *all* the men and beasts." Finally, and tragically, we see the words "all the firstborn."

I'm reminded of a current Middle East dictator named Sadaam Hussein. As he continues to defy and thumb his nose at the Western world, his nation experiences isolation, embargoes, and even thundering missile attacks. Many innocent Iraqi people suffer because of this man's stubborn will.

No dictator, Führer, general, Pharaoh, or president escapes accountability for long, however. God's judgment wheel will turn; it may grind slowly, but it grinds exceedingly fine. The Book of Hebrews tells us that "Nothing in all creation is hidden from God's sight. Everything is uncovered and laid bare before the eyes of him to whom we must give account" (Hebrews 4:13). If this chapter does nothing more than demonstrate to you the thoroughness of God's judgment, it will have done its work. It isn't a happy picture that Scripture paints here, but it is true-to-life. This is the God to whom we must give account.

I have an old book in my study entitled *Living Under the Smarting Rod of God*. It's a book that would probably never be published in this era of "feel-good Christianity," filled as it is with reminders of God's judgment on men and women through the ages. All that I need to tell you to make my point is that the book is over two and a half inches thick.

When God does a job, He does it thoroughly. The plagues did not just trouble the elite of the court; they swept across the entire land of Egypt.

NONE OF THE PLAGUES SOFTENED PHARAOH'S HEART

From beginning to end, Pharaoh's heart remained encased in a cement shell of indifference. Yes, under pressure from his own court, he ended up saying, "Let the people go." But his heart remained case-hardened right up to the end. He maintained a mindset of stubbornness. For all of time and eternity, he will be an example of what it means to resist and reject the goodness of God. Hence the Lord's decision: "Let the plagues begin!"

THE PLAGUE OF BLOOD

> Then the LORD said to Moses, "Pharaoh's heart is stubborn; he refuses to let the people go. Go to Pharaoh in the morning as he is going out to the water, and station yourself to meet him on the bank of the Nile; and you shall take in your hand the staff that was turned into a serpent. You shall say to him, 'The LORD, the God of the Hebrews, sent me to you, saying, "Let My people go, that they may serve Me in the wilderness." But behold, you have not listened until now. Thus says the LORD, 'By this you shall know that I am the LORD: behold, I will strike the water that is in the Nile with the staff that is in my hand, and it will be turned to blood. The fish that are in the Nile will die, and the Nile will become foul, and the Egyptians will find difficulty in drinking water from the Nile.'" (Exodus 7:14–18)

It didn't have to happen. Pharaoh could have acknowledged the signs performed by Moses and Aaron as the finger of God Himself. He could have relented, and his nation would have continued to prosper even without the army of Hebrew slaves. The grief and anguish and loss of life never had to take place.

But that's the story of our world, isn't it? Puny man raises his tiny fist in the Creator's face and says, "I'm doin' it *my* way." And untold heartache, uncounted tears of misery result.

To every Egyptian, the Nile was basic to life itself. Well water in that land was often contaminated—a situation that remains to this very day. So the Egyptian depended on the mighty Nile for all his water needs: water for bathing, cooking, cleaning, laundry, and drinking. On top of that, fish was an Egyptian staple. To strike the Nile, then, was to impact the heart of their diet: fresh water and fresh fish.

God's first punch was a body blow to the heart of Egyptian life.

> So Moses and Aaron did even as the LORD had commanded. And he lifted up the staff and struck the water that was in the Nile, in the sight of Pharaoh and in the sight of his servants, and *all* the water that was in the Nile was turned to blood. The fish that were in the Nile died, and the Nile became foul, so that the Egyptians could not drink water from the Nile. And the blood was through *all* the land of Egypt. (vv. 20–21, emphasis mine)

Just picture that for a few moments, if you can. Your source of water, gone. The fish that provide your family with food, gone. This caused all manner of stress and difficulty across the land. Except for the small amounts of water contained in homes, there was none available. Scripture tells us: "So all the Egyptians dug around the Nile for water to drink, for they could not drink of the water of the Nile. Seven days passed after the LORD had struck the Nile" (v. 24).

Can you put yourself in their place? Seven days and seven nights without your principle source of water. A full week with the grocery stores closed down. At that point, I would be ready to declare, "He is God! Let the people go! I'm thirsty. I'm ready for a fish fry. Let's get on with the program."

But not Pharaoh. Not on your life. As a matter of fact, the king turned on his heels, strolled back into his palace, and shrugged off the whole incident. "Then Pharaoh turned and went into his house with no concern even for this" (v. 23).

The king didn't even give it a passing thought. The Lord's words meant nothing; they were like so much water running off a stone.

THE PLAGUE OF FROGS

Then the LORD said to Moses, "Go to Pharaoh and say to him, 'Thus says the LORD, "Let My people go, that they may serve Me. But if you refuse to let them go, behold, I will smite your whole territory with frogs."'" (8:1–2)

Now I've been up close and personal with a few bullfrogs in my life. As a matter of fact, if you've never dined on frog legs, you're missing a rare and unique treat. (Maybe you'll just have to take my word for it.) But this wasn't an occasional frog steak. This was wall-to-wall croakers!

The Lord told the Egyptians: "The Nile will swarm with frogs, which will come up and go into your house and into your bedroom and on your bed, and into the houses of your servants and on your people, and into your ovens and into your kneading bowls" (8:3).

God help 'em! Frogs in the bread. Frogs keeping them company between the sheets. Frogs in your clothes. Frogs all over the kitchen. Frogs *everywhere*. Can you imagine what that would be like?

In our home in California, I had a three-and-a-half inch plastic pipe running from a low point in my back yard and draining out into the gutter out front. After one of our infrequent rain storms, I noticed that the pipe had stopped up. It wasn't working, and water was pooling up in the back yard. What in the world could be blocking a pipe that size? I wasn't about to dig the whole thing up to check. Out on the street, I got down on my stomach, peered into the end of the pipe and found myself eyeball to eyeball with the biggest frog I've seen this side of the Mississippi. He had taken up residence in the pipe, and stopped up the drain in the process. We're talking the mother of all frogs!

It was bad enough having one large frog move into my drainpipe. What would it be like to have frogs in your cupboards, in the sink, in your closet, and in your bed? You walk down the hall at night to get a drink of water, and you scrunch down on about a dozen of them. Friends, that's a plague. And that's just what happened. "Aaron stretched out his hand over the waters of Egypt, and the frogs came up and covered the land of Egypt" (8:6).

Every drain in Egypt was plugged up. Frogs ruled the country.

Now you would think, "Wow, that ought to do it." But it didn't. The message had been sent, but it wasn't received. Even so, God was gracious. He not only turned the blood back into fresh water, He took care of the frog problem as well.

> Then Moses and Aaron went out from Pharaoh, and Moses cried to the LORD concerning the frogs which He had inflicted upon Pharaoh. The LORD did according to the word of Moses, and the frogs died out of the houses, the courts, and the fields. So they piled them in heaps, and the land became foul. But when Pharaoh saw that there was relief, he hardened his heart and did not listen to them, as the LORD had said. (8:12–15)

With the pressure off, Pharaoh returned to his stubbornness. In spite of the suffering of his people, his heart remained as tough as leather.

THE PLAGUE OF GNATS

This third plague arrived unannounced. The first two plagues were preceded by an announcement from Moses and Aaron. Not this one. As we look back at all of the plagues, it's curious to note that every third plague came on without warning. It seems that God will occasionally predict His plan, but on other occasions He reserves the right to launch a surprise assault. Those are the times that gain our attention.

Here is how it took place: "Then the LORD said to Moses, 'Say to Aaron, "Stretch out your staff and strike the dust of the earth, that it may become gnats through all the land of Egypt"'" (v. 16).

"Gnat" is a word that describes a biting, stinging insect that penetrates the nostrils and ears of its victims. It would be enough to drive you crazy! Have you ever been hiking out on a trail through the woods and walked into a virtual cloud of mosquitoes? It's awful! They're all over you in a heartbeat. In your hair. Down your neck. Up your nose. In your mouth. In your eyes. In your ears. Biting. Whining. Drinking you dry. Or maybe you've been canoeing in some stream or river up in the northern Midwest and found yourself suddenly carpeted with those little black, stinging flies. *Terrible creatures!* You can't get out of there fast enough!

This would have been simply intolerable. And you may notice, as we proceed, that each of these afflictions seems to get progressively worse. The plague on the Nile was a blow to everyone, but folks adapted and got by. The frogs were a horrible nuisance; people were weary of them, sick of them, and grossed out by them. But no one was really hurt.

But with the surrounding swarm of gnats, we're beyond mere discomfort. They would have driven both people and animals to desperation. As Scripture notes, "There were gnats on man and beast. All the dust of the earth became gnats through all the land of Egypt" (v. 17).

Years ago a couple of our children began experiencing some troubling health problems. Through various tests, we discovered they were suffering from several acute allergies. In fact, the allergist told us our children were allergic to dust. Dust! That's like being allergic to *air*. Dust is everywhere. How do you get away from it?

Not long after that discovery, I was sitting in our den as the setting sun shone in through the west-facing windows. As a ray of sunlight shot across the room, I was stunned to see the countless particles of dust floating in the air. I thought to myself, *Wow! What if every particle of dust were a gnat or a mosquito? Who could even contemplate such a thing?*

Even with this, Pharaoh did not soften his heart. Verse 19, by the way, records the last words of Pharaoh's magicians. They have nothing more to say after one last statement to Pharaoh: "Then the magicians said to Pharaoh, 'This is the finger of God.' But Pharaoh's heart grew hard, and he did not heed them, just as the LORD had said" (v. 19).

If I had been a magician in that place, I would have packed my magic bag and caught the next flight out of Cairo. Furthermore, I would have sent my resumé to every king in the civilized world. Enough is enough!

At the end of this third plague, and before the beginning of the fourth, God intervened in an amazing way. From the fourth plague on, the land of Goshen where the Hebrews lived had an invisible shield of protection around it. From then on, God protected the Israelites while He plagued the Egyptians. "But on that day I will deal differently with the land of Goshen, where my people live; no swarms of flies will be there, so that you will know that I, the LORD, am in this land" (v. 22, NIV).

Never doubt it, Christian. The protective hand of God is over your life: "A thousand may fall at your side, ten thousand at your right hand, but it will not come near you" (Psalm 91:7, NIV).

I believe those verses were originally written with satanic invasion in mind. The child of God who walks in the Spirit can move about his or her world without fear of demonic invasion. Walking under the control of the Holy Spirit will free you from the plague of demonic influence. That, I believe, is the whole thrust of Psalm 91.

Here's an example of that in Exodus. The Egyptians found themselves under the black cloud of plagues, but the Israelites, from the fourth plague on, enjoyed divine protection.

THE PLAGUE OF INSECTS

And there came great swarms of insects into the house of Pharaoh and the houses of his servants and the land was laid waste because of the swarms of insects in all the land of Egypt. (v. 24)

The swarm! Sounds like a movie title, doesn't it? Maybe one of those gross horror flicks where a small town gets surrounded and attacked by those ever-present alien beasties. But this was truth, not fiction, and the horror was real.

The Hebrew word for "swarm" means "mixture," speaking of a great mixture of different kinds of insects. Big flying beetles. Spiders dropping off the ceiling. Fleas hopping all over you. Ticks burrowing into your skin. Tiny chiggers crawling under your clothing. Bees stinging you.

As you contemplate that scene, you might say, "If I had to live around that many bugs, they'd have to put me away!" But if you lived in Egypt, even the place where they put you away would be full of crawly creatures, too! There would be no escaping it. The mixture of insects descended on Egypt by the multiplied trillions. Everywhere but Goshen.

And what was the result? "But Pharaoh hardened his heart this time also, and he did not let the people go" (v. 32). This man must have been made of titanium. His stubbornness exceeded belief.

I grew up in Houston, where we had a few Texas-sized bugs, but I can't imagine what it would be like to have that many pests in and around my dwelling. We have friends who lived for a period of time in the panhandle of Texas. They eventually moved on, but lingering in their minds was the vivid memory of the Texas sandstorms that would sweep through their area. On one occasion, a storm blew into town at dusk and raged through the night. In the morning, the skies dawned bright and clear. The lady of the house went to one small closet where her clothes were hanging. Observing the floor, which resembled a small sandbox, she decided she would measure how much sand had drifted into the closet that night. (And this was in a solid, well-insulated home.) After shaking out all her clothes and sweeping up the sand on the floor, she measured out two buckets full of sand.

Sand would be bad enough, but can you even imagine shaking out buckets full of *insects* out of your closet, night after night, day after day. What a plague! Amazingly, Pharaoh still refused to yield.

You know what's equally remarkable to me? The people of Egypt never mutinied against their mule-headed dictator. You never find a time when the population rose up against the one responsible for bringing these plagues into their once-peaceful nation. Humanly speaking, he was the cause. Yet he must have held sway over the people with a powerful spell of awe and fear.

God, however, wasn't in awe of the man at all. Nor was He anywhere near finished with him.

THE PLAGUE ON LIVESTOCK

Behold, the hand of the LORD will come with a very severe pestilence on your livestock which are in the field, on the horses, on the donkeys, on the camels, on the herds, and on the flocks. But the LORD will make a distinction between the livestock of Israel and the livestock of Egypt, so that nothing will die of all that belongs to the sons of Israel.

> The LORD set a definite time, saying, "Tomorrow the LORD will do
> this thing in the land." So the LORD did this thing on the next day,
> and all the livestock of Egypt died; but of the livestock of the sons of
> Israel, not one died. (Exodus 9:3–6)

God had already removed the supply of fish, and for a time He also removed the supply of water. Now there was no red meat or milk. The pestilence struck the cattle, horses, donkeys, camels, goats, and sheep. Think of the bloated carcasses strewn across the land. It made the heaps of green frogs look decorative by comparison!

Yet just over the border in Goshen, the Hebrews' livestock prospered. Their animals never even got sick. How clear could the evidence be? Yet Pharaoh, his own one-man jury, declared the evidence "not relevant." Same song, fifth verse—he hardened his heart yet again.

THE PLAGUE OF BOILS

> So they took soot from a kiln, and stood before Pharaoh; and Moses
> threw it toward the sky, and it became boils breaking out with sores
> on man and beast. (Exodus 9:10)

By this time, the common person in Egypt had to be wondering, *What next? What else could happen?* The Hebrew language describes these boils as "inflamed eruptions, breaking forth into skin pustules." In other words, they were deep ulcers that broke open with pus that ran on the skin. Not even Pharaoh's own magicians were immune: "The magicians could not stand before Moses because of the boils, for the boils were on the magicians as well as on all the Egyptians" (v. 11).

When I was a kid, I remember sustaining a deep stone bruise on my heel—clear to the bone. And from that bone bruise, a deep, pus-filled boil finally worked its way to the surface. Ultimately, it had to be lanced. By that time, I came very close to suffering from blood poisoning. I couldn't walk for a week and a half before it was lanced, and for a while after that, too. What torture! I vividly remember the pain to this day.

My misery grew out of one boil, on one portion of my body. What if you had them *all over?* Think of the anguish such sores would cause behind your knees, where your body bends at the joints, or under the arms, at the elbows, around the waist, on the ankles and feet. You wouldn't be able to walk, or sleep, or even sit down and relax. Perhaps, like Job, you'd find yourself huddled on some ash heap, scraping yourself with a shard of pottery. The pain would become intolerable. And remember, these boils came unannounced. What a frightening experience!

Now, when you have a boil, there is one thing you don't want to happen. You don't want anything or anyone to bump up against you. The pain is bad enough, undisturbed. So what was the seventh plague?

Hail.

THE PLAGUE OF HAIL

> Now the LORD said to Moses, "Stretch out your hand toward the sky, that hail may fall on all the land of Egypt, on man and on beast and on every plant of the field, throughout the land of Egypt." (v. 22)

The hail would have finished off the remainder of the livestock that had survived the fifth plague. Anyone or anything out in the open would have been vulnerable, especially since this was no ordinary hailstorm.

> Now the LORD said to Moses, "Stretch out your hand toward the sky, that hail may fall on all the land of Egypt, on man and on beast and on every plant of the field, throughout the land of Egypt." Moses stretched out his staff toward the sky, and the LORD sent thunder and hail, and fire ran down to the earth. And the LORD rained hail on the land of Egypt. So there was hail, and fire flashing continually in the midst of the hail, very severe, such as had not been in all the land of Egypt since it became a nation. The hail struck all that was in the field through all the land of Egypt, both man and beast; the hail also struck every plant of the field and shattered every tree of the field. Only in the land of Goshen, where the sons of Israel were there was no hail. (vv. 22–26)

This was hail powerful enough to strip bark right off of trees, and in some cases shatter them altogether. (Think of the insurance bills on all those chariots!) Once again, however, Israel enjoyed divine protection. No hail fell on Goshen. Not a single hailstone.

On January 28, 1995, the residents of Thomasville, Georgia, endured what meteorologists call a "supercell hailstorm." Hailstones the size of softballs—up to four inches in diameter—rained out of the sky and tore into that community. Can you imagine being out walking your dog when that storm cranked up? You probably would have thought you'd entered the Tribulation!

The hail in Egypt finally opened a crack on Pharaoh's hard shell... temporarily.

> Then Pharaoh sent for Moses and Aaron, and said to them, "I have sinned this time; the LORD is the righteous one, and I and my people are the wicked ones. Make supplication to the LORD, for there has been enough of God's thunder and hail; and I will let you go, and you shall stay no longer."(vv. 27–28)

The king's little speech sounded good, but Moses didn't buy it. Was it his tone of voice? The way he held his mouth? Those shifting eyes? For whatever reason, Moses knew that Pharaoh was only looking for a back door to a bad situation, and that he hadn't truly repented at all. Moses agreed to ask God to stop the hail, but he looked Pharaoh in the eye and said, "But as for you and your servants, I know that you do not yet fear the Lord God" (v. 30).

Moses probably figured it wasn't over. And it wasn't. Pharaoh hardened his heart yet again, perhaps feeling he could outlast God after all.

Bad decision. The worst was yet to come.

THE PLAGUE OF LOCUSTS

> Then the LORD said to Moses, "Stretch out your hand over the land of Egypt for the locusts, that they may come up on the land of Egypt and

eat every plant of the land, even all that the hail has left." So Moses stretched out his staff over the land of Egypt, and the LORD directed an east wind on the land all that day and all that night; and when it was morning, the east wind brought the locusts. The locusts came up over all the land of Egypt and settled in all the territory of Egypt; they were very numerous. There had never been so many locusts, nor would there be so many again. For they covered the surface of the whole land, so that the land was darkened; and they ate every plant of the land and all the fruit of the trees that the hail had left. Thus nothing green was left on tree or plant of the field through all the land of Egypt. (10:12–15)

What was going on here? Starvation! Little by little, these plagues attacked the basics of the Egyptian diet. What was left after the Nile turned to blood, taking away the water supply and killing the fish? What remained after the livestock perished, and the hail and locusts smashed and stripped every tree and crop? Frankly, nothing.

You've seen national disasters described on television. Southern California, where we used to live, has had its devastating *El Niño* storms and mudslides. Texas, where we live now, has endured droughts, hurricanes, and tornadoes. The damage and loss of life can be appalling.

But this was a national disaster *times ten*. As I mentioned at the beginning of the chapter, this was one of those rare moments in history when God stepped to earth in a specific way to judge His enemies. It had never happened to a nation in that manner since the flood and will not happen again until God says, "Enough," and sends forth His Son with a rod of iron to once again judge the nations.

To make matters worse for the Egyptians, they had only to look across the border into the nearby land of Goshen to see that life went on normally. Cattle grazed in the pastures. Trees blossomed and produced their fruit. Healthy children played in the streets and vacant lots. Fields of grain rippled in the breeze. Not a single locust afflicted the Hebrew community.

I recall a late-night television documentary about locusts. A select team of journalists placed themselves directly in the path of an advancing army of them. (How'd you like to draw that duty? You look on your assignment sheet on Monday morning and you blink twice as you read: "Cover locust plague in Botswana.") The reporters had their microphones on as the swarm drew near and described the sound as similar to that of an approaching 747. As the infestation overran their positions, the roar became so great you could hardly hear the narrator describe the action. It was deafening.

When those creatures—millions of them!—leapfrogged over one another and finally left the area, it was as though the landscape had been burnt. The ground wasn't charred, but every leaf was stripped off every tree. Every green thing had been consumed. You have never witnessed such a complete job of devouring.

Locusts, I have learned, fly in formation. Years ago they located a swarm twelve hundred miles wide over the ocean flying from West Africa toward Great Britain. As you might imagine, they brought great devastation upon the British Isles. In one picture taken from an airplane, you couldn't see any open piece of ground. It was jet black with locusts—an area two thousand miles square.

Exodus 10:14 says Egypt had never seen such an attack of locusts and never would again. Remember how I mentioned that the plagues worsened in their intensity one by one? I'm sure no one in Egypt could imagine anything worse. Yet, if you can believe it, two plagues remained.

THE PLAGUE OF DARKNESS

This is a dark chapter in the history of Egypt and a dark chapter in this book about Moses, too! But God's next action was to make that darkness *literal*. "So Moses stretched out his hand toward the sky, and there was thick darkness in all the land of Egypt for three days" (v. 22).

No one could see a thing. But this was far blacker than the darkness of midnight; this was a darkness so thick you could *feel* it. Scripture tells us the Egyptians "did not see one another, nor did anyone rise from his place for three days, but all the sons of Israel had light in their dwellings" (v. 23).

Some have theorized that the extraordinary darkness was the result of dust particles brought together by some strange electrical phenomenon. Dr. Alfred Edersheim, a Hebrew scholar wrote this:

> Let us try to realize the scene. Suddenly and without warning would the *chamsin* rise. The air, charged with electricity, draws up the fine dust and the coarser particles of sand til the light of the sun is hid, the heavens are covered as with a thick veil, and darkness deepens into such night that even artificial light is of no avail. The floating dust and sand enter every apartment, pervade every pore, find their way even through closed windows and doors. [It is a plague on Egypt's very air supply!] Men and beasts make for any kind of shelter, seek refuge in cellars and out-of-the-way places from the terrible plague. And so, in utter darkness and suffering, three weary nights and long days pass, no one venturing to stir from his hiding.[1]

I can't imagine the oppressive effect this had on mind and spirit. A darkness you could not penetrate, even with a lantern. A darkness that you could feel up against your skin! You and I walk into a dark room and flip on a light. It's automatic. We jump into our cars at night and turn on the headlights. Think of turning on the lights and nothing happens! You can't see your hand in front of your face. It must have felt like blindness or even death. And the Egyptians endured such ink-black madness for three solid days and nights.

Could Pharaoh's heart *still* be hardened? Yes, it could—and was. It finally led to the dramatic confrontation described in Exodus 10:28: "Then Pharaoh said to him, 'Get away from me! Beware, do not see my face again, for in the day you see my face you shall die!' Moses said, 'You are right; I shall never see your face again'" (v. 28)!

And that's the way it turned out. Aside from the prediction of the final plague, which we'll look at in the next chapter, Moses never saw Pharaoh face to face again.

PLAGUES THAT PREACH

Just describing these plagues in survey form has consumed most of this chapter's pages. Yet there is more here than the historical phenomena, amazing and dramatic as it may have been. It's more than an account over which we "oooh" and "aaah," and then say, "Thank goodness we don't live in such a time."

I'm convinced this dreadful display of judgment in Egypt, this battle between a righteous, holy God and the stubborn heart of Pharaoh, has two major truths to teach us.

First, when God judges, He does a thorough job of it.

Second, it is a fearful thing to fall into the hands of the living God.

Let's make this painfully personal. You may be in the danger zone as you read these words. You have played fast and loose with your life, ignoring warning after warning. You have shoved aside essential truths for so long that your heart has become hardened. And the longer you harden it, the more difficult it will be to allow God's light to finally break through.

If that doesn't describe you, we all know people who have placed themselves in such a situation. They have rejected appeals, ignored warnings, scoffed at God's Word, and stiffened their necks to go their own ways, regardless. Something that sits too long under the light of the sun becomes hardened to the sun. Stare at the sun long enough, and you will become blinded by the light. In other words, if you do not respond to it, you will be ruined by it. And that's the way it was with Pharaoh.

This segment of Egyptian history reminds us that you cannot scoff forever. A day of reckoning finally arrives. It is a fearful thing to tread under foot the grace of God. His judgments are terribly thorough. Never doubt it.

But there's a bright side to this dark story, too. When God blesses, He holds nothing back. That's the way it was with the children of Israel in the land of Goshen. As dark as it became in Egypt, the Hebrews were flooded with light. They were a city on a hill, shining through the night, if only Pharaoh had eyes to see it.

You may be one who has enjoyed God's great grace and favor in your life—His protection, provision, daily blessings, and unmerited favor fill your days. You can thank God for a place in the land of Goshen. You enjoy God's protection—a careful plan which distinguishes you from those who live under His wrath. Believe me, nothing in this life or the next is more serious and sobering than the wrath of God. Some are broken—blessedly broken—by that wrath. Others only harden.

Somewhere around the time when I preached a message on this portion of Scripture in Southern California, I remember having dinner with a physician. We met by appointment. He was a Jewish man and probably one of the finest orthopedic surgeons in that area.

For the better part of his practice, he confided, he had given himself without reservation to the making of money. And he made it by the hundreds of thousands of dollars. By the time he was in his late forties, he was extremely wealthy, but he was a man who had no time or thought for God. Work consumed him. And in the process of working eighteen to twenty hour days, for weeks at a time, he began to rely on the very narcotics he administered to his patients in pain.

Over time, this brilliant surgeon became addicted to heroin and various other drugs. What started out as a temporary and artificial high to keep him working extra hours became a harsh, despotic master. When the truth finally came out, he lost his credentials. Following that, in short order, he lost his reputation, his home, his wife, and his children. He lost *everything*. It was as if one plague after another just beat upon him, until he was finally crushed beneath the hands of the living God.

Eventually, through the faithful witness of a believing pharmacist, this broken Jewish physician discovered the answer to his crushing problems. He swallowed his pride, admitted his spiritual emptiness, and gave his heart to the Lord Jesus Christ.

I had the privilege of dining that night with this doctor and the man who led him to Christ. As he poured out his story, the physician blinked through tears of great personal pain. He talked about leaning full weight on the grace of God and the long-term plans for his recovery. Eventually, he wanted to take his tests again, hoping to have his license restored, allowing him to return to surgery. And day after day, night after night, he was on his knees pleading with the God of grace to bring back his wife and family.

After dinner, this man who had been through his own personal ten plagues looked across the table at me. "Chuck," he said, "for the first time in my life, I can really say I have peace. I have come from judgment to a whole new life of grace. And I have to tell you, the most important thing to me now is not my practice. Not the money. Not even my family. It's my vital relationship to God."

As we left that restaurant to head for our cars, he laid his hand on my shoulder. "Chuck," he said, "would you pray for me? Pray that I won't lose any ground in my growth toward maturity."

And I have, many times through the intervening years. He lives in my mind as a perfect example of man who has moved through judgment into mercy.

Life's plagues are tough to endure—painful to the core. But God has no desire to leave us alone in our pain and distress. Habakkuk once cried out to God, "In wrath, remember mercy."

And the Lord has done just that. Jesus, who endured God's wrath to the uttermost on the cross, now invites us to walk arm in arm with Him through the rest of our days. He is our faithful, ever-present Friend. And no earthly catastrophe can ever separate us from the grip of His grace or the legacy of His love.

CHAPTER ELEVEN

The Night Nobody Slept

It was Ralph Waldo Emerson who said, "There is properly no history; only biography." Thomas Carlyle, his contemporary, added these words back to him: "The study of history is nothing more than the study of great men and women."

History *is* biography. And that is especially true of the Bible. Take away the people, and it would be impossible to think your way through the Scriptures. Furthermore, it would be a difficult book to understand, full of abstract concepts unrelated to life. It is *people* who make the Scriptures connect with reality.

Genesis, for example, is nothing more than the biography of twelve men wrapped up in a historical account of God's movement on this earth. Think about those men. You have Adam and his three sons, Cain, Abel, and Seth. That brings you to Noah and his three boys, Shem, Ham, and Japheth. This is followed by the account of Abraham and his son Isaac followed by Isaac's son, Jacob, followed by Jacob's son, Joseph. That's it! That's the basic outline of the Book of Genesis.

When you get to Exodus, it's primarily the biography of one man.

Suddenly the telescopic lens of the Holy Spirit centers upon one individual and stays there through four more books—Exodus through Deuteronomy. As you know by now, it is the biography of Moses, God's personal servant, whom He shaped into a man of selfless dedication.

MAKING HISTORY

Do you ever feel a little overwhelmed when you encounter those great names in Scripture? Do you ever feel as though the men and women in the pages of the Bible were cut from different cloth than you and that you could never be used by God as they were? The idea that you and I could ever "make history" seems almost preposterous.

When you think about it, however, God would be hard-pressed to make history without people. And we must never forget His plan wasn't finished with Moses. Or David. Or Daniel. Or John the Baptizer. Or Peter or Paul or Martha. There is more of His plan yet to unfold and more history to be made until His plan is complete, and history is no more. Until that final day, He is still using people. Kings and common folk. Women and men. Rich and poor. Bold and timid.

Let me ask you, what are you planning to do with the rest of your days?

"Well, Chuck, I'm just tryin' to get through school."

"I'm just working day and night to launch this new business."

"I'm just trying to get our family raised and out the door."

"I'm just punchin' a clock and hoping to live until retirement."

Okay. But what are you doing in regard to eternity?

"Well, I received Jesus Christ."

That's wonderful. That's the most important decision in all of life, and you will never regret it. But what are you going to do with Jesus Christ as you consider your vocation in life?

"What are you getting at, Chuck? He hasn't called everybody to be a pastor or a missionary."

That's true. He hasn't. But He might be calling *you*. And strange as it may seem, that is the whole point of this chapter on the Passover.

THE ESSENTIAL INGREDIENT

The main point, the central ingredient of Exodus 11 and 12, is *obedience*. God spoke, some people heard, and did what God said. As a result, God used them in His plan at that time in history.

That's the bottom line of cross-cultural ministry or any enterprise of God: Hearing what He says, respecting His call, responding in obedience, and leaving the results with Him. You may be able to say that in a much more sophisticated way, but you couldn't say it any clearer. Bottom line, we're talking *obedience* here.

Let's see how obedience—that all-essential ingredient—takes shape in Exodus chapter 11. "Now the LORD [had] said to Moses, 'One more plague I will bring on Pharaoh and on Egypt; after that he will let you go from here'" (v. 1).

I've added the little word "had" to the verse above, to make the chronology clearer. In other words, what God tells Moses in this chapter is something He had already said to him earlier, but it fits into the flow of thoughts as we delve into this matter of the Passover. In the journal that Moses is keeping, called the Book of Exodus, these words of the Lord fit best right here. Let's pick up again on what He had told Moses:

> "One more plague I will bring on Pharaoh and on Egypt; after that he will let you go from here. When he lets you go, he will surely drive you out from here completely. Speak now in the hearing of the people that each man ask from his neighbor and each woman from her neighbor for articles of silver and articles of gold." (vv. 1–2)

Doesn't that strike you as a little strange? The Hebrew slaves were to ask for silver and gold from their Egyptian neighbors? Why? The Israelites didn't realize it yet, but God was getting them ready for a trip. The silver and gold were like a withdrawal from an ATM on the way out of town. And when you think about it, those "wages" were only a meager pay-off for over four hundred years of slave labor for Egypt.

God knew in advance what use that silver and gold would be put to when the new nation arrived at Mount Sinai out in the desert. God already had something in mind that no one had ever dreamed of yet—the Tabernacle, the Tent of Meeting where the Israelites would meet in close proximity with the awesome holy God who had delivered them.

At this point, God didn't tell them why they would need those precious metals. He just said, "Ask for them," and they did. It's called *obedience*.

> The LORD gave the people favor in the sight of the Egyptians. Fur-
> thermore, the man Moses himself was greatly esteemed in the land
> of Egypt, both in the sight of Pharaoh's servants and in the sight of
> the people. (v. 3)

Isn't that encouraging? Just a couple of chapters back, we read about Moses' bad day. The ex-shepherd was under the gun, snarled at by the king and thoroughly hated by the Hebrew leadership. But now we read that he was "greatly esteemed" in Egypt *by the Egyptians*. From the court of Pharaoh on down to the man on the street, people were saying, "Now there's a great man."

Do you know why that was true? Because Moses stood all alone and trusted God (he obeyed), and the Lord gave him favor in their eyes. The Lord delights to do that. Remember Proverbs 16:7? We mentioned that earlier. "When a man's ways please the Lord, He makes even his enemies to be at peace with him." We see that borne out yet again in this amazing development.

Maybe it's the very word you need from the Lord today. It may be that right now in your work you have come to an impasse; there's an issue of integrity at stake and you've determined not to compromise. Because of your stand for Christ, you find that you are resented. I want to assure you that if you handle that situation wisely and tactfully, God will see to it that in the eyes of those who are now your enemy, you will one day be esteemed. They will respect your stand because you are standing alone, doing what is right.

FIVE HARD FACTS

Now, after God had spoken to Moses and told him what to say, after Moses had been told, "You have favor in the eyes of the people," Moses made his way back to the royal chambers for one last interview with the king. In the course of that highly-charged conversation, Moses announced five truths to Pharaoh, which the king promptly rejected (big surprise).

Something is going to happen at midnight.

> Moses said, "Thus says the LORD, 'About midnight I am going out into the midst of Egypt.'" (v. 4)

Moses followed that chilling announcement with a shocker.

All of Egypt's firstborn will die.

> And all the firstborn in the land of Egypt shall die, from the firstborn of the Pharaoh who sits on his throne, even to the firstborn of the slave girl who is behind the millstones; all the firstborn of the cattle as well. (v. 5)

He was telling Pharaoh, "This includes you. Your own firstborn son will die at the stroke of midnight."

There will be national distress.

> Moreover, there shall be a great cry in all the land of Egypt, such as there has not been before and such as shall never be again. (v. 6)

The mourning that will grip Egypt will be without precedent. There had been wars in the past, and there would be wars in the future. Egypt has just endured nine plagues, and there would be national disasters yet to come. But never again would there be a shockwave of grief like this one.

Israel will be protected.

"'But against any of the sons of Israel a dog will not even bark, whether against man or beast, that you may understand how the LORD makes a distinction between Egypt and Israel.'" (v. 7)

Just as in the previous disasters, the Hebrew slave population would be spared.

There will be an exodus.

"All these your servants will come down to me and bow themselves before me, saying, 'Go out, you and all the people who follow you,' and after that I will go out." And he went out from Pharaoh in hot anger. (v. 8)

On that last word "O-U-T," Moses turned on his heels and strode out of the room. He didn't need to apologize for the message, nor the strength with which it was delivered. It was *God's* message. He was invincible as he delivered it. The time of patience was past, and the pronouncement of impending judgment was harsh and severe. It was as if to say, "Pharaoh, you've withstood God long enough. You have dared Him to act, and act He will. You have reached the end of the tether."

PREPARING FOR AN EXODUS

After leaving the presence of Pharaoh, Moses returned and stood before the Israelites. He was through dealing with the king; Pharaoh was now in God's hands. Now he would turn his attention to the people of Israel, helping them to understand God's instructions in these awesome moments before they severed themselves from Egypt forever. He would instruct them and they would cooperate. It's called *obedience*.

To begin with, the Lord wanted the people to establish a memorial. He told Moses and Aaron: "This month shall be the beginning of months for you; it is to be the first month of the year to you" (12:1–2).

From that day forward, the Hebrew calendar would be arranged to reflect the importance of the momentous event that was about to follow.

Speak to all the congregation of Israel, saying, "On the tenth of this month they are each one to take a lamb for themselves, according to their fathers' households, a lamb for each household. Now if the household is too small for a lamb, then he and his neighbor nearest to his house are to take one according to the number of persons in them; according to what each man should eat, you are to divide the lamb. Your lamb shall be an unblemished male a year old." (vv. 3–5)

Notice how exceedingly careful and specific these instructions become.

You may take it from the sheep or from the goats. You shall keep it until the fourteenth day of the same month, then the whole assembly of the congregation of Israel is to kill it at twilight. Moreover, they shall take some of the blood and put it on the two doorposts and on the lintel of the houses in which they eat it.

One of the problems with reading through a passage such as this one is that some of us are too familiar with it. We've read it or heard it so many times that it becomes ho-hum. "So, here we go again with the Passover. Let's go on to some deeper truth."

You and I need to put ourselves in the sandals of those who were hearing Moses face to face. Try to imagine yourself receiving these instructions for the very first time. Remember, the Hebrews had never done anything like this before. They'd never roasted a lamb in that particular way. They'd never gathered its blood in a pan for a special purpose. They'd never smeared it on the doorposts of their homes. They'd never heard of such a thing as an "exodus." Who had? When had a whole nation picked up in a single night and left the country where they have been living for four hundred years? This was all new stuff, and it must have stunned these soon-to-be-freed slaves.

Picture a godly Hebrew family as they hear Moses repeat God's instructions. *"You're to take a lamb, one per family. After cutting the throat of that lamb and draining the blood out of it, you're to keep some of that blood. And with a branch of hyssop, you're to dip in that pan of blood and you're to smear it on the doorpost, on each side. What's the doorpost? Well, if you stand in the center of your doorway and put your hands out to each side, you'll be touching the doorposts. Got it? Okay, and you're also to smear some of that blood on the lintel—that's the horizontal beam just above the doorway. Those are the only places you're to put that blood, understand?"*

Stop and think about those instructions for a moment. What *logical* reason was there for doing those things with the lamb's blood? You say, "Well, God told 'em to do that." That's right! That's the answer. At this point, that is the only reason they needed. There was no power in the dried blood of a slain lamb. Yet God, in His unfathomable wisdom, designed a plan that required only one thing—obedience.

He never asked them to think it through. He never asked them to dialogue about it. He never asked them to consider the idea and decide if they agreed. He simply told them what to do and when to do it. And then He told them what would happen as a result of their strict obedience to His commands.

> For I will go through the land of Egypt on that night, and will strike down all the firstborn in the land of Egypt, both man and beast; and against all the gods of Egypt I will execute judgments—I am the LORD. The blood shall be a sign for you on the houses where you live; and when I see the blood I will pass over you. (vv. 12–13)

Sound familiar? If you're like me, you remember singing that old hymn, "When I see the blood, I will pass, I will pass over you." God told them, "I'm going to visit Egypt. Tonight. I will invade every dwelling where there in no blood on the door. But there will be blood on the doorways of my people, and they will be spared. That's my plan. *Do it.*"

How were they to eat this lamb? God had some specific instructions for the mealtime, as well: "Now you shall eat it in this manner: with your loins girded, your sandals on your feet, and your staff in your hand; and you shall eat it in haste—it is the LORD's Passover" (v. 11).

In other words, they were to be ready for travel. He was telling them,

"This isn't a meal to be eaten lounging around in your pajamas. You must be ready to march! Be dressed for travel, and keep your sandals on." Sandals on—inside a home? Wasn't that out of place? Not on this occasion! They needed to be ready to walk right out the door, fast.

Remember the last time you and your family had to hurry through a meal? ("Chuck," you might say, "that sounds like *every* meal around our place.") Let's say you had to be somewhere at a certain time, and everyone had to just choke down a sandwich on the way out the door. That's the idea here. There was to be no lingering, no casual conversation. All of the Hebrews, from mom and dad down to each one of the kids, had to be ready to move out on a moment's notice.

Why? Because God was about to make history. And these people were going to be part of it. He was telling them, "I'm going to call you out of those homes, and you'll walk away from four-hundred-plus years of slavery without looking back. I am buying you out of bondage, and you're going to be free. Free indeed!"

From that significant day to this present day, the Jewish people would remember Passover. History *was* made that night, and it was made because the people believed God's man and obeyed God's plan.

For that reason, the Lord told them, "This day will be a memorial to you, and you shall celebrate it as a feast to the Lord; throughout your generations you are to celebrate it as a permanent ordinance" (v. 14).

The Lord went on to give them even more details. And after those details, He told them something they were to remember.

> When you enter the land which the Lord will give you, as He has promised, you shall observe this rite. And when your children say to you, "What does this rite mean to you?" you shall say, "It is a Passover sacrifice to the Lord who passed over the houses of the sons of Israel in Egypt when He smote the Egyptians, but spared our homes." (vv. 25–27)

I love this segment of the story. I guess it's the nostalgia in me that captures my attention at this point. Those of us who are parents and grandparents have the very important assignment of helping our offspring grasp the meaning of why we do what we do. We've been there dozens of times.

"Daddy, Mommy, why do we pray before we eat? At Joey's house they never pray, they just dig in. Why do we do that?"

"Dad, why do we go to church every week? Hardly anybody at school does that."

"Mom, what's this juice and cracker thing we do at church? What does it mean?"

"Grandpa, how did that girl know she was supposed to be a missionary? How did God tell her?"

"Grandma, why do you go every week to the soup kitchen where they feed those homeless people? Can't they get somebody else?"

Those are choice parental moments. Classic opportunities. And God tells us to be ready for them. When they come, make them count! Think through your answer. Don't brush it off; treat it seriously. Take the time you need to set the record straight. Help the children to understand the *why* behind your Christian walk and activities. Not only do they need to know, but someday they will need to pass it on to their children.

The instruction Moses gave was to be passed along from generation to generation. After he finished with these specific instructions, Scripture says, "And the people bowed low and worshiped. Then the sons of Israel went and did so; just as the LORD had commanded Moses and Aaron, so they did" (vv. 27–28).

We're back again to the main word: obedience.

THE UNDERLYING, OVERRIDING THEME

I began this chapter with a discussion of hearing and obeying the call of God on your life. The way I see it, the theme that beats like a pulse through this portion of Scripture is obedience, obedience, obedience.

Pharaoh did not—would not—obey. As a result, he exposed both himself and his nation to the judgment of the Lord. The Hebrews, however, heard the Lord's word through Moses and did obey, right down to the smallest detail. As a result, they experienced a great deliverance. They *made* history, while Pharaoh *became* history.

I would like to apply some of these thoughts before we make further tracks in this narrative. My personal conviction is that our greatest struggle is not in the realm of understanding the will of God; it's in the realm of *obeying* the God whose will it is. To be painfully honest, when you and I look back at our lives, we do not find ourselves puzzled and mystified about God's will nearly as much as we find ourselves stubborn and resistant to the One directing our steps. Our problem isn't that we don't know; our problem is that we *do* know but aren't willing to follow through.

That's the basic struggle of the Christian life. The clear truth of God is set before us time and time again. It's available to us, we read it, we hear it explained from the pulpit, in a Christian book, or on a Christian radio program, and we sense the Holy Spirit whispering, *Yes, this means you.* We understand Him clearly, but we resist. When the chips are down, our tendency is to say, "I've got it planned another way."

Let me put this in terms of our involvement with God's worldwide program. The normal question I hear is, "How do I know that God wants me in cross-cultural ministry?" Here's a question that may be more to the point. Ask yourself, "How do you know He *doesn't?*"

At some juncture in our lives—maybe at several junctures—we need to ask ourselves that question. You may say, "Well, Chuck, he's not calling everyone to that task." I know that. But that's not the question here. We're not talking about everyone. The question is, how do *you* know He isn't calling *you?*

STEP BY STEP

To be honest with you, I never asked myself those sorts of questions when I was a teenager. I was going my own way, my own direction, and the last thought on my mind was how God might want to use my life. Frankly, I didn't even care. A number of years later, however, as a young man in the military overseas, unbelievable depravity surrounded me while I was living in the barracks, and God began to nudge me. Then He began to nail me.

An awareness of the need

The first thing He showed me was *the need*. I was encircled by it! On every side of me, there were people who simply did not know the truth. And because of their ignorance, they were living in the scum, disease, and despair of sin. I began to think to myself, *Man, somebody needs to be giving these guys the scoop*. So, without fanfare, little by little, I began doing that within my own small sphere of influence.

Do you know what happened? Wonder of wonders, some people began to respond. Candidly, I couldn't believe it. When I told different ones about God's provision for sin and offer of salvation in Christ, they *believed* it. They actually received that message, and their lives began to change. They turned from darkness to light. Some almost immediately.

An awareness that He could use me

The second step was when I reached out from my sphere of influence and discovered that God could actually use me. Me! He could pick me up as a tool and use me as part of His plan. What a revelation that was for me. And more surprising than that, it was *fun*. It wasn't hard work at all. I couldn't believe it was so delightful and fulfilling.

An awareness that this could be a life's work

Step three came when I started thinking out loud before the Lord about doing this as a full-time job. I said, "Lord, if You have enabled me in Your grace to accomplish these things along with my other work, and I get so much delight and pleasure in doing it, maybe You'd like me to do this for my career. To be honest, that would be a big change for me, but if that's what You want, Lord, I'm available."

During all those months while this process was taking place in my life, I never once had a mystical, spooky, hocus-pocus sort of experience. Never once did I look up in the sky and see the words "Go preach" written in the clouds. There were no bolts of lightning, no visions in the night, nobody laying hands on me and prophesying. I didn't hear voices and I didn't feel any tingles. None of that. It was just a quiet, calm assurance that kept growing and growing in my soul. Through circumstances, through the

Word, and through the Lord's quiet voice in my heart, He seemed to be telling me, "I want to use you. You need to plan accordingly. You need to adapt your life, your marriage, and all your family plans to My approach."

And I said, "Okay, Lord, I'll do it."

As a result, He began to open doors one after another. I never had to force even one of them. One was opened for me, and then another and another and another. And then, before I knew it, I was in seminary (of all places). And then I was standing before God's people, teaching and preaching the Word of God. The whole procedure sort of unfolded. Not once did I try to force something to work out.

It's the most normal process in the world. But the hardest part of the whole operation is *that very first step*. It is that moment when you shake yourself out of lethargy and ask yourself that question, *How do I know He doesn't want me in some aspect of vocational Christian ministry? How do I know? What if He has something in mind for me? Am I willing to hear Him? Am I available? Am I willing?* Again, it's a matter of obedience.

Years ago, I remember reading a book by missionary Don Hillis. The title of the book was *I Don't Feel Called (Thank the Lord!)*. It was a bit of a jab on this whole concept that you have to *feel* something, like some case of holy shivers, before you can take the first step toward a missions career.

Frankly, obedience usually isn't a *feeling* thing at all. There have been times when I haven't felt like preaching. There have been days when I haven't really felt like walking into a classroom here at the seminary. There have been times when I haven't felt like being true to wedding vows. There have been times when I haven't felt like responding to a brother or sister in need, even when I had the resources to help. But you know what? It never really mattered how I *felt*. My feelings will change day to day, maybe hour to hour, like Texas weather. My major need is to obey God's revealed will, plain and simple.

Those Israelites may not have felt like smearing lamb's blood on the lintel and doorposts of their home that dark night of the first Passover. They surely didn't understand the Lord's reasoning. They had no idea that it would point toward a future Messiah who would pay the debt of sin with His own blood and die for the sins of the world. They just did it; they obeyed because they had believed the word of the Lord. They followed the instructions without understanding all the whys and wherefores.

A few hours later, they were very glad that they did. Obedience always pays off.

THE NIGHT NOBODY SLEPT

> Now it came about at midnight that the LORD struck all the firstborn in the land of Egypt, from the firstborn of Pharaoh who sat on his throne to the firstborn of the captive who was in the dungeon, and all the firstborn of cattle. (12:29)

Does that sound chillingly familiar? Yes, that's exactly what God had said would happen. He keeps His word. He overlooked no one who wasn't prepared, not even the king. Scripture says that "Pharaoh arose in the night, he and all his servants and all the Egyptians, and there was a great cry in Egypt, for there was no home where there was not someone dead" (v. 30).

You'd better believe it. Can you hear it? Just listen. In your mind's eye, picture it. The NIV calls it a "loud wailing." It was an eerie, ghastly, deadly night. Death was abroad, and the land was overwhelmed with it.

But over in Goshen? The Israelites were on their feet, eating roasted lamb and bitter herbs, listening to the terrible wailing all across the land. Everyone among the Hebrews was alive. I can imagine dads and moms embracing their firstborn with tears of gratitude. "Thank God, you're alive, son! Praise God we were spared!" The slimy fingers of death invaded like an awful plague, but it didn't touch a single one of God's people.

Scripture says there wasn't a home in Egypt where someone had not died. Think of it! What a shattering night that was! My mind cannot fully conceive it.

Verse 31 says that the grieving Pharaoh called for Moses and Aaron. Can't you picture him? "Get Moses and Aaron in here *now!*"

> [Pharaoh] said, "Up! Leave my people, you and the Israelites! Go, worship the LORD as you have requested. Take your flocks and herds,

as you have said, and go." (vv. 31–32, NIV, brackets mine)

"Get out of here! Scram! Take everything! Don't linger! Do just as you said."

And Pharaoh wasn't the only one urging them to exit. Scripture also says, "The Egyptians urged the people, to send them out of the land in haste, for they said, 'We will all be dead'" (v. 33).

Nobody ever had more help getting their bags packed then those Israelites that night. And since they were obedient and ready to go when the call came, they walked right out of Egypt. What a night! A great host of people filling the streets, marching toward the border while the muffled wails and cries of the grieving Egyptians echoed through the darkness. "Now the sons of Israel journeyed from Rameses to Succoth, about six hundred thousand men on foot" (v. 27).

When you add the women and children to that count, many Old Testament scholars put the number at about two million people. *Two million!* Just think of the logistics. And nobody had any plans for catering the next meal. Think of the sanitation problems. Think of the dietary and medical challenges. Think of the protection from the elements that was needed. Nobody had any contingency plans. They just took off. Those who were able even to think about it on that wild and eerie night must have felt, "If God can preserve us from death when it's raging all around us here in Egypt, He can surely take care of us on this journey into the night." Obedience spawns such faith.

HISTORICAL JOY

Again, you and I have a different perspective because we've read the Book. They hadn't read the Book. At that time, there was no Book. No nation had ever done this before; it was the first time ever. There was no map, no contract, no three-ring-binder with photocopied, step-by-step instructions, titled *Exodus Handbook.* There was nothing guaranteed at all except the presence of the living God represented in a shepherd named Moses, who walked out in front of the biggest flock anyone had ever led.

He was making history. They all were. Multiple centuries later, the descendents of this people would still be singing about that incredible night and the God who had delivered His people:

> "You saw the suffering of our forefathers in Egypt; you heard their cry.... You sent miraculous signs and wonders against Pharaoh, against all his officials and all the people of his land, for you knew how arrogantly the Egyptians treated them. You made a name for yourself, which remains to this day." (Nehemiah 9:9–10, NIV)

When those families left their homes and all that they knew that night to follow the Lord in simple faith and obedience, they had no idea they were making history. They had no concept that their many-times-great grandchildren would be singing of that event, which just goes to show you that you never know what wonders and miracles will result from simple obedience. Saying yes to God and moving out in faith at His command has an incalculable impact on both time and eternity.

What was it like when they left? Many of us have the idea that, if we really step out in faith and begin to follow God into new pathways and new arenas, life will become miserable. We say to ourselves, "My, if I really say yes to His plan and make myself available, it's going to be hard. It's going to be harsh and difficult. I'll be leaving all that's comfortable and familiar and secure, and heading out into the badlands."

In Psalm 105, the psalmist gives some insight from the Exodus that Moses (busy as he was) didn't take time to put into his Exodus journal.

> Then He brought them out with silver and gold, and among His tribes there was not one who stumbled. (v. 37)

That was the spirit in which they departed. Among that great throng, not one person stumbled. There wasn't a weak one in the bunch. They were all ready for the trip. God had preserved them, giving them health and stamina for the journey.

The Night Nobody Slept

> Egypt was glad when they departed, for the dread of them had fallen upon them. He spread a cloud for a covering, and fire to illumine by night. (vv. 38–39)

God took such good care of them. He led the way. He illumined the path.

> And He brought forth His people with joy, His chosen ones with a joyful shout. (v. 43)

Isn't that great? Rather than sadness and fear, there was exhilaration that night. The sweet fragrance of freedom was in the wind. We love to sing the hymn, "O for a thousand tongues to sing, my great Redeemer's praise." If you think that sounds good, how about, "O for *two million* tongues to sing!" You could hear those voices echo far away into the distant reaches of the empty desert as Moses led the way, and the joyous throng followed. Great clouds of dust billowed as Jacob's children walked out of Egypt, walked away from their chains and away from their bondage. (I'm smiling as I write this. I'm thinking, *Yes! Yes! What a way to travel!*)

Just think of that day or night when you came to know the Lord Jesus as your Savior. Can you recapture the emotions of that moment? Remember when that friend gave you the Good News about God's provision for sin and His offer of eternal life? Remember when you realized it was really for *you?* Remember when that pastor or teacher explained the gospel, and for the first time it really made sense? Remember when your dad or mom sat down with you in your bedroom and explained the truth about sin and Christ and eternity, and you said, "Tonight's the night"?

Was that a harsh, hard experience? Admittedly, you left all the familiar things of Egypt behind you, but don't forget you also left your chains! You left your years of slavery, and then you began to taste of God's provision. You began to drink from the deep wells of His grace. Nothing ever tasted so sweet and so refreshing.

It's not over, friend. There's more out there. His plan goes a lot deeper

207

than getting you out of Egypt. Getting you into His family was Plan A. Getting you into His will, for your whole life—that's Plan B. And maybe that's where you are as you read these words. You find yourself about to step into unknown territory and follow God where you have never been before. Looking at it through the eyes of the ancient Hebrews, you're about to make history.

Years ago, I remember speaking to a large gathering of young people at Forest Home conference center in southern California. The kids ranged in age from high school juniors to college sophomores. It was a remarkable time. They didn't come to party or be entertained, even though fun was on the agenda, too. They brought Bibles and notebooks and sharp pencils and wanted to dig into the Book. It was one of those times as a speaker when I just sensed the group drinking it in. It's hard to explain unless you've been in that position as a teacher, but it's an experience you never forget. That group was like a big thirsty sponge, just soaking it up, drawing more and more out of me and the Word.

Even though it was a young, eager audience, we weren't even talking about missions or Christian service; we were digging our way through Nehemiah, wrestling with principles of leadership and obedience to Christ. Afterwards, a young man came up to me and said, "Pastor Chuck, I've got to talk with you about something."

"Sure," I said. "Let's go sit down over there."

We sat down in a quiet place and he said, "I dunno, I . . . I have a funny feeling. It's almost weird, but I think that God wants my life." He looked up at me to make sure I understood. Tears began to pool in his eyes.

"Do you know the Lord personally?" I asked.

"Oh yes," he said. "In fact, I have plans to become a medical doctor."

"Really?"

"Yeah, and you know, I've gotta know what His plan is." And suddenly he began to sob. He was so deeply moved he couldn't even speak. I just reached over and put my arm around him. "Listen," I said, "don't come to our question-answer session tonight. You take off. Get alone with God."

"Well, what do I do?"

"You just tell God what you're telling me," I said. "Ask Him to help you understand what He's saying to you. Ask Him to show you His plan for your life."

The last I saw of him that Friday night, he was walking up the trail into the darkness, to get alone with his Lord. Early the next morning, around the fireplace, he came over to me. "Do you know what?" he said, his face serious. "God wants me to be a medical missionary."

I reached my arm around his shoulders and held him close for a minute. "Hey, that's fantastic," I said.

"Um, well, there's nothing *wrong* with that, is there?"

He looked so serious and scared I almost laughed. "No way, man. You're right on target. Your whole career is going to take on a new dimension."

At the same conference, a man in his forties approached me. He wasn't part of the kids' group at all but came because he knew it would be an in-depth conference where he would have time to think through some of the issues of his life. He was an imminently successful insurance executive with responsibilities ranging across a vast area of southern California.

"Chuck," he told me, "God's really speaking to me. I think He's turning my whole direction for life around. I think He wants to use me somewhere outside the United States."

Later I learned from some of his friends that his life had headed in a whole new direction after that weekend conference. What amazed me so much about those developments was that I had never once mentioned the subject of world missions. The issue on the table was *obedience*. And once people actually began making themselves available to the Lord, opening their lives to His direction, things began to happen. New directions and new pathways opened up for them, as it did for the host of Hebrews who walked out of Egypt on that night of the first Passover.

And what about you? You may have never even considered the possibility that God has a purpose for your life beyond the normal workaday lifestyle in which you find yourself today. But think about it: Why *wouldn't* He call you into some aspect of vocational service for Him? If you don't have the answer, then I suggest you revisit the question.

You've heard it said before, and it's just as true now as when it was first uttered. After all the history books have been written, after time passes out of existence, only two things will remain from this world, only two things are eternal: God's Word and people. It may very well be that He wants you to major in both of those subjects for the rest of your life. You'll never know unless you ask Him.

Want a tip? Take this on as a project. As a regular part of your prayer life, make it a point to ask Him, "Lord, am I in the center of Your plan? Do You want to continue using me in this capacity? Do You have anything else in mind for me, anywhere else? I'm available, Lord. I'm willing to have You change my whole approach to life."

He may tell you, "My son," or "My daughter, you're right where I want you to be. Trust Me, and keep on keeping on. I will bless you and use you."

Then again, He may say, "Yes, now that I finally have your attention, I want to use you in the place of My choosing. Keep your sandals on, and get yourself ready to travel light. Let's go make some history!"

It all starts with obedience.

CHAPTER TWELVE

Between the Devil and the Deep Red Sea

We Americans use a number of words to describe a predicament. If you're from the East, you probably know about "being in a pinch." If you like to cook, you're "in a jam," or "in a pickle." If you're from the South, you're "between a rock and a hard place." There are all manner of such expressions. Foreigners trying to decipher our lingo must scratch their heads in bewilderment as they hear Americans talking about being "up a wall," "up a tree," "in a corner," "up against it," and "hard-pressed."

I recently heard an apt description of a predicament: A predicament occurs when an attorney who specializes in medical malpractice suits finds himself in need of major surgery. Now *that's* a predicament.

It may be that right now you find yourself in a predicament. You might be in that situation because of an unwise series of decisions you have made. Or you might find yourself in a predicament through no fault of your own; it occurred because of circumstances beyond your control. Perhaps you're being impacted from the fallout of another's failure.

Your situation might be related to a child who is not walking with the

Lord. He has grown and left the nest; so he's too old to discipline. Yet you're still the parent, and with all your heart you want that lad to walk with God. To say something might make the problem worse; to say nothing would be less than what you should do. You're in a jam. A catch-22. A predicament.

Your predicament might be related to your work, and if you say something to relieve the pressure, things might get worse. Or it might make somebody look bad if you roll up your sleeves and try to untangle the problem yourself.

Your predicament might be related to something at school or something in your home. It might be a relational issue. Whatever it is, you find yourself squeezed into a tight place, and you see no way out. You're in a predicament.

Thomas Paine referred to such difficulties as "those times that try men's souls." And they do, don't they? Perhaps the lines on your face are beginning to lengthen and deepen, because try as you might, the predicament clings to you like cheap cologne. You can't walk away from it.

If that's your story, I'm happy to report that you will find a measure of comfort in Exodus 14. That chapter describes the most involved predicament Israel ever faced, yet they lived to tell the story. And tell it they did! It became the most celebrated event in all of Jewish history.

So what lessons can you learn when you find yourself in a predicament? It might well be that the *only* solution to your predicament is a miracle. That's what Israel learned.

FOLLOWING GOD . . . TO A DEAD-END

The Israelites had been living in Egypt all their days. Not one Israelite whom God was about to deliver under Moses' leadership had been born and raised outside of Egypt. Their lifestyle was Egyptian to the core. They had picked up the habits, the earmarks, the style, the very smell of Egypt (leeks and garlic!). As a result, God needed to teach His people a new lifestyle. But in order for Him to do that, He first had to get their attention. That is why He brought them to the Red Sea—a predicament with a capitol P.

Before we dig into Exodus 14, let's glance back to a verse from the previous chapter: "Hence God led the people around by the way of the wilderness to the Red Sea" (13:18).

Note the phrase, *"God* led the people ... to the Red Sea." The people of Israel came to this impasse, to this "straight betwixt two," *at God's direction.* Their predicament wasn't an accident. It wasn't a wrong turn. It wasn't a miscalculation. He knew they needed the Red Sea experience to learn some things from Him. And this was one of those valuable lessons they needed to learn early in their journey.

Next, take a look at Exodus 13:21. Moses writes, "The LORD was going before them." So God both "led" them and "was going before them." And how did God go before them? You'll find this interesting:

> The LORD was going before them in a pillar of cloud by day to lead them on the way, and in a pillar of fire by night to give them light, that they might travel by day and by night. He did not take away the pillar of cloud by day, nor the pillar of fire by night, from before the people. (vv. 21–22)

Pretty incredible. You and I have never experienced anything like it, but the Israelites in the wilderness never experienced a moment without it.

Have you wrestled recently with the will of God? I have. Some of my deepest wrestlings involve trying to discern His desire and His way. At times I have looked with envy on the Israelites for a cloud by day and a fire by night. How simple! It was as easy as playing Follow the Leader.

When the cloud moved forward, they moved forward. When the cloud moved to starboard, they moved to starboard. When it moved to port, they moved to port. When it backed up, they backed up. When it stopped, they stopped. Clear as a bell. No question. Nothing to decipher—just follow the cloud.

At night, when you couldn't see a cloud, God transformed Himself into a pillar of fire. So He chased away the wild beasts of the desert, kept His people warm, and gave them unerring guidance. Day or night, all they had to do was look up, and there was God's unquestionable presence. "He went before them," says Scripture.

213

Wouldn't that be great? Suppose you wondered if it was God's will for you to move. What do you do? Just look up. There's the cloud! It's moving toward Baltimore. Pack your bags! Or you wonder if it's God's will for you to work in a given place. What do you do? Just watch the fire. It moves right over to a place of employment and rests there. Time to go over there and apply for the job. Or you've been dating this young lady, wondering if she might be God's choice for your mate. No problem. She opens the door to her apartment and there's the cloud hovering six inches above her pretty head. No question about it. Buy the ring. Pop the question.

That's how simple it was for the Israelites when it came to following God's leading. They never had any questions, never had to make a judgment call. The pillar of fire at night and the pillowy cloud during the day led directly to the Red Sea and put on the brakes. So that's where they went, and that's where they stopped. But why? Why would God box them in and hold them in that tight place?

Exodus 14:1 begins to give us an answer: "The LORD spoke to Moses." You see, God spoke to Moses because this leader had been prepared. Remember, he is eighty years young. He has learned his lessons. He has done his homework in the Midian desert. He has discovered that you don't question God. When the Lord says, "Go to the Red Sea," you get on your horse. You don't wait. So God said to Moses,

> "Tell the sons of Israel to turn back and camp before Pi-hahiroth, between Migdol and the sea; you shall camp in front of Baal-zephon, opposite it, by the sea. For Pharaoh will say of the sons of Israel, 'They are wandering aimlessly in the land; the wilderness has shut them in.' Thus I will harden Pharaoh's heart, and he will chase after them; and I will be honored through Pharaoh and all his army, and the Egyptians will know that I am the LORD." And they did so. (vv. 2–4)

Now, that sounds fairly simple. Before the Exodus the Hebrews had lived in the land of Goshen, in a locality called Raamses. When the Exodus occurred, the Hebrews left Raamses and traveled as far south as Etham. It was there that they camped. And that is apparently where the Lord spoke to

Moses and gave him the message we just read. While they were in Etham, the Lord said, "Go up as far as Baal-zephon." In other words, *"Backtrack.* Retrace all the steps you just took, all the way up to Baal-zephon." (If you've got an ancient map handy, check it out.)

The trouble was, Baal-zephon formed a perfect geographical cul-de-sac. A dead-end street. Just to the north stood some formidable Egyptian fortresses—massive stone structures. No way they could get through there. To the south lay the vast Egyptian desert called Mizraim. No protection there. To the west lay Raamses and Goshen. That's where they'd just been; They couldn't return to Egypt. To the east lay the Red Sea, today called the Gulf of Suez. The northernmost section of that gulf was the Reed Sea, or the Sea of Reeds, most often translated the Red Sea.

Got the picture? They stood staring at the waters of the Red Sea. To the north, strong enemy fortresses. To the south, blazing desert. To the west, Egypt itself. They were boxed in. There was no back door—a geographical trap with no possibility of escape.

WHO HAS TRAPPED WHOM?

God said, however, "Go to Baal-zephon." Militarily, it was the most vulnerable spot to be in. It would be like turning down a dead-end street when you're being chased by a car full of thieves. Humanly speaking, that would be the most foolish decision in the world. Yet that's what God told them to do.

Moses, you see, had walked with God long enough to know that even though the Lord's directions might seem foolish, he wasn't to question them. And God was gracious enough to say, "Look here, Moses. I have a profound plan. As you wander back and forth in the desert, Pharaoh is bound to get word via the grapevine that you're aimlessly wandering around, and he'll think, *Aaah, they're going up north to Baal-zephon. I'll trap 'em there!* That, Moses, is the trap Pharaoh will fall into."

God had it all arranged ahead of time—He always does. The Lord wanted to fight the Hebrews' battle for them. All their lives, they had been fighting their own battles. They had been cinching up to another notch in their belts and taking on all comers, powered by their own strength. But the Lord says, in effect, "No, Moses, I want my people to learn that I will fight their battles for them. All they have to do is to wait and trust. So follow the cloud all the way up to Baal-zephon."

Now the plot begins to thicken. Pharaoh reacts exactly as God had predicted.

> When the king of Egypt was told that the people had fled, Pharaoh and his servants had a change of heart toward the people, and they said, "What is this we have done, that we have let Israel go from serving us?" So he made his chariot ready and took his people with him; and he took six hundred select chariots, and all the other chariots of Egypt with officers over all of them. The LORD hardened the heart of Pharaoh, king of Egypt, and he chased after the sons of Israel as the sons of Israel were going out boldly. (vv. 5–8)

For once, Israel had done precisely what God instructed. They started moving north, thinking, *God is in this. This is gonna be a great experience.* They marched boldly toward Baal-zephon and straight into the jaws of a predicament: "Then the Egyptians chased after them with all the horses and chariots of Pharaoh, his horsemen and his army, and they overtook them camping by the sea, beside Pi-hahiroth, in front of Baal-zephon" (v. 9).

Suddenly the scene changes. Picture it. You're one among two million in the Israelite camp. You have traveled with the people of God to this cul-de-sac in the wilderness. Moses had taken the lead and said, "This is where God wants us to go." All the time you've been thinking, *Well, at least I know there's a way out. We just came up to this area; we can get out the same way we came.* But all of a sudden you hear something in the distance. Thunder? A storm sweeping across the horizon? You look back, only to see a cloud of dust rising, drawing nearer. Wait a minute, that rumbling isn't thunder; it's horses and chariots. Thousands of them! Every chariot in Egypt! Word on the grapevine travels fast: "Pharaoh's coming! It's going to be a massacre!" And panic blows through the ranks of Israel like a gust of cold wind.

Can you almost hear your own testimony in these words? "As Pharaoh drew near, the sons of Israel looked, and behold, the Egyptians were marching after them, and they became very frightened" (v. 10).

What an understatement! The Hebrews weren't merely frightened; they were *very* frightened. We'd say they were scared out of their minds when they saw those Egyptians. "So the sons of Israel cried out to the LORD" (v. 10).

This is the first time we read of the people of Israel crying out to God *en masse*. Isn't it remarkable what a predicament will do to your proud, independent spirit? You walk along with an arrogant swagger, strutting your way through life like a human peacock. But then things begin to change, and it isn't long before you come to the end of your rope. Suddenly you realize, *Hey, I'm in a jam!* So you look up. And then you cry out.

We're not told what they said, but immediately after they cried out to God, they began to look for someone to blame. Isn't that usually the way we all handle a predicament? First, if we're in touch with God we cry out. And second, if relief doesn't immediately arrive, we begin to look for someone to blame.

Naturally, they picked the preacher: "They said to Moses, 'Is it because there were no graves in Egypt that you have taken us away to die in the wilderness? Why have you dealt with us in this way, bringing us out of Egypt'" (v. 11)?

I mean, in a predicament like this, who can resist saying "We told you so"? The Israelites threw it right in Moses' face: "Is this not the word that we spoke to you in Egypt, saying, 'Leave us alone that we may serve the Egyptians'? For it would have been better for us to serve the Egyptians than to die in the wilderness" (v. 12).

In other words, "We would rather be in safety as slaves than to be free men in danger." Read that again. I'd call such thinking nothing other than human perspective. They are no longer looking up.

"DO NOT FEAR!"

Humanly speaking, predicaments are terrible experiences. If you stay in one long enough, you will begin to question the very roots of your faith. By and by you'll begin to look for someone to blame; usually it'll be somebody in leadership. And you'll say, "Look, I took *your* counsel. I did what *you* said. But here I am at the end of my rope. I've tied a knot, I'm hanging on, and I'm dangling. There's no net if I fall. And *you're* the reason I did that!"

That's why I am extremely impressed with Moses' response. He didn't say, as most are prone to say, "God helps those who help themselves." People think that despicable saying comes from the Bible, but it doesn't. It's from the pit. No, God helps *the helpless!* As long as we're helping ourselves, who needs God? It's when we reach the end of our tether, and we're dangling out in space, that we finally cry out, "God, help me!" And God says, "I will. *Let go.*" What's our normal response? "Is there anybody else up there who can help me?" Letting go works against human nature. But God wants us to do just that—to freefall into His everlasting arms and trust completely in Him. It's all a part of His plan.

Note Moses' more biblical response in verse 13: "Do not fear!" What strange counsel. Can't you hear his fellow Israelites? "Hey, Moses, the Egyptians are around the corner. They've got chariots and bows and arrows and pointy spears. And you're saying, 'Don't fear'? What's the matter with you, man? Do you need a change in your eyeglass prescription? Can't you see they're coming? God, save us from this near-sighted shepherd!"

"Oh, I see them fine," Moses replied. "But I'm still saying to you, 'Don't fear!'"

But Moses isn't done. He has a second piece of counsel for his frightened people: "Stand still." And a third: "Watch." And a fourth: "The Lord will fight for you while you keep silent." Did you catch all that? It's a mouthful in any Bible translation. Read it for yourself.

> "Do not fear! Stand by and see the salvation of the LORD which He
> will accomplish for you today; for the Egyptians whom you have seen
> today, you will never see them again forever. The LORD will fight for
> you while you keep silent." (vv. 13–14)

Now, there's a prescription for people in an inescapable predicament! Don't be afraid, stand still, watch God come through, quit talking. The hardest is the fourth, because we just *have* to tell somebody what a predicament we're in. But God doesn't need to be informed. He knows the predicament, and He is waiting for us to wait for Him and keep silent.

When you are in a cul-de-sac, led by God to that tight place, it is there you will discover some good surprises designed just for you. That's why Moses said, "Look, let's stand still. There's a great blessing here for us that we'll miss if we turn tail and run."

You know the human response to panic? First, we are afraid. Second, we run. Third, we fight. Fourth, we tell everybody.

God's counsel is just the opposite. Don't be afraid. Stand still. Watch Him work. Keep quiet. It's then that He does it. He takes over! He handles it exactly opposite the way we'd do it. The Lord just taps His foot, waiting for us to wait.

FOUR MIGHTY MIRACLES

Remarkable as it may seem, the Israelites did exactly what Moses had instructed, and God came through again. (He always does.) He did four mighty things on behalf of the Israelites.

First, He told Moses to go forward:

> Then the LORD said to Moses, "Why are you crying out to Me? Tell the sons of Israel to go forward." (v. 15)

I love that. There's the ocean in front of you; so, forward march! Moses saluted, and as he got his troops together, God did something else.

He moved the cloud from above them to behind them:

Scripture tells us that, "The angel of God, who had been going before the camp of Israel, moved and went behind them; and the pillar of cloud moved from before them and stood behind them" (v. 19).

The biblical account then explains why God did this: "So it came between the camp of Egypt and the camp of Israel; and there was the cloud along with the darkness, yet it gave light at night. Thus the one did not come near the other all night" (v. 20).

What does that mean? It means that the cloud moved from in front of the Hebrews to behind them, by the Egyptians. This awesome, massive cloud formation dropped from heaven to earth and blocked the Egyptians' view. Not only that, but it kept the Hebrews from staring back and quaking with fear. The cloud blocked the one from the other so the Hebrews could listen to God.

It was then that God performed a massive miracle.

He opened a path through the sea:

> Then Moses stretched out his hand over the sea; and the LORD swept the sea back by a strong east wind all night and turned the sea into dry land, so the waters were divided. (v. 21)

I think Cecil B. DeMille's *Ten Commandments* missed the reality of this miracle in his attempt to make it picturesque. Do you know why the wind blew all night? If the waters had parted suddenly, the Israelites would have walked right into a bog. Any riverbed recently drained of water remains an impassable swamp for a number of days, if not weeks. It takes time to dry. That's the reason for the east wind. So as the sea split in two, and its waves formed great, massive, vertical walls on either side, the east wind bore down and dried up the land.

Picture the Israelites as they stood back and watched that divine wind howling down into that riverbed, drying it to dust. God got everything ready for His people. And once God took His hand off that wind, the Israelites moved right in.

Of course, so did the Egyptians. Those gullible pagans! They fell right into God's trap. They thought, *Man, if they can walk between the sea, we can too! Giddy'up, horse.* Scripture says "the Egyptians took up the pursuit, and all Pharaoh's horses, his chariots and his horsemen went in after them into the midst of the sea" (v. 23).

And then God did the fourth thing.

He brought confusion to the Egyptians:

> At the morning watch [that's long before daybreak], the LORD looked down on the army of the Egyptians through the pillar of fire and

cloud and brought the army of the Egyptians into confusion. He caused their chariot wheels to swerve, and He made them drive with difficulty; so the Egyptians said, "Let us flee from Israel, for the LORD is fighting for them against the Egyptians." (vv. 24–25)

Remember what the Lord had said? "When this is over, they will know that I am the Lord." But not all of them would be around to remember anything.

The Lord said to Moses, "Stretch out your hand over the sea so that the waters may come back over the Egyptians, over their chariots and their horsemen" (v. 26). So that is exactly what Moses did. He turned and stretched out his hand over the sea, and at daybreak the sea plunged back to its normal state with crushing force. The Egyptians were caught in the middle of the angry torrent, and as Scripture says, "The Lord overthrew the Egyptians in the midst of the sea."

What a remarkable contrast! The Hebrews, on the other hand, "walked on dry land through the midst of the sea, and the waters were like a wall to them on their right and on their left" (v. 29). Just as the Israelites cleared the seabed, the Egyptians filled it. That's when God said to Moses, "Now! Get that stick in action. Bring the water back." He did, and the waters rushed in.

Nothing short of a massacre took place that day at Baal-zephon, but the Israelites weren't the victims. By the end of the day, not one of the Egyptian soldiers who had pursued the Hebrews had a pulse. Not a single Egyptian lived through God's ambush, and not a single Hebrew was hurt.

Verse 30 tells us the Hebrews later took a walk along the seashore and "they saw the Egyptians dead on the seashore." Please notice, the Bible doesn't say the Israelites killed a single man, because they didn't. It doesn't say they defended themselves, because they didn't. It doesn't even say they *fought*, because they didn't. They waited, they walked through, then they turned and watched God work. Period. And He did. He did it all, precisely as He had planned to do when He first led them into that predicament.

Isn't it remarkable what God can do without our help? Sometimes we think, *My company needs me. My church needs me. My family needs me. Hey, God must need me, too.* No, He doesn't. He can manage quite well without us, remarkable though it may seem. In fact, He prefers us to step aside and leave the striving to Him.

The capstone is captured in verse 31 where we read that God's people stood in awe: "When Israel saw the great power which the LORD had used against the Egyptians, the people feared the LORD, and they believed in the LORD and in His servant Moses."

After the battle an awesome silence reigned. When they saw what God had done, an enormous groundswell of respect spread over that shoreline. They gave God glory, and they looked at Moses through a different set of eyes.

Historians and unbelieving archaeologists have helped us draw additional insights about this milestone event. Archaeological discoveries from obelisks and other records indicate that the Egyptians did not frequent this place for seventeen long years after this miracle took place. They held it in awe. In fact, they did not attempt to regain their ascendancy over Syria for twenty-two years after this incident. Not until the twenty-third year did they seriously try to reestablish their authority over western Syria. The message arrived back home that God had visited the Red Sea, and it remained an unfriendly place for Egyptians for a long, long time.

MIRACLES OF REDEMPTION

The crossing of the Red Sea is to the Old Testament what the Resurrection is to the New. When the prophets and writers of the Old Testament wanted to refer to God's miraculous hand, they returned to this event more than any other. Just so, when a writer in the New Testament wanted to illustrate the power of God, he most often referred to the Resurrection. What the Resurrection is to the New, the crossing of the Red Sea is to the Old. While the scenes are altogether different, both were astonishing miracles of redemption from the hand of God.

LESSONS LEARNED IN A CORNER

This fourteenth chapter of Exodus offers us some timeless lessons. To draw them out, let's begin by considering Romans 15:4, one of the most eloquent

New Testament verses stating the value of the Old Testament. Paul wrote, "For whatever was written in earlier times was written for our instruction, so that through perseverance and the encouragement of the Scriptures we might have hope."

In other words, God put truths into the Old Testament so that we in this era of grace might draw out some profound truths that impact life this very day. I find four such high-voltage thoughts in Exodus 14.

It takes tight places to break lifetime habits

Why does God design Baal-zephons for us today? Because it often takes such tight places to finally free us from thought patterns and behaviors that have held us hostage for years.

It may be that you have developed a rather humanistic lifestyle. Like Moses, you've rubbed shoulders with folks "in Egypt" most of your life. You work with Egyptians. Think like Egyptians. Read Egyptian news-papers. Listen to Egyptian music. Do commercial battles with Egyptian entrepreneurs. You're in the competitive world of Egyptians, so it's only natural that you react like one of them. Right? It's a dog-eat-dog world!

Really? If that is your situation, my friend, then you may be in for some really tight places very soon, if you're not there already.

When God wants to break Egyptian habits, He paints His people into some impossible corners. And I have discovered that the longer the duration of the habits, the tighter the places. The more ingrained the behaviors, the more impossible the cul-de-sacs.

Chesty Puller was a highly decorated U. S. Marine Corps officer. While in command over a large number of men in combat, he inadvertently moved into an area that was crawling with the enemy. Suddenly he realized he and his men were surrounded. To the north lay a platoon of the enemy, as well as on both his flanks. To the rear, another company; all escape routes were closed off. What did Puller do? He just tightened his fist and said, "That's outstanding. They'll never get away this time!"

That's the way it is with God in some of our lessons. In order for those lessons to etch themselves into our hearts, we have to become surrounded, with no escape route. *Then* we learn. That's why you may be in the predicament you're in right now. Perhaps you need a divinely inspired miracle in your life to change a habit pattern that has plagued you for years. God has a Baal-zephon for you to experience before you're released—before the Red Sea opens.

When hemmed in on all sides, the only place to look is up

When there is no escape before or behind, to the right or to the left, we are forced to look up. Remember, the Israelites first called on the Lord only when they found themselves hemmed in on all sides. As Annie Johnson Flint wrote,

> Pressed out of measure and pressed to all length;
> Pressed so intensely it seems beyond strength.
>
> Pressed in the body and pressed in the soul;
> Pressed in the mind till the dark surges roll;
>
> Pressure by foes, and pressure by friends;
> Pressure on pressure, till life nearly ends.
>
> Pressed into loving the staff and the rod;
> Pressed into knowing no helper but God.
>
> Pressed into liberty where nothing clings;
> Pressed into faith for impossible things.
>
> Pressed into living a life in the Lord;
> Pressed into living the Christ-life outpoured.[1]

Maybe that's why you're under such pressure—to bring you to the end of yourself. I'll never forget the counsel of my good and faithful mother. She used to say to me, "Honey, don't worry about So-and-so. He has to come to the end of himself, and then he'll learn." Many times, that's the only way we *do* learn.

If the Lord is to get the glory, He must do the fighting.

This is the most difficult lesson, but it's the most helpful of the four. If you truly want the Lord to get the glory—and that's not just lip service—you must let Him do the fighting. Obviously, there are times and places where you must get involved. Sometimes you are part of the answer. I am not referring to those times. I'm talking about those impossible impasses, when you're between the proverbial rock and hard place, and God has placed you in that predicament, with no escape.

He wants to do your fighting in such situations. He wants you to lay down your arms in full surrender. He wants us to stand still and watch Him work. That way, when the victory is won, the applause goes to Him. He wants to get the glory.

In my personal journal I once wrote this:

> *When I panic, I run.*
> *When I run, I lose.*
> *When I lose, God waits.*
> *When I wait, He fights.*
> *When He fights, He wins.*
> *And when He wins, I learn.*

Had we been in charge of the Red Sea project, we would have handled it differently. Our group of engineers would have pushed back that water a week in advance. We would have installed great, massive fans to dry out the land. We would have erected huge neon signs. Somebody would have brought in concession stands to handle the hot dogs and drinks. You see, when people do it, the project takes on all the trademarks of market-driven hot-shots. The supernatural is eclipsed by human ingenuity.

That's not God's plan. When He wants you cornered, He corners you. And there are no signs. There is no slick ad campaign. There are no great human resources to trust in. There's just an uncrossable Red Sea and an encroaching army of impossibilities. So you wait. And time passes. He will fight *His* way at *His* time. Bite your nails all you want to—He's in no hurry.

Red Seas open and close at the Lord's command, and not until.

Do you know that a clock is one of the greatest detriments to a life of faith? God doesn't tell time as we do. Sometimes He does His work at three o' clock in the morning; sometimes at noon. He even works on Sundays. He does remarkable things, regardless of our time of day. He doesn't bow to our timepiece. He doesn't jump to our alarm bells. He ignores our deadlines and removes our crutches. He will leave that particular Red Sea absolutely closed, without an opening, without a sign, until He has finished teaching us the lessons we need to learn. Once that's accomplished, He has no trouble parting the waters and sending us through.

But Baal-zephon has to do its work. And the results? You won't *see* a miracle—you'll *be* the miracle. That's the best part of all.

Raymond Edman refers to "the discipline of delay" in his excellent book, *The Disciplines of Life*. He writes, "We live in a restless, impatient day. We have little time for preparation and less for meditation or worship. We feel we must be active and energetic, humanly effective; we cannot understand why inactivity, weakness, weariness, and seeming uselessness should be our lot. It all appears so foolish and futile, without plan or purpose." He then makes this profound statement: "The delay that instructs and prepares us saves time, never loses it."[2]

"Hudson Taylor knew the testing that tempers the steel of the soul. He was an invalid, home at the age of twenty-nine. After six years of intensive service in China, he settled with his little family in the east side of London. Outside interests lessened; friends began to forget him; and five long, hidden years were spent in the dreary streets of a poor part of London, where the Taylors were 'shut up to prayer and patience.' As the years of obscurity progressed, and when the discipline was complete, there emerged the China Inland Mission, at first only a tiny root, but destined of God to fill the land of China with gospel fruit."[3]

When we recall the name of Hudson Taylor, does anyone ever mention those five years of obscurity in a poor part of London? Not likely. We're much more prone to emphasize the prominent things about him. But remember this: China was reached because a man was faithful behind the scenes, patiently waiting with his family, waiting for the Red Sea to open.

That's a lesson for all of us. And until we learn it, we're going to stay stuck in the cul-de-sac.

THE COLOR OF YOUR CUL-DE-SAC

Do you feel cornered right now? Up against it? Almost barren? Listen, child of God, your predicament is by His design. It takes those dreary streets of London, those dead-end Baal-zephons, to prepare you for the glorious days of Canaan.

Perhaps you're a single adult. Those can be frustrating, hard years and lonely times. More than anything you'd like to find a spouse, but....

Or maybe you're married. You can be so involved in making a living that you fail to make a life, and then the time is gone.

Or perhaps you feel backed into some physical cul-de-sac where you've languished for weeks, months, years.... still in that wheelchair.

Listen carefully. Read slowly. *Coming* to the Red Sea is just as much a part of His plan as *crossing* it. It may well be that the Lord is breaking a habit born in Egypt, a habit that has no business living in Canaan. Those habits are tough to break. The tears flow as God works in His time. But in the burning of those tears, God becomes very significant and real. And we realize, at last, that a predicament in God's hands is only a highway to the Promised Land.

CHAPTER THIRTEEN

A Heavenly Diet vs. An Earthly Appetite

High school history teachers have a way of making you either love or hate their subjects. I was fortunate. God gave me an instructor back in my high school years who really made history come alive. Mrs. Allen wasn't physically impressive; she probably weighed eighty-five pounds, dripping wet. She wore thick glasses, coughed often, and walked with a limp, but, my, how she loved history, especially American history! And more amazing still, she taught a group of antsy high school kids how to love it right along with her. Her enthusiasm was contagious.

I remember a lot of things Mrs. Allen taught us, but one statement she made is still etched in my brain these many years later. "Students," she told us, "there are two things you can do with history: You can ignore it, or you can learn from it."

Years later, I encountered the words of a cynic who said, "There is one thing we have learned from history, and it is that we have not learned anything from history." That's unfortunate, isn't it? But if you allow for a bit of exaggeration, in principle, he's often right.

Think about the lessons you learned ten, maybe fifteen years ago. Isn't it remarkable how you're still trying to master the same subject material you thought you had nailed down so long ago? We humans are like that. We struggle to learn on a permanent basis life-changing lessons from the mistakes of our forefathers. Instead, we tend to repeat them.

And we're not alone. That was true even among the ancient Hebrews. That's why Paul wrote to a group of first-century believers, "For I do not want you to be unaware, brethren, that our fathers were all under the cloud and all passed through the sea" (1 Corinthians 10:1).

The apostle emphasizes that all of the Israelites who left Egypt with Moses had seen God's hand in great fashion and in a grand display. As we saw in the previous chapter, the Lord led them with a cloud by day and fire by night and wondrously delivered them from bondage in Egypt through the sea. All of them lived to see that mighty miracle with their own eyes. But in verse 5 the apostle tells us, "With most of them God was not well-pleased."

Don't miss that! All of them saw the cloud. All of them went through the sea. All of them actually *experienced* that mighty Red Sea deliverance. But God was not well-pleased with most of them, "for they were laid low in the wilderness."

And then Paul warns us, "Now these things happened as examples for us, that we should not crave evil things, as they also craved." In verse 10 he adds, "Nor grumble, as some of them did, and were destroyed by the destroyer." And then he wraps up his instruction by repeating his warning: "Now these things happened as an example, and they were written for our instruction, upon whom the ends of the ages have come."

When Paul says, "these things happened as examples for us" (v. 6) and "these things happened to them as an example, they were written for our instruction" (v. 11), he is teaching us that not only were the Israelites making history, they were making history for *our* benefit. They took a few tests and failed, and God recorded their scores that we might learn not to do as they did. God did not give Israel a wilderness experience simply to live and die by; He permanently carved their experience into living truth, called the Bible, that we might learn from history and not ignore it. Like reading a powerful epitaph on a granite gravestone, we must learn a lasting lesson from this segment of Hebrew history.

Perhaps you are saying to yourself, "Well, I don't experience too many 'wilderness' problems anymore. I've been through all that. I've come to the place where life is pretty much a downhill slide." If you feel like that, then verse 12 is written for you: "Therefore let him who thinks he stands take heed lest he fall." Pay attention! Even you can learn from history, because our heavenly Father often repeats His messages by taking us through wilderness experiences, just to keep us trusting Him.

SING IT OUT!

After God drowned Pharaoh's entire army in the sea, for the first time in history Israel found herself living in the Egyptian desert, out in the open, completely on her own. The Hebrews had begun their journey to the land of Canaan. God had proven Himself faithful; the nation had walked through the sea on dry land. How awestruck they must have been! As a result, they sang a song of great praise to God. All the way from verse 1 to verse 21 of Exodus 15 they continue to sing. That section of Scripture records this scene:

> Miriam, the prophetess, Aaron's sister, took the timbrel in her hand, and all the women went out after her with timbrels and with dancing. And Miriam answered them, "Sing to the Lord, for He is highly exalted; the horse and his rider He has hurled into the sea."

Have you ever done that? Have you ever, on the spur of the moment, scratched out a song of praise to the Lord? I recommend it to you; it's actually an exciting experience. You say, "Well, Chuck, that's fine for you, but I'm not some kind of eloquent, creative poet. I don't have that ability. Words don't flow through me like that."

Really? How do you know if you never try? The next time you go through an experience, and God proves Himself faithful, stop and think, *Maybe I could write a song.* (Even if it's for an audience of One.) That's how praise songs are born. You and I are living in a beautiful era, when God's

231

people are expressing their praise to God by writing all kinds of new songs and choruses, and even a few fresh hymns. That's what the Israelites were doing in this passage; we're just getting back to it these days.

On the heels of this Hebrew song of triumph and gratitude comes a word denoting a particular time: *"then."* When? After the Red Sea. After the first flush of freedom. After their wonderful song of praise. Scripture records, *"Then* Moses led Israel from the Red Sea, and they went out into the wilderness of Shur."

What a description of the Christian life! All of us have been through the Red Sea. Spiritually speaking, believers have all been placed in God's family through the cross. We have come to know the Lord Jesus. And in coming to know Him we have been delivered for the first time from bondage to the old life. How glorious! Freed from the domination of our old master, we have been given a new song, a new life, a new beginning. But in this beginning we quickly discover we must endure some wilderness experiences. Looking back, we later realize they were deserts designed by God for a very real purpose. But what a come-down after our Red Sea conversion.

BABY STEPS IN THE DESERT

As we consider Israel's first days in the wilderness, perhaps we should remind ourselves of where the Hebrew nation is in Exodus 15. They began their journey in the land of Goshen. If you have a map of that area handy, you might want to glance over it as you pinpoint their location. The Red Sea (or Sea of Reeds) is north of the Gulf of Suez. They crossed that sea, then began a south-southeasterly journey toward Mount Sinai. But before they arrived at the mount of God, they reached the wilderness of Shur in the northernmost section of the Sinai Peninsula. That's where the cloud and fire led Israel into the wilderness, with the shepherd Moses out in front of the flock. It was a vast expanse of desolation stretching south to the wilderness of Etham.

A little later in Exodus 15 we'll read that the Hebrews came down to the wilderness of Sin (better pronounced "Zen"). Clearly, they're in the wilderness—Shur, Etham, Sin. And in the midst of their journey, they will come upon a nice oasis named Elim. We'll pick up on that later.

So that's where the Hebrews were. But *why* were they there? If God took the people through the Red Sea, couldn't He take them immediately to the land of Canaan? Of course! If He was able to part the waters, and enable them to walk on dry land, and deliver them from the Egyptians, wasn't He also able to move them swiftly to the borders of milk-and-honey-land? Absolutely! God can do anything. If He can take you and me through our conversion, He can hasten our journey across this earthly desert and swiftly deposit us into heaven. No problem.

And by the way, wouldn't that be magnificent? Imagine: You come to know Christ, you know nothing of the difficulty of growing into spiritual maturity, no battles, no conflicts, no suffering…and *zing*, suddenly your feet touch down on golden pavement with the songs of angels in your ears. Just as soon as you accept Christ and say "amen," *swoosh!* You're in His presence.

You say, "Well, I'm not so sure about that. I'd like at least to get a taste of the Christian life on earth." That taste really can be wonderful, unless you happen to find yourself in the midst of severe trial. When you're being tested—really tested—you long for heaven. You *ache* for heaven. Many people who have written so compellingly of heaven through the years have been those most bruised by the hurts and heartaches of this earth.

Why does God put us through wilderness experiences before Canaan? For one thing, He wants to test us. That's why God led Israel into the wilderness, according to Deuteronomy 8:2: "You shall remember all the way which the LORD your God has led you in the wilderness these forty years, that He might humble you, testing you, to know what was in your heart, whether you would keep His commandments or not." (Read that again…only this time, slowly.)

God puts us in the wilderness to test us, to stretch our spiritual muscles. Our earthly wilderness experiences are designed to develop us into men and women of faith. Let's face it, our spiritual roots grow deep only when the winds around us are strong. Take away the tests, and we become spiritual wimps. But bring on the wilderness winds, and it's remarkable how we grow, as our roots dig firmly into faith.

THE WILDERNESS IN MINIATURE

Exodus 15:22–27 presents us with the wilderness in miniature. For *forty years* the Hebrew people went through a cycle of events illustrated in these few verses.

First comes the cycle of *abundance*, where the people of God look up. God proves Himself abundantly faithful, and they look up in praise. That's the first part of chapter 15, where Israel sings praises and shouts, "He took us through the Red Sea!" They're looking up.

Second comes *expectation*. When the people of God enjoy abundance, they expect *continued* abundance. They look ahead anticipating wave after wave of blessings. Maybe you have done that recently. God has expressed His grace in a tangible way, and you enjoyed an abundance of something. If you don't watch yourself, you will begin to expect that abundance as your own personal *right*. That's unrealistic and wouldn't even be good for you. I'm sure when Israel left the Red Sea and went out into the wilderness, the people expected continued abundance and continued miracles that would keep them comfortable, safe, and satisfied. They were riding the glory train to Canaan, and nobody imagined that it would grind to a halt along the way. They were looking ahead, anticipating abundance.

That leads us to the third step in the cycle, *disappointment*. Here the people of God look down. Feel the disappointment described in verse 22:

> Then Moses led Israel from the Red Sea [that's *abundance*], and they went out into the wilderness of Shur [there's *expectation;* they looked for another Red Sea experience]; and they went three days in the wilderness and found no water *[disappointment].*

The Israelites began to look down and found no water. They fixed their eyes on their circumstances. Even the water they finally located was bitter and undrinkable. "Therefore it was named Marah" (verse 23). *Marah* is the Hebrew word for "bitter." That made the situation even worse. The Hebrews at last found water, but it was brackish and bitter to the taste. Try as they might, they couldn't choke it down. It was like dying of thirst in the middle of the ocean, with only undrinkable salt water all around.

Their frustration left them disappointed.

That disappointment leads to the fourth step, *complaint*. Verse 24 tells us, "the people grumbled." Caught in the vise of regret mixed with resentment, they looked back. When you complain and grumble as a child of God, it usually occurs because you're looking back to easier days.

That brings along the fifth step in the cycle, *provision*. It's called grace. You don't deserve it, understand, but often when we're fussing and fuming, God steps in to provide us with what we need. That is what happened to the people of Israel. They looked around, and suddenly God stepped in and graciously met their need. "Then he (Moses) cried out to the LORD, and the LORD showed him a tree; and he threw it into the waters, and the waters became sweet. There He made for them a statute and regulation, and there He tested them" (v. 25).

Note especially the last three words: "He tested them." That's why they were in the wilderness in the first place. No child of God "just happens" to move into the wilderness; God sovereignly designs the wilderness as a test, including *your* wilderness.

Verse 26 deserves special attention. We could write across this verse, "Learn from history":

> And He said, "If you will give earnest heed to the voice of the LORD your God, and do what is right in His sight, and give ear to His commandments, and keep all His statutes, I will put none of the diseases on you which I have put on the Egyptians; for I, the LORD, am your healer."

A book published many years ago called *None of These Diseases* took its title from that verse. The Lord told the Israelites, "If you walk in obedience to Me I'll surround you with My protection. You'll be tested, but I promise I'll come through with every provision that you need. I won't say yes to all your greeds, but I will satisfy all your needs." Hence verse 27 tells us, "They came to Elim and there were twelve springs of water, seventy date palms, and they camped there beside the waters." What a wonderful climax! First, the wilderness . . . finally, the water.

Let's review the whole cycle to make sure we have a firm grip on it.

Abundance... *we look up.*
Expectation... *we look ahead.*
Disappointment... *we look down.*
Complaint... *we look back.*
Provision... *we look around.*

It's like an imaginary wheel in time that turns around and around. You and I are somewhere on that wheel right now. Often we begin and end at the same place, only to repeat it. Why? (We're back where we started this chapter.) Because we *don't* learn from history. We should, but in our frail humanity, we don't.

A TRIO OF TESTS

Let's cut to the chase. I dedicate the balance of this chapter to all grumblers. You know who you are. Candidly, I have found myself in your ranks more times than I wish to admit. Exodus 16 and 17 give three life-illustrations of the very cycle we just studied. God put His people through three circumstances—three enduring tests that are worth our attention: time, hunger, and thirst.

The test of time

Verse 1 begins, "Then...." When? After they had been at the oasis, after they had enjoyed the dates, relaxing in the cool shade of the trees, sipping fresh water from the spring. It was *then* the first test occurred.

> Then they set out from the oasis at Elim, and all the congregation of the sons of Israel came to the wilderness of Sin, which is between Elim and Sinai. It was on the fifteenth day of the second month after their departure from the land of Egypt.

Time has passed. If you read the previous passage in chapter 15 with a careful eye, you observe that it took them only three days to find the water they now enjoyed. But now it's been a month and a half—over forty days! I call that the test of time. There they are in the midst of the wilderness with their unrealistic expectations. "We thought we were through with those parched days in the wilderness. We were already there *three days*. Why do we have to go back?"

And guess what? Out rushed the complaints: "The whole congregation of the sons of Israel grumbled against Moses and Aaron in the wilderness" (16:2). Why were they grumbling? Again, they were looking back. Listen to their words in verse 3: "Would that we had died by the LORD's hand in the land of Egypt, when we sat by the pots of meat, when we ate bread to the full; for you have brought us out into this wilderness to kill this whole assembly with hunger" (v. 3).

They're thinking back to those days when there was plenty, when they enjoyed afternoon siestas over a fresh fish sandwich made with Jewish bagels back in "good ol' Egypt." They had all they could ask for and then some.

Sound like your life? If so, it's time to learn a timeless lesson. If you focus on the past, it won't be long before complaints start oozing from your lips. You will remember a long-ago time, bathed in the hazy, rosy glow of memory, when something was easier and more comfortable than it is today. And as you compare then and now, I guarantee it, you will grumble.

I do this; so do you. But it's so foolish! We look back nostalgically on what was once a pleasant situation, at which time (even then!) we were looking back longingly on a more pleasant earlier time. That's dumb, isn't it? You may be grumbling right now about your current situation. But chances are good that two years from now you'll be looking back on *this* moment and saying, "Oh for the good old days! Boy, it was great back then, wasn't it?" We somehow forget that in March of this year we grumbled because we were focusing on February of last year, at which time we grumbled because we were focusing on January of the year before, but that wasn't as good as April of the year before that. *Stop!* We live in light of some dreamy past leisure or pleasure, when in actuality God continues to show Himself strong all along the way. We feel that because we have endured the current test, we shouldn't have to experience it again.

It hurts to endure life's trials, and it hurts worse to repeat such episodes. Yet, without those deep hurts, we have very little capacity to receive godly counsel or make forward progress toward maturity. The test of time is perhaps the most rugged of all.

Over the long haul, God is honing us through such tests. Stretching us. Breaking us. Crushing us. Reducing us to an absolute, open-armed trust, where we say, "Lord, I have come to the end of my own flesh. If You wish me to die in this wilderness, here is my life. Take it. I refuse to look back and complain about where I find myself at this moment. Moses had learned to wait. His congregation needed to learn as well.

The exam continues, as the people of Israel discovered.

The test of hunger

In the last part of verse 3, the Israelites whine, "You have brought us out into this wilderness to kill this whole assembly with hunger." They got hungry; predictably, they started complaining. Yet even though His people were grumbling, God graciously answered their need. He told Moses, "Behold, I will rain bread from heaven for you; and the people shall go out and gather a day's portion every day, that I may test them, whether or not they will walk in My instruction" (v. 4).

What an interesting announcement. "I will meet your need for hunger, but the meeting of that need will bring another test." Have you found that to be true? I have. We find ourselves in the midst of some predicament that we cannot escape. So God says, "I'll provide the way out; I'll show you the way." We accept His answer, His new direction, which introduces us to a whole *new* set of tests and trials of a different kind. So while we are relieved of one wilderness problem, we gain a new one. That's what happened here.

> So Moses and Aaron [knowing that the manna was on the way] said to all the sons of Israel, "At evening you will know that the LORD has brought you out of the land of Egypt; and in the morning you will see the glory of the LORD, for He hears your grumblings against the LORD; and what are we, that you grumble against us?" Moses said, "This will happen when the LORD gives you meat to eat in the evening, and bread to the full in the morning; for the LORD hears your grumblings which you grumble against Him. And what are we? Your grumblings are not against us but against the LORD." (vv. 6–8)

With patience wearing thin, Moses and Aaron say, "Let's get this straight, folks. Who are *we,* that you grumble against *us?* Look, we're just people—flesh and blood, the same as you. Furthermore, this wasn't *our* idea! *We* didn't lead you into the wilderness. That was God's direction. *We* didn't put that cloud up there. *We* didn't light that pillar of fire! So don't complain against *us.*"

Are you prone to complaining? Remember, *God* is the one who has made your circumstances to be what they are. Don't blame someone else. It is helpful to remember that your grumblings go right back to the Lord. Your complaints land at His feet.

Many years ago I heard a children's choir sing a song that really lingered in my mind. Our younger daughter, Colleen, back then a little freckle-faced girl, was standing there on the front row singing this song. She looked over at me several times during the song, and I thought, *Hey, this is a good song for me to hear. I think maybe she's singing that song to me.* The song was called "Grumblers" by Thoro Harris. I still remember its lyrics:

In country, town, or city, some people can be found
Who spend their lives in grumbling at everything around;
O yes, they always grumble, no matter what we say,
For these are chronic grumblers, and they grumble night and day.

They grumble in the city, they grumble on the farm,
They grumble at their neighbors, they think it is no harm;
They grumble at their husbands, they grumble at their wives,
They grumble at their children [that's when she looked at me],
   but the grumbler never thrives.

They grumble when it's raining, they grumble when it's dry,
And if the crops are failing, they grumble and they sigh.
They grumble at the prices and grumble when they're high,
They grumble all the year around, and they grumble till they die.
[Another glance!]

O they grumble on Monday, Tuesday, Wednesday,
They grumble on Thursday too,
Grumble on Friday, Saturday, Sunday,
They grumble the whole week thru.[1]

Ouch! Pretty convicting, isn't it? Some of us make grumbling a habit, even though we may cover it up on Sunday. Whether we're moving along in traffic or have been served a late meal, whether we're planning a last-minute arrangement with someone or working with a difficult group, we're given to complaining and grousing. It's like we have "the gift of grumbling" and feel we ought to exercise it, with gusto!

The only problem is, that *gift* never appears in God's Book. Let's get this straight, folks. There is no gift of grumbling. Neither is there a gift of criticism. The Bible never affirms our griping and snipping and barking over daily situations. Amazingly, the people of God can grumble even when God provides them with food in abundance. Why? Because it isn't the food they preferred. We wanted steak; He provides *bologna*. We preferred lamb; He serves us *liver*. In so many ways, our responses are just like Israel:

> So it came about at evening that the quails came up and covered the camp, and in the morning there was a layer of dew around the camp. When the layer of dew evaporated, behold, on the surface of the wilderness there was a fine flake-like thing, fine as the frost on the ground. When the sons of Israel saw it they said to one another, "What is it?" (vv. 13–15)

Keep in mind, those Hebrews had never read the Book of Exodus, which means they had never heard about manna. This was the first appearance of heaven's catering service. God brought it from above and delivered it to the ground like dew. When they woke up in the morning they looked around and said, "What *is* that?"

> For they did not know what it was. And Moses said to them, "It is the bread which the LORD has given you to eat." (v. 15)

240

"You wanted bread," Moses says to the Israelites. "Well, have at it. There's a wilderness full of it." Verse 35 tells us, "The sons of Israel ate the manna forty years, until they came to an inhabited land; they ate the manna until they came to the border of the land of Canaan." That's what I'd call an abundance.

But you know what? They didn't like that either. Here they were in the middle of the wilderness, with plenty of bread. It just wasn't the bread they preferred. They *loathed* it, even though Psalm 78 calls it "angel's food." Every morning the angels brought down this heavenly-catered meal and spread it before them. The Israelites didn't have to work for it. They didn't have to grind the flour, knead the dough, or bake it over the fire. All they had to do was eat it, but still they didn't like it. Do you know why? Because they looked back and compared it to what they once enjoyed. And so they grumbled:

> "We remember the fish we ate in Egypt at no cost—also the cucumbers, melons, leeks, onions and garlic. But now we have lost our appetite; we never see anything but this [yech!] manna!" (Numbers 11:5–6, NIV, brackets mine)

Just imagine: They baked it, boiled it, broiled it, put it in sandwiches, ate it raw, cut it up, made dumplings out of it—everything you could think of, until there was nothing left to do with it. They never went hungry, but you know what? They *still* didn't like it.

That's the way grumblers are. They gripe when they don't have it, but when they get it, they gripe because it isn't their preferred variety. And when they get their preferred variety, they gripe because they'd rather try something else.

To be painfully honest with you, that is the response of *carnality*. When God graciously chooses what we are to eat, gives us an abundance of it, and we don't like it, by and by the old flesh kicks in, and we gag on His provision. Operation carnality!

The test of thirst

Exodus 17 gives us a third part to this exam:

> Then all the congregation of the sons of Israel journeyed by stages from
> the wilderness of Sin, according to the command of the LORD, and
> camped at Rephidim, and there was no water for the people to drink. (v. 1)

Before, there was no relief from the heat. Next, there was no food. Now,
there's no water. And how do the people respond? Do they complain as
before? Yes, but this time it gets even worse. Verse 2 tells us, "Therefore
the people *quarreled* with Moses."

The dissatisfaction and carnality have escalated. "Quarrel" is a stronger
word than "grumble." Before they said, "Who will give us food?" And they
grumbled. Now, they threaten. They frown and angrily command Moses,
"Give us water that we may drink!" And Moses says to them, "Why do you
quarrel with *me?*" Who did they think he was, anyway? How could *he* provide
them with water? If they had a quarrel with someone, it was with the Lord.

"Why do you test the Lord?" Moses asks them. Realizing how
short-sighted they were, he attempted to turn their eyes on the Lord. That's
the job of a spiritual leader by the way—to consistently and repeatedly turn
his people's eyes to the Lord. Moses does this beautifully all way through
the Exodus. He wants the Israelites to look to God, not to him, and certainly not to their circumstances. That's why he warns them repeatedly
about "testing the Lord." But they refuse to listen: "The people thirsted
there for water; and they grumbled against *Moses* and said, 'Why, now,
have *you* brought us up from Egypt, to kill us and our children and our
livestock with thirst?'" (v.3).

Moses knows a threatening scene when he sees one. Therefore, he cries
out to the Lord: "What shall I do to this people? A little more and they
will stone me" (v. 4). These are not the exaggerated words of a frightened
leader; this is the literal truth. The people had grown so angry that they
were ready to kill their leader.

And once again, in the midst of disappointment and complaint, God
graciously answers with abundance:

> Then the LORD said to Moses, "Pass before the people and take
> with you some of the elders of Israel; and take in your hand your

staff with which you struck the Nile, and go. Behold, I will stand before you there on the rock at Horeb; and you shall strike the rock, and water will come out of it, that the people may drink." And Moses did so in the sight of the elders of Israel. He named the place Massah and Meribah because of the quarrel of the sons of Israel, and because they tested the LORD, saying, "Is the LORD among us, or not?" (vv. 5–7)

When you boil grumbling down to its basic common denominator, you realize it is actually asking the Lord, "Are You here, or not?" It is a case of open, unrestrained, verbal doubt. Because Moses wanted the people to remember their error, he named the place Meribah, "quarrel," to remind them with Whom they argued. Whenever they told the story at some future time, they'd have to remember their quarrel with God. Like some of our slogans of the past couple of centuries, "Remember the Alamo," "Remember the Maine," "Remember Pearl Harbor," Moses was saying "Remember the Meribah." In other words, "Remember when you quarreled and argued with the living God."

I can't help but be impressed all over again at Moses' outstanding leadership.

AFTER THE EXAMS

What lessons can we learn from these unsettling experiences in the wilderness? At least three come immediately to mind.

It takes a humble attitude to learn from earthly tests.

God not only wants us to *endure* tests, He wants us to *learn* from them. But we don't learn without humility. The proud don't learn. In fact, Proverbs says, in effect, "Don't even bother to beat a fool. He won't learn from the beating"(see Proverbs 28:26). The fool isn't humble. The fool remains proud. And so the fool stews in the juices of his own ignorance.

Some of you can read about these events, get up, and resume your life of grumbling as though you had never heard God speak. It can happen in any believer's life, anywhere in the world, going through any test. Biblical truth works, but it must be applied, regardless of your circumstances. Humility accelerates the learning process.

It takes a heavy attack to break a daily habit.

Daily habits are not easily broken. (Some call those habits "addictions.") And nothing is set in concrete more deeply than "Egyptian habits." The Israelites had feasted on a diet of Egypt, and they loved it so much they simply could not be satisfied with anything less. Or make that, they *would* not be satisfied. That is why God brought them through the cycle time and again, year after year.

Have you said to yourself lately, "Why don't we get *through* this situation and get on to something else?" Do you know why we don't? Because we refuse to learn from the same wilderness experience. Somehow, we just won't let it penetrate our hearts. But God never wastes His time or His tests on His people. He knows how long to plan the test, how often to repeat it, and how difficult the examination must be.

It takes a heavenly appetite to enjoy a heavenly diet.

An earthly appetite naturally responds to a heavenly diet with grumbling. Of course! Carnality hates God's catering service. It takes a heavenly appetite to accept heavenly food. You cannot order such an appetite through the mail, call an 800 number and get it through UPS, or pick it up on the sale table at your local Christian bookstore. A heavenly appetite comes only from heaven; the Lord is the one who will reshape your desires as you kneel in submission and obedience before Him.

YOUR WILDERNESS GOES WITH YOU

Each of us has his or her own wilderness cycle. Some struggle with a quiver full of small children at home. Others have no children. Your test is not related to the home at all; it may be connected to your employment. With some it's wrestling with relationships; you're abrasive and have difficulty with people. That's why God keeps you *with* people and grinds away so that your long-standing Egyptian habit might be altered. With others it's finances; you live continually under the gun of insufficient funds. With others it's a problem related to academics and school issues. That's your wilderness.

Years ago, while speaking at a college in Florida, I had a question/answer session with several students. As we wound down the session late that evening, one student asked a question that set me back in my chair a bit. He asked, "What's it like out in California? Is it really as good as I hear? Is anybody ever tested in California like we are in Florida?" He was serious! It was so typical of how some idealistic students view their world.

We laugh when we read such a question because we rightly wonder, *What does it matter?* If we were suddenly to pull up our roots and move to Tahiti (great idea, huh?), we'd carry with us the same cycle. It wouldn't be long before we'd repeat it in Tahiti. Move to Miami or Seattle, Boston or San Diego, North Dakota, central Mexico, China, or Chile, and the story would be the same. Why? Because we carry ourselves with us wherever we go... and therein lies the rub.

Your wilderness does not separate from you merely because you fly several thousand miles to some other spot. Wherever you go, your Egyptian appetite goes with you. God is in the business of not only putting you through the Red Sea at salvation, but in getting you to Canaan by way of the wilderness. Conversion is often a brief trip to the altar, but maturity is always married to time.

Remember that this week. You have never lived the seven days in front of you, and you will never live 'em again. Life is like a coin. Spend it any way you want to, but you can spend it only once. God would like you to learn from your experience in the wilderness. He wants to change your appetite, change your habits, change your style and, in the process, change your entire life.

As I've been saying, such deep, inward changes do not suddenly occur; they begin at the cross, where you lay down your arms and accept God's gift, Jesus Christ. Now may be your time to say, "Lord Jesus, this is Your moment. I give You my heart, my life, as Your child."

May we never forget the lessons of history, whether they be our personal history or the history of ancient Israel. And may we heed the words of my high school history teacher, Mrs. Allen: "There are two things that you can do with history: You can ignore it, or you can learn from it."

Learning from the past may be hard, but continuing in ignorance is expensive. Better to learn those priceless lessons today than to search for pennies in the scorching wilderness tomorrow.

CHAPTER FOURTEEN

Why Leaders Crack Up

Wherever in the world I have traveled to minister, I have found leaders struggling with a similar problem. Whether it's California, Wisconsin, Florida, Venezuela, Mannheim, or London, this thorny issue springs out of the soil and winds its way around the ankles of leader after leader, slowing their progress, tripping them up. It's a phenomenon that touches the lives of camp directors, presidents of schools and teachers, pastors and campus workers, business people and homemakers. What is it?

It's the problem of delegation. It occurs when leaders try to do too much on their own, when they neglect to bring others into the job to help them shoulder the load.

That may not sound like a very spiritual subject, but it carries serious spiritual overtones. When you are overworked, drained, and exhausted because you have not delegated your workload as you should have, irritation sets in. And following close on the heels of irritation comes confusion, a loss of vision, burn-out, and, tragically, sometimes even loss of family.

For whatever reason, this seems to be a special peril connected to

Christian work—the feeling that one must labor more than he should so as to assuage lingering guilt or to somehow win the approval of God or someone on earth.

We are not alone with this problem; Moses encountered exactly the same difficulty. And I am impressed with God's servant who faced this dilemma and did something about it.

A close look at Exodus 18 can benefit you, regardless of your job or profession. The lessons from this episode in Moses' life apply to everyone—the Christian businessperson, the Christian professional, the Christian teacher, the Christian student, all of us who have areas of responsibility—and especially those of us who tend to do more than we should to accomplish our responsibilities. Exodus 18 is a study in leadership with a solid emphasis on the fine art of delegating.

A WARM REUNION

It all began with a visit by Moses' father-in-law. Such a visit might raise the blood pressure of those who picture their spouse's parents more as *outlaws* than in-laws, but Moses actually welcomed Jethro. Over the years, his father-in-law had probably become one of Moses' best friends:

> Now Jethro, the priest of Midian, Moses' father-in-law, heard of all that God had done for Moses and for Israel His people, how the LORD had brought Israel out of Egypt.
> ...Then Jethro, Moses' father-in-law, came with his sons and his wife to Moses in the wilderness where he was camped, at the mount of God. He sent word to Moses, "I, your father-in-law Jethro, am coming to you with your wife and her two sons with her." Then Moses went out to meet his father-in-law, and he bowed down and kissed him; and they asked each other of their welfare and went into the tent. (vv. 1, 5–7)

Now, that's what I'd call a warm greeting. What an enthusiastic welcome! Moses hasn't seen Jethro for an extended period of time, and

Israel's leader is ecstatic that his father-in-law is coming with Moses' wife and children for a family reunion. Soon the two men began to talk about all that God had done in Moses' life since he left the desert:

> Moses told his father-in-law all that the Lord had done to Pharaoh and to the Egyptians for Israel's sake, all the hardship that had befallen them on the journey, and how the LORD had delivered them. (v. 8)

What a treat that must have been for Moses. Since he first walked into Pharaoh's court with the warning of that first plague, who had he been able to unload on? When you're the leader, it isn't always easy to let down your hair and be real. God's timing in sending Moses' family along was especially gracious. He needs a caring sounding board at this particular time in his life.

Note how Jethro responded to his son-in-law. He showed not an ounce of jealousy. In fact, Jethro rejoiced over what had happened:

> Jethro rejoiced over all the goodness which the LORD had done to Israel, in delivering them from the hand of the Egyptians. So Jethro said, "Blessed be the LORD who delivered you from the hand of the Egyptians and from the hand of Pharaoh, and who delivered the people from under the hand of the Egyptians. Now I know that the LORD is greater than all the gods; indeed, it was proven when they dealt proudly against the people."

And then, in good priestly fashion, Jethro topped off the day by offering sacrifices: "Then Jethro, Moses' father-in-law, took a burnt offering and sacrifices for God, and Aaron came with all the elders of Israel to eat a meal with Moses' father-in-law before God" (v. 12).

What a loving family situation. Here we have in-laws and family members who have come alongside Moses to eat together and rejoice in God's mighty works. I love scenes like this where family members sit around the supper table, enjoying each others' company.

It's a wonderful thing to be rightly related to family members. In-law relationships often figure prominently in sarcastic jokes and snide remarks, but it's a marvelous tribute to the grace of God when warm communion of heart and soul exists between those in the family.

I think if my wife's mother had lived on, she probably would be one of my greatest supporters and fans. She loved me before I ever amounted to anything. She believed in me. I didn't have to prove anything or do anything for her to love me. Tragically, she died of cancer in her mid-forties. I believe if her days had been lengthened and she had lingered in life, she would have been a magnificent encouragement through my years of ministry, as would my father-in-law, with whom I enjoyed a meaningful relationship. Now that I'm associated with Dallas Seminary, I long for that same support and dynamic in the lives of the men and women training for ministry. What a welcome and needed source of encouragement and affirmation. Unfortunately, it is often missing.

We find in Exodus 18 a father-in-law who came alongside his son-in-law to rejoice in what God had done in his life. That same evening when Jethro offered sacrifices to God, it was as if he were saying, "I praise You for blessing my son-in-law like this." If you are a parent in a similar situation, don't underestimate the importance of your support to daughters and sons-in-law and the children who follow after.

After the joy of this happy reunion, Jethro begins to observe Moses in his ministry and leadership. The next day he becomes an objective consultant, a silent partner in Moses' life.

FATHER KNOWS BEST

Let's stop and take a look at what Jethro observed:

> It came about the next day that Moses sat to judge the people, and the people stood about Moses from the morning until the evening. Now when Moses' father-in-law saw all that he was doing for the people, he said, "What is this thing that you are doing for the people? Why do you alone sit as judge and all the people stand about you from morning until evening?" (vv. 13–14)

Great question, Jethro. You're starting to sound like a perceptive consultant! *What is this thing you are doing?* The Living Bible phrases it, "Why are you trying to do all this alone, with people standing here all day long to get your help?"

Have you noticed how a visitor can walk into a situation and sometimes offer an insight that has never occurred to those who've been on the scene for years? Some person fresh off the street gets a tour of the facility and asks an innocent question: "Have you ever considered doing so and so? It might streamline the operation—maybe save some time and expense?" And everybody looks around at each other as if to say, why didn't *we* think of that? If someone with insight and good common sense could watch the way you do your job, it's quite likely that person could help you perform your tasks in a better, more innovative way. You've been doing that job for so long you've formed habits that are time-consuming and aren't all that efficient.

That is what happens with Jethro. He watches as his son-in-law takes his seat as judge. He sees the long lines of people stretching out beyond the tent, waiting to get inside to hear Moses' counsel. As Jethro stands watching this human zoo and stroking his beard, two insightful questions emerge in his mind—questions he asks his son-in-law at the first opportunity.

1. "What is this thing that you're doing?"
2. "Why do you do it all alone?"

His first question relates to priorities. His second relates to personnel. "To begin with, Moses, what are you doing with your time? I see these people lined up waiting on you from morning until evening. What are you doing in a job like this? Is this the best use of your time and gifts? Furthermore, why are you carrying the load solo?"

As you look into the next few months of your own life, ask yourself those two questions. *What am I doing with my time? What are my priorities?* And second, *Why am I doing so many things all alone? Why don't I shift some of that load to others, training them to do it for me or with me?*

To his great credit, Moses gives Jethro's question an honest, straightforward answer. "Because the people come to me to inquire of God. When they have a dispute, it comes to me, and I judge between a man and his neighbor and make known the statutes of God and His laws" (vv. 15–16).

You can't fault Moses for his answer. It was the plain truth. He wasn't rationalizing, he wasn't defensive, he didn't try to bathe it all in a holy glow. He simply said, "Look, I've got a big job. It's as simple as that. I'm called of God to be the judge, to serve over these people. They have a series of complaints, and I'm the complaint department. They come to my desk, and they have to wait until I can get to 'em, one by one. It's an enormous job, Jethro. You need to understand that."

And once again, Jethro responds in a direct, forthright way. "The thing that you're doing is not good," he says (verse 17). Now, to say such a thing took some courage. It would be something like you or me stepping into the White House and giving the president a piece of our mind regarding how he runs the country. Now, maybe you'd like very much to do that, and it's possible you would have some insightful counsel for him that he would be wise to heed. But it would take *a lot* of courage.

In a real way, Jethro's comments took even more courage, for Moses was not the duly elected leader of his people; he was God's appointed vessel. To be specific about it, he hadn't been elected to the job, he was drafted by heaven. He had led Israel through the Red Sea. He had struck the rock and water burst forth. Everyone knew he was God's servant. It was through him that God performed some magnificent miracles.

Yet Jethro dared to say to him, "Moses, what you're doing isn't good. I don't like what I'm seeing here."

The church can never succeed without courage. It takes courage even for close friends to counsel strong leaders, or for elders to hold pastors accountable. That goes for the business world, too. Leaders in business are wise to remain open to the counsel of staff members. No one has all the answers. Of course, not every suggestion will be worth implementation, but usually something will at least be worth consideration. Leaders are wise to open the gate of counsel and say, "I'm listening to what you have to suggest. I'm willing to hear you." It takes humility, but it is both wise and safe. That's what Moses did with his father-in-law.

Which brings up another, more personal question: Are you open to the counsel of your relatives? I think it is highly significant (and sad) that people often seek the counsel of their pastors before they seek the counsel of their parents. They consider what a pastor might say far more significant than what a parent might say. Just a question: When was the last time you went to your parents or in-laws for counsel?

No doubt one reason this worked so well in Moses' family was that Jethro knew his son-in-law inside and out. Remember, Moses had worked for him for *forty years*. Jethro knew Moses' tendencies. He knew his work habits. He knew his strengths, his weaknesses. Those years afforded him some built-in knowledge of that man. So he didn't hold back when he said, "You're not doing the right thing." And then he tells him why: "You will surely wear out, both yourself and these people who are with you, for the task is too heavy for you; you cannot do it alone" (v. 18).

The word translated "wear out" comes from a Hebrew term that means "to be withered with exhaustion" or "to sink or drop down, languish, wither and fall." Isn't that vivid? "If you keep this up, you're going to fade away, Moses. Look, you're already starting to wither. If you don't make a change, you're going to get old and wrinkled. Don't forget young man, you're more than eighty years old!" Jethro warned him, "Look son, you're going to come to exhaustion. And so are the people. I mean, after all, their needs can be met in a lot better way than just standing around in line all day in the hot sun to hear your counsel. You're going to wear out, Moses, unless you make a few changes around here."

This text convicts me like few others.

I, too, am guilty of trying to do too much. These words from Exodus 18 confront my own life. Were it not for the wise counsel of staff members who have surrounded me through the years, and an insightful wife who doesn't hesitate to speak the truth, I would have worn myself to a frazzle a long time ago. (As it is, I still tend to do too much. It's hard to slow down Type A's who have good health along with a lot of energy and drive).

And what happens when a person does too much, works too many hours, and stays at it too many days a week? To begin with, he loses his distinction. You and I are gifted in particular areas. When we try to add additional elements to our basic makeup, we weaken our best efforts. The exercise of our highest-priority gifts begin to suffer because we begin to pad them or add other things to them. Soon our priorities get shifted. Our energy gets drained. We lose direction and—sad, but true—we can even begin to lose control of our families.

In fact, the family is often one of the first to suffer from a parent's excessive workload. I wonder if that isn't one of the reasons the apostle Paul added to the list of qualifications for minister, "one who rules well his own household." Paul asks, "If a man does not know how to manage his own household, how will he take care of the church of God" (1 Timothy 3:5)? Could this explain why so many family members of pastors lose their way? Could it explain why so many kids of "great Christian workers" overtly turn off to spiritual things?

I know of two boys, the sons of a pastor, who did the most insulting thing imaginable to their father's grave. While he was alive, this famous dad added so much to his workload that he couldn't give his sons the time of day. They grew up hating the very gospel their dad spent his life preaching.

It's easy to do this in the pastorate. You can draw water for the baptistery, set thermostats, open and close all the committee meetings, mop the floors, stuff envelopes, light the candles for the wedding, choose the tablecloths for the receptions, visit all the sick, dedicate all the babies, and on and on. It happens not only here in the United States but in overseas mission work as well.

Years ago, Dr. Richard De Haan wrote the following words in a booklet entitled, *Men Sent from God:*

> Some time ago I read an article in which the pastor of a church described his activities during a certain day, supposedly typical of his usual routine. It went something like this: Arriving in the church office at 8 o'clock in the morning, he had intended to spend at least two hours in preparation for his Sunday sermons, a noonday talk at a service club, and five radio talks during the coming week. However, he was reminded by his secretary that he had agreed to write an article for the church bulletin, scheduled to go to press at noon that day. He was also obligated to make three telephone calls. After finishing with these duties, only thirty minutes were left for the preparation

of the messages, since at 10 o'clock he was to meet with the Program Committee of the Ministerial Association.

Just as he began to study, again he received word that the mother of the President of one of the Women's Societies in the church had passed away, and his presence was needed. This, of course, caused him to miss the meeting with the Ministerial Association; but he was able to attend the 12:30 luncheon of the Women's Auxiliary. Following this he spoke to a study class at 1:00. At 2 P.M. he officiated at a wedding ceremony. At 3 o'clock he began his regular visit of the city hospitals. He finished just in time to make the Men's Supper that evening where he gave the invocation. The supper lasted till 7:30, allowing the pastor to get away just in time to attend a meeting of the Every Member Canvas Committee that night. He was on hand simply to make suggestions and boost the Committee morale. Having done that, his day of service was finally ended and he arrived home exhausted, about 9:30 that evening.[1]

And then Dr. De Haan adds this comment, "This was a pastor's own account of the way in which he spent an entire day. Now, without any reflection upon, nor criticism of, this man, since I do not know all the circumstances, I would ask: Was he fulfilling his God-given obligation as a pastor of that church? Is this the way in which God intended that man to spend his day? When a man assumes a pastorate, is he justified in spending most of his time in administrative meetings, board meetings, committee meetings, budget meetings, building-program meetings, luncheons, dinners, banquets, *ad infinitum?*"

The answer is obvious. Pastors must maintain basic priorities to do their jobs rightly. But even in that, they need help.

When I first met with representatives of the First Evangelical Free Church of Fullerton, California, back in the early months of 1971, to discuss becoming that congregation's pastor, I was surrounded by some ten or eleven men on the pastoral search committee. We talked realistically about priorities and the importance of family life, of a pulpit ministry, and of time to prepare heart and soul. They promised at that time—and never went back on their promise—that whatever it took to fulfill staff needs, they would meet those demands so that the ministry of prayer and of the Word of God might not suffer. That was the secret of my survival.

Some churches never learn! Failing to think in broad terms like that, board members are notorious for "getting the most for their money" when it comes to the responsibilities of pastoral ministry. But I thank God those folks with whom I met both knew and practiced a wiser approach. I could say the same of those who interviewed me prior to my accepting the call to Dallas Seminary.

It's that kind of counsel Jethro was giving Moses. So he said, "My son, it isn't good what you're doing. Now listen to me." It took guts to say that. But let's not think Moses' father-in-law was obnoxious about it. He didn't stick his bony finger in Moses' face and demand, "You listen up, whipper-snapper! I have something to say to you!"

No, Jethro was a wiser man than that. Gently but firmly, he said, "I shall give you counsel, and God be with you" (verse 19). In other words, "Son, I'm going to tell you what I think might work better for you. But may God give you the wisdom to do what's right." And then he gave Moses two pieces of advice.

MAKE TEACHING A PRIORITY

You be the people's representative before God, and you bring the disputes to God, then teach them the statutes and the laws, and make known to them the way in which they are to walk and the work they are to do. (vv. 19–20)

In other words, "Moses, you have a teaching ministry. When you minister, explain the plan and will of God. Let the people know what God's Word is all about, so they might hear and imbibe those spiritual truths. Don't force all of 'em to wait in line to hear it from you one at a time. There are too many of them. You teach them as a community."

In a very real sense, counseling is one aspect of an effective spiritual leader. But doesn't counseling occur when God's Word is taught? When a well-trained, Spirit-filled man opens God's Book and declares truths from that eternal text, I'm convinced that people receive counsel from God. The Book of Hebrews tells us that "the word of God is living and active. Sharper than any double-edged sword, it penetrates even to dividing soul and spirit, joints and marrow; it judges the thoughts and attitudes of the heart" (Hebrews 4:13, NIV).

You get biblical counsel from God's Word. And that counsel continues and is supported and strengthened when the pulpit ministry is surrounded by the ministries provided and led by additional staff. I have never seen it fail that when a preacher embroils himself in administrative details and a morass of secondary callings (important as they may be), his pulpit ministry suffers. The pulpit weakens whenever a man turns to secondary areas and begins to be consumed by them. Of course, these things must be done by qualified people. *But they cannot be done by one man.* That is the first lesson Moses needed to learn. And the second lesson applied the first:

DELEGATE THE WORKLOAD

Furthermore, you shall select out of all the people able men who fear God, men of truth, those who hate dishonest gain; and you shall place these over them as leaders of thousands, of hundreds, of fifties and of tens. Let them judge the people at all times; and let it be that every major dispute they will bring to you, but every minor dispute they themselves will judge. So it will be easier for you, and they will bear the burden with you. (vv. 21–22)

Great counsel! Jethro displayed tremendous wisdom in his fatherly advice, and Moses followed suit by listening attentively.

Now, I want you to notice something that I never saw until I began studying this text for this book. Jethro said, "By delegating the job, Moses, it will be *easier* for you, and they will bear the burden with you."

Did you see that word? *Easier.*

The Christian worker is a strange breed. He or she wants it to look as if the work is terribly hard. In fact, the more difficult and strained the look, the better. Christian workers are notorious for what I call the "tired blood" look, better known as the overburdened "missionary image," or maybe even the exhausted "over-burdened religious image." They usually carry an old, worn-out Bible, and walk with a slump, listing to port. They seldom smile—sort of a "please pity me" image. Makes me want to gag.

I don't mean to be super critical. The tragic reality is, some of these folks are overworked and hardly have enough to live on. But I believe you can be in full-time ministry without having to resemble the stereotype. As one of my mentors, Dr. Howard Hendricks, often says, "You can be a Fundamentalist, but you don't have to look like it."

I once had the most delightful time in Venezuela with missionaries who didn't fit the "sad banana" role. They looked like normal, everyday people. You really wanted to be around them. You found yourself going to bed in the evening and saying to yourself, "Hey, that was fun. I so enjoyed my time with these folks. I can't wait until tomorrow!" We actually laughed and told jokes and really relaxed together. They were just *regular* folks.

We can learn a valuable lesson from these dear people. The Christian is not some stoop-shouldered, anemic excuse for humanity. Just because you go into the ministry doesn't mean you should look as if you've just finished your last funeral, and you're next in line. *Honestly!* It's easy to pick up "the look" in seminaries or Bible schools. That's where some learn how to "look humble," then they just slide into the ministry and go downhill from there. And that's too bad.

The happiest people on earth ought to be those in God's service. And they ought to *look* like it. We have every reason to smile more than anyone else. Even though our work is terribly serious, we ought to have more fun and have a better time doing it than anybody in any other career or calling on earth. I think an individual in cross-cultural ministry or a pastor ought to be able to enjoy his or her taste in music and live it up, just like anybody else. Those vocational servants of Christ ought to have broad tastes and interests beyond their basic calling, enjoy their families, enjoy times away, and rejoice in good things. That's why I sometimes suggest to a group of pastors, "Hey, get a Harley!" Talk about shaking up the troops!

Yet it's almost scandalous to say such things, isn't it? Why isn't it being said? Because we operate under an eighteenth-century concept of so-called piety in the ministry that simply is not biblical. It is no sign of spirituality that you work fifteen to eighteen hours a day, seven days a week, and never take a vacation. No one is attracted to an unsmiling, always-grim-looking individual, especially if he never takes a break to enjoy life. You'll crack up if you maintain such an insane schedule. It is no sign of spirituality that you groan your way through life, looking humble and wanting everybody to be impressed with your rundown, overworked, underpaid, haggard appearance. Get a life!

Frankly, those who look as if they've just finished their last piece of bread do not minister to me. Those who minister to me, and those to whom I think I minister, are men and women who truly enjoy life. We really don't need to focus on the negative or the intensities of life; there are enough heart-breaking experiences to go around for all of us.

That's why it's such a pleasant twist when we get to hear from people like Jethro. "Moses, you do this and it'll be *easier* on you," he said. Imagine! Jethro told Moses that God wanted it be easier on him. Now that's what I call rare advice.

Please don't misunderstand me. Ministry is not an easy calling. There *are* times when you must work longer than you should. And those times can occur back to back. But we don't need to remind most pastors of the need to work harder. They need a reminder of another sort. "You're making your job harder than it should be. Share the load. Lighten up! Your work needs to be easier. Let us help you get these things done."

A LISTENING EAR

So much for Jethro's advice. How did Moses receive it? Glad you asked. The good news just keeps getting better: "Moses *listened* to his father-in-law, and did all that he had said" (verse 24).

Can you believe it? Moses' stock goes up in my book about ten, maybe twelve points, right there. His father-in-law said, "Listen to me, Moses," and he listened. "Do this, Moses," and he did it. That's why, by the time Moses was buried, the scriptural record says he "was very humble, more than any man who was on the face of the earth" (Numbers 12:3). No man, no woman is so great that he or she cannot learn from someone who has their good at heart. "Moses listened to his father-in-law." And he was a better man for it.

Scripture also tells us that Moses put Jethro's good counsel to work right away: "Moses chose able men out of all Israel and made them heads over the people, leaders of thousands, of hundreds, of fifties and of tens. They judged the people at all times; the difficult dispute they would bring to Moses, but every minor dispute they themselves would judge. Then Moses bade his father-in-law farewell, and he went his way into his own land" (vv. 25–27).

What an eventful visit! It changed the course of events in the history of Israel. Not only was Moses encouraged and strengthened, not only did he lose a few wrinkles, but others shared in the leadership, and the people began to be ministered to in a far more effective way.

FOUR THOUGHTS TO GROW ON

This biblical account reveals at least four practical insights or principles for bringing our lives and our leadership back into sanity and balance.

Separate the "essential" from the "additional"

Every responsibility or job entails these two critical factors. The *essential* areas involve your calling, which you are not to delegate. You do these tasks to the best of your ability and take whatever time you need to do them right. It's the *additional* part that gives us trouble. We *like* to do more. So we add more and more until finally we reach the breaking point.

Yes, some of us can accomplish a great deal single-handedly. Sir Edmund Hillary, the famous British mountain climber who was first to conquer Mount Everest, once said, "Even the summit of Everest is not beyond the capacity of an unassisted man. But the risks are enormous."

Are you willing to risk health, career, family, and future ministry to push yourself to the limit? In his fine book *Spiritual Leadership*, J. Oswald Sanders spends an entire chapter on the art of delegation. In my opinion, every Christian (leader or not), ought to study that chapter. Listen to his wise words: "The principle is that God assumes responsibility for enabling

His man to fulfill every task to which He has appointed him. Now there are some self-imposed tasks which others can do better than we, and we should relinquish them. But even should they do them worse, we should still relinquish them—a severe test for the perfectionist!"[2]

When you know how to do the job better than anyone else, it is difficult to hand it over to someone who's still learning, who may drop the ball, who sometimes fumbles and trips and requires a clean-up team in his wake. But that's the price you pay, and it is well worth it. It's either that or crack up. Our real problems tend to occur not in our essential area, but in those additional areas that we take on and attempt to maintain.

Restrain yourself more, involve yourself less

As the workload increases, the wise leader doesn't get busier, he gets smarter. He asks for help. This is hard to do when you grow up with a ministry. When you start with a group of six or eight families, and it grows to one hundred, then three hundred, five hundred, then ultimately, fifteen hundred, the one who nurtured the original dream tends to want to keep the ministry small in philosophy. That control tendency is often reinforced by members who remember "the early days." Yet a growing metropolitan ministry must learn to think in a metropolitan way with metropolitan dreams—not foolish, extravagant, extreme dreams, but dreams broader and much different from the ones that reigned when the family was small, simple, and tight-knit.

As a ministry grows, it is easy for leaders to get more involved and increasingly busy, when, in fact, it is wiser to seek out more help from the gifted men and women in the pews. I find it significant that when you study the life of our Lord Jesus in the Gospels, you can't find a single place where it says Jesus was in a hurry. You never read, "Now when Jesus heard this, He immediately went into a rush...." Never happened. He got His men involved, but He never lost sight of His core values or primary mission. I think we could learn something from Him, don't you?

God's servants are not exempt from natural laws

Just because you're a servant of the Lord does not mean you won't get an ulcer or crack up if you refuse to delegate. You cut the corners of good health, and you pay the penalties, just like the rest of humanity. You might be amazed to know how many pastors and pastors' wives develop serious emotional disorders because of this persistent refusal to share the load. We are not immune or exempt from the consequences of an unhealthy lifestyle. The body needs so much work, so much rest, so much relief, and can handle only so much strain. Disregard that, and something snaps.

An old Greek motto states, "You will break the bow if you keep it always bent." Jethro saw weariness on the face of his son-in-law and said, "Look, relinquish some of your duties." Because Moses followed his father-in-law's wise counsel, he didn't wear out. I believe it became easier for him. Moses probably started looking younger. In fact, by the end of his life (at one-hundred-and-twenty!) it could be said of Moses, "his eye was not dim, nor was his vigor abated" (Deuteronomy 34:7).

Efficiency increases as we relinquish

Doing more does not guarantee effectiveness. A much better standard of efficiency is how much we are able to delegate.

It's time for a personal confession. Exodus 18 contains an important message for me. I am a strong, natural leader, and I tend toward covering too many bases. With my high-energy make-up, I could easily take on more than is healthy. Through wise counsel I am discovering the importance of delegating tasks so that I might accomplish my essential calling. I'm grateful for the counsel I have received from those who have helped steer me toward the right path.

WHEN JETHRO SHOWS UP, *LISTEN*

Are you tired of adjusting window shades and licking stamps and driving buses and duplicating tapes and running off Sunday bulletins and doing the hundreds of needful things that any willing servant can do? If so, maybe it's about time that you backed off and took a long look at your short life. Maybe it's time for you to determine what is *essential* and what is *incidental*.

If you're able to enjoy the incidental without hurting the essential, great! But if a trusted counselor is telling you it's time to make a change, listen. I know it's hard to say no when you love to do everything. But if you don't listen to your Jethro and determine to give up some of the things that are wearing you out, you'll pay a terrible price. So will your family.

Ask your Lord to help you know how to say no graciously, how to turn off that drive to add more and more work to your already overloaded schedule. The Lord Jesus Christ is able to give us balance and purpose and discipline. He was the most balanced individual who ever lived. And it is He who gives the counsel that comes through Jethro to Moses and then to us. You can do only so much.

There's nothing spiritual about a heart attack or, worse, an early grave.

CHAPTER FIFTEEN

Sinai: Where Moses Met God

C an you name the most important priority in life? Stated another way, what is the single most important investment you will ever make in all your days on earth?

I have considered those questions many times during the course of my life. Those are the sorts of probing, penetrating queries you begin to ask yourself after coming to faith in Jesus Christ. After making a serious study of Exodus 19, however, I began to ask them in a more urgent, heartfelt way.

At first reading, some might call this an irrelevant section of Scripture. You might ask yourself, "How could I locate life's most important priority in a place like Exodus 19?" And yet it's there.

Moses' meeting with God can teach us much about our own meeting with God. We will discover that the time we spend with the Lord as His children must become Priority Number One.

IN THE SHADOW OF MAJESTY

Exodus 19 opens in the shadow of Mt. Sinai, in the place where the sons of Israel met together before the Lord. But before the people could meet with God, before Moses could climb that mountain to hear and receive God's revelation, Israel had to be properly prepared. A significant part of their preparation had to do with where they met: "In the third month after the sons of Israel had gone out of the land of Egypt, on that very day they came into the wilderness of Sinai. When they set out from Rephidim, they came to the wilderness of Sinai and camped in the wilderness; and there Israel camped in front of the mountain" (vv. 1–2).

Chances are that few of us have ever been or ever will be at Sinai—that series of solid granite peaks soaring into the desert sky at the base of the Sinai Peninsula.

Earlier in this book, I mentioned *God's Wilderness*, the large, pictorial volume my sister gave me. It features several pictorial pages of Sinai. One photo of the southernmost area of the Sinai range carries the following caption: "The awe-inspiring granite peaks at the southern tip of the Sinai Peninsula seem to form a gigantic fist of God proclaiming: 'Here! Here!' The ever-changing, ever-deepening colours of the mountains in this part of Sinai invest this indescribably beautiful region with an aura of sanctity, and one can well believe that here God appeared to Moses."

And then the book adds, "Israeli scholars, who explored the Peninsula in the brief period of Israeli occupation, came to experience a holiness pervading Sinai's mountains, and they believe that it was in this region that the Israelites encamped when the Law was given."[1]

How can we possibly imagine the majesty of such a place? This is a massive, craggy range of mountains—solid granite, gray with all the hues of deep purple, the blackness of night, and the silence of space. Yet that's where Israel, with the ink still wet on their national statehood papers, pitched their tents. Sinai was an important spot in God's plan. The Israelites gathered as a people, approximately two million strong, to hear God's voice in the shadow of these great peaks that reach no less than eight thousand feet heavenward like a gigantic fist.

I have always loved walking along the crashing surf. I take delight in the wild loneliness and the subtle changes of light in the desert lands. But nothing can compare to the mountains to describe the majesty of our Creator. Jutting out above the floor of that great wilderness lies the towering peaks called Sinai, where God planned to meet the people He had redeemed from bondage and now claimed as His own.

God, however, does not quickly run into someone's presence—nor must we thoughtlessly barge into His presence. There is no place for a sleepy, careless attitude in contacting and communing with the living God. We must prepare ourselves for it. The Israelites certainly needed to do so. Remember, they had been grousing and grumbling all through their wilderness journey to this point. What kind of preparation, then, did God require?

PREPARING TO MEET GOD

Exodus 19:3–15 lists four prerequisites God made of His people before they could meet with Him. He brought them to His chosen place of meeting, but before He would give His revelation to them, He required them to do four things:

1. Be willing to obey

> Moses went up to God, and the LORD called to him from the mountain, saying, "Thus you shall say to the house of Jacob and tell the sons of Israel: 'You yourselves have seen what I did to the Egyptians, and how I bore you on eagles' wings, and brought you to Myself. Now then, if you will indeed obey My voice and keep My covenant, then you shall be My own possession among all the peoples, for all the earth is Mine; and you shall be to Me a kingdom of priests and a holy nation.' These are the words that you shall speak to the sons of Israel." (vv. 3–6)

God wanted to be sure His words did not fall on deaf ears. He required His people to display an attitude of willingness: "Lord, I want to obey what You say."

Basing their opinions on Cecile B. DeMille's classic movie *The Ten Commandments,* many people assume that Moses climbed that mountain once, got everything, then came back down with the stone tablets tucked

267

under his arm. A careful study of Exodus, however, shows he actually made *seven* trips. He climbed up and down, up and down, up and down—a very busy man. And he took care of these matters before he ever had his forty-day vigil in God's presence to receive God's handwritten Word.

In his first journey up the mountain, God said, "I want to be sure the people are willing to obey." So Moses came back down the mountain to call "the elders of the people together, and set before them all these words which the Lord had commanded him" (verse 7). And how did they respond? Imagine two million people in unison saying, "All that the Lord has spoken we will do" (verse 8)! That's what they did. "Are you willing to obey?" Moses asked them. "Yes, we're willing," the people responded. Their voices must have echoed through those massive stones. So Moses climbed back up the mountain.

2. Be sensitive to listen

> The Lord said to Moses, "Behold, I will come to you in a thick cloud, so that the people may hear when I speak with you and may also believe in you forever." Then Moses told the words of the people to the Lord. (v. 9)

The Lord told Moses, "Not only do I want the people to be willing to obey, I want them to be sensitive to hear when I speak. That will cause them to believe in you, Moses, when they hear what I am saying."

Now, what is God doing? He is laying the groundwork for communication. He laid out a solid base, a structure of receptivity. They were to be ready to hear. They were to be willing to obey. He did not hasten to reveal His truths before the people were ready to hear it and obey it. But now they demonstrated they were ready for the next step.

3. Consecrate your hearts

> The Lord also said to Moses, "Go to the people and consecrate them today and tomorrow, and let them wash their garments; and let them be ready for the third day, for on the third day the Lord will come down on Mount Sinai in the sight of all the people.... So Moses went

down from the mountain to the people and consecrated the people, and they washed their garments. (vv. 10–11, 14)

Their clean garments were to reflect clean hearts. No soil was to dirty their souls. They were to be clean and pure, without and within. Wearing clean apparel, they were to be ready to hear God.

And then God spoke again: "You shall set bounds for the people all around, saying, 'Beware that you do not go up on the mountain or touch the border of it; whoever touches the mountain shall surely be put to death. No hand shall touch him, but he shall surely be stoned or shot through; whether beast or man, he shall not live.' When the ram's horn sounds a long blast, they shall come up to the mountain" (vv. 12-13).

God instructed Moses to erect a boundary, a fence, a secure and sacred barrier around the mountain so the people would not wander too close.

4. Show a deep respect for God's presence

Moses went down the mountain once more and prepared the people as God had instructed. Then, on the third day, the chosen time arrived. The Lord descended in fire on the mountain and called Moses up for another conference. Soon He sent him back down with this urgent message: "Go down, warn the people, so that they do not break through to the LORD to gaze, and many of them perish" (v. 21).

Only those whom God specifically called were to scale the mountain; all others were to stay below. "Moses said to the LORD, 'The people cannot come up to Mount Sinai, for You warned us, saying, "Set bounds about the mountain and consecrate it"'" (v. 23).

So deep, so profound must be this respect for God's holy presence that no one was even to *touch* the mountain. The people were to wait upon God to speak to Moses and hear the Lord's words through the Lord's servant.

A GOD TOO SMALL?

What a needed reminder! This passage makes it clear that we live in a day of pitifully shallow concepts of God. Some of today's contemporary Christian music leaves the impression that God is our buddy—a great pal to have in a pinch. A film star has said of God, "He's the great Big Daddy upstairs." One pop song asks, "What if God were just a slob like us?" That is not the biblical view of God. That is man's feeble attempt to make God *relevant*.

Do you hear the cheap twang of such a concept of God? These small ideas of Him diminish the beauty of His holiness. Although their desire is to make Him relevant, all such efforts cheapen and degrade the holiness of God. Yet here in Exodus 19 we find the God of the Scriptures so insistent upon maintaining an elevated, exalted position that He marks off a boundary, warning His own people, in effect, "Do not cross that line. Do not become glib with Me. Do not become frivolous in My presence."

For years I have considered the hymn "Immortal, Invisible, God Only Wise" as one of the choice songs of the church. Unfortunately, you don't hear it much anymore. Consider some of its meaningful lyrics, full of substantive theology:

> Immortal, invisible, God only wise,
> In light inaccessible hid from our eyes,
> Most blessed, most glorious, the Ancient of Days,
> Almighty, victorious, Thy great name we praise.

And I love the second stanza even more than the first:

> Unresting, unhasting, and silent as light,
> Nor wanting, nor wasting, Thou rulest in might;
> Thy justice, like mountains, high soaring above
> Thy clouds which are fountains of goodness and love.

The Puritans, that rigorous people of old, possessed a solidly biblical concept of God. Do you know why it is so crucial for us to recover such a respectful understanding? Because a shallow view of God leads to a shallow life. Cheapen God and you cheapen life itself. Treat God superficially, and *you* become superficial. But hold God in profoundest respect, and it is remarkable how deep the roots of your spiritual life grow.

I am deeply concerned over the shallowness of our spiritual walk in the American church today. Spiritual depth is rare in these landmark days at the turn of a millennium. Our time with God might as well depend on a flip of the coin—heads I do, tails I don't. If I feel like it, great. If I don't, well, He's a God of grace; He understands. Frankly, I do not find such accommodating nonsense in Scripture—certainly not in a passage like Exodus 19.

God is holy. Exalted. He is the only wise God, the Creator, the Maker, the sovereign Lord. He is the Master. He tells me what to do, and I have no safe option but to do it. There is no alternative, no multiple choice. We have but one directive, and that it is to do His will. We reaffirm that truth in our times with Him.

When Isaiah saw the Lord, he had to crane his neck to a God high and lifted up. When Joshua came upon Him at the banks of the Jordan, he immediately fell before His feet. When Ezekiel saw Him, he found no words to describe Him, groping within the limits of language to depict Him in the clouds among shining wheels that spun in the glories of heaven.

But not today. Today He's our pal, our understanding buddy, our ever-available bell-boy. No, He is not! The Lord is our God. He does not bow to our hurried pace, but in silence He waits for us to meet *His* demands. And once we slow down enough to meet Him, He is pleased to add incredible spiritual depth to our shallow lives.

One man expressed his reverence like this: "The heaviest obligation upon the Christian church is to purify and elevate her concept of God until it is once more worthy of Him. In all her prayers and labors this should have first place. We do the greatest service to the next generation of Christians by passing on to them undimmed and undiminished the noble concept of God which we received from our Hebrew and Christian fathers of generations past."

What has been *your* concept of the Lord? Who is *your* God? Be honest, now. Does He look anything like the God of Mount Sinai?

WHEN GOD CAME DOWN

I think it is highly significant that when the Sinai meeting began, it was not Moses who went up, but God who came down. When we prepare for our meeting by fulfilling God's requirements, He comes down. He accomplishes the contact. It pleases Him intensely when His children properly prepare for their encounters with Him.

Scripture says: "The LORD came down on Mount Sinai, to the top of the mountain; and the LORD called Moses to the top of the mountain, and Moses went up" (v. 20). And what was it like up there? It's worth a closer look:

> So it came about on the third day, when it was morning, that there were thunder and lightning flashes and a thick cloud upon the mountain and a very loud trumpet sound, so that all the people who were in the camp trembled. And Moses brought the people out of the camp to meet God, and they stood at the foot of the mountain. Now Mount Sinai was all in smoke because the LORD descended upon it in fire; and its smoke ascended like the smoke of a furnace, and the whole mountain quaked violently. When the sound of the trumpet grew louder and louder, Moses spoke and God answered him with thunder. (vv. 16–19)

What a magnificent experience! If you live in an area shaken by earthquakes, you feel a little ripple now and then, get a funny feeling, and then life returns to normal. But how often do you see a granite mountain shaking, or hear constant thunder rumbling from lightning strikes between clouds and earth, or shrink before the long blasts of heavenly trumpets announcing that God is ready to meet you?

Just your regular, ho-hum quiet time, right? In no way. Can you imagine how Moses felt when the Lord said to Moses, "Come up, Moses"? Wow! If you were Moses, what would you do now? How would you do it? How could you carry on? I'll tell you how: with fear and trembling Moses made that historic journey up into the clouds. He'd stood before a burning bush, but that was nothing compared to this epochal experience. The writer of Hebrews says, "So terrible was the sight, that Moses said, 'I am full of fear and trembling'" (Hebrews 12:21).

WHY THIS MEETING?

Why did God want to meet with Moses? The text gives us two good and healthy reasons. They serve as strong reminders for us.

To establish a healthy fear of the Almighty

> Moses said to the people, "Do not be afraid; for God has come in order to test you, and in order that the fear of Him may remain with you, so that you may not sin." (Exodus 20:20)

A healthy fear of God will do much to deter us from sin. When we have a proper fear of the living Lord, we live a cleaner life. Any born-again person who sins willfully has momentarily blocked out his fear of God. You and I can do that. When we actively engage in sin, we consciously put aside what we know to be the truth about God. We suppress the knowledge of Him in our hearts and minds. We lie to ourselves by saying, "We'll get by. God won't mind so much." Yet God used Moses to reveal to His people a reverential and healthy fear of the Almighty.

At the risk of sounding as if I am grinding an ax, I must say that this wholesome fear of the Almighty has turned up missing in our era. And when it is absent, we think we may do as we please. You can live as you please if you know you're not being seen and you won't get caught. But if, down deep inside, you *know* there is a loving and holy God who will not let you get away with sin, you will avoid sin at all costs. That is exactly what the Lord wanted to establish first with the people of Israel—a holy, righteous, pure, and respectful concept of His presence.

When you come to that understanding, and God's light breaks into your life like the pure whitewater of a rushing river, you learn to thoroughly hate and dread those actions that will plunge you again into darkness. The psalmist expressed that thought with these words: "How sweet are your words to my taste, sweeter than honey to my mouth! I gain understanding from your precepts; therefore I hate every wrong path. Your word is a lamp to my feet and a light for my path" (Ps. 119:103-105, NIV).

To communicate written instructions for the people

> Now the LORD said to Moses, "Come up to Me on the mountain
> and remain there, and I will give you the stone tablets with the law
> and the commandment which I have written for their instruction."
> So Moses arose with Joshua his servant, and Moses went up to the
> mountain of God. (Exodus 24:12–13)

Isn't it great that God gave His people written instructions to obey?
This is the first time in all of history that God *wrote down* His Word.
Until the time of Moses, the written Word of God did not exist. But now,
here it was. And to think, you and I possess those written words! What an
awesome and majestic thought. How we take that privilege for granted.

Back before the collapse of the atheistic Soviet Union, my friend John
Van Diest represented the Evangelical Christian Publishers Association at
the Moscow Book Fair. The authorities had granted them reluctant permission to hand out a limited number of Russian language New Testaments,
and long lines of people waited in line to receive a copy. When the supplies
were exhausted, one desperately disappointed man asked if he might have
one of the empty boxes that had once held those Testaments.

"But there's nothing in there!" John protested. "The Bibles are all
gone!" With tears glistening in his eyes, the man replied, "Then I at least
want the box." The Bible was so precious to this man that he treasured
the cardboard box that had held the Scriptures. May our eyes be opened
to the astonishing privilege that is ours to hold the complete written Word
of God in our very hands.

WHAT DID GOD REVEAL?

Now we know why God met with Moses. But what did He reveal? Verse
12 tells us the first revelation: He revealed *His written word.* The first thing
God gave to this man who met with Him was His truth in written form.
He took the time to inscribe it in stone. He broke off a chunk of that Sinai
granite, honed it down so Moses could handle it, and chiseled His revelation
into it with His own finger. It was one of the few times in Scripture we

find God writing anything. He wrote the Law and gave it His autograph: "When He had finished speaking with him upon Mount Sinai, He gave Moses the two tablets of the testimony, tablets of stone, written by the finger of God" (Exodus 31:18).

No one has ever had in his possession a more valuable document than this. Moses possessed the very autograph of Deity—the *autographa* from God's own finger.

A second revelation is described in Exodus 25:8–9. After God revealed the written Word, He revealed the *design of the tabernacle*: "Let them construct a sanctuary for Me, that I may dwell among them. According to all that I am going to show you, as the pattern of the tabernacle and the pattern of all its furniture, just so you shall construct it" (Exodus 25:8–9).

God gave His people the Word of God that they might know His mind and obey. He gave them the design for the tabernacle that He might come and dwell among them. He didn't want to remain aloof high up on a mountain. He wanted to make Himself accessible and available, but, in keeping with His own design, He would dwell in a certain place called the tabernacle.

PRIORITY NUMBER ONE

Within these passages that may seem so dated to our modern tastes, we can gain a grip on some highly significant information. These verses suggest that the number one priority for you this year, the one factor that will determine more than anything else your ability to live a life of victory, is *meeting regularly with Almighty God.*

We've met the Lord. We've been through the Red Sea. We've come through the wilderness, but perhaps we haven't yet come to that mountain, to that place of meeting where we consistently and regularly have time with Him. We often glibly refer to this meeting as a "quiet time." But those meetings with God aren't always quiet. A better expression might be a time of "devotional strengthening."

These passages about Moses' meeting with God suggest four principles that we can apply to our own walk of faith.

1. *To meet regularly with God, you need a place.*

I find it intriguing that the very first thing mentioned in Exodus 19 is that the people came to a *place* where they met with God. If you happen to have a mountain in your back forty, that might be a good place to meet the Lord on your own. Climbing that peak every day would probably do wonders for your spiritual *and* physical health. If a mountain peak isn't practical, however, you might find a handy rock or stump on the grounds of some beautiful Christian conference center. Then again, if you wait for an opportunity like that, you'll not meet with God on a consistent basis. If you wait to meet with God until you can get a reservation at a log cabin by the lake or up in the mountains tucked into a cave or by thundering surf along a smooth white beach, you're going to spend a lot of time wandering through life distant from Him. You need a place that's accessible. Somewhere you can go every day.

Remember, when the Israelites came to the mountain, they were in the wilderness. They camped in the wilderness and that is where they met with God. You need to find a place where you "camp"—namely, your dwelling. You need a place in your home or apartment where you can meet with the Lord.

Let me be even more practical than that. You must *provide* yourself with that place. You need only four things: a desk, a light, your Bible, and quietness. It may be in your bedroom, where you can close the door and be alone. It may be in a corner of your den or at your kitchen table. But wherever it is, you need your own quiet place where you can be all alone with God.

Our family has been convinced of this for a long time. In fact, in our previous home in California, we built it into the decor of our home. Each one of our children had a desk, not a big, massive, attractive thing, but a place to write, equipped with a chair and a light. That was one of the first pieces of furniture we provided for each of their rooms. We provided it even before they knew why they were getting a desk. And we helped them know what to do when they were at the desk with the Lord. It was their rendezvous spot with God. We deliberately planted that into their thinking.

Children don't *just become* godly. They need training. Your kids will see what you do, and even attend church with you, but they will not know how to be godly children, young people, and young adults without being trained. So how about giving some time to that, if you're a parent?

I knew a young fellow from a large family who had no other place to meet with God, so he chose the closet. He rigged up a light, built in a small desk, and met with God there. Kind of close quarters, but it was quiet, and he was alone. At least it had a door! It was his place to meet with God.

The house in which I was reared was very small. My mom's place to meet with God was the bathroom. She put her books near the little stove that heated the room. When she met with God she put a little sign on the door that said, "Do not disturb," and we knew she didn't want to be bothered.

Busy mothers can't have their time with the Lord at breakfast or supper time. That creates havoc. They can't help but be disturbed. So if you're a mother, you have to be practical about this. Choose a time that works for you, but remember, you *need* time with God.

If you're a business person, your best place might be at your office. I know a businessman who goes to his office early every weekday morning just so he can spend time with the Lord. If you were to call him at that time, you would get his answering machine. You would not interrupt his appointment with God. That's his place.

Where is your place? You need such a place where you can sit down and enjoy some uninterrupted fellowship with your Lord. I warn you, if you don't arrange an appropriate place, you probably won't meet regularly with God. You can't have a good meeting sitting on the edge of your bed. You won't do it casually sitting on the arm of the sofa in the busy living room. You need a desk, you need a light, you need your Bible, and you need silence. And you must be firm, deliberate, and uncompromising in preparing a place for your time with God.

2. *You need to be prepared.*

You can't waltz into God's presence with a shrug. You can't amble into such a meeting with an idle mind, hands in your pockets, listening to a ball game on your Walk Man. No, the heart needs to be prepared. I don't care who you are, you can't suddenly prepare yourself in a few quick minutes.

Most of us have difficulty getting ready for our time with God due to all the things whirling through our minds. You need a good thirty minutes a day with the Lord, bare minimum. That's not asking too much. The good news is this: It will make *all* the difference in the rest of your day.

I have no desire for this subject to drift into the foggy realms of mysticism. As far as I'm concerned, it's as practical as getting dressed, eating breakfast, driving to work, or pulling weeds out of your flower bed. You and I need to meet with God every day. As believers, we draw our very life from Him. He's the Vine; we're the branches. Apart from Him, as Jesus bluntly told us, *we can do nothing* (John 15:5).

The Book of Exodus tells us that the people of God expressed a willingness to obey. That's a great place to start. When you sit down at your desk, silently pray, "Lord, I'm willing to obey You. I'm here not to play games, but to invest at least thirty solid minutes in listening to Your voice. I want to be sensitive. I don't care if anybody else knows I'm here; I want to hear what You're saying in Your Word." The Israelites had to consecrate themselves, remember? In the same way, you need to be forthright and explicit about the areas that aren't right between you and the Lord. Deal directly with Him, and in doing so, keep short accounts with sin. The Israelites even washed their garments.

I'll let you in on a secret about me. I don't do well in my time with the Lord if I'm physically dirty. I do better after a shower, early in the morning or late in the evening. I don't do well if, in the sweat of the day, or after I've mowed the grass, I try to sit down and immediately launch into my time with God. It doesn't work like that for me. My body needs to be clean. I need to get prepared to hear from God without being preoccupied with other things.

In order to get my mind and spirit tuned into the right direction, I sometimes keep a book of hymns and choruses near at hand. I've memorized a number of both the solid old hymns of the faith, as well as some of the more meaningful contemporary praise songs, and enjoy singing to the Lord during those moments. Since I can't always remember the words, I keep the songbook handy on my desk.

You can do something similar. Prepare yourself so that when God speaks, you can hear.

3. *To hear from God, you need the Scriptures.*

I'm impressed that God did not give Moses a revelation that said, "Go down to the people and give them a vision." If that had happened you would have had Israelites looking for visions from then on all over the desert. They'd hear visions and see visions and witness visions and share visions, and end up with *visionary mass confusion.* No, God gave His people the *Book.* He said to Moses, "Take these written truths and instruct the people." Objective: clear, easily-discernible *words.*

When you meet with God, open the Book. Don't rely on your memory; rely on those printed pages. And don't flip randomly from page to page or verse to verse, especially avoiding the old open-window method, where you allow the wind to blow your Bible open to some verse that you randomly take as your text for the day. You'll never discover God's mind and heart for you if you employ such a haphazard and irresponsible approach.

Start at the beginning of a book of the Bible and work your way through it, slowly and systematically. Read it aloud. Read it thoughtfully. Listen to what your lips say and ask Him to make what you hear come alive in your life. Block out everything else. Pray it. Personalize it. Sing it. Make it a part of your conscious thought, and forget everything else as you give that time to Him. Remember, it's top priority.

You say, "Well, Chuck, this is all fine, but really I've heard it before. This is nothing new."

All right, you've *heard* it. But why have you stopped *doing* it? I know it's nothing new. Our problem does not lie in finding something *new,* our problem lies in our neglect to practice known truth. As Peter wrote, "So I will always remind you of these things, even though you know them and are firmly established in the truth you now have" (2 Peter 1:12, NIV).

We all need reminding. Why? Because meeting regularly with God will have a major, recognizable impact on your attitude in marriage, your parenting, your career, your tongue, your evangelism, and your diligence in school. It's remarkable what this discipline will do to your study habits. I know, because when I neglect it, it isn't long before I pay a price.

4. *To remember what God says, you need a journal.*

So far you probably could have guessed ahead of time what I would recommend, but this one might throw you. You need a notebook; some people call it a "life notebook." But I'm not talking about some costly tome with gold leaves, embossed name on the front, and a beautiful, leather cover. All you need is a basic composition book that may set you back a couple of bucks. It's a personal, hand-written journal, not a daily diary. You're not recording what you have done, but what God is doing in you and through you. Time with the Lord needs to be accompanied by a pen and some paper. You will never regret cultivating this discipline.

Webster gives a super definition of a journal: "a record of current trans-actions, experiences, ideas, and reflections kept for private use." Now, let me give you a hint. Keep your journal private; don't let anybody read it. Journals are not written to be published; they're written to help us maintain our memory about what God is doing. A journal will help you remember what God has said. Last year you may have entertained some of the most powerful, profound thoughts in your times with the Lord that you have experienced in a lifetime of walking with Him, but they're all gone if you never took time to record them.

I have kept a journal ever since I studied the life of Jim Elliot, the martyred missionary whose testimony was so beautifully arranged by his wife Elisabeth in the book *Shadow of the Almighty*. That book is little more than a published volume of one man's remarkable journey with his God.

Once our kids learned how to write (and actually make sense in what they wrote), we began to teach them to keep a journal. That was a real breakthrough for each of them. We taught them, "God can speak to you, and we want you to put down what He is saying. Just a sentence or two is fine."

Are you wrestling with your romantic life? Are you seeking God's mate for you? Then record your desires. Talk about the man or woman with whom you believe God would have you spend your life. Talk about the wrestlings that accompany the challenge of finding that person. Put your wrestlings into writing. Add those qualities you're looking for. What a difference a journal can make.

One of the ways I have cultivated my pen through the years is by means of my journal. Many of the columns, articles, and books I have written grew directly out of seed thoughts and observations recorded in my *life books*.

Listen to Jim Elliot for a moment. What a gift from the Lord that we are privileged to peek over this godly young man's shoulder. He wrote,

> I walked out to the hill just now. It is exalting and delicious to stand embraced by the shadows of a friendly tree with the heavens hailing your heart and the wind tugging at your coattail. To gaze and glory and give oneself to God, what more could a man ask? Oh, the fullness, the sheer excitement of knowing God on earth, I cannot, if I never raise my voice again for Him. If only I may love Him and please Him, perhaps in mercy He shall give me a host of children, that I may lead them through the vast star fields to explore His delicacies. But if not, if only I may see Him, touch His garments, and smile into His eyes, ah, then, not stars nor children shall matter, only Himself.[3]

Have you ever been in an area of the country where there was a lot of fruit ripening in the sun? Maybe on some cool September morning you've taken a walk through the apple orchards of the Hood River valley, or along the Columbia River in Oregon. Or you've driven past groves of citrus trees, in California or Florida, their branches heavy with fruit. Where you live, the crop might be cherries or peaches, strawberries or raspberries, or even bananas and papayas. It is pleasing to the eye to see such an abundance of sweet, delicious fruit hanging on branch or vine, ready to be plucked. And the fragrance of that fruit makes your mouth water and fills your mind with pleasant memories.

A fruitful Christian life is like that—sweet, refreshing, nourishing, fragrant, sustaining, delightful to be near. But such a life requires careful cultivation of the soil, careful tending of the orchards, careful pruning of the vines. A deeper, more consistent walk with Christ requires time and attention every day. If that happens, you *will* bear fruit. You will experience fewer struggles with evangelism, attitude conflicts, relationship hang-ups, schooling, challenges, authority, or even finding God's will. That is why meeting with God is *priority one*.

A DETERMINATION TO BEGIN

Has the Spirit of God grabbed your attention? It's good to be emotionally moved when God brings a matter to our attention, but it's better to make a conscious decision to *do* something about it. Thinking good thoughts and dreaming good dreams is fine, but nothing really happens in your life until you step out in faith and obedience and make that first move.

Make a plan right now to keep a daily appointment with God. The enemy is going to tell you to set it aside, to do something else. He'll whisper, "You're far too involved with other things, far too busy." But every excuse he suggests is a lie.

If you're too busy to meet with the Lord, friend, then you are simply too busy. I repeat, you *must* carve out the time. Why not establish a plan before you go to bed tonight?

Moses is a man who met with God. He learned that it takes discipline and preparation to do so. It's one thing to know what to do; it's quite another to actually do it. How many of us take a course on prayer but never pray, or learn the techniques of evangelism but never share our faith? In this account of Moses' life we may have learned little new, but we have been confronted with some profound reminders from God's Word. We do not need a clever new technique nearly as much as a swift kick in the pants. We need a rebuke from the Holy Spirit, because we are so slothful and procrastinating and sleepy when it comes to climbing that mountain and meeting for half an hour with the Lord.

May He do a work in spite of us! Despite our bad track record, may He stop us this moment with the reminder that we could become far stronger men and women of God if we would only maintain a time of meeting with Him.

It may be on a craggy mountain peak, in a closet, or as with my own mother, in a locked bathroom with a "Do not disturb" sign on the door. God isn't particular in the least about the place you choose or the amount of time you spend. All He wants is you.

CHAPTER SIXTEEN

Grumblings Against a Godly Leader

One of the great mysteries is the perilous nature of godliness. All who pursue a close walk with God move into dangerous territory. We learned in the previous chapter how crucial it is to spend time with the Lord. Did you know you make yourself vulnerable by doing so? If you determine to invest your life in God and cultivate an intimacy with the Almighty, you're asking for it. You're marching directly into a minefield. It won't be long before you begin to experience what we could call "The Peril Principle."

Webster defines "peril" as "exposure to the risk of being injured; danger." Peril speaks of the *threat* of injury, not its certainty. An activity described as perilous doesn't inevitably happen, but it can.

Maybe you like to sail, and you have a small sixteen-foot vessel in which you put out to sea. On the ocean you face the peril of shipwreck. That doesn't mean you *will* be shipwrecked, it simply means the threat of shipwreck is very present. In the same way, if you drive too fast on a rain-slicked highway in the middle of a thunderstorm, you face the peril of a car accident. That doesn't mean you *will* have an accident, but the chances for it are great. Or suppose you like to play football and you make the team. Now you face the peril of a torn knee ligament or a broken bone. That doesn't mean you *will* get a broken bone, but it does mean you risk such an injury. The threat is intensified.

In this chapter, there is a simple axiom I want to develop from Moses' life: *Those who determine to walk with God become the target of the enemy.*

IN THE CROSSHAIRS

It may be that you have seriously decided to make fresh tracks in your walk with Jesus Christ this year. You have determined to awaken from your long sleep-walk and follow your Lord over new horizons. You framed a promise to God that said, in effect, "Lord, I want to spend time with You consistently. I want to meet with You. I want my life to become godly. I desire to honor Jesus Christ."

If you have made such a commitment, I can assure you that the host of hell has already gotten the word. You are now the target of enemy attack. You face a series of perils that could ultimately lead to injury in your spiritual life.

You are facing inevitable traps. You need not fall into any of them, but they will come. The New Testament makes this clear. Second Timothy 3:12 (NIV) says straight out, "In fact, everyone who wants to live a godly life in Christ Jesus will be persecuted." The Amplified Bible translates the verse like this: "All who are determined to live a devoted, godly life will meet persecution (that is), will be made to suffer because of their stand."

That's a strange promise, but it is a promise nonetheless. Most promises are encouraging; this promise we might call realistic. It says that if you determine to live in a godly way, you will face tests intended to put your decision on the stand.

Peter records a similar promise. He writes, "Be self-controlled and alert. Your enemy the devil prowls around like a roaring lion looking for someone to devour. Resist him, standing firm in the faith, because you know that your brothers throughout the world are undergoing the same kind of sufferings" (1 Peter 5:8-9, NIV).

Your enemy is like a roaring lion, looking for unassuming prey. He preys most greedily upon the godly. If you compromise your walk, you're not really a target of the enemy. Why should he waste his time? You're already halfway in his camp. But if you determine to stand alone and against the tide; if you reject the world's opinion of how to spend your life; if you determine to live according to biblical standards, be sure that your enemy is seeking to devour you. You *will* encounter the darts of the devil.

Someone put it this way: "Whoever desires to walk with God walks right into the crucible." All who choose godliness live in a crucible. The tests *will* come.

So many people can testify, "You know, very recently I made a decision to walk with God. I really thought that from that time on, things would get better. But, as a matter of fact, they've gotten worse."

Years ago a man told me that he made a decision unlike anything he had ever made in his Christian life. He was going to walk with God, regardless. And he said, "Almost from the day those words left my lips, I have been in one problem after another, one test after another, living constantly under the gun of enemy assault."

One evening when I preached on this issue, I learned some friends from Zaire had come to visit. Just after the service I walked over to the room where they were and sat down with them. They declared, "This message tonight was for us. That is exactly where we have been." And they had been thousands of miles away in Zaire! I thought the message was for me, because in my preparation it seemed as if it were tailor-made for my own needs. It's a universal principle: If you determine to live a godly life, The Peril Principle says the enemy will make you his target.

But all is not lost. Far from it! Our great hope and assurance is that the One in us is greater than the one in the world. We do not face such a formidable enemy that we cannot fight him or stand firm and secure in our decision. Our Lord is the God of hope. Psalm 4:3 calls in what I would call "reinforcement for the battle." God's supply line never runs short. When His godly followers are in need, He is there to supply the necessary reinforcements. As you do battle, God will provide for all of your needs: "But know that the LORD has set apart the godly man [and woman] for himself; the LORD hears when I call to Him" (brackets mine).

When you determine that you are going to count for Christ as a godly man, a godly woman, a godly young person, when you determine to be a person sold out to God—not just a run-of-the-mill, mediocre Christian accepting Christ as a fire escape—you become the object of God's special attention. He says He "sets you apart" for Himself. And the verse adds, "The LORD hears when I call to Him." Those two thoughts fit together. The godly often need to call upon God when the perils come. So He says, "I am here and I will answer. I will hear what you have to say."

Still, when you walk close to God, you live with the very real threat of enemy attack. And the closer you walk, the deeper the peril.

RUMBLINGS FROM THE RABBLE

Moses is a man who chose to walk with God and who, therefore, became a target of the enemy. How did this godly man face these inevitable perils? In Numbers 10 the people of God are at Mount Sinai, building a tabernacle, getting their heads together regarding the law of God. They are preparing to leave Sinai and proceed on their way to Canaan, the Promised Land. And Moses intends to lead them there.

But first, the perils. "Now in the second year, in the second month, on the twentieth of the month, the cloud was lifted from over the tabernacle of the testimony....Then the tabernacle was taken down; and the sons of Gershon and the sons of Merari, who were carrying the tabernacle, set out" (Numbers 10:11, 17).

The tabernacle was a portable house of worship made up of tents and supported by poles that could be dismantled, taken down, folded up, and carried on the shoulders of the people of God. When the Israelites came to a place and settled down in their camp, they set up the tabernacle. And when the cloud moved on, they folded up the tabernacle, carried it further, then set it up again. Sounds like a military maneuver, doesn't it? Just as soon as you get it all put away, they say, "Pitch the tent;" so you put it back together. That is precisely the way it was for the people of God.

Now, you might think that these people who had just seen the Law of God written with His own finger, who had just built this exquisite new portable worship facility designed in God's own mind, would be a hundred percent excited to move to the land of Canaan. But they weren't.

Any large group of people who wants to walk with God always seems to attract a smaller group who lacks any such desire. Scripture calls this latter group, "the rabble." You know what the Hebrew word for "rabble" means? It means "riffraff." God really knows how to tag a certain group, doesn't He? You might call these folks "the carnal corral."

In this camp of hundreds of thousands of Israelites and a few foreigners who had joined them in their Exodus from Egypt, one segment was constantly a thorn in Moses' side. Back in Exodus 12:38 God called them, "the mixed multitude." Here He calls them "the rabble." Numbers 11:1 describes a group of Hebrews on their way to Canaan who suddenly balk at following God's lead:

> Now the people complained about their hardships [the rabble is grumbling, so these people are grumbling] in the hearing of the LORD, and when he heard them his anger was aroused. Then fire from the LORD burned among them and consumed some of the outskirts of the camp. (Numbers 11:1, NIV, brackets mine)

When things got hot, these grumblers cried out to Moses, Moses prayed to the Lord, and the fire died out. But they weren't finished yet. Verse 4 says, "The rabble who were among them had greedy desires; and also the sons of Israel wept again and said, 'Who will give us meat to eat? We remember the fish which we used to eat free in Egypt, the cucumbers and the melons and the leeks and the onions and the garlic, but now our appetite is gone.'"

I find myself answering, "That's what you get for eating stuff like that!" Leeks and fish and onions and garlic? No wonder their appetite left. And they complained, "There is nothing at all to look at except this manna" (verse 6).

The belly-aching went on and on, leading Moses directly into his first peril.

THE PERIL OF
DISCOURAGEMENT AND DEPRESSION

Even though you may be a godly person, you can hear that kind of depressing stuff only so long before it begins to demoralize your spirit, dragging you down. You want to walk with God, but you're with a few people who just won't. Invariably they're vocal, petty, and negative. They don't want to go God's way, they want to go *their* way. And they're always looking back to how great things used to be (before *you* came along).

Dr. Howard Hendricks used to say, "Those good old times are what created these bad new times that we're having these days." My faithful mentor is right on target, isn't he? We like to look back on those "good old times," and we don't even want to give the challenging *new* times a chance. The rabble never realizes that.

Moses heard this sad bunch gripe and complain and grumble. He heard it continually. He heard it so much he wanted to gag. "Now Moses heard the people weeping throughout their families, each man at the doorway of his tent; and the anger of the LORD was kindled greatly, and Moses was displeased" (v. 10).

Can't you see Moses walking up and down those lines of tents, listening to the constant complaining? There's griping. There's crying. There are frowns and long faces, wagging heads and grim countenances. And before long it begins to wear the old man down. The text says he was "displeased."

Now, I wish I could say that Moses passed all these perils with flying colors. Three out of four, he did. But here's the one he just didn't handle. I can identify with him. I really understand. Moses wanted so much for his people to see the God he had seen in the burning bush, to trust the cloud that moved unerringly toward Canaan, but they didn't. He wanted them to develop a heavenly appetite that delights in heavenly food, but they wouldn't. Finally, they wore him down, and he became discouraged. It should be no surprise that we hear him blurt this out to God:

Why have You been so hard on Your servant? And why have I not found favor in Your sight, that You have laid the burden of all this people on me? Was it I who conceived all this people? Was it I who brought them forth, that You should say to me, "Carry them in your bosom as a nurse carries a nursing infant"....? Where am I to get meat to give to all this people? For they weep before me, saying, "Give us meat...!" I alone am not able to carry all this people, because it is too burdensome for me. So if You are going to deal thus with me, please kill me at once [he's really low, isn't he?], if I have found favor in Your sight, and do not let me see my wretchedness. (vv. 11–15, brackets mine)

Can you understand how he felt? Have you ever been that low? The deeper you commit yourself, the heavier the burden. The faster the pace, the heavier the anchor. Listen, the greater the dreams God may give you, the more persistent will be the rabble who puts them down. They will complain, and fuss, and fume. And if you listen to 'em long enough, you'll get downright depressed.

I once knew a young man who taught in a West Los Angeles junior high school. He was trying to teach math to a group of kids that included a "rabble" who didn't want to learn anything. He told me, "Pastor Chuck, what I'm really doing is teaching a class on discipline. And in the meantime I throw in a little math." He told me he once spent part of a class getting hold of a kid, finally tackling him on a desk. "I wanted to tell him some things," he said. That actually happened in his classroom.

Do you think that teacher ever faced discouragement? He had a Master's degree in mathematics, was passionate about his subject, and knew how to teach. But he spent most of his time putting out fires unrelated to his calling. Instead of wrestling with formulas and equations, he found himself wrestling with unruly students.

May I give you a tip? (No extra charge for this insight.) As soon as a group gets large enough, the rabble will show up. As that Bible class you teach increases in size, sooner or later you'll get the rabble. You go to a Bible school, a seminary, a Christian college, you'll find the rabble there. You visit a church of any size, you will find the rabble. You start a church, it's only a matter of time. It's true of groups in the church, Sunday school classes, choirs. No matter what, when you get a large enough group together, you will find the rabble.

That means that when you want your life to please the Lord, when you want very much to count for Christ, sooner or later you will be rubbing shoulders with the rabble, with those who don't want to please God at all. And if you don't watch it, you will let them get the best of you, and you will succumb to discouragement and depression.

One of the greatest battles I faced as a seminary student involved the rabble. I was naive enough to believe that the men who taught us were all men of God. I was strange enough to think that if you really applied yourself in study, it would be worth it all. But a small percentage of my fellow students couldn't have cared less about their studies. I had to battle discouragement around those guys. Now, I wasn't the super saint who never sinned and who came through life untarnished. But my goals clashed with a number of fellow students, and we had some confrontations. It was unpleasant, even depressing.

If you *focus* on those confrontations, however, you will stay discouraged. That's what happened to Moses. He heard weeping behind one too many tent flaps and finally whimpered, "Lord, take my life." That's the ultimate expression of depression.

An exhausted Elijah once muttered similar words beneath a scrawny tree in the wilderness. Jonah said the same thing under a withered vine outside the walls of Nineveh. Both were ready to quit; both asked the Lord for a quick death. But the Lord refused to take the life of Elijah or Jonah, and He wasn't about to take Moses' life, either. But He did take care of the problem.

Again Moses had been trying to do too much, so the Lord spread out his work load. You can read it for yourself in Numbers 11:16-25. God took care of his need. But as soon as that peril exited stage right, another one emerged stage left. Right on the heels of the first came the second. That's how it is when we determine to walk with God. The perils can come one after the other.

THE PERIL OF
JEALOUSY AND INDISPENSABILITY

Moses' second peril began with these words in verse 26: "But two men had remained in the camp...." That statement might not mean much to us unless we realize that Moses had told seventy elders of the people to come out and stand by the tent of meeting. God had appointed these seventy men to help Moses carry the load. But when they called roll, two of the men didn't show up. One was named Eldad, the other Medad. Neither was a rebel; in fact, they had been led by the Spirit of God to stay in the camp. Verse 26 tells us, "The Spirit rested upon them...and they prophesied in the camp." A young man saw what happened and scurried to Moses with the breathless report, "Eldad and Medad are prophesying in the camp."

Now, what did he mean? He meant, "Moses, that's *your* job. You're the prophet. And if anybody's going to prophesy, you oughta be the one to do it." That's the way that young man saw it. "Moses, a couple of fellas aren't getting with the program," he tattled. "And, of all things, they're over there doing *your* job." It's interesting to see what happened next: "Then Joshua the son of Nun, the attendant of Moses from his youth, said, 'Moses, my lord, restrain them'" (v. 28).

These young men were jealous for Moses' role. And they said, "Moses, you can't let 'em get away with that. You're the prophet. What are Eldad and Medad doing in there? Who do they think they are, prophesying like that? That's your job." So Joshua says, "General Moses, sir, put a stop to it."

I love it that Moses is more broad-shouldered than that. He replies securely, without a hint of jealousy, "Are you jealous for my sake? Would that all the LORD's people were prophets, that the LORD would put His Spirit upon them" (v. 29)! Talk about unselfish. There wasn't an ounce of insecurity in that man of God.

Are you pursuing godliness? Do you want to count for Christ? Has God gifted you for service? If so, somewhere along the line, you will face the peril of jealousy, the feeling of being "indispensable" to some particular ministry. And some around you will plant seeds of jealousy in your heart that will tempt you to feel indispensable. You'll think, *What's she doing up there? I could teach better than she.* Or, *You know, that man bears watching. He's trying to take over. Everybody knows I'm the leader.* Or, *I can't afford to step down. I started this organization.* Ever heard those words or something similar? Ever said them yourself? Those are words of petty jealousy and proud indispensability.

Listen to me! *Everybody* can afford to step down if God's enthroned. Some of the most jealous, suspicious people in the world are so-called Christian public figures enamored with their own press clippings. It's vital to them that they drop the right names and be seen by the right people and have others think well of them. They crave fame. And God help the one whose fame crowds theirs!

An old poem warns of this danger:

> Sometime when you're feeling important,
> Sometime when your ego's way up;
> Sometime when you take it for granted
> that you are the prize-winning "pup";
> Sometime when you feel that your absence
> would leave an unfillable hole,
> Just follow these simple instructions,
> And see how it humbles your soul.
> Take a bucket, fill it with water,
> Put your hand in it up to your wrist.
> Now pull it out fast and the hole that remains
> Is the measure of how you'll be missed.
> You may splash all you like as you enter,
> And stir up the water galore,
> But stop and you'll find in a minute,
> It's right back where it was before.[1]

You're not indispensable. I'm not indispensable. Nobody is indispensable, except the Lord Jesus Christ. He's the head. He's the Preeminent One. He's the founder. He's in first place. And when He moves one and brings in another or demotes one and sets up another, He calls the shots. That is His sovereign right. The problem arises when we get to thinking *we're* sovereign. My friend, He put you where He wanted you. He gave you that job. He can take it away just as fast as He gave it. Just faithfully do your work, lie low, and exalt Christ.

Moses passed the second test with flying colors; so you might think that would be it for the tests. No more perils. Wrong.

THE PERIL OF
BEING MISUNDERSTOOD AND MISREPRESENTED

It is very possible that Moses' wife, Zipporah, had died, and he married another woman described in Numbers 12:1 as a Cushite. Look at the response to this choice Moses made: "Then Miriam and Aaron spoke against Moses...."

Wait a minute! Who are Miriam and Aaron? Aren't they Moses' sister and brother? True enough. Incredibly, Moses' older siblings started a whispering campaign against their younger brother. Why? "Because of the Cushite woman whom he had married."

This passage troubles some people, because God stood in Moses' defense, even though he married a non-Israelite. Hadn't the Lord specifically forbidden any Israelite from marrying a Canaanite? Yes, He had; but this woman was a Cushite, not a Canaanite. No prohibition had been made against that. The real problem (in their minds) was that Moses hadn't turned to Miriam and Aaron to seek their counsel. They considered themselves indispensable members of the inner circle. They didn't appreciate it when Moses made a decision without consulting them. So they said, "Has the LORD indeed spoken only through Moses? Has He not spoken through us as well" (verse 2)?

You can almost hear the audience go silent as the text declares, "And the LORD heard it." Uh-oh! That's not a comforting thought. In every slander there is a gossiper and a gossipee. And between the two is the Lord. Before the gossipee ever hears the comment, the Lord has already intercepted what was said. Miriam and Aaron misrepresented this man of God who had made a decision about a marriage they couldn't understand and wouldn't approve. And because they felt slighted in the process, they tucked their thumbs under their suspenders and pranced around, implying, "Look, *we* are authorities just like Moses." We'll see about that.

Scripture says, "Suddenly the LORD said to Moses and Aaron and to Miriam, 'You three come out to the tent of meeting.' So the three of them came out" (Numbers 12:4).

When I read those words, an eerie chill runs up and down my back. Remember the days when you were in school and you got a note to report to the principal's office? Oh, man, you'd look for the first fire escape. You just couldn't believe *you* were summoned to the principal's office. And God had said, "You three come to My office. *Now.*"

Of course, Moses had nothing to lose. He was delighted to return to the Lord's presence, but not Miriam and Aaron. When the Lord told them to "come out," you bet they came! And this is what they heard: "He said, 'Hear now My words: if there is a prophet among you, I, the LORD, shall make myself known to him in a vision. I shall speak with him in a dream. Not so, with My servant Moses, He is faithful in all My household; with him I speak mouth to mouth, even openly, and not in dark sayings, and he beholds the form of the LORD. Why then were you not afraid to speak against My servant, against Moses'" (vv. 6–8)?

"I have a unique relationship with My servant Moses," God proclaimed, "and no one will take his place. He will die and pass on, but there will be no one else in this camp as long as he is alive with whom I have a face-to-face relationship. So leave him alone!"

And just to make sure that no one misunderstood the divine message, God left a little calling card behind:

> But when the cloud had withdrawn from over the tent, behold, Miriam was leprous, as white as snow. As Aaron turned toward Miriam, behold, she was leprous. Then Aaron said to Moses, "Oh, my lord, I beg you, do not account this sin to us, in which we have acted foolishly and in which we have sinned. Oh, do not let her be like one dead." (vv. 10–12)

And how did Moses respond? In verse 13 he calls out to the Lord, "O God, heal her." What humility! Moses had been betrayed and slandered by his sister, but when he saw her leprosy, he said, "God, cleanse her body." And then it was time for *God's* response. Verse 14 records a statement unlike any other ever made by the Lord: "If her father had but spit in her face, would she not bear her shame for seven days? Let her be shut up for seven days outside the camp, and afterward she may be received again."

In other words, "Let this chastisement run a course of one week." And so Miriam was excluded from the camp for seven days, and the people did not move on until she rejoined them.

Numbers 12 reminds us how God protects a godly person. You don't have to run your own defense; God runs the defense for you. Let me assure you, you will be misrepresented. You will be misunderstood. But when that happens, don't try to cover all the slanderous things said against you. Let God be your defense.

I think it's especially interesting that Moses was slandered in the personal realm of domestic privacy. After all, who he married was his own business, right? Yet domestic life seems to be the area of scandal the rabble most often feeds upon, especially among the godly. God never does tell us why Moses married her. But I take it that since God defended his decision, Moses and God had talked about it, and Moses chose the woman God wanted him to marry. But Aaron and Miriam couldn't accept it so they put down their little brother.

Here is a warning every one of us needs to heed: Be *exceedingly careful* about what you say regarding the private business of God's people. If you do not know the facts and you are troubled about appearances, talk to the individual one-on-one, or better still, say nothing at all.

I am appalled by what some people say about the individuals others choose to marry. One of the saints of the last generation lost his wife and after a few years of being alone, he married a woman several years his junior. Some nosey busybody came up to him and said, "The nerve! How could you have the nerve to marry somebody that much younger than you?" And in his gravelly voice he answered, "Listen, honey, I'd rather smell perfume than liniment any day."

Wonderful answer! I wish I knew what the woman said in reply. She probably said nothing (if she was smart). Just be sure you've got God's woman or God's man and then forget it. Invariably someone will pick on you because of your choice. The same thing applies to your kids. Ignore what people say; just go right on. It will help if you remember the words of some wise soul: "Maturity is moving from a soft skin and a tough heart to a tough skin and a soft heart." Sage advice. Don't let your heart get hard, but allow your hide to get tough. You'll never be the godly leader you could be if you have thin skin.

There was still another peril that awaited Moses soon after this one passed.

THE PERIL OF BEING IGNORED AND REJECTED

When the Israelites came to the threshold of the land of Canaan, God told them to spy out the land. He sent them out from the wilderness of Paran to do some reconnaissance of Canaan. Twelve spies went out, spending forty days to look around. On their return they said, "We went in to the land where you sent us; and it certainly does flow with milk and honey, and this is its fruit" (Numbers 13:27).

The spies displayed example after beautiful example of fruit from the land of Canaan. Moses' heart beat faster because he could picture the people going into the land and taking it as God had promised. Yes! It was really going to happen! What God had told him out in the deserts of Midian was finally going to be fulfilled.

But just that quickly, something went terribly wrong. As the spies continued their report they said, "Nevertheless, the people who live in the land are strong, and the cities are fortified and very large; and moreover, we saw the descendants of Anak there" (v. 28).

Who were the descendants of Anak? They were giants, a race of huge men. And they scared ten of the spies out of their wits. "We were going along and all of a sudden we came upon these *giants*. We've been running ever since, back to you guys, to tell you about it."

Many years ago when we served a church in New England, we had a pair of interns who might have given Anak a run for his money. The guy was about six-foot-six inches tall while his wife was six-foot-one. When she put on high heels, you thought you had fallen into some gigantic pothole. They were really up there.

One afternoon after church, when both were all dressed up, they entered a grocery store to get a few things before Sunday lunch. As they pushed their cart down the aisle, all of a sudden a little kid came tooling around the corner. He screeched to a halt, took one look up at them, then screamed "Giants!" and fled in the other direction.

That's what happened here. The spies' report disheartened the people, and Moses' heart sank right to the bottom. Although Caleb and Joshua insisted, "Don't listen to these guys about the giants. We have a giant God who can take us right into the land," they refused to hear. They had their own ideas of what to do. "So they said to one another, 'Let us appoint a leader and return to Egypt'" (14:4).

There it is—the peril of being ignored and rejected. The people didn't want Canaan. They didn't want Moses, either. They wanted to go back to the chains in the carnal land of Egypt, because to enter the Promised Land meant they would have to face the giants. How serious were they about their full-scale retreat? When Caleb and Joshua tried to talk the people into entering Canaan, and Moses and Aaron fell on their faces in the presence of all Israel, the Bible says "all the congregation said to stone them with stones" (Numbers 14:10). In other words, "Get rid of 'em. If they don't do things our way, send 'em to the hereafter. Hand me one of those rocks!"

The violent, heart-breaking, grossly unfair behavior of the people in this critical moment might very well have dumped Moses into a fourth and final peril.

THE PERIL OF RESENTMENT AND REVENGE

What a chance for Moses to say, "Lord, zap 'em!" If anyone had a right to feel resentment and revenge, it was Moses at that moment. Immediately the glory of the Lord appeared in the tent of meeting and God said to Moses, "How long will this people spurn Me? And how long will they not believe in Me, despite all the signs which I have performed in their midst? I will smite them with pestilence and dispossess them, and I will make you into a nation greater and mightier than they" (vv. 11–12).

Now that *had* to be a tempting proposition! Start over with a clean slate. Bury those grumblers and whiners in the wilderness and start fresh with a new nation. What would Moses do? If the Lord had made that offer to me, I might have said, "Umm. Lemme think about it a minute. That's not a bad idea, Lord. Could I bring Caleb n' Joshua along, too?"

But not Moses. This humble servant replied, in effect, "But Lord, Your testimony's at stake here. The Egyptians will hear about it, and what will the nations say?" No resentment, no revenge. Not even a mild offense. In fact, Moses actually *defended* this stiff-necked nation and asked the Lord to stay His hand against them. And the Lord did so.

When someone shoots at you as a godly person, this final peril of resentment and revenge will eat at you like an acid. Many a man of God, filled with resentment and revenge, turns the pulpit into a hammer to fight his battles against the rabble. Bad plan. How much better to leave it with God, as did Moses.

THREE TRUTHS ABOUT A GODLY LIFE

Before we leave this remarkable portion of Moses' life story, let me suggest three statements that may be of help in *your* life story.

The godly life is never easy.

Rewarding? Yes. Fulfilling? Yes. Worthwhile? A thousand times yes. But it's never easy. Think twice before you enter the Christian ministry. Think twice before you sign on to serve in a cross-cultural ministry or at a Christian school, because a whole realm of difficulty awaits you. Beware, all thin-skinned saints!

The godly life is often endangered.

Someone once said the life of the apostles was like the path of a bleeding hare making its way across the snowy hills—just a trail of blood. If you're looking for a safe, secure, no-hassles sort of existence, the narrow road winding into the steep hills of godliness may not be your path of choice.

The godly life is always eventful.

A Christian friend of mine with an active, adventurous family shook his head ruefully and said, "My mother-in-law just loves coming to visit. She says, 'Something always happens every time I'm here. It's all so *exciting.*'"

The truth is, if you really want to break the boredom syndrome, commit yourself to Jesus Christ. Life will start comin' at you! You will become effective, empowered from heaven, and the battle will rage. You never find people on the front lines going to sleep. They're in the fray. The war's exploding. It's terribly eventful when your life counts for Christ. Psalm 34 says, "Many are the afflictions of the righteous, but the LORD delivers him out of them all" (v. 19).

I can promise you one thing: If your walk with Christ is consistent, all hell will break loose. But all heaven will come to your rescue! And you'll be right in the middle of cosmic, high-stakes warfare.

If you like leeks, garlic, and fish, topped off with a cup of warm water from the Nile, you'd be better off making predictable bricks in "good old Egypt." But if you're willing to sign on as one of the Lord's commandos behind enemy lines, life will never be the same. You may only get a quick meal of manna while you're dodging spears, but it will never be boring.

In fact, it's the only way to live!

CHAPTER SEVENTEEN

A Moment of Rage

In stunned disbelief one early morning years ago, we read the headlines over our first cup of coffee: "Twelve Bodies Found." A madman had bludgeoned to death a dozen people and buried them in shallow graves along the Feather River in Northern California. After a gruesome investigation the body count went up several more.

There have been so many such headlines since that spring day decades ago. Bloody rampages in fast food restaurants, neat suburban neighborhoods, government buildings, courtrooms, post offices, and even more recently, in public schools and playgrounds. The weapons have become more fearsome, the killers and victims have become so much younger, but the recoil from such tragedy is much the same as it has always been.

I can still remember that hot Texas morning on August 1, 1966, when Charles Whitman carried a portable armory to the observation deck of the University of Texas library tower. Before he finished his deadly work and was killed himself, he had shot to death no less than sixteen innocent pedestrians on the streets of Austin. A few months before that, Richard

Speck slipped into a Chicago townhouse and strangled or stabbed to death eight student nurses.

When we hear accounts like that, we shake our heads in disbelief. How do you process such logic-defying information? Who can identify a *reason* for such carnage? Not even the psychiatric professionals who examine the killers can find much meaning behind their deadly acts of violence. As much as we hate to admit it, our American landscape is strewn with the litter of murder and violence.

I was reared in the city that topped the nation's murder rate through all the days of my childhood: Houston, Texas. I remember reading about murders as if they were commonplace events. As we get older we wonder how men and women can, with their own hands, take the lives of their innocent human brothers and sisters.

I think *Time* magazine put its finger on what might be the best answer. In covering a murder story a number of years ago, its editors published a picture of the murderer above the caption, "A Moment of Rage."

Social commentators warn that people today are sitting on emotional powder kegs. We've gone from *short* fuse to virtually *no* fuse. How else can you explain the phenomenon of "road rage," where one motorist points a gun out the window and shoots another driver who happens to make him angry. Whether you're a university professional or in private practice; whether you're a student or working in some kind of blue- or white-collar job—you're living over a tank of nytro. Should any slight thing jostle the explosive mixture, something suddenly has to give. Often it's the life of yet another human being.

FIVE LEVELS OF ANGER

Psychologists have done many in-depth studies of anger. While they've come up with no guaranteed answers—for there is no ultimate answer aside from Jesus Christ—they have helped us analyze the emotional dynamics of anger. They have told us that anger rises along five steps, each step more intense than the last.

Anger, we are told, begins with *mild irritation*. This stage is marked by uneasiness, brought on by some unpleasant disturbance. It may be as mild as a traffic jam or the pressures of rearing a group of noisy children in the same small home, in tight quarters with not enough money or patience or sleep. So mild irritation begins to build.

That can lead to *indignation*, a deeper level of intensity. Indignation is a reaction to something that seems unfair or unreasonable. It can be expressed in violence, as sometimes happens at sporting events, when someone in the stands throws a beer bottle onto the field or court and strikes a referee. The fellow in the stands is angry because he believes the umpire's call was unreasonable. So he expresses himself in that form of overt *indigniviolence*.

The third level is *wrath*, which psychologists say never goes unexpressed. No one restrains wrath. When your anger reaches this level, you have a strong desire to avenge, to fight back, or to defend, and you will not hold back. Wrath wears many faces, all ugly.

Uncontrolled anger soon becomes *fury*, the fourth level. Fury introduces violence. It may include a momentary loss of control—even a temporary loss of sanity. In a moment of fury we strike out against someone else. I watched a television documentary several years ago that paraded before the viewer one case after another of murders in the Los Angeles area. Most of them happened inside homes, between husbands and wives. Unresolved domestic conflicts often lead to fury.

The fifth stage is *rage*, the most intense level of angry expressions. Rage, we are told, is the most dangerous form of anger. It can so overcome a person that it inspires acts of brutal violence, sometimes performed without conscious awareness. Experts say a person filled with rage can commit murder while hardly realizing he or she is doing it; psychologically, the person blacks out.

HELP FROM THE INSIDE OUT

The pastorate is not an easy position to fill. On occasion you must deal with the raw, ragged edge of life. Many years ago I was sitting in my church study when a man came in to meet me by appointment. Visibly shaken and carrying the marks of a recent fight, he told me he had just beaten his daughter, then his wife. When he left home, his daughter lay unconscious, and his wife was sitting on the side of the bed, sobbing and covered in blood. It reminded me of another occasion where I sat inside a jail cell, eyeball-to-eyeball with a man who had killed his child with his own hands in a few moments of rage.

With deep remorse, both of these men told me, "Something just snapped inside. Something exploded. And in that moment of *rage* I did that." They both openly confessed their crimes.

Ironically, the man who took his child's life said, "You know, the strange thing about living in this state is that the authorities won't take my life for what I did, although that's what I deserve. I will live on with the memory of being a murderer."

Now, before we sit in judgment upon any of these men, we must confess that we all have within us the very same potential for violence. The only difference is the matter of control. Those of us who have given our lives to Christ know we have Someone inside of us who enables us to control our anger. Don't kid yourself; if we were given free reign to let our anger run its course, we would use our fists or some lethal weapon and take the lives of others. But Christians have within them the person of the Holy Spirit, who brings a needed restraint and unprecedented control to our lives. He serves as an inner governor, who tells us, "That's far enough."

If you are reading these words and don't know Christ as Savior, I must tell you that I have no hope to give you in this area of anger. I have no encouragement to offer, whether you express your anger through profanity or fist fights or something more vicious. The living Lord is the only one I know who can come in like a flood and smother the flames of a vicious temper.

It may be, however, that even though you're a Christian, you still wrestle with violent explosions of temper. You're ashamed of it, you feel guilty about it, but you really don't know what to *do* about it. If that describes you, I want to insist that you *can* find control. You *can* find an expression for your anger apart from violence. For if that were not true—if we didn't have such a hope—then our faith wouldn't offer much hope at all.

But Christ does offer hope to those of us who struggle with anger! A whole ocean of it. Still, we must take advantage of the resources He offers us. If we fail to do our part, we will continue to struggle, just as Moses did.

THE STORY OF AN ANGRY MAN

Most of us don't normally think of Moses as a man given to violent temper. Yet I believe the record shows he never did get complete control of his anger.

This surprising observation may benefit us in at least two ways. On the one hand, it may give us some hope that if a man like Moses struggled with anger, we don't need to feel so badly that we struggle with it, too. But on the other hand, I hope it shocks us into realizing the terrible ramifications of an uncontrolled temper. Moses controlled his anger periodically, but when he allowed it to express itself, it tended to explode. In fact, I wonder if his anger didn't at times reach the level of rage. If you learn nothing more from this case study in the life of Moses, I hope you learn the sad consequences of an uncontrolled temper. I hope this episode motivates you to let the Spirit of God gain full and complete control of your life.

To begin observing Moses' lifelong anger patterns, let's return briefly to his childhood.

Murderous anger

> The child grew, and she [that is, Moses' mother] brought him to Pharaoh's daughter and he became her son. And she named him Moses, and said, "Because I drew him out of the water." Now it came about in those days, when Moses had grown up, that he went out to his brethren and looked on their hard labors; and he saw an Egyptian beating a Hebrew, one of his brethren. (Exodus 2:10–12, brackets mine)

About the time Moses reached his fortieth birthday, he saw an Egyptian slave-driver beating an apparently defenseless Hebrew. The beating was an unfair, unreasonable act, and Moses the Hebrew quickly became indignant. Fury boiled up like a geyser. Verse 12 tells us, "He looked this way and that, and when he saw there was no one around, he struck down the Egyptian and hid him in the sand." As we saw in a previous chapter,

Moses committed an act of murder, then dug a shallow grave and hurriedly shoved sand over the dead body.

The Book of Acts proves that anger is not simply an expression of those who are ignorant and uneducated, for it reminds us that Moses "was educated in all the learning of the Egyptians...a man of power in words and deeds" (Acts 7:22). Don't think for a moment that an advanced education is all you need to restrain an anger problem. It goes much deeper than that. You cannot educate your anger out of existence.

As the text goes on to say of Moses, "But when he was approaching the age of forty, it entered his mind to visit his brethren, the sons of Israel. And when he saw one of them being treated unjustly, he defended him and took vengeance for the oppressed by striking down the Egyptian" (vv. 23–24).

Did you notice the motive behind Moses' act? He "took vengeance" in his own hands. That's why he murdered the Egyptian.

Immediately after this incident, Moses escaped to the desert. For the next forty years he cooled his heels in the school of self-discovery. While there he learned many valuable lessons, yet he still did not learn how to control his temper.

Unnecessary anger

After he returned to Egypt to lead the Exodus, Moses had nine encounters with Pharaoh before the tenth and final face-off prompted the death of Egypt's firstborn. When Moses visited Pharaoh between the ninth and the tenth plague, he became violently angry with the king. Although the Lord had told Moses, "I am going to harden Pharaoh's heart," Moses became furious with Pharaoh. Exodus 11 reports that after his final warnings to the stubborn king, "he went out from Pharaoh in *hot anger*" (v. 8).

Moses' blood had reached the boiling point. We might say he was "fried." But our modern expression doesn't begin to do justice to the underlying Hebrew terms, for they are the strongest words available to express anger. Moses walked out of that place in the throes of *fury*.

Now, why was that? God had already told Moses, "Look, I'm going to harden Pharaoh's heart. You don't need to get mad at him. All you have to do is tell him, 'Man, you're condemned. There's no way out but to let

My people go.'" But Moses couldn't handle the assignment. Not content merely to give the message, he proceeded to give it furious expression, beyond God's intention or desire.

Destructive anger

Sadly, the story doesn't stop there. Months later, the people of Israel had moved out of Egypt and come to Sinai. Moses had climbed the mountain to receive from the Lord the tablets of the Law. Meanwhile, the people he left below grew weary of waiting. The Israelites began to get jumpy and jittery in his absence and finally said, "Let's build a golden calf and worship it." So, in unbelief, the people began to prance around and commit obscenities in front of their new idol. At the height of their revelries, Moses returned to the Israelite camp:

> Then Moses turned and went down from the mountain with the two tablets of the testimony in his hand, tablets which were written on both sides; they were written on one side and the other. The tablets were God's work, and the writing was God's writing engraved on the tablets. (32:15–16)

Remember, these tablets, written by Almighty God Himself, were the most precious documents man ever had in his possession. Think of having a book written in stone by the finger of God! Imagine possessing a document that God personally penned, signed, and deposited to your trust. That is what Moses had. In his own hands he held the precious documents of the inspired Torah. As he came down from Sinai with these tablets, he saw his people dancing before the golden calf. And his old anger flared.

"It came about, as soon as Moses came near the camp, that he saw the calf and the dancing; and Moses' anger *burned* ...."

You ask, "Well, *shouldn't* he have gotten angry?" Absolutely. That is what we call "righteous indignation." It's the kind of anger a father feels when he sees his child in willful disobedience. The father has a right to feel angry toward such an act of defiance. But how do you express that anger? Ah, that's the question!

Look at what Moses did. He took the precious documents of God, and, in a moment of fury, "he threw the tablets from his hands and shattered them at the foot of the mountain" (Exodus 32:19). And he wasn't finished yet. Exodus tells us, "He took the calf which they had made and burned it with fire, and ground it to powder, and scattered it over the surface of the water, and made the sons of Israel drink it" (32:20). Picture that! We can hardly imagine such a thing.

But let's go back to the tablets. Isn't it strange that we have heard this story all our lives, and yet we've never stopped to think that this act of Moses' was simply an act of out-of-control temper? For all our lives we have excused Moses for what he did; but God didn't excuse him. If you study the subsequent text, you will find that God never approved of what Moses did. In fact, when Moses was given the Law again, God said, "Cut out for yourself two stone tablets like the former ones, and I will write on the tablets the words that were on the former tablets which you shattered" (Exodus 34:1). In other words, "This time you make the tablets, Moses. I made them once already." In quiet tolerance, God continued to deal with His child in this area not yet submitted to His control.

Rebellious anger

Now fast-forward many years. The people of Israel are again on the edge of the land of Canaan. By this point the Hebrews have been wandering for thirty-nine years and complaining every step of the way, it seems. When the nation had arrived at the border of the Promised Land almost four decades before, the people refused to go in because of unbelief. They didn't believe God could give them the strength to overcome their enemies and defeat the giants who roamed the fields of Canaan.

As a result of this disobedience, God said to them, "This whole generation is going to die off; none of the adults will go into the land except Caleb and Joshua. I am not going to send any of you from the older generation, because you have not believed in My power."

Now, recall that the nation was made up of about two million people. Let's say half of them were adults who were to die off in the next thirty-eight to forty years. If just half of them expired in the next four decades, the

Israelites would have been burying people every day. Yet despite the fresh burials, despite the tombstones that stretched across the Wilderness of Zin, the people of Israel continued to complain. No doubt on frequent occasions Moses grew beside himself with anger, irritated over their impatience.

It was just like a mother who tells her child, "Look, don't do that again. Don't do that *one more time*." But as soon as the mother returns to her room, the child is doing it one more time. So she deals with it. Two weeks later, she comes along, and the child is doing it again. So she deals with it again. Less than a week passes, and it's going on again, and again, and again, and again. Who wouldn't grow irritated?

That's how Moses felt with the Hebrews. And by the time Numbers 20 rolls around, he's had it. The man is *seething* within. He walks on the razor edge of white-hot fury.

> Then the sons of Israel, the whole congregation, came to the wilderness of Zin in the first month; and the people stayed at Kadesh. Now Miriam died there and was buried there. There was no water for the congregation, and they assembled themselves against Moses and Aaron. (vv. 1–2)

A familiar scene, isn't it? When things don't work out according to everyone's plan, call out the ol' lynching party for those in charge.

> The people thus contended with Moses and spoke, saying, "If only we had perished when our brothers perished before the LORD! Why then have you brought the LORD's assembly into this wilderness, for us and our beasts to die here? Why have you made us come up from Egypt, to bring us in to this wretched place? It is not a place of grain or figs or vines or pomegranates, nor is there water to drink." (vv. 3–5)

It's the same, tired old refrain. They're still griping, still carping, still complaining about their lot in life, and how neglected they are. How miserable. How abused. How pitiful. How unfair. Moses had heard it all a thousand times before. What the people didn't realize, and what Moses himself may not have realized, was that they were about to push their leader over the edge. Observe very carefully what follows, keeping in mind Moses' persistent struggle with anger:

> Then Moses and Aaron came in from the presence of the assembly to the doorway of the tent of meeting and fell on their faces. Then the glory of the LORD appeared to them; and the LORD spoke to Moses, saying, "Take the rod; and you and your brother Aaron assemble the congregation and speak to the rock before their eyes, that it may yield its water. You shall thus bring forth water for them out of the rock and let the congregation and their beasts drink." (vv. 6–8)

What could be more clear? There was nothing ambiguous about those instructions. "Take the rod, go out to the rock, *speak* to the rock, and get out of the way. Water will be on its way." But remember, Moses is hot. He's bitterly angry at all those complainers, and very, very close to losing control. In fact, he's at wits' end. So he takes the rod, as the Lord commanded, goes out to the rock, as the Lord commanded, but then deviates to his own angry course:

> So Moses took the rod from before the LORD, just as He had commanded him; and Moses and Aaron gathered the assembly before the rock. And he said to them, "Listen now, you rebels; shall we bring forth water for you out of this rock?" (vv. 9–10)

Now, wait a minute! Did we miss something? Where did Moses get the okay to deliver that scathing address? The truth is, He didn't. Then where did it come from? From anger. *Brimming* with hostility, and reacting in unbelief, he takes that rod and preaches an angry sermon to the people. His short fuse prompts him to take advantage of an opportunity to level these *rebels* with simmering verbiage.

I think there's even a hint of blasphemy here. "Shall *we* bring water out of the rock?" he asks. But Moses, when did *you* ever bring water out of a rock? Isn't *God* the one who summons water? True enough. But when you give in to rage, you sort of black out; you set aside your right mind and are driven by the unchecked emotions of anger. So the text states, Moses "lifted up his hand and *struck* the rock *twice* with his rod" (20:11, italics mine).

God had told him to *speak* to the rock; Moses *struck* it, not just once, but *twice*. And I frankly doubt whether he even cared if water came. He probably hoped it wouldn't. He was so angry, he wanted their throats to stay dry. He wanted them to choke and writhe in their thirst. "Do you think we'll give *you* water, you low-life scumbags? Hah!" So he belts the rock—Wham! Wham!—and much to his surprise, out comes water. Scripture tells us that "water came forth abundantly, and the congregation and their beasts drank" (v. 11). Absolutely amazing! Amazing *grace!*

But that's the way God's grace works, isn't it? Have you ever acted in rash unbelief, and yet God went ahead and opened up the door in spite of you? Talk about super humiliation. It happens when you're out to lunch spiritually, when you're walking in the flesh and you know it. You knew when it began and you knew the depth and intensity of your carnality, but God graciously gives you what is best anyway. It's remarkable, isn't it, this thing called grace? It was grace that brought forth that clear stream of fresh water for the rebellious Israelites, as well as for ill-tempered Moses.

ANGER'S BITTER FRUIT

Don't think for a moment that God overlooked or excused Moses' temper tantrum. He couldn't. Therefore, He didn't:

> But the LORD said to Moses and Aaron, "Because you have not believed Me, to treat Me as holy in the sight of the sons of Israel, therefore you shall not bring this assembly into the land which I have given them." (v. 12)

As we read these words we're tempted to think, *Isn't that punishment a little harsh? A bit severe? All Moses did was hit a rock. And after all, he was provoked! Those people were ornery enough to test the patience of Job.*

If you read on into Deuteronomy, you will find that Moses prayed three times that the judgment might be reversed. Finally God said, "Don't pray for that again. My answer is no." The words came with finality.

You see, God had tolerated Moses' anger, patiently worked with him, honed him, tooled him, and still Moses let his anger flare. He had been losing his cool since he was forty. He simply never learned this lesson. God tolerated it and patiently put up with it as Moses continued to lose his cool and break tablets and strike rocks. Until at last God said, "No more, Moses. That's enough!"

WHAT WE CAN LEARN

The apostle James offers better counsel than you'll ever receive on a psychiatrist's couch. He writes, "Everyone must be quick to hear, slow to speak and slow to anger; for the anger of man does not achieve the righteousness of God" (James 1:19–20).

In his heart, Moses must have known that. Deep within, he must have been aware that his own raging temper could not advance the righteous cause of a holy God. Yet through the years, he never allowed his patient Lord to slay that destructive monster within, and in the end it rose up and consumed him. How tragically sad!

What can we learn from Moses' unwillingness to tame his anger? I suppose there are dozens of points to ponder, but let me highlight three of the most important ones that stand out in my mind.

1. An act of disobedience stems from unbelief.

God said Moses disobeyed Him "because you have not believed Me" (Numbers 20:12). Moses did not say, "I don't want to do it Your way, Lord." It wasn't that simple. His disobedience grew out of his unbelief.

When you know God's will and you willfully move in another direction, that is unbelief, plain and simple. You're saying before the Lord, "I do not believe Your plan is the best." That is why God said to Moses, "Because you have not believed Me. . . ." When Moses walked out of the presence of the Lord, rod in hand, and the glory of God still hovering about him, he had no intention of speaking to that rock. He was fuming. He'd had it!

He planned to disobey. As he walked out he turned a deaf ear toward God and said, in effect, "My plan is better than Yours. I'll strike this rock." In doing so, He demonstrated what he really believed—that God didn't know the best way to handle those rebels.

F. B. Meyer, a trustworthy commentator of Scripture from a previous generation, wrote this regarding unbelief: "It is a solemn question for all of us whether we are sufficiently accurate in our obedience. It is a repeated burden of those sad chapters of Hebrews, which tell the story of the wilderness wanderings—the cemetery chapters of the New Testament—that 'they could not enter in because of unbelief.' But throughout the verses the margin suggests the alternative reading of 'disobedience'; they could not enter in because of disobedience, because, you see, disobedience and unbelief are the two sides of the same coin—a coin of the devil's mintage. They who disobey do not believe; and they who do not believe disobey."[1]

So it is that the New American Standard version renders Hebrews 3:18–19, "And to whom did He swear that they would not enter His rest, but to those who were *disobedient*? So we see that they were not able to enter because of *unbelief*" (italics mine).

I can't explain why it happens, but to my shame, I must admit I've done the same thing. Haven't you? There are times that I get so angry and become so determined to do my will that I block out God's better plan. I do it out of sheer stubbornness. My jaw is set and my teeth are clenched. Looking back later, however, I invariably admit the act held no satisfaction for me. With deep remorse I realize my sin was rank unbelief, not mere disobedience.

2. A public act of disobedience diminishes God's glory.

God declared that Moses' unbelief failed to treat God "as holy in the sight of the sons of Israel" (Numbers 20:12). In other words, "You've tainted My holiness, Moses. You have encouraged these people to forget that I am a holy God." This is an especially important consideration for a servant of God whom He places into leadership. Perhaps that is why James counsels, "Not many of you should presume to be teachers, my brothers, because you know that we who teach will be judged more strictly" (James 3:1, NIV).

313

All God's servant-leaders live in a divine goldfish bowl, as it were. We are on display. If you serve as an officer in your church, if you are known for some leadership position in a Christian institution, you are a public letter displayed before the world. Your act of willful disobedience publicly casts a shadow upon the glory of God, and He is jealous that such a dreadful thing never happen.

One man wrote, "The plain and sobering lesson is that God deals more stringently with the sins of leaders, especially when their public actions involve His glory." There are times when that thought haunts me.

3. Any such act, though forgiven, bears painful consequences.

After Moses, prompted by anger, committed this sin, the Lord declared, "you shall not bring this assembly into the land which I have given them" (Numbers 20:12). God told His servant flatly, "You will not step foot into the Promised Land."

Now, wait a minute. Didn't God forgive Moses of the sinful act he committed? Yes, indeed. And more to the point, you might be asking, "Won't God forgive *me* if I disobeyed Him just today?" Yes, He will. But let's suppose you have committed this sin frequently (as in Moses' case) and your unbroken habit has brought reproach upon the name and the glory of Christ. He forgives that sin each time it's honestly confessed, but the repeated sin's earthly consequences can be terribly painful.

Did God forgive David for his dreadful sin against Bathsheba, along with the murder and deception in the year that followed his adultery? Yes. But if you study the life of David, you'll notice it can be outlined like the peak of a roof. In the first part of his rule, David went all the way up. The son of Jesse never lost a battle, as the boundaries of Israel rolled out from six thousand to sixty thousand square miles. His reign was like an unstoppable express train of success, rolling on and on, *until Bathsheba.*

Suddenly he began to lose on the battlefield. The wheels came off the wagon. Everything changed. Unrest and disharmony erupted in his home. His leadership skills faded. He lost favor with his son and was forced to run from Absalom. He literally became a fugitive in his own kingdom. Terrible consequences!

God does not look favorably upon the smearing of His glory by His child. He may be longsuffering, but He will not always remain patient. Forgiving? Yes. But never forget, there are times even forgiven sins bear terrible consequences.

GOD OF ALL MY MOMENTS

Wouldn't you love the ability to go back in time and change something you did or said? I know there have been moments in my life—awful moments when I acted on the impulse of the flesh—that I would dearly love to call back. But alas, I cannot.

Don't you imagine, during those days prior to his homegoing, Moses would have cheerfully given his right arm to relive that incident at the rock? *"Oh Lord, if I could only back up and do that all over! I would have cried out for Your help to control my anger. I would have been more concerned for Your glory. I would have done exactly as You instructed."*

But he couldn't go back. In a single moment of rage (think of it!), he forfeited his right to lead Israel and threw away the opportunity to enter the Promised Land. As I ponder that tiny slice of time in Moses' life, my mind ranges through the Scriptures to other such moments:

- What would Eve give for another chance before the tree in the Garden?

- What would Jephthah give to call back the reckless vow he made on his way to battle the Ammonites?

- What would David give to relive that night on the rooftop, when he first saw Bathsheba?

- What would King Uzziah give to call back that day when he bulled into the Temple and pushed past God's priests to offer a forbidden sacrifice?

But the sad fact is, we cannot go back. None of us can. We cannot undo sinful deeds or unsay sinful words. We cannot reclaim those moments when we were possessed by rage, or lust, or cruelty, or indifference, or hard-headed pride. Like Moses, we may be forgiven for those sins and have them blotted out of our record by the blood of Christ. Even so, we must live with the consequences of our words and our actions. What we sow, the Scriptures warn, we will also reap.

This is a sobering reminder to me that life on earth is really nothing more than a string of moments, one after another. And I do not want my testimony for Jesus Christ to be shattered by a single moment of indulging my flesh. I don't want *one moment* of rage or pride or arrogance to cast a shadow over a lifetime of walking with my Lord. Frankly, I fear that possibility. And do you know what? I *want* to fear that possibility. When I stop fearing it, I am in grave danger.

David once prayed, "Keep back Your servant from presumptuous sins; let them not rule over me; then I will be blameless, and I shall be acquitted of great transgression" (Psalm 19:12). The Living Bible renders that verse, "Keep me from deliberate wrongs; help me to stop doing them. Only then can I be free of guilt and innocent of some great crime."

What a great prayer! "Lord, you know my capacity to throw everything over in one stupid, fleshly act. Keep me from it! Restrain me. Guard me from trashing it all in one horrible moment of rage or lust. If You guard me and keep me, Lord, I'll never have to look back and mourn over committing such a deed."

No, we can't go back. Our gracious Lord has covered our past with His own blood, given on the cross for us. David reminds us that, "As far as the east is from the west, so far has He removed our transgressions from us" (Psalm 103:13).

But we *can* learn to walk much closer with Him, day by day, hour by hour, moment by moment. We *can* keep short accounts with Him and lean on the Holy Spirit to guard our hearts and shield us from destructive, life-shattering sins. He will do it. He has promised to provide us with a way of escape so that we can bear up under any temptation (Hebrews 10:13)—*any* temptation at *any* moment.

If this becomes our way of life, my friend, when God says speak to the rock, we *will* speak, not strike. And the water that flows from those moments of obedience will refresh a multitude, including ourselves, with no aftertaste of regret.

CHAPTER EIGHTEEN

Filling the Shoes of Moses

It's hard to be the replacement for a hero. And the greater the hero, the more difficult the task. It's no fun to step into the oversized shoes of a legend.

The man or woman who follows a great predecessor is often forgotten, even though he or she may be quite capable. Put yourself in the place of Andrew Johnson, who had to assume the presidency after Lincoln was cut down by an assassin. What an assignment! No matter what he said, no matter what he did, he would always come off looking less than the best. That's the way it is when you follow a giant.

Can you tell me who took the place of Gen. Douglas MacArthur when President Truman called him home from Korea? Try as I might, I can't come up with that name, either. Who moved into Number 10 Downing Street after Winston Churchill left office? I certainly can't recall.

Or how do you think the pastor felt who was called to take the place of the great Peter Marshall in Washington, D.C.? You can't even name him, can you? Neither can I. How about the man who followed Donald Barnhouse at the Tenth Memorial Presbyterian Church of Philadelphia?

Or how about the one who assumed the post of Bible teacher Henrietta Mears? Does anyone recall the name of her replacement? Or how about the ones who took over the duties of Harry Ironside or G. Campbell Morgan or Charles Haddon Spurgeon, or sat in the faculty chair vacated by the late, great B. B. Warfield of Princeton Seminary? Difficult roles to fill! So difficult, in fact, that those who replace great leaders are often referred to as "sacrificial lambs," since they seldom remain very long.

Dawson Trotman founded the Navigators, a parachurch ministry focused on Christian discipleship. He was a man of great discipline, boundless enthusiasm, steely determination, and broad vision. It was he who first arranged and organized the follow-up ministry still used by Billy Graham's crusade team.

At the young age of fifty, Trotman was called home through a drowning accident in Schroon Lake, New York. Just before he drowned, he told his wife he'd seen a premonition of his death, so the two of them sat down and together mapped out the future for the Navigators, sort of like buying the nails and wood for your own coffin.

The person God chose as Trotman's replacement was Lorne Sanny, a man markedly different from Trotman in personality, appearance, physique, style, and expression. Who would have thought that a Sanny would follow a Trotman? Certainly not Sanny. He often said that when the ministry's leaders came to him and said, "We feel God has placed you on the heart of this work," he wanted to flee in the opposite direction. But what an outstanding choice!

I also think of Richard Seume, who filled the pulpit of Emmanuel Baptist Church in Richmond, Virginia, for over a dozen years. He was eloquent, handsome, tall and dark, an evangelist at heart, and a heart-warming devotional expositor with a winsome personality. In God's marvelous providence, Seume was suddenly plucked from Emmanuel and sent to the Wheaton Bible Church in Wheaton, Illinois, a move that took most of us by surprise.

The good people at Emmanuel waited and waited for God's man. Finally God called Dr. Stanley Touissaint—a name I doubt many would recognize, but a man who was instrumental in shaping my skills (and the skills of many others at Dallas Seminary) in handling the Greek New Testament—to that pulpit in Richmond. He isn't tall and dark or as handsome as Seume. In fact, he has a short, rather stumpy appearance, brought on by a battle with polio he fought in his early years. He walks with a limp, but what an outstanding man of God! He isn't a warm devotional speaker, but a classic professorial type—more of a teaching expositor. Though quite different from Dr. Seume, God used Dr. Touissaint for several effective years at Emmanuel. Thankfully, he is now back at Dallas Seminary—*where he belongs!*

The truth is, the individuals who take over the duties of great men and great women are usually quite different from their predecessors but are nevertheless appointed by God to do the job that needs to be done. Frequently God uses them to change the direction of a group or organization, which is not an easy or welcomed task but often a necessary one.

For example, you probably can't name the person who replaced Hudson Taylor at the China Inland Mission, but that new leader reshaped the whole mission. God used a successor in the wake of a very successful predecessor to do a whole new work.

Now, I don't know God's plan for your life. Neither do you. But for all you know, He is training you and shaping you *this very moment* to step in and serve as a pastor or an officer or as a board member or as a student body leader, to fill the shoes of someone who has done a bang-up job. Sure, you're different from that person. But if God is calling you into that unenviable place of His appointment, He can use you in a remarkable way.

How do you replace a great man or great woman? What do you do when it comes time to choose a successor for an effective leader, whether the leadership position concerns a school, a business, a ministry, or a political role? How do you conduct an effective search and make the right decision, especially when the shoes you need to fill belonged to a giant?

It's a simple fact that all great leaders must eventually be replaced, even men like Lincoln. Or Roosevelt. Or MacArthur. Or Walvoord. Or Billy Graham. Or Moses.

And while those departures take many of us by surprise, they never take God by surprise. When a man of God fades from the scene, nothing of God fades. He always has His Joshuas waiting in the wings.

GOD'S CANDIDATE

Moses, you'll recall, was barred from entering the Promised Land not only because he indulged his rage or because he disobeyed God by striking the rock instead of speaking to it as commanded. Through that act of disobedience, he had publicly tarnished the glory that belonged to the Lord. And God had said, "That's enough, Moses. You're going to be replaced. I'm calling someone else." It must have been a heartrending time for Israel and certainly painful for its long-time leader.

But who was qualified? Who could ever take Moses' place? He would have to be an incredibly strong leader, someone unintimidated by the memory of Moses' greatness. The hurdles of those many outside challenges and the difficulties from internal opposition must not frighten him. The replacement had to be a man on whom the hand of God rested. In Numbers 14 we read of such a man.

By this point in the narrative, the Hebrew nation had come to the edge of Canaan and sent out twelve spies to check out the land. When the spies returned, ten of them said, "Forget all that talk about conquering this land. There are giants in there!" God was so displeased with the people that He said to Moses and Aaron,

> "How long shall I bear with this evil congregation who are grumbling against Me? I have heard the complaints of the sons of Israel, which they are making against Me. Say to them, 'As I live,' says the LORD, 'just as you have spoken in My hearing, so I will surely do to you; your corpses will fall in this wilderness, even all your numbered men, according to your complete number from twenty years old and upward, who have grumbled against Me. Surely you shall not come into the land in which I swore to settle you, *except Caleb . . . and Joshua*'"
> (Numbers 14:27–30, italics mine)

Who was qualified to take Moses' place? Only two men had the necessary credentials. Only two leaders had received years of training at the feet of Moses and had watched God's hand in the lives of the people: namely, Caleb and Joshua.

320

So why didn't God name Caleb as Moses' replacement? Why Joshua? I think Numbers 11:28 reveals the likely reason for His choice. Scripture calls Joshua "the attendant of Moses from his youth."

It is highly significant that Joshua served Moses in such a way. No doubt Caleb was every bit as godly, courageous, and qualified as Joshua, but he had not been honed and mentored by Moses. Think of what it must have been like to have worked as Moses' servant from your early years. Talk about an unusual privilege! As a matter of fact, that is how most men entering the ministry used to be trained. A hundred and more years ago, a man preparing for the ministry did not normally go to seminary. He simply moved into the home of an older, more experienced minister and imbibed the principles of godliness, the disciplines of study and prayer, the wisdom of dealing with knotty problems related to the ministry, and the direction involved in leading a congregation from the older man's life. He learned what he needed to know by rubbing shoulders over an extended period of time with a seasoned minister.

Charles Spurgeon habitually trained younger men at his footstool, as it were, then released them to the ministry. G. Campbell Morgan did the same. And that's not a half-bad plan. Seminaries are realizing the wisdom of this today. Most require their students to be involved in pastoral internships where they get first-hand ministry experience under the direction of veteran pastors and seasoned pastoral staffs.

That's why Joshua was better qualified than Caleb to succeed Moses; he'd been personally trained for the task. Now, I don't believe he *knew* he was being groomed to take Moses' place. (It probably would have scared the younger man spitless to think he was in training to lead the nation into the Promised Land.) But that is exactly what God was up to during those long years of Joshua's serving Moses.

THE LORD'S WORK MOVES ON

Numbers 27 illustrates a simple, basic principle: *When a man of God dies, nothing of God dies.* When a man of God is moved on to another position, nothing of God moves on. It is all too easy for a person who remains in the same position for many years, being used of God to accomplish much in

321

his ministry to replace (almost) God in the minds of people. Then when that person is moved to another ministry or dies or fails, many of those who idolized their leader fall by the wayside. God teaches us in Numbers 27 that when He moves a man on, like Moses, and buries him on the mountain, nothing of God is buried. The Lord remains hard at work; His plans move forward, His affairs competently tended by other hands.

When Donald Barnhouse passed on, nothing of God passed on in the work and ministry of Tenth Memorial Presbyterian Church. Nothing of the Navigators died when Trotman died. Nothing of China Inland Mission ended when Taylor was called home. Why not? Because God lives on. Invariably, one of His servants picks up the torch and carries it forward. It is so easy to develop tunnel vision, rather than to see God at work in the lives of gifted individuals down through time.

In Numbers 27 we find Moses on the edge of death, viewing the land he would not be permitted to enter. What a bittersweet moment that must have been!

> Then the LORD said to Moses, "Go up to this mountain of Abarim, and see the land which I have given to the sons of Israel. When you have seen it, you too will be gathered to your people [an Old Testament way of saying he will die], as Aaron your brother was. . . ." (vv. 12–13, brackets mine)

God told His servant, "When you have seen the Promised Land, you will die." Now, some people might read such an announcement and think, *How cruel can you get?* It sounds to them like a young man falling in love with a woman, only to have God say, "Take one final look at her this evening. Then tomorrow she's going to marry somebody else." Or like saying to a hungry dog, "See this fresh T-bone? Well, you can't have it." Why would God do such a thing to Moses?

First, God is not a mocker, nor is He cruel. We never find Moses submerged in self-pity. We never see Moses shaking his fist and saying to God, "Why have You done this to me?" No, God was not teasing Moses but blessing him. He was showing Moses that He keeps His word.

322

You see, for forty years God had been telling Moses, "I'm going to lead these people into the Promised Land." And so, appropriately, on the edge of that land, the Lord told Moses to climb up that mountain range and look across to Canaan. In doing so, he would see that God keeps His word. It was as if God told His servant, "Moses, you forfeited the right to enter the land by your disobedience and unbelief. You took the glory that belonged to Me, and you did so publicly. I can't have that kind of man take My people into the land. Nevertheless, I want you to see that I keep My word."

Something happened in the heart of Moses when he gazed upon that land. Feelings deeper than nostalgia stirred his soul. From the depths of his shepherd's heart, Moses realized the people of Israel needed a leader. Fierce enemies awaited them in Canaan—high walls, iron chariots, intractable foes, subtle temptations.

As a rule these Canaanites were a godless people. Historical documents and archaeological finds have shown that pornography quite likely got its start in Canaan, as did the wholesale perversion of sex. The grapevine was just as fast and devastating in those days as it is today, and Moses knew those old pagans were wicked to the core. He also knew that, in order for the people of God to be preserved from both military and spiritual defeat, they needed a strong and uncompromising leader.

But knowledge is one thing; action is another. In his last moments on earth, Moses demonstrated once again how he could excel at both. In his last official act, he once again revealed the magnanimity of his heart. Listen to a man unselfish enough to think ahead:

> Then Moses spoke to the LORD, saying, "May the LORD, the God of the spirits of all flesh, appoint a man over the congregation, who will go out and come in before them, and who will lead them out and bring them in, so that the congregation of the LORD will not be like sheep which have no shepherd." (vv. 15–17)

Moses made two requests of the Lord regarding his successor. He knew that this leader would need two irreplaceable qualities.

A MAN OF GOD'S CHOOSING

First, Moses requested that this successor be God's own choice. He said, "May the Lord appoint a man. . . ."

It would be easy to skim right over those simple words. But think about what Moses might have said. He might very well have pulled a short list out of his back pocket and said, "If You don't mind, Lord, I'd like to bounce a few names off You and see what You think."

Strong leaders tend to wrestle with the desire to appoint their own successors. I've seen it happen, and I've seen it fail over and over again. When a strong leader appoints his own successor, he usually appoints someone very much like himself. Yet it is frequently God's plan to appoint a different kind of man to bring a whole new dimension that would otherwise remain undeveloped.

Moses was wise enough to see that danger and said, "Lord, let him be *Your* appointment. You tell me who You want." He didn't hold up to God a handful of candidates and say, "Choose a card. I have four in mind; whichever one of these four You choose will be fine." Instead he said, "I have no suggestions. You make the man known to us, and we'll appoint him." Moses knew Israel's leader must be a man singled out by God Himself.

That's especially important when you consider who God is. Moses calls Him, "the God of the spirits of all flesh." God is unlike man in that He sees straight through to the spirit, while we see only the thin, outward wrappings. God reminds us of this truth in 1 Samuel 16:7, where He says, "Man looks on the outward appearance, the LORD looks on the heart."

Samuel got a full taste of what that means centuries after Moses' era when it came time to find a successor to Saul, the first king of Israel. Saul was a tall man, head and shoulders above everybody else. Most likely, he was handsome, winsome, and impressive. He would have been a great political candidate for our own era. With his big physique and chiseled good looks, he would have been a natural for TV ads and magazine covers. He probably would have had a deep bass voice that would have had "soccer moms" lining up to vote for him.

But physically attractive as he may have been, the man was a moral and spiritual wreck. He discredited himself because he walked in the flesh. So God removed him from office and said to Samuel, "Go find My replacement, Samuel. He'll be in the house of Jesse."

Obedient prophet that he was, Samuel saddled up and took off down the road for Jesse's ranch near Bethlehem. When he arrived, he saw Eliab, the eldest son in Jesse's family. He looked at Eliab and said to himself, "Bingo! There's the man. The Lord's anointed is standing before me." But the Lord said, "Hold it! Not so fast." (Swindoll paraphrase). Immediately He made it clear to Samuel, "This man is not My choice."

Do you know what Samuel was looking for? Interestingly, he had in mind another just like Saul. Eliab had the same stature and rugged good looks of Israel's first failed king. But God said, "No way! You back off a minute. I have already selected My man." And whom did He pick? Someone totally *unlike* Saul—a young shepherd boy, a teenager overlooked even by his own dad. Jesse hadn't thought of bringing David in to introduce him to the prophet along with his other sons. Samuel had to ask Jesse, "Are these *all* your sons?" Brought back to reality by the question, Jesse replied, "Oh, yeah. I almost forgot. I've got one more. He's out in the back forty with the sheep." (That's what happens when you've got a corral full of kids.) As you recall, young David had the inner qualities needed as Saul's replacement.

God sees the inside of the person, not just the outside. And that makes all the difference. But there was also a second request in Moses' prayer.

A MAN WITH A SHEPHERD'S HEART

Moses asks for a man "who will go out and come in before them, who will lead them out and bring them in, that the congregation of the LORD may not be like sheep which have no shepherd" (v. 17). In other words, "Lord, we need a man who realizes he must be in touch with the people before he can minister to them. He needs to be a people person."

Moses was saying, "These people don't need a mystic. They don't need a man preoccupied by his love for research, as important as that may be. These folks don't really need a slick-type CEO or a super-efficient organizational genius. They need a *shepherd*. They need a man who knows people, who will minister to people, understand people, and know how to guide people."

In whatever capacity you might minister—as a Bible teacher, as a student preparing for the ministry, as a woman of God ministering in your area of giftedness—your ministry is primarily *people*, not shuffling papers, not crunching numbers, not making phone calls, not writing letters, not planning programs, or noodling over strategies for the next decade. Of course, all of those things must be done. I must sign and/or write an average of forty to fifty letters a week and get involved in planning sessions, too. Administrative details need to be handled. (As few as I can get by with!) But as I frequently remind the students at Dallas Seminary, "Remember this: The ministry is people." I learned this lesson through the hard knocks of dealing with life in the ministry and by making some ridiculous mistakes because I wasn't attuned to the hearts of people.

Do you know the most common thing I hear from individuals just beginning to come to church? They want very much to get to know some of us on staff, and they'll say, "You don't know me, but I come on Sunday to hear you preach." And they almost apologize, as if to say, "Hey, I'm sorry to take your time, but I just want to shake your hand." I go out of my way to say to each one, "You are as important as anybody else in this entire church. There is no insignificant member of the family of God." I don't say this to make a good public relations statement nor to make an impression. I say it because I believe it. Whoever you are, whatever you do, you are special before the God who has chosen you.

I love the old album recorded many years ago by the Bill Gaither Trio called *Especially for Children*. It came in two volumes and featured a song titled "I'm a Promise." I know there are two volumes because we wore out Volume 1 and had to run out and get Volume 2. My son Chuck, then five years old, insisted.

Chuck loved those records more than I did. He would listen to the same record day in, day out, almost without pause and without a break. He was relentless. Eventually we found the answer—headphones!

Hour after hour Chuck sat in our large, overstuffed chair in the family room with those oversized headphones clamped over his ears, belting out, "I am a promise, da da da."

Take a minute to read the lyrics that so captivated our youngest:

> I'm a promise, I'm a possibility,
> I'm a promise with a capital P.
> I can be anything, anything God wants me to be.
>
> You are a promise, you are a possibility,
> You are a promise with a capital P.
> You are a great big bundle of potentiality.

(I *love* that line!)

> And if you'll listen, you'll hear God's voice,
> And if you'll try, He'll help you make the right choice.
> You're a promise to be *anything* He wants you to be.[1]

To tell you the truth, Chuck could have played that old phonograph record until the grooves went flat, and I wouldn't have minded. Why? Because the song has it right. People have no idea of their potentiality. That's part of the problem in our day with breakdowns of identity. Men and women, boys and girls, don't understand who they are in God's sight.

Apparently, however, that wasn't young Chuck's particular problem. His church choir teacher rapped on my door one day and said, "I want to tell you something that happened with your youngest. We were talking about going to heaven. I was telling all the children how great it would be. Chuck stood there all by himself, listening. I was saying, 'When we're in heaven, we're going to be made like Jesus. We're going to have *a whole new body*, and we're going to be just like Him. We're going to be *different* from what we are now.'

"Chuck raised his little hand to speak and declared, 'I don't wanna go to heaven.' 'You don't want to go to heaven?' I asked. 'Why not?' He said firmly, 'Because I *like* my body.'"

I thought, "Good for you, son!" Hey, you *ought* to like your body. God gave you that body, and I don't care if you're a six-foot-five-inch, thirteen-year-old girl. Listen, "You're a great big bundle of potentiality!" God knows exactly what you are and what you need.

And one of the things you need is a shepherd who believes in you as much as you need to believe in yourself. That's why Moses said, "Please, God, don't send us a sterile scholar! Don't pick some slicked-back corporate executive in a tailored Louis Roth suit. Send us a man with a great heart for people. Send us somebody who will take care of the flock." That's a crucial balance that can *never* be learned out of a textbook or in a seminary classroom. I can name dozens of teachers, scores of superb preachers, and many able administrators. But I can't name many true, caring, servant-hearted shepherds.

So Moses prayed that God would appoint the right man, and that the man would be a shepherd of God's flock. And you know what? God had just the man in mind: "So the LORD said to Moses, 'Take Joshua....'" (verse 18).

I love that! God was never biting His nails in heaven, wondering who would take Moses' place. He didn't need to consult a personnel agency, do an internet search, or launch a corporate head-hunting expedition. He knew from the beginning who He would call. He already had Joshua's resumé on top of the pile. He'd been training him for years.

Church boards and mission organizations often wonder who could possibly replace a retiring "star." They wrestle with who might take the reins. Perhaps they have a person in mind whom they think is shaped for it, but wise are those who wait on God to be sure. "Lord, we've got a few ideas, but who would *You* appoint to shepherd the flock? Will you reveal that to us, Lord?"

When you wait upon God like that in faith, don't be surprised at how directly He puts forward a specific name. That's what he did with Moses' request: "Take Joshua the son of Nun, he is a man in whom is the Spirit, and lay your hands on him" (v. 18).

God didn't give Moses a multiple choice. He didn't run one personality against another and say, "Choose between these five men; the majority vote wins." The Lord said, "*Take Joshua* and place your hands on him. He's got what it takes. He has My Spirit within him. He is My choice."

Why did the Lord direct Moses to lay his hands upon Joshua? In Bible times the laying on of hands conferred authority upon the recipient. The practice was a visual picture of ordination, if you will, and connected the leadership of one generation to that of another. That is why Paul, in the New Testament, tells Timothy, "Do not lay hands upon anyone too hastily and thereby share responsibility for the sins of others; keep yourself free from sin" (1 Timothy 5:22).

The rite does not pass on physical power, but it does establish a spiritual connection of conferring authority. To make sure no one missed the significance of His command, the Lord instructed Moses to have Joshua stand before the priest and before all the congregation at a public commissioning service. "You shall put some of your authority on him, in order that all the congregation of the sons of Israel may obey him" (v. 20). In other words, "Moses, let it be publicly known that you support this man."

As soon as Moses received his orders, he obeyed them. "Moses did just as the LORD commanded him; and he took Joshua and set him before Eleazar the priest and before all the congregation. Then he laid his hands on him and commissioned him, just as the LORD had spoken through Moses" (vv. 22,23).

Moses followed the Lord's plan without argument. That impresses me. He didn't say, "But Lord, I would rather have Caleb." He heard God's choice and accepted it. Then he took God's man and introduced him publicly as Israel's new leader.

What a set of big shoulders! I don't detect a scintilla of self-pity or resentment or bitterness at this point in his biography. No sour grapes. Not a hint of envy or jealousy. I don't think he got Joshua in the tent a few hours later and whined, "You lucky dog" or, "It isn't fair." That's not Moses' style. He said (no doubt with a broad smile), "Joshua, you're God's man. I'm proud of you." He couldn't get out of Joshua's way fast enough.

That's a good model for all of us. If you live to see your successor step on the scene, applaud his or her arrival and then *get out of the way*. Back off. Refuse to haunt the old hallways. Let God minister and work in the beautiful fashion only He can manage. And support that individual with all your heart and soul. Do it verbally. Do it privately. Do it publicly. Do it personally. After all, he or she is God's appointment, God's man or woman. You've had your day, now it's time for him or her to shine.

GOD'S STEADY HAND IN YOUR TRANSITIONS

I see three crucial lessons in this episode from Moses' life that can help us in our own walk of faith.

When God removes, He replaces.

Let me repeat a line I stated earlier: When a man of God dies, nothing of God dies. When God reaches down and plucks one flower, He nutures another one. When He pulls up one plant, He has another ready to bloom. He never runs out of qualified replacements.

No matter who you are, you have a part in this process. Let me encourage you to pray for the churches that are looking for pastors. Pray for the schools that need presidents and/or faculty members, the mission boards that need directors, and the Christian organizations that need leaders to step into places of public responsibility. Pray for those whom God will call to fill unique positions in His kingdom plan. Pray for the new officers who will be stepping into the shoes of former office holders. Pray that God's people will endorse and embrace God's appointments. Humanly speaking, the future of the church hangs on its qualified leadership. Pray that we will have leaders of God's choosing.

And if you are approached regarding a ministry appointment in your own church, or in some significant appointment outside your comfort zone, think seriously about it. Cover it with prayer. Don't give a quick answer. Consider this: It just may be that God is in it. Think of it as Joshua must have when God said, "You are to take Moses' place." Replacing a godly leader is an awesome responsibility. Treat it as such.

When God appoints, He approves.

The beautiful thing about the Lord is that when He takes control, He blesses. He approves when we seek His counsel for a replacement. When the Lord said to Moses, "You take Joshua," He didn't have to add, "I will bless him." Why not? Because Joshua was *God's* selection. The blessing came with the appointment.

It's an humbling experience to be chosen by God for a position of great responsibility. You answer to Him. You punch no timeclock for men to examine. Your work is known only to Him. Nobody follows up to check on you.

I find too many churches making one of two common mistakes when they search for a man to follow a great leader. First, they try to get someone just like that individual. Or second, they panic and grab the first available man who comes along. *Both approaches are lethal.* The best choice is always God's choice.

When God sustains, the leader succeeds.

Joshua's life perfectly illustrates this truth. God sustained Joshua's life, and the Old Testament does not record a single one of his sins. Now, don't misunderstand. I'm sure Joshua sinned, but the record makes it clear his life was not characterized by gross failure. His success was due to God's sustaining him.

By the way, when God is given proper control of a ministry, there is no such thing as failure. Isn't that an exciting thought? "You mean we won't have lean days? We won't run into headaches and opposition?" I didn't say that. I said there will never be failure if God is in charge of a ministry. Why not? Because when He sustains it, the ministry succeeds, and so does His chosen minister.

GOD OF EVERY DETAIL

I am always amazed to hear how the Lord uses His Word in the lives of His people. I don't know your circumstances. I don't know how God intends to use this episode from the life of Moses in your own life.

It may be that these words fall on a very hungry heart. Or perhaps you have been strengthened and encouraged with the thought that you're very special to God, that none of His children are insignificant. Or maybe you're engaged in the awesome task of finding a man or a woman for a position that carries a great weight of responsibility, and you've been reminded that you are dependent, more than ever, on God for His Joshua. Or perhaps *you* are that Joshua, and you've been asked to accept a responsibility broader than you ever dreamed.

Whatever your circumstances, I want to remind you that our heavenly Father cares about areas of your life that would seem insignificant to a distant deity. He's never too busy to hear your hurts, to wipe away your tears, to whisper words of encouragement, and to put His big shoulder under your load.

As I write these words, I'm praying that our sovereign God might be a very personal comfort to you this week. I pray especially for you who are wrestling with loneliness and discouragement. Even though you're surrounded by people, deep within there's an ache. Friend, God can meet your need as only He can, even as He did in the heart of Moses just a few hours before the great man's death.

If you're God's Joshua, you don't need to worry that you'll be forgotten. You don't need to worry that the shadow of your predecessor (or successor) will eclipse you and your ministry in the years to come. In fact, you don't need to worry about *anything*. If you're God's Joshua, you're right where you ought to be. Remind yourself that God is sovereign. He has everything under His control. He will have His way in His time, for His glory, which includes your life, your position, and your future. Worrying over any of this is a waste. He's got *every detail* covered—every one.

Think of it this way: There's no such thing as God's being *almost* sovereign.

CHAPTER NINETEEN

Obituary of a Hero

O ne afternoon many years ago, my oldest son Curt and I went looking at tombstones. I had been giving final thoughts to the thirty-fourth chapter of Deuteronomy, prior to preaching on it, and was having difficulty getting into the spirit of it.

I walked through our family room at home and saw him lying on the floor, resting.

"Curt," I said, "I'm going to go look at tombstones."

"Can I go with you?" he asked.

"Sure, son. That would be fine."

So we got in the car and drove out to a nearby cemetery, where we walked around for about an hour and a half. Have you ever done that? It may sound ghoulish, but you get quite an education when you read the epitaphs on tombstones. It's fascinating!

One tombstone in Loma Vista, California, has just three words: "You can't win," then gives a name. That tells you something, doesn't it? Another one says, "Our darling son, May 3, 1940 to May 7, 1940." Full of emotion.

I love to wander through cemeteries when I visit historic cities. Call me

MOSES: A MAN OF SELFLESS DEDICATION

eccentric if you wish, but visiting these graveyards has become one of my favorite pastimes. I find it intriguing to read what was chiseled into granite about people now long gone from this old earth.

A friend of mine who shares this unique interest recently e-mailed me a few pages of actual epitaphs for my collection. Bear in mind, someone had to get down close to the tombstone and wipe away the dirt and moss to read these inscriptions:

A lonely widow evidently composed this epitaph in a Vermont cemetery:

> Sacred to the memory of
> my husband John Barnes
> who died January 3, 1803
> His comely young widow, aged 23, has
> many qualifications of a good wife, and
> yearns to be comforted.

On a tombstone in England, somebody saw this chiseled inscription:

> Sir John Strange
> Here lies an honest lawyer,
> And that is Strange.

In a Georgia cemetery:

> I told you I was sick!

The grave of Ellen Shannon in Girard, Pennsylvania, reads almost like a consumer tip:

> Who was fatally burned
> March 21, 1870
> by the explosion of a lamp
> filled with "R. E. Danforth's
> Non-Explosive Burning Fluid"

And what are we to make of the message on the grave of Ezekiel Aikle in East Dalhousie Cemetery, Nova Scotia?

> Here lies
> Ezekial Aikle
> Age 102
> The Good
> Die Young

One thing I've noticed: Every tombstone represents the passage of time in exactly the same way. Wherever you go, you find no difference. The time we spend on this earth is always represented by a small horizontal dash, and that's all. The person could have lived to be eighty or ninety, but a tombstone wraps up all of life in one little dash. That's life, and then it's gone.

I suppose I began to think seriously about death shortly after my dad passed out in the middle of a worship service one Sunday morning almost a quarter of a century ago. He was hospitalized, and things went from bad to worse. First came a heart attack. That led to several strokes, causing paralysis, which made it difficult for him to swallow. Further complications allowed a virus to set in, which led to a fever. And then he contracted pneumonia.

One cold Wednesday night before he died, I visited him in his dimly-lit hospital room. I watched white-clad nurses bustling about their routines and looked at the man dying on a metal bed. The next day I returned and saw a man without teeth, without conscious awareness, staring straight ahead with a distant, hollow look in his eyes. This man who once held my hand, whom I, many years later, held and touched and embraced, was leaving us. Just a short dash, and soon he was gone.

That experience, coupled with my quiet trip to the tombstones, suddenly began to make me feel a part of the scene that unfolded on Mount Pisgah, up there where Moses died. It grips you quietly, but down deep. I think it's wrong to approach a section of Scripture as though you're about to complete a lesson or, for that matter, a book. God's Book is a book of *life*. And with the exception of the death of His Son, the Author of Scripture never lingers long over death. I can count on both hands, with fingers left over, the number of lengthy obituaries found in the Word of God. God's people simply die, and then a whole new dimension of life begins.

But when you study a man as great as Moses, when you bury him at the end of the study and then look back on where you've been, you find that you've boiled things down to some very real basics. Much can be gleaned from reading an obituary. So God invites us to ponder Moses' burial and tombstone to discover heaven's estimate of this great servant of God—a man of selfless dedication.

THE VIEW FROM THE TOP

Chapter 34 of Deuteronomy begins by telling us of the place and purpose of Moses' death: "Now Moses went up from the plains of Moab to Mount Nebo, to the top of Pisgah... " (v. 1).

The summit of Mt. Pisgah reaches a height of 4,500 feet. That's almost a mile. Not too many one-hundred-twenty-year-old men can climb up a mountain almost a mile high and live to tell the story. Yet Moses could. He did it, scrambling hand over hand. There was no trail wide enough to accommodate a walker, and Moses didn't need one anyway.

If you're wondering what condition he was in, that feat alone will provide the answer. When was the last time you climbed a mountain? It's probably been awhile. Maybe you've never done it. I have done it only twice and never plan to do it again. Each time I was huffing and puffing and blowing the house down all the way up that crazy thing, and it wasn't even 3,000 feet high. I felt like a martyr.

Yet here was Moses, almost a century and a quarter old, climbing to the summit of a 4,500-foot-high peak and having a great time when he got up there. You don't find any self-pity in Moses. He knew he was going to die; God had told him so. And the Lord had already placed a man, Joshua, in his place. For the first time in his final forty years, the great burden of leading the nation was off his back. With lightened shoulders, Moses could take each step on the slope in stride. He knew very well that he was about to breathe his last.

Moses teaches us that the believer has no reason to fear or run pan-ic-stricken into the streets when it comes to dying. We all die; that's what life is all about. We're really not ready to live until we're ready to die. So when we're ready to die, *let's just do it.*

I realize, of course, that the thought of dying brings up all kinds of strong feelings. Everything within us longs to hang on to dying loved ones. That clinging desire is poignantly reflected in this poem.

What's wrong with me, Lord?

Week after week
I begged You to take her.
In agony I wept and waited
While she grappled
With insidious pain.
I watched the gradual decline
Of her once strong and lovely body.
I saw her lines of weariness,
Her constant discomfort.
I listened to her broken sobs
As she pleaded for release.
I felt the pressure
Of her trembling fingers
When the gripping pain intensified.
I sensed her growing weakness,
Her deep depression.
Through sleepless nights
I listened to her labored breathing.
In the darkness I cried to You—
Over and over I cried...
Then yesterday morning, Lord,
At the first streak of dawn,
You answered my prayer.
Gently You took her to Yourself—
You rewarded her with fullness of joy.

Thank You, Lord.
Yet even while I thank You,
I wish I could have kept her
Just one more day.
What's wrong with me, Lord?[1]

As I arrived at the last verse of Deuteronomy 34, I didn't want Moses' story to end. I wanted to hang on to him for a few more chapters. I didn't want him to make that final climb up the steep slopes of Pisgah.

Do you ever find yourself wanting to cling to a loved one about to make that last journey? Sure you do. That's part of the flesh deep within us—to keep, not give, to hold on to, not to share. I wanted to hold Moses near and hear his voice just a little longer. I wanted him to linger, but God says, "That's enough. Now, he is Mine." And so He escorts him up to the peak and gives him a final view, the likes of which you and I cannot imagine. We will never see the Promised Land as Moses saw it—that virgin soil that had yet to stick to the sandals of Israel.

Imagine the vista that stretched before him. Moses looked out and "the LORD showed him all the land, Gilead as far as Dan, and all Naphtali and the land of Ephraim and Manasseh, and all the land of Judah as far as the western sea, and the Negev and the plain in the valley of Jericho, the city of palm trees, as far as Zoar" (vv. 1–3).

God gives Moses the e-ticket tour. He starts by looking north, then turns and looks west, then twists around and looks south, and finally turns his head and looks east. Moses is like a beacon in a lighthouse, turning around in a circle. It's a moving scene, even in its geography. Through it all Moses must have clucked his tongue and mumbled to himself, "My, look at that. Beautiful! Beautiful! O, Lord, look at that. What a land!"

In the final analysis, the death of a believer opens up a panoramic, heavenly vista that boggles the mind. It's a whole new dimension. Paul tells us, "No eye has seen, no ear has heard, no mind has conceived what God has prepared for those who love him" (1 Corinthians 2:9, NIV). That is what Moses was looking forward to as he took in this final visual feast of the Promised Land, a piece of real estate he would never set his feet upon.

And then God said, "That's it, Moses. Now come on home."

> Then the LORD said to him, "This is the land which I swore to Abra-
> ham, Isaac, and Jacob, saying, 'I will give it to your descendants'; I
> have let you see it with your eyes, but you shall not go over there."
> So Moses the servant of the LORD died there in the land of Moab,
> according to the word of the LORD. (vv. 4–5)

Moses gave up the spirit. Hero or not, all of us come to that moment
when we leave the body behind and move on to another realm. When I
think of Moses' passing, a double message comes to mind.

THE ALONENESS OF DEATH

Not its *loneliness*, but its *aloneness*—there's a difference. Loneliness suggests
an empty longing, reaching in vain for someone else. Aloneness means
nobody else goes along. That is what I see here. It's a solo flight.

You never take a companion along when you travel through death; you
go all alone. The Talmud says, "Man is born with his fist clenched, but he
dies with his hands open." You don't take anything with you; it all stays
behind. Moses' life, not his possessions, was his legacy. He died high up
on Mt. Pisgah, and he died all alone.

If we're honest, we have to admit that most of us are strangers to being
alone. We have radios, TV, and a fax. We have e-mail, a telephone, and
probably a cell phone or beeper. We have a car, multiple contact points
with friends, and bunches of rendezvous places to meet. It's a sign of our
times to be gregarious. We like involvements. My poet friend, Ruth Harms
Calkin, offers an interesting insight on this matter:

> You know, Lord, how I serve You
> With great emotional fervor
> In the limelight.
> You know how eagerly I speak for You
> At a women's club.

You know how I effervesce when I promote
A fellowship group.
You know my genuine enthusiasm
At a Bible study.

But how would I react, I wonder,
If You pointed to a basin of water
And asked me to wash the callused feet
Of a bent and wrinkled old woman
Day after day,
Month after month,
In a room where nobody saw
And nobody knew?[2]

That's a different story, isn't it? Everything is great just so long as we don't have to be alone. Perhaps that's what makes death so frightening to some. We are so seldom alone. But on the top of Mt. Pisgah, Moses is alone. Joshua wasn't permitted to come along. Aaron was already gone. Only one lone figure stumbled his way over the rocks on the pathless ascent to the summit.

THE SECURITY OF DEATH

Moses died "according to the word of the LORD." Everything ended for the old man exactly as God had arranged it.

I am absolutely comfortable with the fact that God not only knows our times, He knows the ends of our times. Therefore I do not live in fear when I board an airplane. I have no apprehension when I climb in the car for a long trip across the Texas panhandle, or a drive up to Oklahoma, or journey into New Mexico. I don't even fear the Los Angeles freeways or the North Dallas Tollway. I know that in God's plan, He has arranged the extent of my life and, in fact, the very day of my death.

Perhaps you have a ways to go in accepting that thought. Maybe the idea is a little too heavy for you. If so, you quite probably tend to fear the thought of death. Allow me to offer a word of encouragement.

Look at verse 5 once again, but this time put two phrases from that verse side by side. Read the following together: "Moses the servant of the LORD...the word of the LORD." They're near enough to each other to be taken as sort of a rhythmic movement. "The servant of the LORD, according to the word of the LORD, died." They fit together, and that is what brought great security to his death.

That the two thoughts of aloneness and security should fit together seems strange to us, especially at the time of death. Yet, if we want to conquer our fear of death, they *need* to come together in our thinking. They certainly did in the thinking of the apostle Paul. That's why he was able to write, "I eagerly expect and hope that I will in no way be ashamed, but will have sufficient courage so that now as always Christ will be exalted in my body, whether by life or by death. For to me, to live is Christ and to die is gain" (Philippians 1:21–22, NIV). Many of us magnify Him in our lives, but it's another story when it comes time to die. It needn't be.

Moses died alone, but securely. The report of his death is spread throughout the final six verses of Deuteronomy 34. First, Scripture gives us his age: "Although Moses was a hundred and twenty years old... " (v. 7). A century and a score—twelve decades. Yet upon his death, all of Moses' education, all of his fame, all of his fortune, all of his experience, all of the things we would normally hold on to, went with him. None of those things lingered behind.

A WIDER PERSPECTIVE

Death has a way of putting things in proper perspective, doesn't it? That's one of the things I love about the ministry—no two days are ever the same. I often traffic in eternal paths: birth, death, deep sickness, tragedies. I live at the cutting edge of life. Dealing with the dead is just as familiar to the man of God as making the final sale is to a salesperson, or fixing a meal is to a homemaker, or changing a set of plugs is to an auto mechanic. Pastors could run the risk of becoming callused in handling death as a business, but I must say I don't ever remember burying anyone one-hundred-twenty years young.

I left the hospital late one night after my dad's heart attack and spoke a word of appreciation to the nurse who had been so kind to my father in his unconscious state, even when my dad didn't know she was there.

"You know," I said, "he's lived eighty-three great years."

"Yes," she replied, "there aren't too many who die near the age of Moses."

She had no way of knowing I was meditating on that event even as she spoke. I couldn't help thinking, "That's right. I've never buried anybody over a hundred years old. There aren't too many of 'em left."

Most of the centenarians I do know of aren't in the best of health. They're blind, crippled, deaf. Not many mountain climbers are in their nineties. And Moses was a hundred and twenty! We think, *My, he must really have been crippled up.* But that's not what the record states. Scripture reports that "his eye was not dim, nor his vigor abated" (v. 7). The Living Bible says that "his eyesight was perfect and he was as strong as a young man."

My reaction? What a way to live! A hundred and twenty and you don't need glasses; a century and a fifth and you don't need crutches. Moses never did sit around in a rocking chair rubbing on liniment and drinking Ensure. He kept moving on, just as Caleb did, staying fit right up until the end.

You know our problem? We get old before we're old. We start living as if we're ancient before we turn seventy. It's a crime! A guy will get a Ph.D. and feel that he's over the hill because he worked on his degree for a number of years. You're in a going business, doing your part, and your sixty-fifth birthday rolls around. You ask yourself, *Am I getting too old for this?* Nonsense! Longfellow wrote,

> "It is too late!" Ah, nothing is too late—
> Cato learned Greek at eighty; Sophocles
> Wrote his grand Oedipus, and Simonides
> Bore off the prize of verse from his peers
> When each had numbered more than fourscore years;
> And Theophrastus, at fourscore and ten,
> Had begun his Characters of Men.
> Chaucer, at Woodstock, with his nightingales,
> At sixty wrote the Canterbury Tales.

Goethe, at Weimar, toiling to the last,
Completed Faust when eighty years were past.
What then? Shall we sit idly down and say,
"The night has come; it is no longer day"?
Why, age is opportunity no less
Than youth itself, though in another dress.
And as the evening twilight fades away,
The sky is filled with stars, invisible by day.

LIVE TO THE HILT!

You're just as old as you want to be. I think it is a shame that we don't live as Moses lived. The late Jim Elliot said, "Wherever you are, be all there. Live to the hilt every situation you believe to be the will of God." If you're a student, live it up! If you're in business, go for it! If you lose your job, have at it! *Really* be unemployed. If you're having a baby, throw a party! If you release your only child to marriage or business, let her go! Live on! Be "all there," wherever you are.

Stop and think, *What's the alternative?* Climbing into a closet and pulling the door shut behind you? Sadly, I meet men and women every day who have chosen that path. I know they have because, unlike Moses, their eye is dim and their vigor abated.

Even more important than the physical, however, is the spiritual. What did God write on Moses' tombstone about this category of His servant's life? What does Moses' heavenly obituary say? "Since then no prophet has risen in Israel like Moses, whom the LORD knew face to face" (verse 10). When Moses' successor, Joshua, wanted to get direction from God, he had to go to the high priest. Not Moses. Amazingly, he got hold of God's direction through eyeball-to-eyeball contact with the living Lord. His life of one hundred-twenty years was a face-to-face walk of dedication.

Are you past sixty? If so, how is your walk with Jesus Christ? Are you two still on speaking terms? Do you still carry His Book around? Do you still spend time in it? "Oh, well, I'm retired." From the Book? From your walk with Christ?

The Lord says in the New Testament that the older women should minister in a significant, life-impacting way to the younger women (Titus 2:3–4). Yet I can't name that many younger women who have had that experience. And many want it so desperately. Do you know why such a sad situation exists? Because most older women today believe the lie that they have outlived their usefulness or can't relate to the younger generation. Not true! Someone sixty and seventy years young can remain incredibly useful for Christ.

When I was just launching into my ministry, some of my best counsel came from men in their sixties and seventies—men who had pored over God's Book until it was plastered in their character. I used to pray with one man who literally had worn the print off the page in many of the Psalms, just from spending protracted time in that book. When we prayed together it was like kneeling alongside David.

We who sat under the tutelage of the late Dr. Merrill F. Unger at Dallas Seminary knew it was worth it just to be covered by his prayers. Dr. Unger used to pray, "Lord, many of these men are so discouraged today." And the fellow sitting behind me would say, "Boy, that's me, Lord. That is me, right now." Dr. Unger would continue, "and many of these fellows cannot make it financially." "That's me again, Lord. That's me again." We would be entering into this man's power-packed prayer life. Some might think it boring to pray together for five minutes. Not with Merrill Unger! It was a whole seminary education to spend even five minutes under that man's prayer. We followed profs like Unger and Hendricks and Pentecost around like shadows, just to be near them.

I want to hang around men who know the Lord even as Moses did. And Moses knew Him face to face. Now, you and I aren't promised a face-to-face knowledge of God on this side of heaven. Paul writes, "For now we see in a mirror dimly, but *then* face to face; now I know in part, but *then* I shall know fully just as I also have been fully known" (1 Corinthians 13:12). The "then" the apostle writes of is that future time when we shall receive our glorified bodies, and we shall be like Jesus. That's not now. Unlike Moses, we cannot know the Lord face to face quite yet.

On the other hand, the apostle can pray that "the eyes of your heart may be enlightened, so that you will know what is the hope of His calling, what are the riches of the glory of His inheritance in the saints, and what is the surpassing greatness of His power toward us who believe" (Ephesians 1:18–19). He can ask the Lord "that you may be filled with the knowledge of His will in all spiritual wisdom and understanding, so that you will walk in a manner worthy of the Lord, to please Him in all respects" (Colossians 1:9–10). He can say on a personal level, "I count all things to be loss in view of the surpassing value of knowing Christ Jesus my Lord… that I may know Him and the power of His resurrection and the fellowship of His sufferings, being conformed to His death" (Philippians 3:8,10). And he can write of Moses,

> But if the ministry of death, in letters engraved on stones, came with glory, so that the sons of Israel could not look intently at the face of Moses because of the glory of his face, fading as it was, how shall the ministry of the Spirit fail to be even more with glory?… For if that which fades away was with glory, much more that which remains is in glory. Having therefore such a hope, we use great boldness in our speech, and are not as Moses, who used to put a veil over his face that the sons of Israel might not look intently at the end of what was fading away… But we all, with unveiled face beholding as a mirror the glory of the Lord, are being transformed into the same image from glory to glory, just as from the Lord, the Spirit (2 Corinthians 3:7–8,11–13,18)

We can know the Lord deeply, in a way that not even Moses could. And yet the Scripture says that Moses spoke to the Lord face to face. That is the legacy that this great man of God left behind, a legacy and a beautiful memory that his people never forgot. You wonder, *Did those complaining Hebrews really love him, or was he just a convenient target—a lightning rod for their discontent? Did they view him as some distant, profound man of God?*

The answer is found in verse 8. When he died, "The sons of Israel wept for Moses in the plains of Moab thirty days."

Think of that! Why, when many a person dies today, the heirs already have the will sectioned out in thirty days. They didn't do that in Moses' day; they were busy mourning. Oh, how the Israelites loved their deceased leader. His ministry among them so inflamed their hearts that it took a full month for them to mourn his memory. But finally that mourning came to an end.

That ought to be true in our own lives. If you lose a loved one, go ahead and mourn. Cry your eyes out. Don't weep as those who have no hope, but weep for your loss. Grieve their earthly departures. Get it all out. And then stop.

The day I visited the tombstones with Curt, I saw two people in two different places talking to tombstones. I had a good friend who, at the time her husband died, was so broken she spent a lot of time at his tomb. When my mother spoke to her about faith in Jesus Christ, she responded beautifully to His claims, and a few days after her husband's death she became a child of God. And God led her to have a graveyard ministry. Almost to the day of her death, my friend spent her weekends at the cemetery, witnessing to people who were talking to tombstones.

After a death comes a burial, and so it was in the case of Moses. But verse 6 contains one of the most remarkable statements about the whole remarkable career of Moses: "And He [God!] buried him in the valley in the land of Moab, opposite Beth-peor; but no man knows his burial place to this day" (Deuteronomy 34:6, brackets mine).

Moses is the only person in the Bible whom God personally buried. Did you know that? And then the Lord hid the tomb. Why did He do that? Because that grave would have become a second Mecca. They would still be beating a path up Nebo to this day, building shrines, selling popcorn and peanuts, offering all sorts of rides, maybe running a tram up there, with big banners announcing, "Moses' burial place!"

"No way," the Lord said. "Put him in that grave, seal it over, and conceal it, so they'll never know where it is." This was so crucial to the Lord that it even sparked an angelic confrontation. Jude 9 contains one of the stranger accounts in the Bible concerning this event. Jude writes, "But Michael the archangel, when he disputed with the devil and argued about the body of Moses, did not dare pronounce against him a railing judgment, but said,

'The Lord rebuke you.'" Apparently the devil had his own plans for Moses' body, but God said, "Nope. His body is mine just as much as is his soul, and I'm burying the corpse where no one will ever find it. End of story."

All things have their proper wrap-up, as does the story of Moses:

> Since that time no prophet has risen in Israel like Moses, whom the LORD knew face to face, for all the signs and wonders which the LORD sent him to perform in the land of Egypt against Pharaoh, all his servants, and all his land, and for all the mighty power and for all the great terror which Moses performed in the sight of all Israel (34:10–12).

"All...all...all." The word is written all across that passage. Joseph Renan, the famed French philologist and historian, said of Moses, "He is a colossus among figures of humanity."

When we read this part of the epitaph and think of all the mighty power and all the miracles that Moses did, many of us tend to think, *Moses is in another league. I can't touch him. This life I've observed amounts to just another theoretical study. It almost mocks me, because I'm not like Moses.*

What a colossal error we make if we come to such a faulty deduction. Moses was unique, certainly, but he was just a man in the service of God. Still, we can learn much of personal benefit from his life and death.

THREE SECRETS REVEALED

Let's begin to wrap up our study of Moses with three helpful observations.

The secret of fulfillment in life is involvement.

Don't let this first observation fall on deaf ears, even if your hearing isn't what it used to be. One of the worst curses that has ever struck our country is the curse of a retirement attitude. It's not retirement as such, but the attitude that says, "Do not disturb; I've earned my rest," or "I'm finishing my years; don't bother me."

Sometimes that comes out in the thought, *I really don't have much more to contribute.* No wonder the suicide rate of the over-sixties is so high, and that includes many who have plenty of money. The secret of fulfillment is involvement—pitching in, getting busy in God's many-faceted work.

As we've already discovered in this study, only two things on earth are eternal: people and the Bible. When you're planning on retirement, don't plan on checking out with people or with God's Word. If you do, you'll be moving away from that which is eternal, and that's the wrong direction, my friend. So stay in touch. Give until you don't have anything else to give, and then tap into God's reservoirs and give some more. This is what lengthens the meaning and purpose—and sometimes the years—of life.

The secret of reality in life is humility.

If involvement gives life *length,* then humility gives it *breadth.* Moses presents us with a beautiful picture of real humanity mixed with deep humility and genuine godliness. Moses never believed his own press reports. He never got lost in his own track record. He never got up in the morning to see what the headlines had to say about his performance the day before. True, he set incredible records that have not, and never will be, touched, but he never got lost in his own pride. He stayed real, believable, and humble.

Humility gives life breadth. So stay touchable. Stay available. Stay believable. Solomon wrote, "Let another praise you, and not your own mouth; a stranger, and not your own lips" (Proverbs 27:2). Praise may come, but don't let it come from your own voice box.

The secret of happiness in life is perspective.

I think this is the best of the three. If involvement gives life length, and humility gives it breadth, then perspective gives life depth.

Let me level with you. I know that some of you reading this book right now face a bleak situation. You're not sure about the future. Maybe you're in a dilemma regarding your career. It could be that a health problem has you by the ankles. Perhaps you recently lost a romance that looked like it was budding. Or it might be that you have come to an impasse in your marriage, and you don't see a way through. You feel as if you're trapped in a locked closet, and you can't get out.

If you feel like that, then pay special attention to the story that follows. Consider what this well-known writer says about perspective, because I believe that a great deal of depression is brought on by an improper perspective:

> When I first began driving to my hospital office in 1966, I noticed a nice-looking young man who invariably stood at the window of an old apartment house, which is located across the street from the doctors' parking lot. Morning after morning this same man, whom I would judge to have been in his middle forties, appeared at the same open window as I drove past. He was always there when I went home at the end of the day as well. I began to wave or smile to the man in the window, and he would return my greeting with a similar gesture. Though it seems unlikely, we developed a friendship in the absence of any personal knowledge of one another, without a single conversation between us.
>
> My curiosity finally compelled me to get better acquainted with the man behind the smile. One noontime I walked from my office to the building where my congenial friend lived and climbed a dark stairway to the second floor. I knocked on the door, and it was opened by "the man in the window." He introduced himself as Tommy and invited me to come into his two-room apartment. During the next hour he told me his story. He had been a successful executive until devastated by a massive coronary thrombosis about six years earlier. His heart ailments were compounded by emphysema and other physical disorders, which prevented his engaging in any form of work. I also noticed that his right arm was deformed, being much smaller than his left. Tommy, I learned, was rarely able to leave that tiny apartment. He was not married and seemed to have no relatives or close friends. His situation was not unlike being sentenced to virtual solitary confinement in a two-room cell.
>
> The beautiful part of Tommy's story is how he chose to cope with his personal tragedy. He had every reason in the world to be depressed and despondent, but he exuded confidence and optimism. He had decided that he would make friends with as many people as possible

among those driving to and from their work, and that comprised his entire social life.

I said, "Tommy, what can I do for you? Do you need anything? Can I help you in any way?"

He said, "Thank you, sir, and I appreciate your offer. But I'm doing all right. I really don't need anything."

There was not one ounce of self-pity apparent anywhere in our conversation, and he steadfastly refused to let me treat him as an invalid. His only acknowledgment that life was difficult came in response to my question, "Do you ever become discouraged with your situation here?"

Tommy replied, "Well, in the morning when everyone is coming to work, I enjoy greeting the people at the start of a new day. But when they're heading on their way home at night and I'm saying good-bye, I sometimes feel a little blue." That was the only negative statement I ever heard him utter. Tommy had obviously made up his mind to accept life as it was.

For something more than fifteen years, Tommy stood his watch above the noise and traffic of the street, and we remained good friends. I stopped my car beneath his window on January 3 this year, to greet him after I had been gone for a brief Christmas vacation. Without thinking, I asked him, "Did you have a good holiday?"

Tommy replied, "It was great."

I learned later that he had spent the entire Christmas season in the solitude of that room, watching the harassed shoppers and commuters below him.

A few weeks later, Tommy failed to appear at his usual place at the window. The second morning he was absent again, and both the shades were drawn. I learned from the parking lot attendant that Tommy had collapsed and died during the previous weekend. My friend was gone. His funeral had already been held, though I doubt if anyone attended it. Now as I drive past the apartment building each morning, I can hear Tommy saying the last words he ever spoke to me, "It was great."

> My point in writing to you about Tommy is to illustrate the fact
> that depression is usually a matter of perspective.[3]

My long-time friend, Dr. James Dobson, penned those words years
ago, and I've thought about that story ever since. You may have a rather
rough life, but you probably don't have it as rough as Tommy, because
you're sitting there reading this book. Somehow you are able, either with
someone or all alone, to acquire the book, open its pages, turn on a light
and either read or listen to the words on its pages. You may face a difficult
tomorrow, and if you don't watch it, you can easily succumb to self-pity.
It all depends on your perspective.

You see, in great measure, happiness in the Christian life depends on
how we perceive it. In the eyes of Tommy, life was great. How is it with
you? If you die before me, and I visit the place where you are laid to rest,
what will your tombstone read? Perspective pervaded Moses' life, and that's
why his epitaph gives us so much hope.

A WORTHY GOAL

Death comes to all of us. And unless our Lord comes in the clouds for us
first, that day of departure will arrive...maybe sooner, maybe later. We
have no control over that, but we *do* have control over the way we live, right
up to the moment we leave this world.

When we are given to self-pity, let's remind ourselves of Tommy and
the thousands of other Tommys stretched across this planet who live every
day with hope. We have a God worth living for, and certainly worth dying
for. Furthermore, it's time to adjust our perspective when we begin to live
as though that were not true.

Moses teaches us that, regardless of whether we live or die, God remains
worthy of our praise. It must be our goal, then, as it was the goal of Moses,
to bring honor to Him, whether by life or by death.

And then the tombstone will take care of itself.

351

CHAPTER TWENTY

Moses' Faith, Moses' Choices, and Me

I was returning from lunch several days ago with a couple of seminary students. As we made our way back to the campus, one of the men tossed a question my way that no one had ever asked me before: "With which Bible character do you most easily identify?" he wondered.

It was a good question. Tough, but good. He didn't ask, "Which one is your favorite?" or "Which do you prefer to preach on?" or "Who could be called your hero?" He wanted to know, "If you could get inside his skin, with which Bible character would you most identify?"

You ought to ask yourself that question. I still haven't given that student my answer. I honestly don't know who the person would be; I'm still thinking about it. But if I were to be asked, "Who are the top five Bible characters you most *admire?*" one would certainly be Moses. What a tremendous servant of God, a giant in every respect.

Here is the man who led the Exodus, witnessed the parting of the Red Sea, led a congregation of two million through a trackless wilderness, sustained himself on "the bread of angels" for years on end, followed a towering pillar of cloud by day, and sat beneath the fire of God hovering over the camp at night. "He was mighty in word and deed," declares Stephen.

As we saw in one of my earlier chapters, Moses' parents so inculcated godliness in their son that even at the height of his political stature, he refused to depart from his childhood training. He had great roots. A friend of mine likes to say, "When he grew up, he even looked like Charlton Heston." He was a man who had everything going for him.

Of course, he had weaknesses. If you examine the details of his life long enough, you'll surely find reason to say he experienced periodic failures. But who hasn't? The same thing could be said of any one of us, including God's spokesman. I don't think we can fully appreciate the greatness of this man without coming to appreciate how much he gave up and what it meant for him to model such selfless dedication.

As we learned early on, young Moses had everything going for him. He was the pride and joy of ancient Egypt. No business executive can imagine handling enough money to compare with what went into Moses' coffers in one year. We cannot fathom the extent of his treasury. We cannot imagine the pomp that preceded this adopted grandson of the Pharaoh. Or the palace where he resided. Or the power in his grip, simply to say, "Let them die" or "Let them live," and no questions would be asked. We have no words to describe the man's exalted status. He had it all. In our terms, *he had it made.*

Yet, isn't it strange? There is no sphinx in Egypt erected to Moses' honor. There is no impressive pyramid, no mortuary temple of stone that bears his name. Remember, these people honored their dead. The Egyptians had a saying: "To speak the name of the dead is to make him live again."

So where are Moses' monuments? Why didn't they build in his honor an enormous body of a lion, 240-feet long and 60-plus-feet high, with Moses' face carved 15 feet across? Why only of Thutmose and Raamses and Tutankhamen and Queen Hatshepsut? Why not Moses? The Prince of Egypt was the Pharaoh-elect. Yet you can walk from the easternmost section of Sinai down to the westernmost region of the Libyan plateau and not find a single statue in honor of Moses. Why not?

I think the answer is woven into the fabric of Hebrews 11. What the hot, arid sands of Egypt miss, the timeless Word of God contains: "Now faith is the assurance of things hoped for, the conviction of things not seen... " (11:1).

"By faith Moses, when he had grown up, refused to be called the son of Pharaoh's daughter, choosing rather to endure ill-treatment with the people of God than to enjoy the passing pleasures of sin, considering the reproach of Christ greater riches than the treasures of Egypt; for he was looking to the reward. By faith he left Egypt, not fearing the wrath of the king; for he endured, as seeing Him who is unseen. By faith he kept the Passover and the sprinkling of the blood, so that he who destroyed the firstborn would not touch them" (11:24–28).

It is because of the *decisions* Moses made that there is no timeless statue in Egypt bearing his name. Review the salient scenes from Moses' remarkable life as we consider three of those life-changing, history-shaping decisions.

FIRST DECISION: REFUSING TO SUSTAIN THE SINFUL

Hebrews 11:24 tells us, "By faith Moses, when he was grown up, *refused.* . . . "

Visualize this strong young man, Hebrew within but fully Egyptian without. He would easily pass for the up-and-coming Pharaoh. But when Moses reached adulthood, a seismic change took place. The phrase translated "when he had grown up" literally means "having become great." That's even more vivid! "Moses, having become great, made a decision. . . . "

Picture it this way: Every person, every individual, many times in life comes to a fork in the road, a crucial fork. Great banners wave at us to follow one route as opposed to another. One road is broad, wide, attractive, and well-trafficked. The other is narrow, rugged, unpopular, and lonely. The fork requires you to make a decision. Your choice leads to another fork a little farther down the road, and the decision you make there leads to yet another.

Moses came to his first major fork in the road when he had become great. He was forced to make a choice. He had to decide whether he would allow the Egyptians to continue to call him the Pharaoh-elect. He had to decide between the seen and the unseen. Firmly he made that choice. The Scripture says he "refused to be called the son of Pharaoh's daughter." Literally, it says he "denied it to be said the son of Pharaoh's daughter."

What an astonishing event that was! Perhaps it took place one day when Moses stood up in court. Maybe he said it to the soft-footed servants who waited on his every whim. Perhaps he announced it to his adoptive grandfather, who ruled as the all-powerful Pharaoh. Or maybe he spoke his decision to his adopted mother, the daughter of Pharaoh. However it happened, one day he declared, "No longer call me your son. I yield my right to the throne. I refuse to be called Pharaoh-elect any longer."

Moses' decision reminds me of Daniel, who centuries later stood alone in a pagan royal court—a Hebrew through and through, yet surrounded by a Babylonian lifestyle—and said, "I will not eat the king's food. I will not adopt the king's lifestyle. I will not follow the king's route. I am first and foremost a believer in Yahweh. He has my allegiance, my unqualified loyalty. I will live for His glory and, if necessary, I will die for His honor."

In a word, Moses had integrity. He came to this first fork and made a decision to refuse "to be called the son of Pharaoh's daughter." But how could he do that? After all, he was a red-blooded man. The "catch" of the kingdom. He had whatever he wanted, whenever he wanted it. He had the world by the tail. How could he give it all up?

The words "choosing," and "considering" in verses 25 and 26 give us the insight we need to answer that question. How could Moses, by faith, refuse what he did?

Choosing

Verse 25 says he made a choice. The word translated "choosing" comes from a Greek term that means "to take for oneself a position." In other words, Moses came to that epochal fork in the road and had to "take for himself" a position before he could go to the right or the left. Without taking a position, he would have remained paralyzed by neutrality.

Part of the reason we do not make right choices is because we have not taken a position for ourselves on the priority principles of life. We have not decided where we stand on matters of character, morality, values, godliness, and commitment to Christ. And so we teeter. We drift. We slide this way and that way. We stall our steps at the neck of the fork, waiting for something to break free. Or we make a choice on the basis of our feelings alone, or on the response of others, only to regret it later.

Joshua, Moses' successor, must have imbibed his mentor's decisiveness. Prior to his death, he stood before the elders of Israel in the land and challenged them to make up their minds about the most crucial issue of life. "If it is disagreeable in your sight to serve the LORD, choose for yourselves today whom you will serve: whether the gods which your fathers served which were beyond the River, or the gods of the Amorites in whose land you are living; but as for me and my house, we will serve the LORD" (Joshua 24:15).

Elijah, standing alone on the peak of Mount Carmel, said much the same thing to the assembled Israelites: "How long will you waver between two opinions? If the LORD is God, follow him; but if Baal is God, follow him" (2 Kings 18:21, NIV).

Moses did not waver between two opinions. He thought through his position, came to a conclusion, and made his choice. What did he choose? He chose "rather to endure ill-treatment with the people of God than the passing pleasures of sin."

Life is full of choices. We must choose a radio station, choose a television channel, choose how we'll spend our afternoon, choose a mate (if indeed we are to be married), choose whether to have children, choose a career, choose a school, choose a degree program, choose where to live, choose how to live, choose our friends, choose our church. We face constant and unending choices, some of them life-changing.

Moses, having taken a position concerning his walk with the Lord, next made a decision that was neither culturally popular nor materially advantageous. He pulled off the headgear of the Pharaoh, walked away from the palace of the queen, ignored all of the prerogatives that were his to enjoy for the rest of his life, and chose to live with the people of God.

Don't think for a moment that the Bible is simply embellishing the text when it talks about "enjoying the pleasures of sin." The pleasures of sin are *always* more enjoyable than a walk of righteousness, at first. Your heart beats faster when you're near the sin. It is voluptuous and seductive, it feeds the flesh, and it makes you feel good. Don't let anybody ever tell you that it doesn't. It brings a burst of satisfaction, for awhile.

A very attractive woman stopped me following a service one Sunday and said, "I'm visiting from out of town, I just came to know Christ, and I'm having real trouble believing that God can love me." Tears began streaming down her careworn face as she admitted, "I have made all the wrong choices. I have been involved with drugs and several men who had everything but God. Now I'm reaping the consequences." With that she just buried her face in her hands and sobbed audibly. As attractive as she looked, she appeared older than she really was. Hard miles will do that to you.

No doubt her first few miles were pleasurable. Fun. Thrilling. Fascinating. But one thing about sensual pleasures: The Bible insists they're "passing." They don't last. And when they vanish, as they surely will, they leave behind an ocean of pain, heartache, and regret. This woman pursued her passing pleasures, and they kept her going to the next man and the next drug and the next thrill. It's like falling over a terraced hillside where you rush downward, accelerating with each bump, bump, bump until you hit bottom and can go no further.

Moses chose the path of godliness rather than the "passing pleasures of sin." How could he do that? What was it inside Moses that caused him to make such a choice? The answer is in another word worth a closer look.

Considering

The word "considering" in verse 26 helps us to understand Moses' rationale. The term means "to think beforehand." Moses saw ahead, looked further than the fork in the road, and allowed his imagination to run on ahead. He came to the fork and realized, *If I continue to be called the son of Pharaoh's daughter, if I continue to be called the Pharaoh-elect, if I continue to amass this fortune and win these awards and gain the acclaim of these people, I will find myself in a place where I cannot turn back without damage to the nation or my own soul.* Why? Because with such status comes the alluring perks that whisper, "Come on. Hey, come on, everybody does it." Moses said, "No. I see far enough down the road to know that such a life will not be good. It will ultimately erode into bad."

Moses considered "the reproach of Christ greater riches than the treasures of Egypt; for he was looking to the reward." The original text suggests that Moses looked away from everything else and fixed his full attention on one thing: the reward God offers to people of faith.

If you're a football fan, you know something of what this is like. In the final seconds of a close game between fierce rivals, you don't get up, stroll over to the fridge, and browse the shelves for a snack. Rather, you look away from everything else and focus on the guy with the ball. Is the opponent going to score? Or is your team going to win? Moses looked away from everything else and fixed his eyes on Christ. That's how he made the right decision.

If you dink around with all the possibilities, if you loll around in the passing pleasures long enough, you'll lose your focus on Christ. It will happen! Listen, it happens to the best of God's men and women. Don't say you're not vulnerable. Don't think you're immune. We could easily etch into stone the names of forty or more famous Christians of our own generation who no longer walk with Christ because they failed to fix their gaze on Him alone.

We have no real choice but to focus exclusively on Christ. I think of Jim Vaus, the infamous wiretapper—a wild and crazy guy. He was working part-time for gangster Mickey Cohen and part-time for the Los Angeles Police Department—a case of law and crime working together. The problem is, Jim Vaus had to live with Jim Vaus.

He stumbled into a tent meeting in downtown Los Angeles one evening back in 1949 and was converted to Christ. His conversion quickly drove a wedge into his duplicity. He could no longer set up the crime or the government. He could no longer live with both hands in different pots. Why not? Because he had come to see that Christ must be Lord of every part of life.

Have you come to that place?

The reason there is no sphinx in Egypt bearing the image of Moses is that he refused to sustain the sinful. No earthly monument, not even a handprint pushed into wet cement, bears the image of Moses. He's forgotten in Egypt, but he's greatly honored in heaven.

SECOND DECISION: LEAVING THE FAMILIAR

Moses' second decision centers around the word "left." The writer of Hebrews says, "By faith he *left* Egypt, not fearing the wrath of the king; for he endured, as seeing Him who is unseen." Moses turned his back on the familiar.

Do you see his fixation? The sharp focus? This was no Sunday-go-to-meetin' kind of a guy. No sleepy-eyed do-gooder. This man fixed his attention on Yahweh. He locked on, like a radar installation locks on to an approaching warplane, or like a heat-seeking missile pursuing a fleeing enemy jet. By this fixation, he determined in his heart to leave the familiar. "By faith he left Egypt."

Egypt. I've never been there. I don't know much about Egypt, but I do know something about El Campo. I was born in that little South Texas town. I know its little roads and trails. I know the little drugstores and a few folks who once lived there. The information is imprinted in my mind because my roots are there. But I left El Campo as a child, so I really don't know the town as well as those who have lived there all their lives.

Maybe you have worked at the same company for thirty-five or forty years. All you know is that company. How would it be for you to just up and quit one day and get another job? Would you feel a little insecure? I would imagine so.

Or perhaps you have lived in the same house as long as you can remember. You've reared your kids in that house. And if you have your way about it, you'll die in that place. Because it's *your* place and you have deep roots there.

I have a pastor friend who took over from a man who held forth in that church's pulpit for thirty-seven years. "Chuck," he says, "his voice is in the woodwork. His handprint's on the pulpit. They're mashed all over it." For thirty-seven long years the same man pastored that one church. You can be in a place so long that your presence seems to permeate the place long after you've left.

That is what Egypt was to Moses. He knew nothing but the land of the Nile. He had never been to Canaan; he knew only Egypt. But he left it. Why? How could he? Because of faith. *God* led him out. *God* moved him. Moses determined to leave the familiar even though Egypt coursed through his blood. Negatively, he didn't fear what the king would do to him. Positively, he looked ahead, seeing the One who is unseen.

A major battle for most Americans is that of things, places, houses, belongings, and territory. We sink the roots of our security into these things. Now, there's nothing wrong with roots, but we can grow to love them too much.

So, how does a son and daughter-in-law explain to a set of parents that they intend to leave all that security behind and move to Europe? The young man and woman have earned their degrees. They've had two healthy babies. They're just getting started in a promising profession, and suddenly they announce to Mom and Dad they're heading overseas.

"*Where* are you going?"

"We're leaving for Spain."

"*Why* are you going there?"

"We're going by faith."

"Yes, but look at all you have here. We just helped you get into your house. We paid the $25,000 down payment. We got you moved in. We got you going. We have good medical help here. *Why do you want to go to Spain?*"

"God is calling us there."

"But look, things are so different over there. Have you seen the cars they drive in Spain? Do you know what they eat in Spain? And what about the language?"

"Well, we know we have to go to language school."

"*You're kidding!*"

"No, we're not."

"And *why* are you doing this?"

"Because that's where God wants us."

How can you explain a couple who would do such a thing? How do you explain someone who is willing to pull up their roots and move to who knows where? It could be the bush in Ethiopia, the middle of Europe, the southernmost tip of South America, the center of Canada, or an Indian reservation right in the heart of America. How can you explain a couple who will leave all the "good stuff" behind? If you ask them, they will say, "Because we're going to *the better*."

Am I saying this is for everybody? No, but I am saying it's for many. The major battle is leaving Egypt. It's a risk of faith. It's tough because we are born and bred to hang onto *stuff!* Yet, if your place burned down today to a concrete slab and smoldering black rubble, nothing of real value would have been destroyed as long as all the lives in your home had been saved. Why? Because you have relationships and memories, and you build everything from there.

Moses left Egypt. He burned the bridges. He didn't look back. He did not fear the wrath of the king. He simply took off. I love the way one man put it: "We live by faith or we do not live at all. Either we venture or we vegetate. We risk or we rust."

There is no sphinx in Egypt today because Moses left Egypt. Who needs Egypt when God says, "There's an Exodus in My plan"? If you are committed to Egypt more than to an Exodus, then you are not committed to God.

THE THIRD DECISION: DOING THE UNUSUAL

This is probably my favorite of the three. He refused sinful pleasures, he left the familiar, and then he *did the unusual*.

Try to picture what this man did. Act as if there has never been a Passover, because when he did it, there never had been. "He kept the Passover and the sprinkling of the blood, so that he who destroyed the firstborn might not touch them" (Hebrews 11:28).

We watched in previous chapters as Moses returned to Pharaoh time after time saying, "Let My people go. Let My people go." But the king steadfastly refused. Finally, God said to Moses, "I'm going to bring death to them. Then Pharaoh will let the people go. I will strike every home with death, except one special group of homes."

And how would the people in this special group of homes be saved? You remember how we described that scene earlier in the book. The slain lamb. The blood on the doorposts. The meal eaten in a hurry, with sandals strapped on and a walking stick in hand. These were all brand new directions for Moses and the Israelites. They had never been done before.

"Moses," God said, "make sure you have your staff in your hand, your cloak under your belt, your sandals on, and be ready to *run!* Because I'm sending death across that land, and you're going to hear the screams of grief from one end of Egypt to the other. But if you put blood on your doorposts, I'll pass over you."

"You gotta be kidding. *Blood?*"

"That's right."

"Maybe *my* blood?"

"No! Lamb's blood."

"*Lamb's* blood? You're telling me that I don't even have to lock my door?"

"Don't lock your door."

Now, here's a guy with an advanced degree in hieroglyphics. He graduated from the Temple of the Sun. He has a chest full of medals. And he's out there smearing blood on the side and top of his door!

"*What* are you doing?" someone asks.

"I'm keeping death away."

"Oh, yeah. Sure. Ri-i-i-i-i-ght."

Can you imagine the looks the Hebrews must have had? Today we look at the actions of the Israelites as if they were high and holy, and indeed they were. But imagine the mockery these Hebrews had to endure.

"Oh no, Death's 'a comin'! Close the windows, Martha. Let's all go down to the gym and hide out tonight. I mean, there are stone walls down there. Ha ha ha!"

"Well, we're just putting blood on our door."

"*Why?*"

"Because—I know it sounds unusual—but God says if we sprinkle blood here, death won't come in."

"Ooooo. Sounds so scary. Look at me! I'm tremblin' all over." The mockery continued until nightfall—that fateful night.

The screaming started. It began in Memphis and swept all the way up through the valley toward the land of Goshen. You never heard such screaming. Kids dying like flies. And here is this little Hebrew couple, standing there with a staff and a cloak and sandals, munching on roasted lamb, about to make an Exodus. What an unusual thing.

And remember, Moses had no tradition to fall back on. How could he do it? How could he keep that first Passover exactly as God instructed him to?

He did it in the same way Noah could pound pegs into the ark when there had never been rain. He could do it in the same way Abraham and Sarah could look for a city with a foundation whose builder and maker was God when they had never been to the land of Canaan. He could do it simply because God said, "Do it."

DIRECTIONS AT THE CROSSROADS

The writer of Hebrews devoted six verses in the "Hall of Faith" chapter to a man named Moses. He didn't pen those words to discourage us, dishearten us, or to set the bar so high that we would sigh and say, "Ah, what's the use? I could never live like this man." On the contrary, those words appear in the sacred text to recharge our batteries and fill us with fresh determination to invest our lives for eternity.

Moses refused to compromise his commitment; so can we.

Moses willingly left the familiar to follow God's call; so can we.

Moses did the unusual at God's command, turning a deaf ear to the scoffers, critics, and nay-sayers. And so can we!

Moses' life is a simple roadmap for people just like us—regular, every-day, garden-variety folks, young and old alike, single and married, retired and youthful. And the directions we extract from that map can help us at three critical crossroads of our lives.

1. To have the discernment it takes to refuse the sinful, faith must overshadow my feelings. My feelings say, "Run!" Faith says, "Stand still."

My feelings say, "Try it!" Faith says, "Stay away from it."

My feelings say, "Give it up. Throw in the towel." Faith says, "Hold on!"

We live in a day of feelings. "Whatever you *feel* like, get at it." The Academy Award-winning song a couple of decades back captured that philosophy with the words, "It can't be wrong, when it feels so right...." Oh, yes, it can! Faith says, "Hold it. You have come to a fork in the road. If you take that journey, you will buy into a lifestyle that is wrong. Stop. Back up. Look again."

Maybe you find yourself right there. You have already made some poor choices. If so, it's time to back up. It's time to retrace your steps right back to that place where you made the wrong turn. That takes discernment and courage, but you can do it. God will give you the strength.

2. To have the determination it takes to leave the familiar, faith must be my security. If faith is our security, we can pack up and leave for Spain when God calls us to do so. Or Siberia, for that matter. I can name dozens of couples, and singles, too, who have done something just like that. Their faith has become their security. Their walk with God is the steady rock beneath their feet, not the safe and familiar floor of their own home. Remember Corrie ten Boom's words? "I've learned to hold precious things loosely, because it hurts when God pries my fingers and takes them from me." Hold your possessions loosely, even your children. The old hymn says it well:

> Give of thy sons to bear the message glorious,
> Give of thy wealth to speed them on their way;
> Pour out thy soul for them in prayer victorious,
> and all thou spendest Jesus will repay.[1]

Are you rearing your children to keep or to give? Sometimes our kids' greatest battles in moving into cross-cultural ministry is parents who won't let them go. Give them up! What a tremendous investment. If you want the determination to leave the familiar, you must make your faith your security.

3. To have the discipline it takes to do the unusual, faith must silence the critics. Trust me on this one. The critics *will* be there. Count on it. It will require discipline to take the journey and to live with the mockery, the condescending comments, the inevitable second-guessing. You must have the kind of discipline it takes to say, "Lord God, You are the One who set me on this course, and until You say otherwise, this is the direction I'm going to walk. My critics are getting louder and more in number and closer. Silence them. Or at least, stop my ears." Elton Trueblood said it best: "Faith is not belief without proof, but trust without reservation." We like to think that we are people of faith. And yet the quality and even the integrity of our faith may have been challenged by this study of the life of Moses. Perhaps we've been mouthing statements of faith without really believing what God tells us about Himself and His way for us.

If we desire the kind of faith expressed by Moses, the kind of faith that enables us to forfeit the security of this world for the security God desires for us, we must develop a deep-seated, quiet confidence in Him who works all things after the counsel of His own will.

Fortunately, that's easier than it sounds, for He does all things right. Moses discovered that by long experience. And so can you.

I want to live my life so eternally committed to my Savior and so available and free to Him that all it takes is a whisper from heaven, and I'm obeying. I want that for my wife, my children, and my grandchildren. I want that for us as a people of God.

Let me return to the question we started with: If you could put yourself into the skin of any Bible character, which one would it be? In these closing lines, I urge you to put yourself in the skin of Moses. Consider what he gave up and what he received in return. There was no monument to this man of selfless dedication. No towering sphinx. No imposing pyramid. Egypt was more than willing to forget that such a man ever existed. He was buried on some lonely peak on the barren slopes of Mount Pisgah, without so much as a single flower on his grave.

He willingly traded the earthly monuments and acclaim, the perks, the power, and the pleasure for a reward in an invisible realm. He cashed it all in—every shekel of it—for a relationship with the living God.

It was the best trade anyone could have made. What he lost, he couldn't have kept anyway, and what he gained, he could never lose.

Moses couldn't do any better than that.

Neither can we.

CONCLUSION

Moses: A Man of Selfless Dedication

W hat a journey we have traveled together! Our companion along
the way has been that venerable old leader of the Exodus—
Moses himself. When we started, we hardly knew the man.
Now that we've completed the journey, he may seem to you like a new-
found friend. Perhaps, even a close friend. I hope so.

For me, the journey has been a nostalgic one. I have deliberately let my
mind enter his world. I've paused along the way to ponder painful moments.
I've entered into different scenes, lingered over those times when our friend
struggled, felt the sting of disappointment at those times when his heart
was crushed, and smiled with him when he enjoyed God's surprising power.
I think I could almost feel the mist when he led those startled Hebrews
through the Red Sea onto dry ground.

The journey has also been a difficult one—more difficult than usual.
While in the midst of this project, as I was writing about the plagues in
Egypt, I received an early-morning call from Dallas Seminary. A water
main under the street adjacent to the school had broken in the middle of
the night. Once the city had fixed it and turned the water back on, the

sudden burst of pressure caused a valve in the second-floor bathroom of one of our older buildings to break and begin to spray water into the room and down the hallway.

Hour after hour the flow of water went undetected. During that time, water flowed down into the first floor, where thousands of my books were shelved, then on down into the basement below that room, where hundreds of my research volumes were shelved. Once the damage was discovered and I had been notified, visiting the scene reminded me of those Southeast Asian monsoons I had endured many years ago, where the humidity and dripping water splashes and soaks into everything.

I'll not take the time or space to describe all that was involved in the clean-up or how many of those precious works were destroyed (thankfully, most can be restored), but this writing project went on, unhindered. It was almost as if the Lord wanted me to experience my own set of plagues during these months alongside Moses and the Hebrew people. So, in a sense, I feel a special kinship with them in the things they endured.

As we journeyed to the end of his life, standing at last on the windswept slopes of Pisgah, I felt as though I had lost an intimate traveling companion. My heart beat faster as I witnessed the secret burial, read his epitaph, and reviewed his remarkable one-hundred-twenty-year pilgrimage. Not unlike that dark day when I said goodbye to my own father, and we laid him to rest, bidding Moses farewell was a moving experience I'll not soon forget. There is much one can learn from the silence of a tomb.

Clarence Macartney's words speak eloquently of such moments: "I have no dread of a cemetery," he wrote. "Sometimes it is better to be there and have fellowship with the dead who are buried than to walk down the streets of our cities and meet the unburied dead; that is, those in whom faith and hope and love and purity have long been dead, leaving only the animal alive. In the cemetery the Bible of life is open and a passionless voice reads to us its great lessons and tells us to apply our hearts unto wisdom. Sometimes we can learn more from the silence of the dead than from the speech of the living."

He continues, "Whether it be a little churchyard, where under ancient elms the dead lie close to holy walls, or the dark spaces of some hoary cathedral, where the dead sleep under sculptured sarcophagus and lettered marble, or some wilderness battlefield where the nation had gathered the bodies of the soldiers who there gave their last full measure of devotion, or some rural hillside where the wind blows free, or some quiet acre by the banks of a river that flows silently and swiftly away like man's life—wherever it may be, the resting place of the dead has always something worthwhile to say to the living."[1]

From the silence of Moses' burial site come enduring, worthwhile lessons. Yes, the great servant-hearted leader has died, but the things he has taught us will never lose their significance. His life remains forever one of those solid blocks of granite whose deep and abiding etchings no storm can erase or earthly disaster remove. And in times like these, we need such points of reference.

Thank you for traveling with me. If you have made the journey through each of my other biographical works, then you are able to mark this one as your fourth in the Great Lives from God's Word series. By God's grace and through His enablement, there will be more. But for now, may this one take root and grow within you. And may the story of *Moses: A Man of Selfless Dedication* inspire you to do as he did so well: to endure, "as seeing Him who is invisible."

ENDNOTES

CHAPTER ONE
MISERY, MIDWIVES, AND MURDER

1. C. F. Keil and F. Delitzsch, in *The Pentateuch*, vol. 1 of *Biblical Commentary on the Old Testament*, trans. James Martin (Grand Rapids: William B. Eerdmans Publishing Company, n.d.), p. 375.
2. Dr. and Mrs. Howard Taylor, *Husdon Taylor's Spiritual Secret* (London: China Inland Mission, 1955), p. 107.

CHAPTER TWO
BORN AFTER MIDNIGHT

1. As mentioned by Henrietta C. Mears, in *What the Bible Is All About* (Ventura, Calif.: Gospel Light Publications, 1966), p. 33.
2. Winston Churchill, as quoted in *Bartlett's Familiar Quotations*, 15th ed., revised and enlarged, ed. Emily Morison Beck (Boston: Little, Brown & Co., 1980), p. 746.
3. F. B. Meyer, *Moses: The Servant of God* (Grand Rapids: Zondervan

Publishing House, 1953), p. 20.

CHAPTER THREE
GOD'S WILL, MY WAY

1. Phyllis Thompson, *D. E. Hoste* (London: China Inland Mission, n.d.), p. 122; as quoted by J. Oswald Sanders in *Spiritual Leadership*.
2. F. B. Meyer, *Moses: The Servant of God* (Grand Rapids: Zondervan Publishing House, 1953), p. 31.
3. Meyer, *Moses*, pp. 31–32.

CHAPTER FOUR
LESSONS LEARNED FROM FAILURE

1. Winston Churchill, as quoted in *Bartlett's Familiar Quotations*, 15th Edition, revised and enlarged, ed. Emily Morison Beck (Boston: Little, Brown & Co., 1980) p. 621.
2. A. W. Tozer, in *The Reaper*, February 1962, p. 459; as quoted by J. Oswald Sanders in *Spiritual Leadership*.
3. Os Guinness, *The Call: Finding and Fulfilling the Central Purpose of Your Life* (Nashville, Word Publishing, 1998), p. 162.
4. Matthew Henry, *Commentary on the Whole Bible: New Modern Edition*. Electronic Database. Copyright © 1991 by Hendrickson Publishers, Inc. Used by permission. All rights reserved.

CHAPTER FIVE
THE DESERT: SCHOOL OF SELF-DISCOVERY

1. Natalie Ray, "No Lover," in *Eternity Magazine* (Philadelphia: Alliance of Confessing Evangelicals, 1975), n.p. Used by permission.
2. —————, "How Firm a Foundation" (n.d.)
3. J. Oswald Sanders, *Robust in Faith* (Chicago: Moody Press, 1965), p. 62.

4. Amy Carmichael, from *Rose from Brier* (Fort Washington, Penn.: Christian Literature Crusade, 1973), p. 12. Used by permission.
5. V. Raymond Edman, *In Quietness and Confidence* (Colorado Springs: Scripture Press, 1953), p. 63.
6. Martha Snell Nicholson, "Guests," in *Poems That Preach* (Wheaton: Sword of the Lord Publishers, 1952), p. 33.

CHAPTER SIX
BURNING BUSHES AND SECOND CHANCES

1. Hezekiah Butterworth, "The Bird with the Broken Piñion," in *Poems That Preach* (Wheaton: Sword of the Lord Publishers, 1952), p. 93.
2. Amy Carmichael, "Make Me Thy Fuel," from *Toward Jerusalem* (Fort Washington, Penn.: Christian Literature Crusade, 1961; London, England: Society for Promoting Christian Knowledge, 1950), p. 94. Used by permission.

CHAPTER SEVEN
WHO? ME, LORD?

1. As quoted by V. Raymond Edman, in *The Disciplines of Life* (Colorado Springs: Scripture Press, 1948), p. 43.
2. As quoted by Nelson G. Mink, in *Pocket Pearls* (Wheaton: Tyndale House Publishers, Inc., 1987), p. 16.

CHAPTER EIGHT
GOD'S WILL, GOD'S WAY

1. Daniel Iverson, "Spirit of the Living God" (© 1935, R 1963 Birdwing Music; administered by EMI Christian Music). All rights reserved.
2. F. B. Meyer, *Moses: The Servant of God* (Grand Rapids: Zondervan Publishing House, 1953), p. 42.
3. Adelaide A. Pollard, "Have Thine Own Way, Lord" (n.d.)

CHAPTER NINE
GOING FROM BAD TO WORSE

1. J. Oswald Sanders, *Spiritual Leadership* (Chicago: The Moody Bible Institute, 1967, 1980), p. 108.
2. William Cowper, "Light Shining Out of Darkness."

CHAPTER TEN
PLAGUES THAT PREACH

1. Alfred Edersheim, in vol. 2 of *The Bible History—Old Testament* (Grand Rapids: William B. Eerdmans Publishing Company, 1959), p. 77.

CHAPTER ELEVEN
THE NIGHT THAT NOBODY SLEPT

1. —————, "When I See the Blood" (n.d.)
2. Charles Wesley, "O for a Thousand Tongues" (n.d.)

CHAPTER TWELVE
BETWEEN THE DEVIL AND THE DEEP RED SEA

1. Annie Johnson Flint, "Pressed Out of Measure" (n.d.)

CHAPTER THIRTEEN
A HEAVENLY DIET VS. AN EARTHLY APPETITE

1. Thoro Harris, "Grumblers" (©1926 Thoro Harris).

CHAPTER FOURTEEN
WHY LEADERS CRACK UP

1. Richard W. DeHaan, *Men Sent from God* (Grand Rapids: Radio Bible

Class, 1966), pp. 26–27. Used by permission.
2. J. Oswald Sanders, *Spiritual Leadership* (Grand Rapids: The Moody Bible Institute, 1967, 1980), p. 206.

CHAPTER FIFTEEN
SINAI: WHERE MOSES MET GOD

1. Beno Rothenberg, *God's Wilderness* (Nashville: Thomas Nelson Publishers, 1962), p. 2.
2. A. W. Tozer, *The Knowledge of the Holy* (San Francisco: Harper & Row, Publishers, 1961), p. 4.
3. Elisabeth Elliot, *Through Gates of Splendor* (New York: Harper and Brothers Publishers, 1957), pp. 265–266.

CHAPTER SIXTEEN
GRUMBLINGS AGAINST A GODLY LEADER

1. Anonymous, as quoted by A. Dudley Dennison, Jr., M.D., in *Windows, Ladders, and Bridges* (Grand Rapids: The Zondervan Corporation, 1976), pp. 113–114.

CHAPTER SEVENTEEN
A MOMENT OF RAGE

1. F. B. Meyer, *Moses: The Servant of God* (Grand Rapids: Zondervan Publishing House, 1953), p.42.

CHAPTER EIGHTEEN
FILLING THE SHOES OF MOSES

1. Bill and Gloria Gaither, "I Am a Promise" (Alexandria, Ind.: Gaither Music Company, 1975). All rights reserved. Used by permission of Gaither Copyright Management.

CHAPTER NINETEEN
OBITUARY OF A HERO

1. Ruth Harms Calkin, "What's Wrong With Me?" from *Tell Me Again, Lord, I Forget* (© 1974 Ruth Harms Calkin), p. 21. Used by permission.
2. Calkin, "I Wonder" from *Tell Me Again, Lord, I Forget*, pp. 14–15. Used by permission.
3. Dr. James Dobson, *What Wives Wish Their Husbands Knew About Women* (Wheaton: Tyndale House Publishers, 1975), pp. 177–180. Used by permission. All rights reserved.

Ordinary People, Great Lives

The Great Lives from God's Word series explores ordinary men and women whose lives were empowered by God when they surrendered to Him. Learn from the great lives of our faith and how their stories can help us become who we were created to be.

This best-selling series from Charles Swindoll focuses on the lives of *David, Esther, Joseph, Moses, Elijah, Paul, Job,* and finally *Jesus,* the greatest life of all. Also available are *Fascinating Stories of Forgotten Lives* and the 365-day devotional *Great Days with the Great Lives.*

Visit your favorite bookseller to complete your collection.

INSIGHT FOR LIVING

THOMAS NELSON
Since 1798

JESUS

The Greatest Life of All

Jesus Christ. He is, without question, the most influential person in history. Millions of people claim the truths of the religion that bears His name.

But who exactly *is* Jesus? A popular religious teacher? An ancient martyr? Many today are unsure. Even scholars debate whether the Jesus of history is the Christ of faith. Now, more than ever, we need a clear understanding of the person and work of the man millions call *Savior*.

In this biographical study in the best-selling Great Lives from God's Word series, beloved pastor and Bible teacher Charles Swindoll introduces you to the carpenter from Nazareth as you have never seen Him before.

This fascinating biography, filled with biblical and historical insights, takes you on an unforgettable journey through the complex and provocative life of Jesus of Nazareth. His unique birth. His astonishing power. His controversial teaching. His shocking death. And His world-changing resurrection.

Refreshingly honest and deep, this in-depth profile reveals Jesus with great clarity and offers practical applications for your own life. Whether you're just curious about Jesus or a longtime follower of His life and teachings, you'll experience Him in a new way as you join Charles Swindoll in *Jesus: The Greatest Life of All*.

DAVID

A Man of Passion and Destiny

What does it mean to be someone "after God's own heart"? David, Old Testament shepherd, king, and psalmist, offers an answer in the shape of his own life.

In many ways he was a most extraordinary man—intelligent, handsome, abundantly gifted as a poet, musician, warrior, and administrator. Yet in other ways he was a most ordinary man—often gripped by destructive passion, rocked by family chaos and personal tragedy, and motivated by political expediency. How did David become the national hero of God's chosen people? Why is he the one character in the Bible described as "a man after God's own heart"? Charles Swindoll explores the many facets of David—from his teenage years and dysfunctional family life to his overwhelming passion for God.

David's life offers hope to all of us. It shows that God can do extraordinary things through ordinary men and women. And *David: A Man of Passion and Destiny* offers an insightful perspective on what it means to be truly spiritual, to become like David—men and women after God's own heart.

PAUL

ESTHER

A Woman of Strength and Dignity

Everyone loves a transforming story. Rags to riches. Plain to beautiful. Weak to strong. Esther's story is that, and much more. It is a thought-provoking study of God's invisible hand, writing silently across the pages of human history. Perhaps most of all, it is an account of a godly woman with the courage, wisdom, and strength to block an evil plot, overthrow an arrogant killer, and replace terror with joy in thousands of Jewish homes.

In *Esther: A Woman of Strength and Dignity*, Charles Swindoll interweaves an ancient, real-life story with insight not only into the virtues of Queen Esther, but into how the qualities that formed and empowered her can be ours. We discover the practical process Esther must have gone through as she prepared herself for her life-and-death appearance in the king's throne room. And we enjoy watching the demise of the calculating and cruel Haman, who—like many biblical villains—died in the very trap he had set for someone else.

Through this captivating portrayal of Esther, not only do we encounter the grace, faith, and courage that identified her as a woman of God—we also discover how every Christian can live a transformation story.

The apostle Paul. Converted terrorist, inspired author, amazing teacher, and patient mentor. This colossal figure strode boldly onto the stage of the first-century world and left an indelible signature of greatness never to be forgotten. His life? Magnificent! And his ministry? Impressive. While assigned sainthood by some today, by his own description he was "the chief of all sinners." No other person in the Bible, aside from Christ Himself, had a more profound influence on his world and ours than Paul.

He was a man of real grit, with a firmness of mind and spirit as well as unyielding courage in the face of personal hardship and danger. Tough, tenacious, and fiercely relentless, Paul pursued his divine mission with unflinching resolve. And God used him mightily to turn the world upside down for Christ in this generation.

But Paul's message and his style were also marked by gentle grace. This man, who tormented and killed the saints of God, understood and explained grace better than any of his contemporaries. Why? Because he never got over his own gratitude as a recipient of it. God's super-abounding grace transformed this once-violent aggressor into a humble-but-powerful spokesman for Christ. A man with that much grit desperately needed that much grace.

Perhaps that's why Paul's life is such a source of hope for us. If the chief of sinners can be forgiven and become God's chosen vessel, can He not forgive and use us as well? He can if we, too, become people of both grace and grit.

ELIJAH
A Man of Heroism and Humility

JOSEPH

A Man of Integrity and Forgiveness

In a world where faith is fading and integrity is rare, the life of Joseph shines like a brilliant star in the nighttime sky, showing us that following God brings hope even in the worst of circumstances. In *Joseph: A Man of Integrity and Forgiveness*, Charles Swindoll reveals a man buffeted with the same kinds of problems we face today—or worse. A man whose tenacious faith in God ultimately won him great honor and achievement.

No family today is more dysfunctional than Joseph's. No one faces greater temptation than what Potiphar's wife offered this man of faith. No faith is challenged more than Joseph's as he sat on death row in an Egyptian prison. Yet Joseph stood firm, modeling for us what is possible when ordinary people maintain their connections with God.

Swindoll traces the life of this intriguing man from the famous multicolored coat, through the jealous rage that prompts his brothers to sell him into slavery, to his astounding rise to a position of national power. He follows Joseph through temptation and imprisonment to his ascension in Egyptian society after he explains the king's dreams, revealing a grim and threatening future and proposing a plan for saving the nation . . . and the brothers who deceived him.

It is a story that reads like an epic novel, filled with intrigue, tension, temptation, and torrential emotions. We are heartened today because although we face the same kinds of difficulties, Joseph's life also shows us we can triumph.

Where are great leaders like Elijah today? Uncompromisingly strong, yet self-controlled? Disciplined, yet forgiving. Audaciously courageous, yet kind. Heroic in the heart of battle, yet humble in the aftermath. Rarely does someone model these invaluable traits more obviously than God's mighty prophet Elijah, whose calling was anything but calm and free from conflict.

Exploring the depths of Elijah's fascinating life as a prophet of God, Swindoll does not gloss over his human weaknesses. Rather, he presents an honest picture of this ordinary man who God transformed into His personal spokesman to confront idolatry and evil in the ancient world. It's a life worth emulating.

In a world that has lost its way and lacks godly, balanced leaders, we are more than ever in need of a few Elijah-like men and women who are not afraid to live courageously among their peers as they walk humbly with their God.

Charles Swindoll's wish is that *Elijah: A Man of Heroism and Humility* will help "establish deep within you a desire to stand strong for what is right as you bow low before Him who is worthy of your trust and obedience."

FASCINATING STORIES OF FORGOTTEN LIVES
Rediscovering Some Old Testament Characters

JOB

A Man of Heroic Endurance

Job, a study in pathetic tragedy . . . a hapless victim of unfair treatment. His disastrous circumstances overwhelmed him. His boil-covered body tormented him. His so-called friends belittled him. His distraught wife discouraged him. Even God seemed to desert him—letting Satan have his devilish way. And Job sat patiently by, enduring it all. Not a portrait of a hero. Or is it?

Could a man with ordinary internal fortitude stay faithful as Job did? Could a wimp endure the excruciating pain, suffering, and loss that this man did? No hero? Think again.

After a year of focused research into the life of Job, Charles Swindoll says, "Job appears boldly in the ancient book of the Bible that bears his name, and yet most of us have not taken the time to examine his life in depth. But a careful study of Job's life will convince us that this is another of God's amazing men with heroic character qualities worth emulating."

Travel with Swindoll into the horrific world of *Job: A Man of Heroic Endurance.* "Even if it was written in Scripture long ago, you can be sure it's written for us" (Romans 15:4 THE MESSAGE). So pay close attention to Job's life. Who knows what God will do next in *your* life?

Would you rather be a person of significance or a person of prominence? Think carefully! The answer to that question will shape your entire future.

Charles Swindoll says, "Somehow life has taught us poorly. We're trained to think that the most significant people are star athletes, actors, and musicians—the ones we applaud, those whose autographs we seek, those who have worldly renown. They aren't. Not really. Most often, the people really worth noting are those who turn a 'nobody' into a 'somebody' but never receive credit."

What is forgotten far too often is this: *Success in God's kingdom and in the church depends upon faithful people the public rarely knows.*

The Old Testament contains numerous *Fascinating Stories of Forgotten Lives*—unsung heroes whose actions, sacrifices, or battles failed to ascribe them worldly renown. These great lives, however, reveal *significant* people whom God honors in the pages of His Word and, therefore, deserve our serious attention and emulation.

- Adino took out eight hundred armed, skilled fighting men *with his sword.*
- Eleazar attacked the Philistines *by himself* for so long that his comrades had to pry his sword out of his grip.
- Shammah, while his companions ran like scared cats from their enemies, *stood his ground—alone—and was victorious.*

And yet, did you recall any of their names? They're not on the rolls of the rich and famous. Still, they are *significant.* As Swindoll examines little-remembered Bible characters and events, he will help you discover biblical principles and practical applications for living so that you can be who you are in God's estimation—a person of true significance.

GREAT DAYS WITH THE GREAT LIVES

Daily Insight from Great Lives of the Bible

"We desperately need role models worth following," says Charles Swindoll. "Authentic heroes. People of integrity. Great lives to inspire us to do better, to climb higher, to stand taller."

Great Days with the Great Lives is a collection of biographies taken from the Great Lives from God's Word series. Each day provides a Scripture reference and devotional thought based on the experience of some of the greatest heroes of the Bible—men and women whose authentic walk with God will teach us, encourage us, and warn us.

These profiles in character from one of America's most beloved teachers, Chuck Swindoll, offer us hope for the future. They show us that God can do extraordinary things through ordinary men and women like us. They teach us what it means to be genuinely spiritual people—people after God's own heart.

Join Charles Swindoll for a full year of *Great Days with the Great Lives*—an exploration into the hearts and lives of God's heroes who continue to instruct and inspire.